□ KNIGHT □

Charles Whited

KNIGHT

A Publisher in the Tumultuous Century

"Now that the old man is gone," one Times-Press official is reported to have said, "let's get Jack."

SUCH AN AMBITION seemed attainable at the time. C.L. left an estate of $515,000, most of it in Beacon Journal stock. John had to borrow money to pay his inheritance tax. He was not "the rich man's son" some imagined, although I inherited," he once remarked, "was opportunity."

Knight already had proven ability as a newspaper builder. Like other leaders, upon syndicated entertainment features as "flotsam and jetsam which neither amuses nor instructs the outstanding mind" and often ignored them for days at a time to make room for weighty articles.

Earlier, when the Times-Press had relinquished an Associated Press franchise acquired with other assets of the Akron Evening Times, he grabbed it without consulting his father and then instituted a late-afternoon edition. The outside sheets were printed on green paper.

C.L. scoffed at the gaudy "night final" but when circulation rose sharply, he remarked, "Son, for all I care, you can make the damned thing red, white and blue."

IT WAS John who proposed building a new plant at East Market and South Summit streets.

He solved a short-term cash crisis after C.L.'s death by giving employees half their pay in scrip accepted at business places that owed the newspaper advertising bills.

The Toledo Blade was winning its competitive battle with a Scripps-Howard newspaper, the News-Bee. Knight talked to its editor, Grove Patterson, a friend. "It's not what we're doing," Patterson said. "It's what they're not doing." The News-Bee had cut expenses and it showed — in reduced local news coverage. The Blade expanded.

THE TIMES-PRESS, too, had retrenched. Knight became aggressive. He spent more money on new features and a larger news staff. His editorial policies reached a new high of popularity in a changing political climate during a protracted strike in 1936 at Goodyear. A former mayor, C. Nelson Sparks, wanted to organize a citizens' Law-and-

some excellent features. I hired about five members of the staff of The News

the News was a newspaper which C.L. had bought years before, the Independent at Massillon.

The Herald paid off the $2 million loan — most of it secured by the Beacon Journal — in a few years. "In all the years it's been more that I've held a majority of its stock," Knight would say.

KNI acq the Her establi what Alexa years it all "the principle" by which good newspapers because its owner said of him a vigorous successor who could be depended upon to keep the property alive and its

what might have been the most personally satisfying deal of his career.

In 1938, the Scripps-Howard organization decided that the only way the Times-Press could become profitable would be to achieve a newspaper monopoly in Akron. It made an offer to buy the Beacon Journal — which Knight rejected, saying, "I won't sell." After a time, the Scripps representatives answered, "Then we will." An American Newspaper Guild report in that year said Scripps-Howard got 38 percent of the stock in a newly named publishing company. It wasn't until 1963 that Knight Newspapers Inc. purchased that 38 percent — for $8 million.

THE BEACON JOURNAL moved from East Market and South Summit to the Times-Press building at East Exchange and South High streets, which had the facilities for printing a Sunday edition. Until then, the former had been a six-day paper.

Aware of protests in some quarters about the "unhealthiness" of "a one-newspaper town," Knight offered to sell the East Market plant and equipment at a reasonable price to any citizen or group who wanted to set up another daily publication. There were no takers.

His next move was to resign from the county Republican executive committee. From that day forward, "the one newspaper" carried no political label.

IN DETROIT, two years later, the 81-year-old Stair was getting ready to retire. He had published the century-old Free Press, a morning paper, for 34 years and wanted it placed "in good

ton News, the Coral G

In 1969, the Macon T Macon News and the quirer and Philadelphia added to the KNI family

A giant expansion st Knight Newspapers and tions, with 19 dailies in 1 n Knight-Ridder N igh and the Ridder nds." Particularly, he ssing on the paper to her. He knew that K Herald and the Beac lly independent and th chances to run for ida and Ohio.

Knight's distaste for ticians, in the main, spr

and he found Congress sive. So after one term h nor of Ohio (second in a

"Having been associa those years, and noting ple who surrounded hi achieved a great distaste of ever running for pol though he encouraged m

AFTER A SERIES of Stair sold the Free Press million, taking his note down payment of $100,0 willing, even eager, to p

Knight changed the l a rock-ribbed conserva one reflecting his own b ism. The gains in circul tling. In less than four he had signed were ret ings, far in advance of dates.

On one occasion, Kn himself as "a true libe liberal with his fellow m

THE HEIR PRINCI play again when Secreta Frank Knox died in Apr Chicago Daily News went had become run down be absences in Washingt would-be buyers turned i

Knox, in his will, inst utors to sell to the bide ered best qualified to ca per's character and tradi the one offering the mos

Knight was examined tors for more than two

E. P. DUTTON   NEW YORK

Published in the United States by E. P. Dutton,
a division of NAL Penguin Inc.,
2 Park Avenue, New York, N.Y. 10016.

Published simultaneously in Canada
by Fitzhenry and Whiteside, Limited, Toronto.

Library of Congress Cataloging-in-Publication Data
Whited, Charles.
Knight: a publisher in the tumultuous century / Charles Whited.—
1st ed.
p. cm.
Bibliography: p.
Includes index.
ISBN 0-525-24723-8
1. Knight, John Shively, 1894–1981. 2. Publishers and publishing—
United States—Biography. 3. Newspaper publishing—United States—
History—20th century. I. Title.
Z473.K68W48   1988
070.5'092'4—dc 19
[B]   88-17643
                                                             CIP

Designed by REM Studio

1 3 5 7 9 10 8 6 4 2

First Edition

*Life is an inexplicable mixture of joys
and sorrows, triumphs and defeats,
exhilarations and dark moods, love and
hate. The full man has experienced them all.*
—John Shively Knight, 1894–1981

CONTENTS

CONTENTS

Sixteen pages of photographs follow page 182.

□KNIGHT□

PROLOGUE

Cloud masses lowered over downtown Akron, Ohio, threatening rain. The gray granite bulk of the Beacon Journal building brooded on its urban hillside, a block of Art Deco topped by an incongruous spike of revolving neon displaying time and temperature. At 11:10 A.M. on June 16, 1981, the temperature registered eighty-one degrees.

In his third-floor office, beneath the spike, John S. Knight stood at a sloping countertop absorbed in a daily habit of sixty years, scanning his own newspapers for errors. Today's batch included the *Miami Herald*, the *Philadelphia Inquirer*, the *Detroit Free Press*, the *Charlotte* [North Carolina] *Observer*, and the first edition of the *Akron Beacon Journal*, fresh off the press. Baldish and erect, Knight wore a suit of banker's gray, a white shirt, and gold cuff links. His hair was a white wisp, combed straight back. His patrician features sagged from age and deteriorating health.

He was eighty-six years old and had fewer than seven hours to live.

His eye skimmed the front page of the *Beacon Journal*. At midpage it stopped, snagged by a grammatical flaw. Knight grunted in irritation, grabbed up the page, and strode past his secretary, muttering, "I'm going to find out about this."

In that off-hour, the newsroom was almost empty, a place of editorial clutter and vacant computer terminals. Knight waved the page at entertainment editor Ted R. Schneider, Jr. "Who edits this newspaper? I need an editor to tell me if something here is good English."

Schneider paled. A few other staff members joined them. Knight pointed out the offending item, a subheadline describing the East Expressway as "An old roadway with obsolete design which was fit into a heavy industrial area."

"Shouldn't that word be *fitted*?"

A discussion developed. One copy editor defended the phrase as a direct quote from a public works official. A headline supervisor agreed.

Knight stalked back to his office, unsatisfied.

He was not well. Angina attacks caused him frequent pain and distress. He wore nitroglycerin patches taped to his chest. His health had worsened since the death of his third wife, Betty, five months earlier. He was fatigued from a recent trip to Detroit to celebrate the 150th anniversary of the *Free Press*. He was socially in demand and this evening planned to dine with a widowed friend, Stella Hall.

He left the office in the early afternoon. Chauffeur Forrest ("Bud") Boggs drove him toward Portage Country Club for lunch. June was Akron's loveliest time of year. In silence the old man watched the passing splendors: the maple, beech, and walnut trees in full leaf; the rolling Ohio hills adorned in new grass and flowers. The city's landmarks were achingly familiar to him.

John S. Knight was unique, they said: stubbornly independent, a study in contrasts. Though often aloof and prudish, he was admired by women. Overbearing, he nonetheless inspired strong

men to seek his favor. Associates accorded him a godlike deference, but the love of his one surviving son was entangled in
personality conflict.

He was rich and famous. Journalism had given him its major
honors, including the Pulitzer Prize. And yet many people saw
him as an enigma: part liberal populist, part conservative. He
sought the society of Old Guard wealthy, but often expressed
dissenting opinions on social issues. His soul was Republican, but
he had bitterly opposed the Vietnam War and endorsed Democrat Lyndon Johnson for president. Though a longtime dues-
paying member of the NAACP, in Miami Beach he resided on a
millionaire's island that once prohibited property ownership by
blacks or Jews, but refused to sign the deed restriction. He puck-
ishly termed himself a Prolicon: "pro" for progressive in outlook,
"li" for liberal toward humanity, "con" for fiscal conservative.

He had once aspired to be a screen actor, was an artful public
speaker, and yet professed a painful shyness with strangers. He
was called "hard-boiled," accepting wrenching personal disasters
with unblinking stoicism, but wept over a colleague's tragedies.
He was vulnerable to flattery. He hated to be alone, but had few
intimate friends. His moods could shift from gracious to glacial,
but interviewers found him engagingly candid.

Journalism esteemed him for uncompromising integrity, a
model for the craft. He had spent a lifetime deploring scoundrels
in public life and "weak-willed toadies" in the Fourth Estate. He
saw the duty of the press as absolute, an unbreachable pledge of
public trust, and by example vastly expanded the concept. And
yet he was a zestful crapshooter and horseplayer, a driver of hard
business bargains who admitted to having cheated at dice.

With the help of brilliant subordinates, Knight in fifty years
had parlayed the small, Depression-ridden *Beacon Journal* into
a publishing empire. By this spring of 1981 the Knight-Ridder
corporation claimed a circulation of 3.2 million daily newspapers
in thirty-three U.S. cities, plus suburban papers, TV stations,
news wire, investment news services, and newsprint production.
Annual revenues exceeded $1 billion. His personal holdings were
worth $200 million.

And yet he confessed that he himself was one of the mysteries of life he had been unable to fathom: "The forces and motivations that impel a person to act as he does are often baffling. But they make him what he is."

On this climactic day in Akron, Knight lunched at the country club and then went across the street to Blair House, where he lived in a lofty apartment with a panoramic view. It was after 5:30 P.M. when he arrived at Stella Hall's cottage in nearby Portage Woods. She was not quite ready and served him Dubonnet wine. He wore a new suit, which she dutifully admired. They chatted about the wine and his ration of one glass per day by order of cardiologist Dr. Henry Kraus. Knight put down his glass.

"Get ready, now," he said. Then: "It's cold in here."

"I'll turn down the air conditioner."

"No, don't . . ."

There was an odd noise in his throat, like an expelling of air. He slumped in his chair, eyes half closed.

"Jack, did something go down the wrong way?"

He did not reply.

"Jack?"

She felt for his pulse. There was none. She ran to the telephone, glancing at her desk clock. It was ten minutes to six. Frantically, she dialed Dr. Kraus's number.

John S. Knight was dead.

Telephones jangled across the Knight-Ridder empire. Computer printers rasped out advisories. In the newsrooms of Miami, Macon, Philadelphia, Lexington, Detroit, Wichita, St. Paul, Long Beach, and San Jose, editors called for prepared obituary material and remade front pages. From a massive store of Knight quotations and writings they compiled examples:

"I am an individualist," he had said. "I know what I know, I know what I think. I'm not afraid of anybody. I have my own code, how I live, and I live up to it."

That evening, only a few noted in the *Beacon Journal*'s final edition a small grammatical footnote to Jack Knight's memory.

In a subheadline on the story about the East Expressway, the word *fit* had been changed to *fitted*.

fortune seemed a little more evenhanded in its treatment of John S. Knight. He grew closer to his brother and son. The few honors that he had not already won as a journalist and a human rights advocate were heaped on his shoulders.

Then, on Aug. 8, 1974, his wife of 42 years died after a long illness. And there was more to come.

The news of the death of John S. Knight Jr. in Germany was kept from Johnny's wife, the former Dorothy Wells of Columbus, Ga., until after the birth on April 13 — about two weeks later — of a boy who was named John S. Knight III.

Knight. Through the medium of the Editor's Notebook they discussed the campus violence of the '60s and the course of the Vietnam War. They exchanged letters frequently, played golf together and talked for hours.

Paul Jensch, managing editor of the Daily News, said of young John. "He was really a charming guy. He knew who he was. He knew he was an heir to a fortune and to a key job in the organization if he earned it. But he didn't take himself too seriously."

It was obvious that John S. Knight hoped through his grandson to see that

John S. Knight III and lives. I can't think of change. I can't think of down. So I am not myself guilty.

"I am not going to quer me." he told Thoi to start a new life."

He returned to Fl after his grandson's announced he would ma Augustus. They 1976, in the chapel of Sea at Bal Harbour Lifestyle editor of the

VOICES OF THUNDER

latter cum laude in 1968 with a degree in history, then went on to study philosophy, politics and economics at Oxford University in England, where he earned a master of arts degree, with honors, in June 1970.

During high school and college he worked summer vacations at several Knight papers, including the Beacon Journal.

His first full-time newspaper job came at the Detroit Free Press in 1970. He gained experience in the circulation

center of Philadelphia, John S. Knight III was stabbed to death during a robbery by three men. There were homosexual overtones.

At the time, his grandfather was visiting at the home of Mr. and Mrs. Edwin C. Whiteheads of Greenwich, Conn. Mrs. Whiteheads is a daughter of the then Betty Augustus, widow of Cleveland millionaire Ellsworth H. Augustus. Knight and Mrs. Augustus had known each other for 35 years though a mutual interest in thoroughbreds and horse racing.

Mrs. Knight died while watching the R the LaGorce Island ho

WHEN HE STEPP torial chairman of Kni 1976, his title became Knight-Ridder and the His decision to qui by Thomas and others "The trouble wit Knight's position." Tho ly that they stay on to hat the business can't

Man cannot escape his bloodline: the traits, good and bad, implanted from birth, shaped in life's experiences, and borne to the grave. Throughout the process, from boyhood to manhood to old age, John S. Knight was especially conscious of this influence, for he had matured under the domination of one parent. His life would be long and rich and filled with the association of bright men. Some were pleased to thrive in the shadow of his personality, a fine balm for the ego. Yet the most important man in his life, the one whom he wished to please above all others, had given him scant honor, never wholly acknowledging him for achievement, always leaving him with a nagging sense of disfavor. This was his father, Charles Landon Knight.

Even as he himself grew old, with the man long dead, Jack Knight pondered the riddle of that overwhelming personality whom he adored but never really knew. "My father, complex, brilliant, colorful and unpredictable: he was a man of many moods, from deep pessimism to joyful ebullience. I learned more at his table than from any university." It was an adoration touched with fear; for Knight, the son, found the tumultuous nature of Knight, the father, more than he could fathom. And so did the world at large.

They called him "C. L."

He had been born on a farm in Georgia two years after the Civil War. He matured into a fiery Ohio editor, politician, and practitioner of personal journalism; sired two sons, John and James; and died in slow agony of cancer at Akron on September 26, 1933. The great and near-great were present to honor his passing, for the man's complexities touched them all. Gregarious by nature, yet strangely detached; conversant with gamblers, rounders, and ladies of the night, he was also a compulsive Bible reader, worshiping no specific god, and an ardent poker player who could not bear to lose. An Akron politician, informed that C. L. Knight had died, commented, "I'm glad the sonofabitch is gone. No self-respecting worm would eat his rotten carcass." The man then took part in the funeral as a leading mourner.

The late publisher's *Akron Beacon Journal* devoted an entire edition to memorializing him. Among the columns of type praising his name, however, there also appeared a cryptic, unsigned commentary:

> . . . C. L. Knight walked alone, intensely a part of the world, intensely aloof from it. At once warrior and recluse, he met the challenge of the day's events, took up unpopular causes, questioned those that caught the current fancy, played a lone hand, courted no friendships, asked no favors and wrote what he damned well thought, regardless. A curious man, this, our neighbor and not our neighbor; for twenty-five years and more, a man we did not know.

He left to his widow, Clara, and two sons, John Shively and James Landon Knight, a debt-ridden newspaper in the depths of the Depression that paid employees in tokens, called scrip, which local merchants accepted as IOUs. In later years Jack Knight would bristle at suggestions that his wealth was inherited: "All I inherited was an opportunity."

Some contemporaries insisted it was more than that.

C. L. Knight claimed to be a descendant of St. John Knight, a former soldier of Oliver Cromwell who migrated from England to Massachusetts in 1662. St. John's great-grandson moved to Georgia a century later to found a southern branch of the family at Milledgeville.

It was a legacy of crusty independence. C. L. Knight's father, William, a Georgia state senator, introduced a bill in 1837 to abolish slavery, but the measure was uproariously defeated in the legislature. Senator Knight would free his own slaves eight years before the Civil War.

C. L.'s boyhood left him with bitter memories of a South left ravaged by war and Reconstruction, its heroes disgraced. Among notables who visited the Knight home at Milledgeville were former Confederate leaders Jefferson Davis and General Albert Sidney Johnston. Davis made such an impression that in later years C. L. would write a biography, *The Real Jefferson Davis,* depicting the wartime Confederate president as a maligned idealist who had defended slavery because of a fervid belief in constitutional principles.

Knight finished high school in Milledgeville, taught school briefly, worked on a ranch and in a lumber camp. He attended Vanderbilt University at Nashville, Tennessee, and Columbia College in New York, taking a law degree in 1889, then traveled abroad writing free-lance magazine articles.

He wrote in a flowery style spiced with classical and biblical writ. Restless, he turned to law. In 1893, aged twenty-six, he launched a practice at Bluefield, West Virginia, defending small-time lawbreakers and doing legal chores for coal companies.

It was not an auspicious start. The only interest Bluefield offered was Clara Scheifley, a petite, bookish Pennsylvania girl visiting relatives in the town. Knight was impressed by her ability to recite long literary passages from memory. They married on November 22, 1893. The new bride helped her husband in the law office and also enabled him to make connections in the tightly knit local society, where coal executives built pretentious homes and sent their children off to private schools. The Knights' first child, John, was born in Bluefield, October 26, 1894.

C. L. Knight gave three years to the law, augmenting his income by free-lance writing. Bluefield so soured him that he quit the profession and, in 1896, left southern Appalachia for good.

Knight turned to the newspaper business, founding a small paper, the *Journal,* at Winston-Salem, North Carolina. When that failed, he moved the family to Clara's home state of Pennsylvania. The former lawyer found work as a subeditor on the *Philadelphia Times,* a politically rambunctious morning newspaper of 100,000 circulation. His feisty idealism appealed to *Times* editor A. K. McClure. The paper waged such a lively feud with Philadelphia's Mayor Fitler that city hall tried to cut off the *Times*'s water supply when it moved to a new plant. Knight won promotion to chief editorial writer. Restless again, he quit the *Times* in 1900 and moved to Springfield, Ohio, to work as assistant editor of the *Woman's Home Companion* magazine. Co-owner T. J. Kirkpatrick soon promoted him to editor in chief. Kirkpatrick then sold his magazine interest, bought the *Akron Beacon Journal,* and invited Knight to join him in the enterprise.

Akron was a lusty manufacturing town of forty-five thousand with a legacy of boom and bust. Historically the place attracted rugged individualists who prospered or went broke in a competitive atmosphere as extreme as northern Ohio's climate. Set in the mineral-rich hills forty miles south of Cleveland, the town had flourished with such ventures as canal shipping; iron, coal, and coke production; and the manufacturing of clay pottery, sewer pipe, stoves, mowers, reapers, nails, matches, machine tools, flour, cereal, and shipping containers.

C. L. Knight found the city a yeasty, real-life drama of capitalistic rough-and-tumble. Fascinated, he prowled Akron's byways and probed its history.

In the 1830s, immigrant laborers had dug the great canal linking Lake Erie and the Ohio River, scaling Akron's hills with navigational locks and opening the way for an inpouring of opportunists, entrepreneurs, and scoundrels. The German immigrant Ferdinand Schumacher, a miserly eccentric, built a dynasty in oatmeal, the forerunner of Quaker Oats. John Frederick Seiberling, son of a Pennsylvania shoemaker, made a fortune in mowers and reapers, only to lose it all and leave his sons to found their own dynasty. Ohio C. Barber, the match king, became so incensed when accused of not paying his taxes that he moved his huge Diamond Match factory out of Akron, creating his own town of Barberton. Frail B. F. Goodrich, a young surgeon with a different kind of dream, so charmed local business satraps that they lent him $13,000 to relocate his struggling little rubber factory from Melrose, New York, to reshape the destiny of Akron for all time.

By the late 1800s, the city was booming. Workers poured into the factories on a polyglot tide. Industrial moguls built turreted Victorian mansions with verandas and stained-glass windows, entertained at lavish dinner parties, and wore evening clothes to the opera. Then the bubble burst in financial panic. Jobless multitudes simmered and fumed. At the turn of the century, a thwarted lynch mob destroyed city hall with fire and dynamite, killing two.

Hard times still lingered as Kirkpatrick and Knight took over the *Beacon Journal* on October 12, 1903. The paper had a rundown plant and a daily circulation of seven thousand, paid and unpaid. Kirkpatrick became the *Beacon Journal*'s general manager, Knight its business manager.

For C. L., now a stocky man of thirty-six with heavy forehead, a shock of backswept hair, and piercing eyes, Akron offered room for flamboyant personal journalism. In an introductory speech to the printers union, he declared his ideals: "We are ourselves free and our paper shall be free, free as the Constitution we enjoy, free to truth, good manners and good sense. . . ."

Akron liked his style. It matched the robust local heritage. Old-timers remembered with affection the crusading fire of the original *Summit Beacon,* whose founder, Hiram Bowen, sixty years earlier had lambasted his opponents as scoundrels and knaves. A Bowen successor, teetotaling sometime sheriff and mayor Samuel A. Lane, had fought with equal vigor to rid Akron of swindlers and gin mills. Always, the newspaper had been hard-rock Republican. Knight, the lifelong southern Democrat, noted this fact and quietly switched to the GOP.

As the paper's business manager he had no editorial voice, the current editor being a holdover from the previous ownership. Knight confined his writing to completing his Jefferson Davis biography. Socially, Akron found him difficult. Though fond of poker parties and spirited talk, he formed no close attachments and often withdrew to his home, to read Gibbon and Plato in Olympian solitude. Other men were nonetheless drawn to him. Gradually he attracted financial backing to take over the *Beacon Journal.* A prime supporter was banker Edward R. Held. In later years Held's son-in-law, lawyer C. Blake McDowell, Sr., would be a key legal strategist in building Knight Newspapers.

In 1907, C. L. Knight was able to buy Kirkpatrick's interest, and two years later, at age forty-two, he took control as editor and publisher. He quickly began to make his presence felt with furious editorials that he scrawled with a pencil stub on legal pads. It seemed a loosing of long-suppressed outrages. "Why should the public go to the polls," he rumbled, "when there is nothing to vote for except a jackass and another bond issue?" And "Government's pestiferous gadflies swarm over the land destroying its substance even as swarms of locusts, called down upon the Pharaoh by Moses, destroyed the fields of Egypt." Akron nodded and chuckled.

The Knight family lived in a Victorian frame house on West Market Street. The boy, John, lagging in school, was set back two grades. Clara Knight planted flowers, read her books, and cultivated friends. There were those who saw her quiet nature in John. C. L. dominated, his dinner-table conversation weighted with politics and world affairs. Domestic life often was shattered by some calamity, such as an unexpected breakdown of the *Beacon Journal*'s balky, gas-fed press and angry protest from afternoon subscribers whose papers were not delivered until 8:00 P.M. The publisher's response could be apoplectic.

In the shadow of such a father, John Knight's childhood was marked by acute shyness. He became the butt of neighborhood bullies. "Had my boyhood been spent in today's mixed-up society," he would recall years later, "Mother would have hired

a psychiatrist to find out why John wasn't like the other boys."
C. L., weary of the sniveling, ordered his son to go on the attack.
John, more fearful of his father's displeasure than a bully's fists,
gave as good as he got. Life took a turn for the better. Even his
school grades improved. He affected a protective outer shell that
he would keep for life.

C. L. Knight's son explored an expanding world from his
classrooms at Crosby Elementary School, writing compositions in
lined copybooks. He demonstrated an eye for precision. "My
desk is 20 inches long and 12 inches wide," he noted as an eight-
year-old. "It is made of pinewood and iron. The iron is to hold it
up and keep it firm." At age eleven, he was expressing a snobbish
vexation with the dull-witted. "Dangerous people are the ignorant. They do not know the difference between right and wrong
and can easily be led astray." In copybook margins, teachers
chided him for lapses: "Poor. I do not like your writing." And,
"Try again." And, "I don't like those dirty finger marks."

It was a childhood to be warmly remembered. As Knight
would reflect many years later, "The days were carefree. Radio
and television had not been invented. The automobile was an
object of wonder. We probed Indian mounds for arrowheads,
shot squirrels, swam in unpolluted rivers. Schoolwork empha-
sized reading; I had read more than 100 books by the age of 12."

Around him, industrial Akron underwent a startling rejuve-
nation as the golden age of bicycles—the town had twenty thousand of them by the 1890s—was supplanted by that of the automobile. B. F. Goodrich's rubber company switched production
from fire hoses to tires. Frank Seiberling, thirty-eight, stood in
the ruin of his father's bankrupt mower and reaper business and
saw a chance to recoup; in three days, he and his brother Charles
went door-to-door selling $45,000 worth of stock to found Good-
year Tire and Rubber Company. An Ohio farmboy and former
buggy tire salesman named Harvey Firestone arrived with a
$20,000 bankroll and plans to launch yet another rubber-making
enterprise.

The outpouring of technological energy did not escape the
notice of C. L. Knight's elder son. As a preadolescent he had
thrilled at the dash of Akron's fire department, which sent its
smoking, horse-drawn engines thundering through the crowded

streets. But the maturing process jaded him, and at fifteen his pleasures took more complicated, and expensive, forms. "According to my tastes, in order to make a boy happy at Christmas you must possess a good deal of knowledge about electricity and telegraphy and have money. The perfect gift is a complete wireless telegraphy outfit transmitting and receiving up to two hundred miles."

By now, Jack Knight had a year-old baby brother, James, born in 1910. But the fact did not merit mention in his school essays. Infinitely more significant was the experience of driving his father's Franklin automobile. "It is a grand sensation to feel yourself gliding away in a big, roomy, silent, powerful car, as if on wings."

Motorcar mania swept the nation, carrying Akron's economy along with it. Prosperity sent rubber smoke gushing from factory chimneys in east and south Akron. To escape the stench, wealthy families retreated westward into the hills. Rubber magnate Frank Seiberling spent millions building Stan Hywet Hall, a revised English Tudor mansion dominating three thousand acres of hilly woodlands. As the fortunes of the *Akron Beacon Journal* improved, publisher Knight built a home near Seiberling's on historic Portage Path, where Indians once carried their canoes eight miles overland along the ancient river route between Lake Erie and the Ohio River.

It was a time of high adventure and sensational news, flashed by telegraph. Jack Knight was nine years old when the Wright brothers' flying machine took off from the sand dunes of Kitty Hawk, North Carolina; twelve when San Francisco was devastated by the 1906 earthquake; fourteen when Admiral Robert E. Peary dashed to the North Pole; seventeen when the *Titanic* sank with fifteen hundred souls.

Powerful social elements were on the move. Akron's rubber labor force boomed to twenty-two thousand. The city erupted in strife in the winter of 1913 when rubber workers, marshaled by the radical Industrial Workers of the World, struck for better wages and working conditions. The standoff dragged on for weeks with street mobs' singing and parading. Local vigilantes prowled the icy streets armed with clubs. C. L. Knight's *Beacon*

Journal refused to take sides, calling for mediation. Rioting injured sixty people before the crisis ended in stalemate.

For all the rising ferment, it was still an age of innocence. As Eleanor Roosevelt would later recall, "Babies dropped from heaven or were brought in the doctor's satchel." *The New York Times* warned editorially of dire unspecified consequences if women were allowed to vote. In the White House, trustbuster Theodore Roosevelt complained of "the dull, purblind folly of the very rich man." The president of Princeton University, Dr. Woodrow Wilson, observed dourly, "Nothing has spread socialist feeling in this country more than the use of the automobile."

A rising American middle class was caught in contradictions. Schools clung to traditional values. As angry workers marched, schoolboys read *The American Boys' Handy Book,* including a chapter on how to stage "Puss 'n' Boots." Knight's essay topics were more advanced than most pupils', who even in their early teens still wrote about fairy princes and forest creatures. Home reading helped. The Knight home was well supplied with books, including such shocking works as *The Scarlet Letter.* C. L. sent his elder son off to the Tome boardingschool in Port Deposit, Maryland, to improve his Latin and classics reading. It was a dismal interlude. By fall 1913 Jack was back at Akron Central High, playing end on the undefeated state championship football team. The squad outscored opponents 201 to 6. The only opposing touchdown came around young Knight's side of the line.

Politics were in upheaval. His father's editorial skirmishes provided hard lessons in the hazards of taking strong stands. Democrat Woodrow Wilson launched his drive in 1912 to unseat the GOP's three-hundred-pound president William Howard Taft, whom C. L. Knight despised as corrupt. Declaring, "We are witnessing a renaissance of spirit!" Wilson defeated Taft in the November elections, ousting the Republicans from the White House. Knight licked his political wounds, brooding, "Taft has left his party a heap of junk."

Abroad, a tempest gathered that would change the world order for all time.

Jack Knight graduated from Akron Central High in the spring of 1914 and spent that summer working at the *Beacon Journal* in an Akron of droning electric fans, rattling trolley cars, the new hit song "Sylvia" blaring from wind-up Victrolas, and newspaper headlines of impending disaster in Europe. On July 28, even as *The New York Times* described war as "unthinkable," Austria opened fire on Serbia. One after the other, Germany, France, Belgium, and England called their sons to arms. By early September, as Jack boarded the train for Cornell University, guns rumbled on the fields of battle half a world away, and the fate of his generation was cast.

Jack's life at Cornell was pleasant, if academically undistinguished. He talked of taking a bachelor's degree and studying law at Harvard, but his university career was not crowned with success. He was cut from freshman football because he was too light. He failed to make team manager because rowdies stole the Cornell mascot bear from his temporary custody during the Harvard game. His grades were short of Honor Society standards. He lacked required singing and dancing talent for the Savage Club. He joined another fraternity because his choice catered to athletes and did not invite him. Success eluded him in English class, where the instructor informed him icily, "You think you can do as little work as possible, write a term paper and get by. Well, you'll never get more than a C-plus from me."

Diligence was not his strong point. Handsome, well-dressed, and rich, Knight padded his curriculum with easy subjects. His achievements occurred outside the classroom. He met actresses Elsie Ferguson and Beverly Bayne at his fraternity's Junior Week party, danced with Irene Castle, rode a white horse in the Spring Day Parade, and performed as an extra in Pearl White's silent film series, *The Perils of Pauline,* shot in Ithaca.

C. L. Knight was unimpressed by his son's college performance, but more earthshaking issues commanded the publisher's attention. Alarmed by the nation's drift toward war, by early 1917 he was writing thunderous editorials terming the conflict in Europe "a blundering and calculated crime against humanity" and predicting it would "reap a harvest of debt, death and taxes."

It was a risky effort. These were times of rising hatreds. Civilian war hawks badgered Americans to demand entry into the war. "Four-Minute Men" loosed verbal barrages at public gatherings. Prowar editorials filled newspapers and magazines. Congress enacted a Sedition Act to punish with fines and imprisonment anyone using "disloyal or abusive language" against the government or resisting the war. Fifteen hundred Americans ultimately would be arrested. State laws outlawed teaching German in schools and purged German books from libraries. Patriots stopped eating sauerkraut. German-Americans, of whom there were thousands in Akron, feared to speak their native language in public. "This is preposterous," wrote editor Knight.

Rumors circulated that he was a German agent. The U.S. Justice Department sent agent W. H. Garrigan to Akron with orders to provide Washington with tearsheets of *Beacon Journal* editorials and keep watch on the publisher. In later years Garrigan would go into the insurance business in Akron and count himself among C. L. Knight's admirers. But in the early spring of 1917, as America hurtled toward war, he read the editor's words and clipped and filed and reported. "Do these people who are clamoring so noisily for war have any conception of what it means?" the *Beacon Journal* asked.

A group of local patriots decided they had had enough of Knight's treason: they would tar and feather the editor and run him out of town. Knight was warned, bought a shotgun and shells, and waited in his house. "They might get me," he said, "but before they do, I'll get several of them." The plot never materialized. On April 6, 1917, the United States declared war. The following day, the *Beacon Journal* dropped its resistance and called for full public support of the nation in conflict, urging readers to plant Victory Gardens. Ohio governor James Cox appointed Knight as Summit County food and crop commissioner.

At Cornell, the ROTC paraded in uniform. Students rushed to recruiting stations. John S. Knight, a twenty-two-year-old junior, spurned his father's attempts to procure a commission as captain in the National Guard for him. When the spring semester ended, he enlisted as a private in Cleveland.

He was swept up in the floodtide of American youth leaving home to go to war. The mood was jubilant, the launching of a glorious adventure. As laden troop trains streamed across country, the nation celebrated with parades and bond rallies. Martial music blared from loudspeakers. Preachers were "afire with war spirit." Carpenters swarmed onto remote tracts of government land to build military camps.

For former collegian Knight, military life began in the muggy heat of Fort Crook, Nebraska, "changing into rumpled woolen uniforms, peeling potatoes and doing squads right, passing out under a blistering sun after taking typhus shots, shooting craps in the latrine, receiving knitted socks and sweaters from home, getting passes into town."

His typing ability won him a billet as company clerk. He managed to transfer from the infantry to motor transport, training at Indianapolis with a unit of tough former taxicab and truck drivers. Brawling, profane, and expert at shooting dice, they made quick work of the bright boy from Cornell in their payday crap games. Knight learned the art of palming dice to improve one's odds of making a point.

It was a unit of heavy trucks, grease, fumes, and dirt, offering little excitement and less glory. Looking higher, Knight applied for the fledgling balloon corps. His application vanished into the bureaucratic maw. That December he shipped out with the truckers at Halifax, Nova Scotia, aboard an ancient transport vessel, the *Megantic,* bound for Le Havre, France. They arrived there on January 7, 1918.

The winter was a snow-blown misery for American troops training for combat. By spring, U.S. divisions were in action with French armies. Knight was a truckmaster sergeant, his unit convoying supplies over miserable roads in support of the First and 26th divisions. The First, a regular army division, went into battle in May to help the British repulse a German attack at Montdidier. Knight's truckers, behind the lines, watched the terrible tide of wounded and dead stream back from the front.

Bored by inaction, he enrolled in Infantry Training School and then was accepted as an officer candidate. He was commissioned a second lieutenant on July 9 and assigned to the 113th Infantry Regiment of the 29th Division.

The Western Front was a tortured maze of trenches stretching four hundred miles from Switzerland to the North Sea, pulverized by shell fire and drenched in blood. The summer of 1918 continued the carnage with the infusion of American troops. The National Guard 29th Division had only arrived in France in late

June. A month later, accompanied by its new second lieutenant, the division was assigned to the Vosges sector for battle training. Commanders sent out sporadic patrols against German lines and exchanged desultory gunfire. Casualties were frequent. Between August 31 and September 7, Knight's green troops conducted raids and captured prisoners.

The division was withdrawn from the Vosges sector and placed in reserve near the town of Verdun, out of combat. A few miles to the north, nine U.S. divisions poised to attack an area of massive German trench works. Before dawn on September 26, Knight and his fellow reserve troops were awakened by distant thunder as twenty-five hundred Allied guns opened the battle of the Meuse-Argonne. Six days later, in a cold, drenching rain, the division received battle orders. Unaccountably, Second Lieutenant Knight was ordered immediately transferred for training in the Air Service. The action was never to be explained, leaving the curious to speculate about whether C. L. Knight pulled strings back in Ohio, or important military friends interceded in France, or Jack Knight's old application for the Air Service, submitted the previous year in Indianapolis, miraculously came through. As he rode a truck toward the airbase at Tours, the 29th Division was hurled against strong German gun emplacements. In three weeks of bloody fighting leading up to the Armistice, the division would suffer more than five thousand casualties. The lieutenant from Akron spent the time training as a gunner in a cratelike De Havilland biplane high over the lovely chateau country. He would remain in France until May 1919, six months after war's end.

From payday crap winnings, he sent home nearly $6,000 in cash.

When he arrived in Akron on June 27, 1919, C. L. was hosting an evening poker game with town cronies. The publisher greeted his uniformed son and asked politely, "Care to take a hand?"

Lieutenant Knight smiled. "Don't mind if I do." He won a $600 pot.

2

JOYS AND SORROWS

Clannish Akron matrons regarded Katherine McLain as one of their own. Bright and self-assured, she had grown up in the nearby town of Massillon. Her wealthy father, Frank McLain, famed as a national champion bicycle racer, owned a wholesale grocery business and had invented the locknut in his garage. Katie was a graduate of Wheaton College, a horsewoman, and a golfer. She had interests in literature, art, and children and was enormously popular.

Jack Knight had known her casually for years. As a handsome young fashion plate and war veteran, he escorted other local beauties to dances and parties, where Katie McLain favored him with flirtatious glances. He felt himself drawn to the circle of people who always surrounded her, but was restless and unready for serious romance. Besides, she was engaged to marry a young man on the staff of Ohio governor James Cox. Knight turned his attention to his own uncertain life and tried to put Katie McLain out of his mind.

There was opportunity in Akron. The city was swept up in a new boom. Seventy thousand worked in the rubber plants. The block-long works belched black smoke by day and glowed eerily at night, "—the roar and growl and mutter as of metal monsters caged in colossal brick prisons, swelling to the mighty voice of the city." The young veteran smelled the familiar stench of rubber in the air, a heady odor of prosperity. Job seekers jammed incoming trains and the masses choked downtown sidewalks. Prices skyrocketed. Landlords rented beds to workers in eight-hour shifts. The city counted 122 millionaires.

Jack could always go to work for his father, and that sort of thing was expected of a well-to-do young man. But he could not be like C. L. The *Akron Beacon Journal* publisher had become an institution of personal journalism, railing editorially on this cause and that. Now it was angry defiance of the Anti-Saloon League. So passionately did C. L. feel about the issue that he turned from teetotaler to imbiber, stocking his basement with booze. Hard-drinking poker parties brought weekly debauches to the house on Portage Path, at which the publisher gambled with deadly intensity. Losing, he would bolt from his chair and vanish to another room, to sulk and read the Bible while his guests played on. Yearning for agrarian peace of mind, he bought at 238-acre farm near picturesque Hudson, Ohio, where he entertained with big political cookouts. There were dark rumors of amorous trysts with women of easy virtue, sometimes behind the locked doors of his newspaper office. The whispers deeply offended his prudish elder son. In matters public, the publisher bemoaned "the dominance of fools." He deplored America's postwar glut of materialism, feminism, automobiles, warped values, Red-baiting reactionism, the Ku Klux Klan, and religious intolerance.

Jack wished for his own identity. He felt purposeless. Drawing his army dice winnings from the bank, he boarded a train for California. There he dallied with film acting, partied with starlets and producers, played golf and polo. But this was not the answer either, and he quickly became bored. Years later he would brush aside the experience as "a lotus-eating life, eminently unrewarding." Ironically, C. L. Knight saw his son's drift and briefly felt his own urge for change. He talked of selling the *Beacon Journal* and escaping to a black walnut grove in California. As his younger son, James, would recall long afterward, "Father suddenly fancied himself going back to the life of a Southern planter, overseeing his groves on horseback." C. L. took Clara and ten-year-old James to Santa Barbara, where they met Jack. The latter affected little interest in what was to be done. It was Clara who drew the line on C. L. "You're not selling the *Beacon Journal*. That will be for the boys to decide." She herded them all back to Akron.

Clara inquired politely whether Jack intended to go to work.

"I've thought about it," he said.

His mother smiled. "Your father would like to talk with you."

The old awe of his father remained strong. Jack sensed himself inadequate. The elder Knight came quickly to the point. The logical thing was for Jack to start making something of himself at the *Beacon Journal*.

Jack was dubious. "I'll do it on one condition."

"What's that?"

"If I don't like the work, I can get out; if I'm no good, I'll be kicked out."

He went to work as a cub reporter and occasional copyreader.

The *Beacon Journal* had fierce competition against two rival local newspapers. The daily *Akron Press* was liberal and prolabor; the *Times* followed the rubber companies' line. The *Beacon Journal* charted a middle course, but with a considerable handicap: publisher Knight had discarded his Associated Press (AP) wire service before the war, contending that the AP was pro-British. National news was now thinly supplied by a single-circuit International News Service wire.

John Knight was no stranger to the newspaper. Since age fourteen he had hawked election-night extras on the street and worked in the composing room during school vacations. He knew employees by their first names. But now he was being groomed for management, a process of painful enlightenment. "I discovered how little I knew about newspapers and practically everything else," he would recall, "—how damned stupid I was, how ignorant and poorly informed."

The 1920s roared. In politics, two Ohioans surged to the forefront as presidential candidates, Republican U.S. senator Warren G. Harding against Democrat Ohio governor James Cox. The state was powerfully and emotionally split.

Jack Knight liked Governor Cox's progressive spirit, but Harding was the Republican, and the *Beacon Journal* was not one to bolt its party. Akron buzzed over an exchange between C. L. Knight and Harding. "Whoever told you that you'd make a good president?" asked the irreverent publisher. "My wife," Harding replied coolly. The GOP senator was pledged the paper's unstinting support. After Harding took office in 1921, however, C. L. would come to regret it.

Journalistic rookie Jack Knight felt out of his depth. As a reporter he covered some sports, but wrote so poorly that he used a pseudonym. He spent Sundays gleaning other newspapers for ideas, finding little difference between innovation and imitation. "If I can borrow, adapt or steal a great idea, that's journalism at its peak." He wrote on politics, worked on the city desk, set up headlines, and did page makeup. The last presented a special challenge, because the paper chronically went to press late. Knight stormed into the back shop, shouting, "By God, let's make these pages move!" Printers, by nature resentful of front-office bosses, liked this brash heir-apparent. The pages moved.

Akron was unimpressed. The fledgling editor overheard a businessman's dubious assessment. "Old C. L.'s a damn good newspaperman, but the boy won't amount to much."

He found himself taking on editorial responsibility sooner than expected. C. L. decided to run for Congress in Ohio's Fourteenth District. It was a bitter campaign. Opponents lashed at his "unpatriotic" war record; the publisher struck at his rival, Martin L. Davey, as a lackey of the Ku Klux Klan and the Anti-Saloon League. "My opponent," Knight declared, "has drawn into this cause every man having a grievance against me, every grafter that my paper ever thwarted from preying upon the people, every war contractor, every man who would rather be a subject of King George than a citizen of the United States. . . ." He won by seven thousand votes and went to Washington in March 1921, leaving his son as managing editor of the *Beacon Journal.*

Jack Knight disliked the new order of things. Previously he had told his father, "I couldn't be a politician and run a newspaper too." The elder Knight was stung. The differences between them were deep-seated. Jack had once asked C. L. which candidate for sheriff they intended to back in a forthcoming race. "The one," his father replied, "who gives us the county printing business." The cynicism of it galled him.

His burden as managing editor was not overwhelming. Veteran editors and a seasoned staff kept things running well. Young Knight had plenty of time to be out in Akron society. And it was there, among the young smart set, that he found romance with Katie McLain.

They seemed to go together naturally, the handsome bachelor Knight and the headstrong young woman from Massillon. But friends were skeptical. Gossips recalled with relish how in one of her flings Katie had been betrothed to an heir to a yeast fortune. All went well until she attended a house party with her fiancé and friends in New Hampshire, suddenly changed her mind, climbed out her bedroom window that night, and ran away. Two days later she called her frantic parents from Baltimore announcing that she was safe. Now tongues wagged afresh as she threw over another well-connected suitor to keep steady company with John S. Knight. "Oh, I love you!" she wrote to him in a note. "How could any two people be so happy and so blessed?"

They were married on November 19, 1921, in a formal wedding with bridesmaids, ushers, flowers, and an overflow crowd.

Life for John S. Knight took on fresh new abundance.

Katie was a wonder. She flourished in marriage and seemed possessed of inexhaustible energies. She won the women's golf championship at Portage Country Club. Her expert horsemanship stirred Jack's interest in breeding and training. They were formidable bridge partners.

They moved into a large new home at 400 South Portage Path, lushly landscaped and set back from the street. It was soon a center of social activity, as she organized parties and dinners and gave the rooms her own decorative touches. In time, her enthusiasms for art and literature would draw luminaries of the day: writer Heywood Broun came to call, as did lawyer Clarence Darrow, an admirer of C. L. Knight's editorials. Katie was as much at ease entertaining politicians, industrialists, and business tycoons as she was fixing sandwiches for herself and Jack on the veranda on a Sunday afternoon. Even crusty C. L. was dazzled by his daughter-in-law. "Well," he told his son, "you did something right."

The newspaper interests expanded. To strengthen his political base, C. L. acquired a small morning daily, the *Sun,* in Springfield, Ohio, competing against the dominant afternoon *News* owned by Governor Cox. In April 1922, Jack took charge as the *Sun's* editorial director.

He soon made his first major tactical error.

The Ku Klux Klan thrived in Springfield. One hot summer day, members paraded down the main street, masked and robed. Knight stood glowering from beneath the brim of his derby hat. "Take off that goddamn hat!" a bystander snapped. Knight told him to go to hell. Outraged, the young editor tracked down a secret Klan membership list and published it on the front page of the *Sun.* It included the names of prominent townsmen. Advertising and subscriptions tumbled, *Sun* reporters were frozen out of local news events, and Knight himself became a focus of town dislike. The *Sun* would suffer for the next dozen years of Knight ownership.

The incident strongly influenced John S. Knight's publishing policies. Never again would he order abrupt changes in a newly acquired newspaper. Rather, he resolved to seek change gradually, studying the community and gradually building editorial strength. Press freedom was essential, but there was little freedom for a paper struggling to survive. He would borrow a remark attributed to Tulsa editor Dick Jones: "The penniless newspaper, like the penniless young lady, is more susceptible to immoral proposition. . . ."

In 1922, Katherine gave birth to their first son. They named him John S. Knight, Jr. People said the baby was the image of his father.

The "Ohio Gang" ruled Washington. Harding cronies charted public affairs in backroom smoker parties. C. L. Knight enjoyed insider privileges at the White House among men who had played poker on Portage Path. But he hated life in Congress. A rookie congressman was expected to be seen but not heard. Congressman Knight battled the status quo in angry speeches from the floor, taking renegade positions against strongly backed tariff bills ("An absurdity—and the House had to swallow it in one ugly, unpalatable mass.") and huge naval appropriations ("The most extravagant and useless military program ever forced upon an unwilling people!"). He became a notorious absentee from roll call votes, and retorted: "I am not a clock puncher. Neither will I go through the trained rat performance which some newspapers and possibly some congressmen think constitutes representing the public."

In Akron, Jack ran the *Beacon Journal* in the face of multiple frustrations. He had an inferior news wire service. His staff was molded to the attitudes and style of the absent C. L.—"More royalist," young Knight remarked dryly, "than the king." A jaded public saw the *Beacon Journal* as politically slanted and unreliable. This was a reflection on the perennial power struggle over who ran Akron, the rubber barons and downtown merchants or C. L.'s local political machine.

In Washington the congressman's own disenchantment was growing. As whispers of corruption in the Harding administration rippled through the cloakrooms, C. L. talked of resigning his congressional seat. Back home, a coalition of progressive Republicans urged him to run for governor. In June he announced his candidacy in the party primary. "Ohio is dominated by an oligarchy of politicians," he thundered. Ohio's top GOP functionary, national committeeman Rudolph Hynicka, "should have been in the penitentiary twenty years ago." It became a free-for-all campaign as fresh candidates kept jumping unexpectedly into the race. Thus Knight's foes stacked the field to erode his support. In the autumn 1922 election he suffered a narrow but bitter defeat. Leaving Congress, the grim-faced Knight told a press conference, "I look forward to getting back to a decent business, to my newspapers and the society of my Duroc hogs out on the farm who understand some things that are lost on statesmen."

A year later, in August 1923, a depressed President Harding took an arduous train trip across the country. Stricken with ptomaine poisoning, he died in San Francisco. Vice President Calvin Coolidge, a dour and mediocre man, came to power. In the rush of public mourning, it seemed the dead president could not be praised enough. "A martyr in fidelity to the interests of the people," declared the normally aloof Charles Evans Hughes. But Senate investigators were probing mounting evidence of multimillion-dollar graft in the Harding administration, to be known as the Teapot Dome Scandals.

C. L. Knight vowed never again to seek political office. His son John was even more convinced that active politics and journalism did not mix. The job of newspapers was to monitor government, not run it.

In 1924, Katie gave birth to their second son. They named him Charles Landon Knight II, after his grandfather. He was a headstrong child, strongly resembling his mother.

Except for her intervals of pregnancy, Jack and Katie were constantly on the go. Akron's wealth surged. The building boom broke all records. They danced, played golf, partied, went off on jaunts to Washington and New York, entertained lavishly at their home. He took fierce pride in his young wife, basked in the society of bright, successful men and women and would look back wistfully long afterward to "the gay Twenties: Prohibition, raccoon coats, derbies, flasks at football games . . . and Cal Coolidge's White House pancakes."

At the *Beacon Journal,* C. L.'s retreat from active management had allowed Jack to develop his own way of doing things. He dressed up the paper with more features, comics, better local news coverage. His father saw no merit in such fluff, considering the newspaper's function to inform, not entertain. To avoid being overwhelmed, Jack had learned to stand his ground with icy persistence. Disgustedly, C. L. editorialized: "Where we once, as in the days of Dana, had the journalistic gem casket, we now have a garbage can of flotsam and jetsam which neither amuses nor instructs an inquiring mind."

Something was working in the *Beacon Journal*'s favor, however. In 1925 the rival *Akron Times* was bought out by Scripps-Howard, owners of the *Akron Press*. The two papers merged to become the *Akron Times-Press*. A new editor arrived, vowing to "take Akron journalism out of its swaddling clothes."

As the decade waned, C. L. relinquished more and more authority. Winters sent him and Clara south to Sarasota, Florida, where he built a fine home. By 1927, persistent growth made it necessary for the paper to move to a larger plant. The absent publisher was not consulted on drapes and furnishings for his new office. Returning from Sarasota, he sulked in the empty old building for three weeks. Finally persuaded by Jack to inspect the new plant, he grudgingly pronounced it fit for human habitation and moved in.

In February 1928, Katherine gave birth to a third son. He was named Frank McLain Knight, for his maternal grandfather. The infant was sickly.

Katie herself had not been well. After the birth, she complained of tiredness and looked pale. Still, there were many things to do and little time to spend resting. She had organized a Junior League for Akron and promoted charity boxing, and both projects demanded her attention. The Children's Hospital needed volunteers. She continued to promote the arts, helping out with fund-raising bazaars and receptions. Her mother-in-law, Clara, noticed Katie's persistent weakness. But no one took it seriously.

Jack was swept up in his ever-expanding career.

The *Beacon Journal* engaged its rival *Times-Press* in a circulation battle, acquiring even more comics and features and spurring the staff to greater efforts. A major break came when the *Times-Press* dropped the local Associated Press franchise—its parent organization, Scripps-Howard, being intent on building up its own United Press wire service. Jack grabbed up AP and launched a special afternoon street edition, printed on distinctive green paper. C. L. snorted his disgust. "Green! It's sickening." Jack stood firm, pointing to a dramatic increase in *Beacon Journal* sales. The publisher retreated. "Hell, for all I care you can color the damn thing red, white, and blue."

It was time to do something about the *Springfield Sun,* which continued to lose ground against Governor James Cox's afternoon *News.* Jack was ready to sell, but needed a buyout offer from Cox. Acting on a sudden brainstorm, he spread rumors that they planned to expand the *Sun* into an afternoon paper and drive the *News* out of business. He hired a huge flatbed truck and ordered it loaded with heavy Linotype machines and other equipment. As the machinery rumbled through the heart of Springfield, a building contractor began busily taking measurements of the *Sun* plant and tearing out walls. Townsfolk watched intently, and gossip raged.

Cox sent an emissary. Would the Knights be interested in selling the *Sun?* Soon afterward they accepted his check for $275,000. It was $55,000 more than C. L. had paid for the paper.

One did not leave such profits lying idle. Jack looked around for other opportunities. In Katherine's hometown of Massillon, the local *Independent* was for sale. He went down to bargain with one of its owners. After lengthy haggling, the man rocked back and eyed Knight shrewdly.

"We're only ten thousand dollars apart, son. How are we going to resolve this?"

The young editor shrugged.

"Ever shoot dice?" the Massillon man asked pleasantly.

Knight's face was impassive. "I'm afraid I don't have a lot of time for that, sir."

The other produced a pair of well-worn ivories. "Care to roll 'em?"

Knight flexed his fingers. "I'll shoot you for ten thousand, one roll."

He rolled a seven.

He handed the dice back to his shocked host with an engaging smile.

"Beginner's luck," he said.

The winter snows ended. Elms and maples greened along Portage Path. Jonquils flecked the gentle hills with yellow. Jack's mother, Clara, wrote in her diary about the April rains and the hyacinths coming into bloom in the front garden.

Katherine Knight was feverish, felt listless, and lost weight. Doctors recommended a rest cure in the southern mountains. Leaving the children with Jack and the servants, she went with her parents to North Carolina. By early May she was at the majestic Greenbrier Hotel and cottages at White Sulphur Springs, West Virginia. She breathed clear mountain air, took cod-liver oil and sunlamp treatments, drank mineral water, and wrote homesick letters to Akron.

> May 5—*My Darling: I can't wait to be home again. The hypos tone me up wonderfully, despite making me look like a leopard with spots and smell like a fresh cod. Are the boys good or bad? I love them so much. I'm ashamed for allowing myself to get into this condition.*

> May 13—*Darling: Whatever is wrong with me, if this treatment doesn't cure it nothing will. Your sweet letter came this morning. . . . What I have is not at all infectious. The doctor says mine is a closed case and I'm no danger to others.*

> May 20—*My Dear: It has been pouring down rain all afternoon and evening, a lovely, soft rain that sounds nice in the trees around my windows. I hope you have been going places and doing things. I love you so terribly much.*

> June 6—*Dearest: I can't stand it much longer, being away. I wish I could hurry and get over this so I can show everyone how nice I can be . . . I can hardly wait until I'm Katie Knight again, and not a half-cracked egg.*

Summer came. The fevers persisted. Returning to Akron, she had no strength for activities and suffered from the heat. Among her frequent visitors was socialite Blanche Seiberling, who was impressed by Katie's frail beauty. There was talk of Jack's running for a seat in Congress. Katherine smiled wanly. "I expect big things of him too, but not in politics." And then she was gone again, to Saranac Lake, New York, for more rest and treatment. Jack hired a railroad car and uniformed nurses for her journey.

Doctors were unable to provide a positive diagnosis. X rays showed no active TB lesions. She went to Roosevelt Hospital in New York for a checkup. Specialists studied evidence of kidney infection and possible tubercular meningitis, a chronic disease with little prospect for recovery. They advised rest, mineral waters. As autumn deepened, she lived at a sanitorium at Saranac Lake. Her weight loss continued and she complained of headaches and loss of memory. Jack visited her for their seventh wedding anniversary on November 19 and then returned to Akron. She spent Thanksgiving at Saranac in the company of her mother, a housekeeper, and a nurse. The *Beacon Journal* staff sent her a turkey dinner and she wrote: "My Darling: People are really too kind. I don't deserve it. . . . My love for you overflows. Always, your Katie."

Akron watched and waited. John S. Knight turned thirty-four, a wealthy fashion plate moving in a circle of expanding influence. Outwardly, he affected a stoic acceptance; only close friends and family knew his way of retreating behind a hard protective shell.

The end came in the second week of January 1929. Katie suffered blinding headaches, loss of memory, and difficulty in walking. Jack took her by ambulance from Saranac Lake to Roosevelt Hospital for emergency surgery. Doctors removed a tumor mass from her brain. The operation went well, with little blood loss or damage to surrounding brain tissue. But the tumor was identified as a tuberculoma, a slow-growing malignancy spread from a primary cancer elsewhere in her body, possibly the kidneys or intestines.

Katie seemed to rally. By that evening her vital signs had strengthened. Her doctor, Alfred Taylor, left the hospital in an optimistic frame of mind. Five hours later, she died.

The funeral of Katherine McLain Knight took place in their house on Portage Path. Floral tributes filled the parlor around her casket and overflowed into other rooms. Jack Knight sat in tight-lipped silence with his three small sons, the youngest not yet one year old. When the service was over, the motorcade moved westward along Market Street in dreary January cold, past snow-patched fields and gray wooded hills to Rose Hill Cemetery. And then the family and intimate friends returned to the home of C. L. and Clara Knight, where the children had been living for months.

John S. Knight ordered the house he had shared with Katie on South Portage Path emptied and locked. He never returned to it.

He was flooded with messages of condolence. Word of the death reached Blanche Seiberling in Miami Beach, where she was spending the winter. She wrote a letter that Knight would keep all his life:

> *A great sorrow builds or destroys. Don't let this one destroy you, Jack. You have much to give the world. The memory of a beautiful, brave woman will keep you climbing, climbing, always upward.*

He did not return immediately to a full work schedule, becoming preoccupied instead with golf, practicing on the driving range and putting greens with the Portage club professional. Knight had caddied on that course at age eleven and played there as a teenager. Golf became an obsession now as he worked his strokes, his chip shots, his putts.

In June 1929, six months after Katie's death, he won the men's golf championship at Portage Country Club. Friends celebrated late into the night. They engraved his name on a plaque and hung it in Portage's 19th Hole Lounge. It would be the first of six such plaques.

People said Jack Knight looked like a new man.

He never again spoke publicly of Katie McLain. It was as if he resolved to turn a painful page of life and never look back. And yet the deep anguish was always there, occasionally showing through the chinks of his armor. And he would write long afterward, "Life is a leveler. The good years bring happiness and pride of achievement, the bad leave permanent scars."

fortune seemed a little more evenhanded in its treatment of John S. Knight. He grew closer to his brother and son. The few honors that he had not already won as a journalist and a human rights advocate were heaped on his shoulders.

Then, on Aug. 8, 1974, his wife of 42 years died after a long illness. And there was more to come.

The news of the death of John S. Knight Jr. in Germany was kept from Johnny's wife, the former Dorothy Wells of Columbus, Ga., until after the birth on April 13 — about two weeks later — of a boy who was named John S. Knight III.

Knight. Through the medium of the Editor's Notebook they discussed the campus violence of the '60s and the course of the Vietnam War. They exchanged letters frequently, played golf together and talked ———.

Paul Jensch, managing editor of the Daily ———, said of young John, "He was really a charming guy. He knew who he was, ——— knew he was an heir to a fortune and to a key job in the organization if he earned it. But he didn't take himself too seriously."

It was obvious that John S. Knight hoped through his grandson to see that ———

John S. Knight III and ——— lives. I can't think of ——— down. So I am not myself guilty.

"I am not going to ——— me," he told Thomas to start a new life."

He returned to Florida ——— his grandson's ——— nounced he would ma——— beth) Augustus. They ——— 1976, in the chapel of Sea at Bal Harbour ——— Lifestyle editor of the ———

3

TIMES OF TEMPEST

latter cum laude in 1968 with a degree in history, then went on to study philosophy, politics and economics at Oxford University in England, where he earned a master of arts degree, with honors, in June 1970.

During high school and college he worked summer vacations at several Knight papers, including the Beacon Journal.

His first full-time newspaper job came at the Detroit Free Press in 1970. He gained experience in the circulation center of Philadelphia, John S. Knight III was stabbed to death during a robbery by three men. There were homosexual overtones.

At the time, his grandfather was visiting at the home of Mr. and Mrs. Edwin C. Whiteheads of Greenwich, Conn. Mrs. Whiteheads is a daughter of the then Betty Augustus, widow of Cleveland millionaire Ellsworth H. Augustus. Knight and Mrs. Augustus had known each other for 35 years though a mutual interest in thoroughbreds and horse racing.

Mrs. Knight died ——— while watching the R——— the LaGorce Island ho———

WHEN HE STEPP——— torial chairman of Kni——— 1976, his title became ——— Knight-Ridder and the ——— His decision to qui——— by Thomas and others ——— "The trouble wil——— Knight's position," Tho——— ly that they stay on to——— hat the business can't ———

The 1920s roared. The era was wild; prosperity unlimited. Every American dreamed of striking it rich on the stock market. There were 1.5 million stock accounts, of which 600,000 were on credit. "The business of the country," Calvin Coolidge had said in a rare burst of articulate speech, "is business." Anybody who thought otherwise was deemed a gloom-and-doomer, a sorehead, or worse. And yet C. L. Knight's deep skepticism would not be stilled. His editorials warned darkly that the public had gone mad on the market, recklessly siphoning off vital bank funds and risk capital. "The whole condition is so basically unsound that we really face a crisis. . . ." A money-hungry public preferred the rhetoric of President-elect Herbert Hoover: "We shall soon with the help of God be in sight of the day when poverty shall be banished from this nation."

Disaster struck on October 23, 1929. The final hour of trading on Wall Street was marked by a sudden and spectacular fall in prices. The decline continued on October 24, "Black Thursday." Brokers were flooded with sell orders. Pandemonium broke loose. At the close, 13 million shares had been sold for a loss of $13 billion. The economic wreckage had begun.

It was two days before Jack Knight's thirty-fifth birthday.

The Great Depression was just around the corner.

At home, the boys adapted to life without a mother. Johnny, Jr., was the dominant brother. Two years older than Landon and five years senior to Frank, he was bigger, stronger, more aggressive, a natural athlete. The two younger boys looked to Johnny for leadership.

Their father had buried the pain of Katie's loss deep inside himself and moved his sons into their grandparents' house on Portage Path. There, C. L. Knight's cronies came in for weekly poker parties and argued boisterously. On mornings after, the boys would come downstairs to find playing cards strewn over the floor.

Uncle Jim, their father's brother, was a twenty-year-old attending Brown University in Providence, Rhode Island. The children were close to their grandmother and the servants. The house was big and solid with a wide veranda, formal rooms, mahogany woodwork, fireplaces, and leaded windows looking out onto the ample yard and gardens. The yardmen sculpted boxwood hedging into the Three Bears. Clara Knight planted tulips, peonies, gladioli, and roses. In each of her books, she placed a pressed flower.

As the boys roamed fields and wooded hills, spring weather broke winter's icy tedium, and then the summer arrived. Uncle Jim came home from college full of talk about quitting school to work full time at the *Beacon Journal.* Grandfather C. L. grumbled at this. As the weather warmed, he often left the office early to put on his old clothes and putter in his half-acre vegetable garden behind the house. Five-year-old Landon trotted at his side, down the rows of parsley, tomatoes, and sweet corn.

The day came when Johnny and Landon left Akron for Coronado, California, where their maternal grandparents now lived. They would stay for nearly two years. It was an idyllic time.

The Frank McLains owned horses and a beach house. The boys became expert riders and swimmers. Though smaller than Johnny, aggressive Landon frequently taunted him into fistfights and always lost. One day as they swam, he was caught in an undertow and would have drowned if Johnny had not pulled him out. They did not speak of the incident afterward, but Landon never forgot.

Finally, in 1932, word came to Coronado that the boys were to return to Akron to live.

Their father had married again.

It was a joining of adult needs and common interests. Gone, now, the flippancy of youth. Life had matured and wisened them both: Jack through the ordeal of Katie's illness and death, leaving him with three small sons; Beryl Zoller Comstock from the failure of her first marriage and divorce, with a five-year-old daughter, Rita, to be brought up and educated.

Beryl was nearly two years older than he; tall, attractive, her hair prematurely gray. A Washington diplomat would describe her as being "like a classic poem; all grace and style, yet warm and human." There were those who doubted Beryl's warmth, but undeniably she possessed style.

Beryl Zoller had been born in a southern Illinois coal-mining town. Her father, Robert Zoller, and his brother made a fortune working seemingly exhausted mines. They moved to Chicago, where Beryl grew up in wealth. Educated at private schools and the University of Chicago, she was married in 1915 to Jackson D. Comstock, a young executive for a rubber company. The couple moved to West Virginia, where their daughter was born. They were divorced in 1929, the year of Katie Knight's death. Jack Knight met Beryl while attending a charity ball in Akron with his mother.

The marriage of Jack and Beryl in Chicago, January 24, 1932, provided what one written profile of her later would describe as "a light for both in a darkened world." In a letter to Jack years afterward, Beryl Zoller Knight would recall their difficult early marriage, "the five years in which we loved, worked and met our troubles together, taking them for granted, thinking it would always be that way. Now, we know that happiness must be cherished and cultivated. How easy life can be, if we are not sick of heart and low in mind. . . ."

At first, the troubles seemed endless.

Hard times came to Akron. As nationwide orders for rubber goods slackened, factories cut back production. By the end of 1930, some 14,200 workers had lost their jobs. That fall, the city allocated funds to hire the unemployed. An advertisement for 60 workers to clear underbrush brought 900 applicants.

If 1930 was bad, 1931 was terrible. Local welfare agencies were swamped. Jobless families dug into savings. Mortgages were in default. Bank withdrawals were so heavy that Akron deposits plummeted by $14 million. When Central-Depositors Bank & Trust Company teetered at the brink of insolvency, local businessmen and banking officers secretly hauled in $3.5 million cash from Cleveland by heavily armed motor convoy to prevent a run on the institution.

From his office window at the *Akron Beacon Journal,* Jack Knight looked down upon lines of ragged men waiting for free soup from the Eagles Temple kitchen across the street. An Akron industrialist sneered publicly that "any man can find work if he really wants it." Hundreds besieged his factory office asking for jobs. They were told to look elsewhere.

C. L. Knight spent his time agitating for such causes as repeal of Prohibition, and against government waste and taxation, with occasional thrusts at "papsuckers and scoundrels" in general. "Examine both political parties under a microscope," he wrote, "and if you can find any difference between them except the emblem on the ballot, I will swallow both the elephant and the jackass without pinning back their ears."

He was irritated when his younger son, James, quit college to work full time in the business office of the *Beacon Journal.* C. L. assigned Jack Barry, business manager, to train him and declined further involvement. Barry had little taste for the task. Young Knight wound up handing out pencils and paper clips to the staff, nosing around the back shop looking for things to do, and being generally ignored. He went to work regularly, nonetheless, and did not complain.

As the nation's economic disaster intensified, the old publisher seemed unable to offer the usual grandiose remedies, suggesting merely that industry provide a shorter work week at no reduction in wages. An army of ten thousand jobless veterans of World War I poured into Washington demanding early payment of the government's promised bonus of $1,000 per man. C. L. was one of the few U.S. editorialists to support them. "Those who shouted loudest and profited most from that war," he protested, "now move heaven and earth to block the bonus payment."

But his outrage seemed to be cooling; his energy sapped. Rarely did the old puckish wit arise afresh.

C. L. Knight was terminally ill.

In November 1932, as Roosevelt's election triumph crushed the Republican party and swept Hoover from the presidency, C. L. was admitted to Akron City Hospital for major cancer surgery, his second of the year.

The old publisher steadily weakened, accepting callers in his hospital room and later at the house on Portage Path. They came in sorrowful procession: mayors, judges, financiers, the governor, lawyer Darrow, all the old cronies and poker players. The final six months were hell, as he fought death with a stubborn will. On a sunny day in March, the thin, slightly nasal voice of America's new destiny cut through the static of his bedside radio. "Let me first assert my firm belief," declared the thirty-second president of the United States, "that the only thing we have to fear is fear itself."

C. L. Knight, the former Democrat turned Republican, the populist and progressive maverick, listened with mixed feelings. Again in his lifetime Republican conservatism had been out of step with public necessity. Sometimes the patient managed to sit up, smoke a pipe, and drink a bourbon, peering whimsically from beneath shaggy brows while friends argued the issues generated by FDR's first hundred days. Old Guard conservatives were livid. "I tell you, C. L., that man will be the ruination of America."

In the fetid swelter of late summer, he groaned and fought for breath, slipping inexorably toward the end.

Akron sweated in August heat. Electric fans droned. The clatter of horse-drawn ice wagons brought children swarming to scoop up bits scattered by the deliveryman's pick. Sheriff Ray Potts's deputies dreaded serving eviction notices on families. Day after day, the officers carried peoples' worldly possessions out of their houses and piled them onto the sidewalks, while men stood in stunned silence and women wept. By the end of this terrible year of 1933, the deputies would perform the task three thousand times. Twenty-five thousand Akron people were out of work, and the great chimneys no longer gushed smoke around the clock.

Several cases of polio were reported among Akron children. The outbreak became an epidemic. Some children died.

The four-day national bank holiday that spring had devastated public morale. When it ended, three Akron banks did not reopen. By summer, *scrip*—an IOU token that could be spent in lieu of cash—made its appearance in the city. At the *Beacon Journal,* Jack Knight told employees he was cutting wages. "But everybody will be kept on the payroll." Ben Maidenburg earned $50 a week as a weekend and special sections editor: he was reduced to $30, half of it in company scrip.

In late August, nine-year-old Landon complained of fever and headache. Normally the boy was peppy and headstrong. At home, he rebelled against the regime of his stepmother, Beryl, and stepsister, Rita. Beryl Knight did not demonstrate great warmth for children. Uncle Jim did not like her at all.

During the week before Labor Day, Landon went several times to the nearby Harvey Firestone home to walk ponies between chukkas of the rubber baron's late-summer polo matches. Sometimes a boy could ride one of the ponies. While walking, Landon unaccountably lost his balance and fell down; then he tumbled from a horse. Word got back to his stepmother, and a doctor was called. The boy was put to bed with a severe headache. The doctor was baffled. Landon .heard someone say, "It might be what his mother had." He was taken to Akron Children's Hospital for diagnostic tests.

Charles Landon Knight II had polio. The disease initially left him paralyzed from the neck down.

Half a lifetime later, an interviewer would ask John S. Knight what one needed to move ahead in life. "A trained mind," he would reply, "—an analytical mind, with the ability to look at a problem objectively, consider all of the factors involved, weigh the possible solutions and come to a decision." One applied the same disciplines, he believed, in matters of deep personal travail. And so in this bitter autumn of 1933 he absorbed continued onslaughts, outwardly unblinking and resolute. Friends said that each blow seemed to harden the man's resolve. He plunged deeper into work.

C. L. Knight died in his bed on September 26. The funeral was a massive ingathering of loyalists, hangers-on, friends, foes, the mighty, and the obscure. The next day's entire edition of the *Beacon Journal* was given over to the event. Dignitaries extolled the publisher's virtues and judiciously ignored his faults. In the rush of printed matter, few but John S. Knight took note of one special quotation of his father, resurrected for the occasion. "It is our duty to hold high our ideals of public service or else get out of the newspaper business," C. L. Knight had written. "Better it is that you should set fire to your plant, leave town by the light of it and take to raising speckled peas on a windy hillside . . . than to remain a human cash-register editor."

As the patriarch went to his grave near Katherine's in Rose Hill Cemetery, the condition of his grandson stabilized in Akron Children's Hospital. Beryl Knight, the stepmother whom Landon regarded as lacking maternal warmth, sat up nights at his bedside giving him alcohol rubs. When they took him home, Beryl continued to work with the nurses, rubbing and exercising Landon's useless limbs, coaxing partial feeling back into the young body.

The John S. Knights were now a family of six, one of them an invalid. For added space, they moved into the grandparents' home on Portage Path and Grandmother Clara took their smaller house on Merriman Road. Landon underwent daily whirlpool baths, and, at Beryl's suggestion, Jack had a swimming pool built for him. Some muscle activity returned. The boy developed strength in his arms and shoulders. But like thousands of other Americans, including President Franklin D. Roosevelt, Landon Knight would be crippled for life by polio.

The death of C. L. Knight compounded financial difficulties at the *Beacon Journal*. He left no will. Although the estate was valued at more than $500,000, including $116,000 in cash, Jack Knight had to borrow $800,000 to pay the taxes. He called a family conference. The *Beacon Journal* showed no profits; there was no money to distribute among shareholders. "We'll have to tighten our belts and ride it out." This came at an especially bad time for brother Jim, who was planning to marry his sweetheart, Mary Ann Mather.

At the rival *Akron Times-Press,* an editor was heard to say, "The old man's gone, now let's get Jack." It was never quite clear to John S. Knight how they planned to do this; for with slack advertising and falling circulation, the *Times-Press* was cutting back sharply on employees' salaries, number of pages, and coverage of the news.

Knight, now president and editor of the *Beacon Journal,* opted to gamble. With the bankers' blessings, he hired more reporters; added columns, comics, and features; and expanded news coverage. Again it was a game of percentages, weighted by the theory that the public would buy a high-quality newspaper even in hard times. The next two years in Akron saw the beginnings of economic turnaround. As revenues rebounded, the *Beacon Journal* climbed out of the red while the *Times-Press* sank deeper into it.

And suddenly it was 1936, another pivotal year.

The Republican party was desperate for a candidate who could dislodge Roosevelt. Old-line GOP leaders, getting ready for their summer national nominating convention in Cleveland, eyed Kansas governor Alf Landon. Knight, disenchanted with the Old Guard, threw his support instead to Idaho's Senator William E. Borah, who was floating trial balloons in Ohio.

It was an odd alliance. Borah, nominally a conservative Republican, had been a notorious fence-straddler on Senate issues. Knight was not especially enthusiastic, but saw in Borah a chance to break the conservative stranglehold on primary politics "which denies the people of Ohio the right to express their will." A visiting Chattanooga political writer assessed the editor's role. "John Knight dislikes the programs of the Roosevelt administration but regards continued control of his own party by the Big Business–Wall Street crowd as dooming it as a national political force. By backing Sen. Borah, he hopes to arouse Republican liberalism all over the nation."

Borah's Ohio campaign was a disaster. Only the Summit

County district, spurred by thundering *Beacon Journal* editorials, turned a marginal victory. Three months later, party loyalist Knight was introducing Alfred M. Landon to a packed Akron armory, hailing the Old Guard's candidate as "representing a liberal, forward-looking viewpoint and imbued with the practical ability to keep the ship of state on an even keel." As it turned out, candidate Landon had trouble keeping his own campaign on an even keel. The shrewd Roosevelt depicted him as a toady for "business monopoly and organized money" and even heaped ridicule on the Landon campaign symbol, a Kansas sunflower: "It is yellow, has a black heart, is useful only as parrot food and always dies before November." Roosevelt scored a plurality of 11 million popular votes and an electoral vote landslide. Democrats seized control of 75 percent of both houses of Congress.

Labor in Akron was a sputtering powder keg. For decades sporadic attempts to organize the rubber plants had gone nowhere. Hard times now dealt massive blows to the industry. U.S. motor vehicle production plummeted; tire demand fell off 40 percent. As profits dried up, rubber companies were forced to make deeper cuts in manpower and wages. Idle workers were angry and resentful.

A worried Knight followed closely the march of events. Congress sought solutions with the National Recovery Act, part of which gave workers the right to collective bargaining. Labor organizers converged on Akron with a flurry of work stoppages designed to force union recognition on the rubber industry. In 1935, the Wagner Act further strengthened union power. That November a strike shut down an insulation plant at Barberton, an Akron suburb. Pitched battles broke out between sheriff's deputies and strikers. Finally matters subsided in sullen compromise. Neither the *Beacon Journal* nor the *Times-Press* took an editorial position in the dispute.

By winter of 1936 trouble spread to Goodyear, idling 13,800 workers. Five hundred pickets clustered at plant gates in subzero weather. More than a thousand workers defied the strike and entered the plant amid torrents of abuse. Goodyear was a prime target for John L. Lewis and his militant new Congress of Industrial Organizations (CIO). Akron filled with outside labor muscle—steelworkers from Pittsburgh, coal miners from West Virginia—bolstering Lewis's drive.

Knight saw the mood grow uglier. Goodyear president Paul Litchfield called the strike "defiance of constituted government to protect a man in his right to work." Sheriff James T. Flower, Jr., warned that if he tried to break up the picketing, "East Market Street will run red with blood." Goodyear's main plant was a fortress. Loyal workers slept on desks and makeshift cots, as did Litchfield and his chief aide, vice president, and plant manager, Edwin J. Thomas, a genial but tough-minded man who had first gone to work for the company as a teenager.

In the *Beacon Journal,* Knight began pushing for settlement. Tempers became explosive as a former Akron mayor, C. Nelson Sparks, went on radio denouncing "radicals and Communists" and vowing to lead armed citizens against the strikers. Knight responded with a front-page editorial, "No Room for Vigilantes," calling Sparks's saber rattling "an invitation to rioting and violence." The message hit Akron's troubled streets with such impact that the rival *Times-Press* reprinted it. Then, accompanied by *Beacon Journal* business manager Jack Barry, Knight drove to Goodyear's main plant and pushed through the crowd. He was met by Litchfield and Thomas. The Goodyear officials were coolly polite.

"Let's get this thing settled," Knight said. "The town's a powder keg. Damn it, we're on the verge of civil war out there."

Litchfield let Thomas do the talking. The vice president, himself a native of East Akron, had known Knight casually since boyhood. "Jack, nobody wants this strike settled more than we do. It's new for us. There are a lot of issues at stake. You can't settle them overnight."

"At least get started," Knight said.

It was Thomas's turn to flare. "Don't pressure us! You're sitting there comfortable as hell at your *Beacon Journal* and not helping very much. We can't give the company away and we've got long-term relationships to think about. You go back and run your *Beacon Journal* and we'll run Goodyear."

The standoff seemed unbreakable. And yet both sides were ready to give way. Thomas reopened talks with the union. Loyal employees leaving the plant were spat upon and assaulted, a circumstance that did not sweeten the feisty executive's mood. Still, there was a beginning. After six weeks of bitter impasse, Goodyear's plants resumed production.

Financially, the *Beacon Journal* was doing well; editorially, it lacked something. The strike crisis reminded Knight that a responsible press could exert powerful leverage for good. In a moment of vanity, he nominated his own newspaper for a Pulitzer Prize, citing several editorials on the strike issue and claiming that the *Beacon Journal* had helped to avert "anarchy, suppression of civil liberties, violation of constitutional guarantees, coercion of labor by management, management by labor, and disruption of civil life. . . ." His nomination was rejected by the Pulitzer board.

In the absence of C. L., the paper had no strong voice and tended to be editorially impersonal. A staff writer who could have emulated the late publisher's style went unused. Jack Knight made a painful self-assessment. Was he turning into one of those "cash-register editors" his father had so despised? He talked about editors' obligations in a speech to college students. "Far too many newspapers are languorous when they should be alert, cynical when they should be enthusiastic, cowardly when they should fight. The vigorous editor has an opportunity to inspire the people. . . ."

Knight seemed restless and ready to expand his horizons.

4

"THE EDITOR'S NOTEBOOK"

It was, by his own lights, a love-hate relationship between man and word. Writing did not come easily to him. "I'm a bleeder," he would confess. "I sit there and struggle with the typewriter, smoking cigarettes and drinking Cokes and ruining my gut." Writing was work. To write opinion under one's own name, moreover, meant personal exposure to censure, argument, and ridicule. Hadn't his father experienced enough of that?

How much simpler it would be to leave writing to the writers and busy oneself with business and community matters. He hired reporters to write and editors to correct their grammar. Besides, a newspaper column involved much more than the writing: one had to generate ideas, interview newsworthy people, and answer letters from readers, pleasant and unpleasant. And yet he felt a need to express himself. He was, after all, a newspaperman.

It had complex roots. Too many editors, he said, were more concerned with profit than with issues. C. L., for all his faults, had taught him that an editor ought to be more than figurehead. The editor was a thinking, rational being, and readers were entitled to know where he stood. As Knight would recall in an interview many years later, "Newspapers were becoming impersonal institutions, like banks."

Thus, in the 1930s, he had emerged as a critic of journalism. "Despite lofty talk about elevating journalism, newspapering as an art has bogged down dismally in the past ten years," he said. Journalism schools were turning out ignoramuses; editors lacked discipline, independence, and that inexplicable something called "a nose for news." He quoted Kentucky journalist Mark Ethridge: "I like an editor with fire in his guts." It was the editor's duty to question, to probe, to be skeptical.

For years he had tried his hand at editorials and ghost-authored "Intercepted Letters" and acerbic vignettes. A well-aimed thrust brought indignant howls from aggrieved public figures. Former Akron mayor C. Nelson Sparks had been livid over an unsigned Knight item. "My Dear Jack: Whoever told you that tale that you used is a damned liar. What must a guy do in private life to keep from being pot-shotted continually?" Knight relished the joust. "We fawn not upon the mighty," he said.

The Goodyear strike had spurred his thinking. Akron needed a voice. Ideas were generated by other ideas; they were not born in a vacuum. On December 1, 1936, he typed out seven paragraphs on the subject of the lagging Community Chest drive and showed it to editorial writers Herschel C. Atkinson and W. Sprague Holden. "I'm starting something new on the editorial page." He was mindful of his limits, he said, and knew the thing would be difficult. "Some days there might not be anything to write about but a tree on a hill." He would call it "The Editor's Notebook."

The first effort began: "One wonders why the Better Akron Federation didn't iron out its problems with the labor unions long before the time for holding the annual Community Chest drive had actually arrived. . . ." The issue was hardly earthshaking, the style pedantic and no match for C. L.'s "concentrated thunder, with biblical overtones," as editorialist Holden liked to remember it. But for Knight and his readers, the effort was to launch forty years of "Notebook" writing, in a style that would range from the wistfully poetic to the angry and agonizing. Ultimately, the "Notebook" would gain for him journalism's highest award, but by then he would be almost too old for the heart-swelling pride of achievement.

And so it was a modest and parochial first attempt as Knight began turning out a daily column for the *Akron Beacon Journal* and its ninety thousand readers. The mill, he discovered, consumed a vast amount of grist.

At a Woman's Club luncheon, the columnist heard a visiting lecturer review Margaret Mitchell's new novel *Gone With the Wind*. Afterward, he could not resist a swipe at Akron's snobs. "Our speaker assured the good ladies that they didn't have to apologize for reading the novel. This last, I assume, was to provide them protective veneer against the verbal thrust of factory town intelligentsia, who pride themselves in never disturbing the covers of a book that 'everybody reads.' " Barely was one column written when he faced the next. He found himself addressing issues in endless variety, from Akron's crowded streets ("How much longer must we stand for a hick town policy in the regulation of traffic?") to the abdication of Britain's King Edward to marry American divorcée Wallis Warfield Simpson ("The King's farewell . . . made other lovers in history look like second-raters."). And he reflected on the dire events taking shape in Europe: "It is all very interesting to hear a critical talk on 'Germany Under Hitler,' but it would be intensely more informative if another speaker could give you Hitler's side of it from the same platform."

The daily rigors had a loosening effect. His initial self-consciousness gave way to a surer, more personal touch. Local doctors aroused his ire when they deplored as unethical the publicity given a young Akron surgeon in a *Beacon Journal* photoessay. Replied the "Notebook," "If ever there was a profession shot through with jealousies, it is medicine. Ethics? What about all the patients whose sufferings go unrelieved because the doctor can't be reached on Sunday? Where are their precious ethics then?" His attention turned to a *New Yorker* article, by former *Beacon Journal* staff reporter Ruth McKenney, describing Akron as "dirty, seething with class warfare, an architect's hell and a city planner's nightmare." JSK's civic pride was stung. "Sloppy reporting," brooded the "Notebook," "that would never get past a newspaper city desk." In a follow-up article, he reflected on Akron as a town of uncommon resiliency.

> Akron reminds me of boxer "Rubberman" Johnny Risko in his palmy days. He was awkward, wide open half the time and swung from the floor. Better boxers beat a steady tattoo against his ribs and sent him sprawling to the mat. But the bell usually found him back on his feet. Akron is like that. The city has taken heavy punishment; but like good old barrel-chested Johnny Risko, we're still in there fighting.

Initial daily columns rarely exceeded five inches, but as the writer became more adept, personal revelations began to emerge. Conscious of his receding hairline, JSK wrote wistfully about Dr. André A. Cuteo's claims for a hair-growing machine. The contraption resembled an aluminum football helmet and produced snickers from barbershop louts. Nonetheless, wrote the columnist hopefully, "if he can produce even a mild sprinkling of fuzz on a shining pate, I'll sign up." Sad to say, Dr. Cuteo's wonder machine failed.

As the writing expanded and deepened, unexpected quality began to emerge. Thus he reflected at considerable length on the tragedy of an old friend whose triumphs and reversals smacked of an F. Scott Fitzgerald novel.

> I first knew him at an eastern preparatory school. He was sophisticated, wealthy, a good student, a trifle spoiled, a bit arrogant. Our views were dissimilar, but we shared a mutual respect. During the war, he made a brilliant record in the air service. By 1923, he was a Wall Street bond salesman, well dressed, charming when he cared to be. He forged ahead in New York. The old studied arrogance won him important connections. By 1929 he was a junior partner, cultivating the "right people." His star shone brightly. Then came the crash.

He found himself out of job and ill-equipped to face the realities of life. He began a daily round of speakeasies, a series of women, the downward slide.

Our last talk was in 1932. His pride and lack of candor were barriers between us. It was hopeless. Two years ago he was working for a pari-mutuel operator in Havana. Then I heard he had gone to South America. Word came yesterday that he was dead in Rio of a heart attack.

I wonder . . .

Knight became engrossed in the study of style. He discovered William Allen White's *Forty Years on Main Street,* a collection of editorials by the great journalist from the *Emporia* [Kansas] *Gazette.* He relished the power of White's pen. "The charm of his writing lies in his unfailing good humor, warm humanity and a sympathetic understanding of his fellow man." Knight especially enjoyed White's infrequent swipes at fellow journalists, such as a biting commentary on the demise of one Frank Munsey. "Frank Munsey, the great publisher, is dead," White had written. "Munsey contributed to the journalism of his day the talent of a meat packer, the morals of a money changer and the manners of an undertaker. He and his kind have about succeeded in transforming a once noble profession into an eight per cent security."

Mail increased in both volume and temper. A column decrying "the abandon with which people desire to have Mr. Roosevelt do all of their thinking" drew caustic response. ("Dear Mr. Knight: Before Franklin D. Roosevelt, you Republicans were sending this country down the drain.")

He trod the thin line between editorial principle and self-interest. When the city authorized business development a block from Knight's home, neighbors beseeched him to join their protest. "My telephone has rung constantly," he wrote wearily. "While I personally support their objections, it would not be ethical to involve the newspaper because I own property nearby. My sympathies are with them. I hope they win."

They lost.

When the Knight family took an automobile vacation trip in

spring 1937, the column went along too. Readers of the *Beacon Journal* learned that the bartender at the Mayflower Hotel in Washington, D.C., could not make a good milk punch, and that golfers at the exclusive Burning Tree Club included some fierce gamblers. At Jekyll Island, Georgia, Knight viewed the elegant retreat of aged Morgans, Bakers, and Vanderbilts and pronounced it "geriatric paradise."

The trip's highlight was Miami and Miami Beach. Wealthy, attractive, and social, Jack and Beryl were at home in teeming South Florida. By day he went after giant sailfish and tuna in the Gulf Stream, bet on Thoroughbreds at Hialeah, and golfed with Firestones and Fords. By night they toured the clubs and matched dice skill against the house. Reported the "Notebook": "Insignificant-looking Mert Wertheimer of the Royal Palm made a cool million by taking out a license, legalizing his place, under an ancient Florida law. By the time competitors tumbled, the licenses weren't being issued any more."

He wrote quickly, glibly, an outsider looking in. It was the work of a man having no thought of one day becoming a Miami community pillar, his newspaper crusading to shut the illegal casinos in which he now played as a carefree vacationer.

The uninvolved could easily poke fun at the local establishment. "An amusing byplay is the rivalry between Miami Beach's two best-known clubs, Bath and Surf. Childish as it may seem, they hate each other. It seems a hell of a lot of fuss over finding a place to take a swim in the ocean." Ultimately, Knight would join both private clubs and never again belabor them in print.

He was back in Akron in May when the giant German dirigible *Hindenburg* exploded on landing at Lakehurst, New Jersey, killing thirty-three. The disaster shook the rubber city, where two doomed American airships, *Akron* and *Macon*, had been built by Goodyear under direction of Knight's neighbor, the former German Zeppelin scientist Dr. Karl Arnstein. "Years of pioneering in the field," the "Notebook" dourly observed, "are crowned with failure."

The columnist continued to expand his range. As he joined U.S. editors meeting in Washington, a "Confidential Pink Sheet" gossiped that President Roosevelt had been found slumped at his desk in a coma, but revived. "Pink Sheet" author Dick Waldo was expelled by the National Press Club and charged censorship. Editors split. Knight, though no lover of FDR, considered the "Pink Sheet" bad taste, reminiscent of scurrilous whispers in country clubs about "Red Eleanor" and a Roosevelt divorce. "The President's official acts are open to criticism. But snooping around the back door of the White House can hardly be considered a notable contribution to American journalism." Fifty years later, his *Miami Herald* would expose the bedroom adventures of presidential aspirant Gary Hart.

In mid-July, he flew to South Florida on business and gave Akron readers a verbal glimpse of the marvels of air travel. Cleveland to Miami in ten hours! The big DC-3 flew at the pulse-pounding speed of 180 miles per hour and altitudes of nine thousand feet. "Breakfast in Akron and dinner in Miami would have been impossible a few years ago. Who knows what the future holds?"

He was the father of three growing sons and an energetic stepdaughter. The eldest, Johnny, Jr., and Rita, were fourteen years old. The family provided occasional column fodder. "Only people who have children, or are in constant contact with them, experience the incredible changes of succeeding generations." Today's youth was crazy about model airplanes, radio drama, and Charlie Chan movies. "It is a far cry from my pedestrian boyhood."

The world of grown-ups sometimes seemed less logical, however. President Roosevelt needled certain unnamed publishers as being right-wing "Lord Macaulays" at heart, while posing behind façades of democratic idealism. "Highly unfortunate," Knight harrumphed, "that a man of Mr. Roosevelt's talents would engage in promoting class strife."

Akron was a town of strong social structure. Gertrude Seiberling's Tuesday Musical Club fairly oozed gentility. The Portage Country Club stood heavily for the Old Guard. Men of substance joined luncheon clubs. Knight, having little stomach for the typical club, formed his own, calling it the Mayflower Club after the downtown Mayflower Hotel. His luncheon chums consisted, nonetheless, of hand-picked bankers, business moguls, industrialists, and professional types. Meetings would convene for more than half a century. But even having his own club, Knight wondered at the folly of it all.

"These clubs are more innocuous and tiresome than ever," he lamented in print.

> How many times have you heard the issues of the day presented by intelligent speakers holding opposite views. Neither have I. It seems to me that the most stuffy Rotarian would rather hear rivals debate closed shop in the rubber mills than be punished by some fat "success" revealing how little he learned in Europe this summer. ... Among other benefits, it would increase attendance.

Another day, another column. Some days were better than others.

> People who make me tired:
> Lawyers who make speeches in behalf of safety campaigns, then ask the newspaper to go easy on a client caught drunk driving.
> Society ladies who wouldn't be caught dead serving on the same board with a representative of organized labor.
> Country club Tories who are sure the nation is going to hell, but avoid doing anything about it because they "don't know anything about politics."
> Candidates who pump your arm off just before the election, and never see you the rest of the year.
> Teenagers who never earned a nickel, referring to the family car as "that old crate."
> Doctors who tell you not to worry.

fortune seemed a little more evenhanded
in its treatment of John S. Knight. He
grew closer to his brother and son. The
few honors that he had not already won
as a journalist and a human rights advocate were heaped on his shoulders.
Then, on Aug. 8, 1974, his wife of 42
years died after a long illness. And there
was more to come.
The news of the death of John S.
Knight Jr. in Germany was kept from
Johnny's wife, the former Dorothy Wells
of Columbus, Ga., until after the birth on
April 13 — about two weeks later — of a
boy who was named John S. Knight III.

Knight. Through the medium of the Editor's Notebook they discussed the campus violence of the '60s and the course of
the Vietnam War. They exchanged letters frequently, played golf together and
talked

Paul Jensch, managing editor of
the Daily News, said of young John, "He
was really a charming guy. He knew who
he was. He knew he was an heir to a
fortune and to a key job in the organization if he earned it. But he didn't take
himself too seriously."

It was obvious that John S. Knight
hoped through his grandson to see that

John S. Knight III and
lives. I can't think of
change. I can't think of
myself guilty.

"I am not going to
start a new life."

He returned to Fl
nounced he would ma
beth) Augustus. They
1976, in the chapel of
Sea at Bal Harbour
Lifestyle editor of the

GAMBLE IN MIAMI

latter cum laude in 1968 with a degree in
history, then went on to study philosophy, politics and economics at Oxford
University in England, where he earned
a master of arts degree, with honors, in
June 1970.

During high school and college he
worked summer vacations at several
Knight papers, including the Beacon
Journal.

His first full-time newspaper job
came at the Detroit Free Press in 1970.
He gained experience in the circulation

center of Philadelphia, John S. Knight III
was stabbed to death during a robbery
by three men. There were homosexual
overtones.

At the time, his grandfather was visiting at the home of Mr. and Mrs. Edwin
C. Whiteheads of Greenwich, Conn. Mrs.
Whiteheads is a daughter of the then
Betty Augustus, widow of Cleveland millionaire Ellsworth H. Augustus. Knight
and Mrs. Augustus had known each other
for 35 years though a mutual interest in
thoroughbreds and horse racing.

Mrs. Knight died
while watching the R
the LaGorce Island ho

WHEN HE STEPP
1976, his title became
torial chairman of Kni
Knight-Ridder and the
His decision to qui
by Thomas and others
"The trouble wit
Knight's position," Tho
ly that they stay on t
hat the business can't

Knight admired M. Smith Davis. The man could sell anything.
Bluff and florid, Davis had a hulking build, white hair, and an
expansive personality. From a base in Cleveland, he functioned
as financier, broker, and middleman in the buying and selling of
businesses. His specialty was newspapers, but if you were in the
market for a radio station he could arrange that too. Like all
master salesmen, he concentrated on cultivating potential buyers. The aggressive buyer created his own market and made
things happen. Such a man, intuition told Smith Davis, was John
S. Knight.

By the summer of 1936 Knight had settled the *Akron Beacon
Journal*'s debts. He was forty-one years old, building cash reserves and looking for new investments. Commercial radio fascinated him. Of the 30 million families in the United States,

nearly 25 million owned radios. Aside from its entertainment value, radio now brought important news events to America's living rooms, from President Roosevelt's national Fireside Chats to the transatlantic ravings of German dictator Adolf Hitler. All this was a far cry from the wireless telegraphy of Knight's boyhood.

Smith Davis had made a name for himself refinancing a small chain of Ohio-based newspapers. Knight liked the man's audacious style. That spring he asked Davis's advice about buying an Akron radio station. Davis felt the timing was not right. But the shrewd broker stayed in touch, for he knew that the publisher relished a calculated gamble. Kneeling at dice among well-heeled friends in the locker room of the Portage Country Club, Knight boasted of being the world's best crapshooter. And yet privately, whether at dice or in business, he always respected the percentages. "Only a fool," he said, "plays against the percentages."

Davis turned up again at the *Beacon Journal* one sunny March day in 1937 with an investment proposition. A Boston financial house planned to issue some special Florida bonds. Would Knight be interested in buying?

"What are they?" Knight asked.

"Newspaper bonds, for the *Miami Herald.*"

The publisher smiled. He had just returned from the vacation in Miami Beach and liked what he saw. The *Herald,* though drab in appearance and poorly managed, had enormous potential. "I don't want any newspaper bonds, but I might buy the newspaper." It was spoken partly in jest.

Davis talked about the *Herald,* its ownership by a Indiana-born lawyer, Colonel Frank B. Shutts (the "colonel" was an honorary political title, bestowed by a Florida governor), and the bountiful weather, contrasting so dramatically with Akron's in winter. Knight made mental notes. The *Beacon Journal* and the *Massillon Independent* were making money. For expert help he could enlist the talents of lawyer C. Blake McDowell and *Beacon Journal* manager John H. Barry, the one for hardheaded negotiations, the other for uncanny business sense.

"When would you like to go to Miami?" Davis asked.

"Well, next week?"

It was an eight-hour flight by one of the new commercial airliners.

Miami's Frank Shutts was a foxy, gray-haired lawyer of sixty-six with thick glasses, intense pride, and nagging personal problems. Glaucoma, aggravated by diabetes, eroded his eyesight. He was heavily in debt, even though his law partners had prospered representing railroads and utilities. Signed photographs of dignitaries lined his office walls. While he'd had no formal journalistic training, Shutts instinctively avoided compromising the *Herald* with the private ambitions of his cronies; nonetheless they carried great weight. His concept of newspapering differed markedly from that of Jack Knight.

"As I told Mr. Davis, I'm not interested in selling," Shutts said. "I'm just trying to refinance my operations." He hoped to secure personal credit of around $1 million.

Knight nodded noncommittally. He had researched the colonel's background and was aware of his considerable strengths. The son of an Indiana postmaster and shoe cobbler, Shutts had arrived in Miami in 1909 from Aurora, Indiana, as an attorney for the U.S. Treasury Department. Miami was then a sun-blasted village with dirt streets and voracious mosquitoes. Shutts was named receiver for a failing newspaper, the *Miami Morning News-Record.* He borrowed $29,000 from Florida railroad tycoon Henry Flagler to buy the paper and changed its name to the *Miami Herald.*

He had stumbled into a gold mine.

By 1925/26, when the Florida land boom brought explosive growth to Miami, the *Herald* carried more paid advertising than any newspaper in America, outstripping three local competitors, including the afternoon *Miami Daily News.* The boom went bust in late 1926, and a hurricane devastated Miami with great loss of life and property. The *Herald* teetered at the brink of ruin, saved only by Shutts's remarkable ability to borrow large sums from friends on the strength of his word.

While the rest of America basked in Coolidge prosperity, Miami struggled, a resort town in the doldrums. To lure tourists, community leaders winked at a host of sinful pleasures, from wide-open gambling to illicit liquor and prostitution. Slot machines whirred. Cigar counters took horse bets. Gertie Walsh's whorehouse was touted as the best in America. Despite Prohibition, rum-running was rampant. There was widespread corruption of politics and police. Warring gangsters designated Miami as neutral turf. Chicago rackets czar Al Capone took over the entire top floor of a downtown hotel and then bought a mansion on exclusive Star Island in Biscayne Bay.

Shutts's *Herald* avoided "sensational" news that could hurt the economy. Crime was soft-pedaled. Word of impending bank closings went unreported. In the early 1930s, a reporter's eyewitness account of a killer's hanging, obtained by sneaking into the forbidden gallows area disguised as a hearse driver, was kept out of the paper; the judge issuing the ban was a friend of Shutts. The paper affected a dull makeup of condensed type and single-column headlines, imitating *The New York Times.* Shutts continued the trend even after 1934, when a strong competitor burst upon the scene: the tabloid *Miami Tribune,* published by Moses L. Annenberg.

A streetwise veteran of Chicago circulation wars, Annenberg was said to have powerful underworld connections. His *Tribune,* brash and muckraking, claimed a soaring readership and was spurred by a hell-for-leather city editor, Paul Jeans. In the tumultuous scheme of things, however, it lacked the solid advertising base to make the paper profitable. This was despite the fact that Miami tourism was booming again.

Knight and Shutts toured the *Herald* plant. The buildings were badly run-down, the newsrooms so hot in summer that editors and reporters worked drenched in sweat, sometimes wearing bathing suits. Mosquitoes poured through screenless windows. Deskmen wrapped their legs in newspapers against the pests. If Colonel Shutts had to fix a price for this, Knight wondered, what might it be? "I would have to get at least three million," Shutts replied. They went to his house for bourbon and lunch. It was surprisingly modest, a two-story cube built in 1912 and the only home the Shuttses had ever owned.

Knight balked. Three million dollars was more than he intended to pay. How about $2.5 million?

Shutts chuckled to his wife. "We're half a million dollars apart. What's half a million dollars to a man like Mr. Knight?"

Knight also directed his comment to Mrs. Shutts. "What's half a million dollars to a man like Colonel Shutts?"

He went home to Akron, the issue unresolved.

It was another turbulent summer. The Akron rubber plants enjoyed a shaky labor peace. The U.S. Supreme Court had upheld workers' rights to organize under the new Wagner Act. Union boss John L. Lewis of the CIO, who quoted Shakespeare and fought with his fists, won strong concessions. Roosevelt called for massive programs of public works, flood control, relief, housing. In private social bastions such as Akron's Portage Country Club, New Deal haters called FDR "another Stalin."

Jackboots tramped in Europe.

As June warmed the hills of Summit County, Knight found himself in noisy confrontation with Walter B. Wanamaker, an Akron judge presiding over a local vice and gambling trial. Wanamaker wanted to question the defendants secretly for more gangland information and asked the press to keep silent. He was rebuffed by both the rival *Times-Press* and the *Beacon Journal*. Knight was singled out for stinging rebuke in open court: "The underworld can breathe a sigh of relief and extend its thanks to John S. Knight." The publisher retorted in kind: "We suggest that the judge take a vacation. His actions indicate that he needs it badly."

If the flurry scored no popularity points with the judiciary, it did spur Knight's public image. Ohio Republicans, anxious to recoup from the 1936 Landon disaster, began to tout him as a prospect for governor. The *Times-Press* raised a trial balloon, its correspondent writing from the capital in Columbus, "Mr. Knight is a . . . liberal-minded person in step with the world." Knight chuckled. The *Times-Press* was hailing its most implacable competitor. He bought another comic strip, brightened the weekend pages, and saw readership rise another notch. For the *Times-Press,* the screws turned a bit tighter.

And then Smith Davis was back, glad-handing and backslapping, a fresh gleam in his eye. "Colonel Shutts couldn't get his financing worked out. If you're still interested, Jack, he'll sell the *Herald* for the right price."

Knight called in Blake McDowell.

The Akron lawyer's interest in Knight business was whetted by his family holdings in *Beacon Journal* stock. As Knight's fortunes improved, so did McDowell's. His first move was to audit the *Herald*. The study was a revelation. Publisher Shutts had put the paper so much in debt he would need $1.5 million just to bail out. His major creditor, Cincinnati financier Richard LeBlond, had lent the colonel $750,000 to keep the *Herald* out of bankruptcy. None of that had been repaid. Shutts also owed money to a Miami bank, a Boston bank, and assorted friends. Debts were so numerous that he had no accurate accounting of them all.

McDowell learned that Shutts had tried to sell the *Herald* to publisher Eugene Meyer, who had bought the struggling *Washington Post* in 1933. Meyer looked over the Miami plant and turned it down. Shutts then considered handing over the paper to *Herald* employees, but this proved unfeasible. Moses Annenberg had tried to buy it for $3.5 million, but was rebuffed. Shutts, fearing violence from Annenberg, had hired a watchman at his house.

By late summer Knight was having qualms. He would have to borrow heavily for the *Herald,* staking the *Beacon Journal.* He was a stranger to Miami. Would he be out of his depth? He worried about competing head-to-head with Annenberg. It was gambler's caution, calculating the odds. The rival *Miami Tribune* might be a scandal sheet, but its owner was a tough adversary. Thirty years earlier, Chicago's circulation wars had been orchestrated by Moe and his brother Max. Now, Annenberg's annual income from various sources was $6 million, making him one of America's richest men. A year before, in 1936, he had bought control of the *Philadelphia Inquirer.* Moe Annenberg could make short work of a newcomer from Akron.

Knight expressed his misgivings to Smith Davis. The broker sought to put them to rest by arranging for Knight to accompany him to New York and visit publisher J. David Stern, Annenberg's most bitter competitor and owner of both the *New York Post* and the *Philadelphia Record.* The *Record* was locked in a fierce circulation battle with Annenberg's *Philadelphia Inquirer.* Stern accused Annenberg of importing Chicago hoodlums to raid *Record* distributors. A big giver to the Democratic party, Stern had tried unsuccessfully to put the FBI onto his arch-enemy and did persuade Pennsylvania's governor to protect *Record* trucks with National Guardsmen. (Stern so loathed Annenberg that ultimately he would telephone his friend Franklin D. Roosevelt in the White House and get a federal investigation of his rival's income tax records. The tax case would send Annenberg to prison for nearly three years, until his parole in July 1942, when he was dying of a brain tumor.)

Stern was pleased to wine and dine Jack Knight. If what they said about the Akron publisher were true, he could revitalize the *Herald* and make things uncomfortable for Annenberg in Miami. Along with Smith Davis, the men lunched in Stern's penthouse office atop the *New York Post,* with a magnificent view of the city. For Knight, such surroundings made for a heady sampling of the power of a big city press. Stern hammered on the theme that his enemy was not invulnerable. That evening, the group met again for dinner at Stern's Park Avenue apartment, after which Stern suggested that they all go to the Joe Louis–Tommy Farr heavyweight championship fight in Yankee Stadium. Knight remarked that it was impossible to get tickets. Stern picked up the telephone, and quickly obtained three ringside seats. Such casual exercise of power impressed the man from Akron.

The fight, which Louis won by a fifteen-round decision, provided grist for another "Editor's Notebook" column. "The Brown Bomber's left jab found Tommy Farr's badly marked face a convenient target, literally tearing it to ribbons. Farr, the ex-coalminer from Wales, never had a chance." They capped the evening with a round of Manhattan nightclubs, where maître d's greeted Stern with unctuous deference.

During the flight back to Ohio, Knight again was nagged by doubts, rejecting Davis's attempts to reassure him. The strange malaise hung on for days. He complained of chest pains, and said that a man in such condition had no business buying another newspaper. He made a quick trip to the Mayo Clinic in Rochester, Minnesota. After an examination, doctors pronounced him physically fit and his heart sound.

Events moved relentlessly ahead.

Lawyer McDowell visited Colonel Shutts's rented summer home at Lenox, Massachusetts. The *Herald*'s owner stuck doggedly to his price. McDowell probed Shutts's debts and financial objectives. He learned that the aging publisher wanted desperately to build up cash for his family. The lawyer radiated folksy charm, paying heavy court to both Colonel and Mrs. Shutts. Under pressure, Shutts finally agreed to reduce the *Herald* price if his creditors would trim back what he owed them. Negotiations wore on.

In Cincinnati, real estate magnate Richard LeBlond chatted amiably about Shutts. He was so fond of the publisher that he had never tried to recoup his $750,000 note: "Anything I can do to help the colonel . . ." He was even willing to erase $250,000 of Shutts's debt and write off all interest.

And so Shutts came down to Knight's price of $2.5 million. McDowell persisted. The colonel actually owned only 60 percent of the *Herald*. If he reduced his selling figure to $2.25 million, Knight in return would pay him an annual consultant's fee of $12,000 for ten years. This would provide the Shutts family a direct cash income over the decade, instead of a wait for a share of long-term mortgage payments. Like a man befogged, Shutts agreed. Still McDowell was not finished. On the day of closing the *Miami Herald* sale at New York's Waldorf-Astoria Hotel, auditors expressed concern that Shutts's slipshod bookkeeping might result in additional unpaid future claims against the newspaper. To avoid this, McDowell proposed that Shutts place $200,000 of the *Herald* selling price in escrow. Wearily, the colonel assented. At last it was done. John S. Knight paid $2.5 million in borrowed money, with the *Beacon Journal* as collateral. He still thought the price too high.

At his mother's insistence, Knight assigned his brother Jim to take part in managing the Miami paper. Initially, however, the shrewd John H. Barry would be in charge. Barry was a cherubic-faced former schoolteacher from New York State. Fastidious and penny-pinching, he had managed *Beacon Journal* finances since 1911. It was said that he had even stopped C. L. Knight from dipping into the cash drawer for pocket money, demanding that the publisher sign a chit for what he took.

Jack Knight's ability to recoup from debt after the death of his father was largely due to Barry's financial acumen. In later years, the publisher would regard the skills of Barry and McDowell as his major inheritance. "My father had the sense to pick good men and give them freedom to function."

James Knight and his wife, Mary Ann, flew to South Florida in late September with instructions to prevent anything from being carried off before the formal takeover. After inspecting the *Herald* plant, Knight shook his head. "There's nothing here to carry off." Among things that would have to change, he noted that general manager George Harper kept pigeons cooped on the roof and engaged in amorous trysts with his secretary behind the closed doors of his office. As a result, future *Herald* executives would be obliged to work in open enclosures or glass-walled offices.

On October 15, 1937, the Knights took control of the *Miami Herald.* In a front-page editorial, the new publisher pledged to operate the paper "in behalf of the general public, uncontrolled by any group, faction or selfish interest and dedicated solely to the public service. . . . We hope to be tolerant, just, friendly and fair."

Miami gossips whispered that John S. Knight was a front man for Moe Annenberg.

With his headline-screaming tabloid, Moses L. Annenberg practiced roughhouse journalism in Miami. It was a town suited for sensationalism. Behind the palm trees and floral abundance, Miami was celebrities, sex, ripe politics, crime, gunfights, gambling, prostitution, police payoffs, a corrupt judiciary, and a corps of picturesque, often hard-drinking news reporters and editors eager for scoops. Big, breaking stories—the *Hindenburg* disaster, the Lindbergh kidnap case, John Dillinger shot dead in Chicago—sent newsboys into the streets shouting extras.

Newspaper street sales were lucrative. In winter, downtown Miami was a busy crush of tourists, streetcars, and horn-blasting automobile traffic. Men wore spectator shoes and ice cream suits, and women turned out with white parasols and cloche hats for the evening promenade on Flagler Street, followed by dinner and a show. In Bayfront Park, Maestro Caesar LaMonica's concert band played "Moon over Miami." City lights cast a pastel glow. Lighted causeways were strung like pearls across the black velvet of Biscayne Bay.

Annenberg relished competition. Old-timers remembered the time he had had three different copies of the *Tribune* printed in advance for the execution of Bruno Hauptmann, kidnapper of the Lindbergh baby, with headlines reading EXECUTED!, RE-PRIEVED!, PARDONED! The papers were sorted and stashed in a downtown warehouse days ahead of time. As the moment neared, Annenberg hovered over the wire machine, fiercely puffing an aromatic Turkish cigarette, an open telephone line at hand. When the bulletin came, he grabbed up the phone and announced, "He's executed. Let 'em go!" *Tribune* extras were on the street in ten minutes.

By summer 1937, Annenberg had lost his appetite for Miami. This was due partly to circumstance, partly to tragedy. The circumstance was his purchase of the *Philadelphia Inquirer* the previous year, and the bitter feuding with J. David Stern. The tragedy was a head-on automobile crash in April 1937 which killed the *Tribune*'s vibrant city editor, Paul Jeans. If Annenberg was the financial spirit of the *Tribune*, Jeans was its journalistic soul and body. His death left such a vacuum that the publisher no longer even visited the paper regularly when he was in Miami, much less frequent its offices.

Again, Smith Davis presented an idea to John S. Knight. "I think you ought to buy the *Tribune* from Moe Annenberg."

Knight asked him what advantage was to be gained.

"You can get a monopoly on Miami. Oh, sure, Governor James Cox has the *News,* but the *Tribune* is the key. With it out of the way, you can turn the *Herald* into a fantastic success. Besides, a town of two hundred thousand can't support three newspapers."

Knight and Davis made an appointment to see Annenberg at his *Inquirer* offices in Philadelphia. Annenberg greeted them affably. In years to come, Knight would recount the verbal exchange:

"Mr. Annenberg, I would like to ask you just three questions."

"Go ahead."

"Do you think there's room for three newspapers in Miami?"

"No."

"Would you sell the *Tribune*?"

"Yes."

"How much do you want for it?"

"One million dollars."

"I don't have a million dollars. As you know, I've just bought the *Miami Herald.*"

"Then what do you have?"

"We own a small paper in Massillon, Ohio, the *Independent.*"

"Where the hell is Massillon, Ohio?"

"Twenty miles from Akron, between Canton and Wooster. Circulation is around ten thousand but the paper nets fifty thousand a year. I believe you are losing two hundred and fifty thousand a year in Miami."

Annenberg nodded. "What's your proposal?"

The haggling would take weeks. Again, Knight delegated the details to Blake McDowell. Annenberg finally would drop his price to $600,000 for the *Tribune* and accept the *Massillon Independent* as part payment.

Knight returned to Miami in a buoyant mood. Things were definitely going his way. It did not occur to him to question how long the trend would last.

fortune seemed a little more evenhanded in its treatment of John S. Knight. He grew closer to his brother and son. The few honors that he had not already won as a journalist and a human rights advocate were heaped on his shoulders.

Then, on Aug. 8, 1974, his wife of 42 years died after a long illness. And there was more to come.

The news of the death of John S. Knight Jr. in Germany was kept from Johnny's wife, the former Dorothy Wells of Columbus, Ga., until after the birth on April 13 — about two weeks later — of a boy who was named John S. Knight III.

Knight. Through the medium of the Editor's Notebook they discussed the campus violence of the '60s and the course of the Vietnam War. They exchanged letters frequently, played golf together and talked for hours.

Paul Knopf, managing editor of the Daily News, said of young John. "He was a real charming guy. He knew who he was. He knew he was an heir to a fortune and to a key job in the organization if he earned it. But he didn't take himself too seriously."

It was obvious that John S. Knight hoped through his grandson to see that

John S. Knight III and lives, I can't think of down. So I am not myself guilty.

"I am not going to her me," he told Thoi start a new life."

He returned to Fl ounced he would m beth) Augustus. They 1976, in the chapel of Sea at Bal Harbour Lifestyle editor of the

6

CASTLES IN THE SAND

latter cum laude in 1968 with a degree in history, then went on to study philosophy, politics and economics at Oxford University in England, where he earned a master of arts degree, with honors, in June 1970.

During high school and college he worked summer vacations at several Knight papers, including the Beacon Journal.

His first full-time newspaper job came at the Detroit Free Press in 1970. He gained experience in the circulation

center of Philadelphia, John S. Knight III was stabbed to death during a robbery by three men. There were homosexual overtones.

At the time, his grandfather was visiting at the home of Mr. and Mrs. Edwin C. Whiteheads of Greenwich, Conn. Mrs. Whitehead is a daughter of the then Betty Augustus, widow of Cleveland millionaire Ellsworth H. Augustus. Knight and Mrs. Augustus had known each other for 35 years though a mutual interest in thoroughbreds and horse racing.

Mrs. Knight died t while watching the R the LaGorce Island ho

WHEN HE STEPP torial chairman of Kni 1976, his title became Knight-Ridder and the His decision to qui by Thomas and others "The trouble wit Knight's position," Tho ly that they stay on to hat the business can't

The *Miami Herald* plant was a run-down firetrap. Of the three buildings only one, built in the early 1920s, was equipped with an elevator. The business staff was laden with deadwood and holdovers, hired willy-nilly. Some, Knight discovered, had little productive work to do but remained on salary. The newsroom was a strange mix of characters, many of them drifters and misfits. Ancient cigarette-burned desks sagged beneath the leavings of editors and reporters come and gone—dusty copy paper; outdated almanacs, directories, newspapers, and yellowed typed copy; ashtrays filled with dried cigar butts, broken pencil stubs, paperclips; drawers filled with empty whiskey bottles. In a corner one still found an ancient brass cuspidor encrusted with dried tobacco spittle. The toilets were smelly cubicles of hand-scrawled obscenities. Beyond, in the mechanical areas, ink-stained men toiled in paper hats over presses that rumbled and groaned, feeding fresh newspapers in bound stacks to waiting trucks at the loading docks.

Knight's newly appointed general manager, John H. Barry, launched his assault on disarray, both human and fiscal. Within a week of his arrival, former business manager George Harper and his secretary both had resigned, workmen were busy sawing office walls down to half-height, and the pigeons were banished from the roof. Barry reported to Jack Knight in Akron: "Last week's payroll showed 403 people, which to me is outrageous. We're taking steps to reduce the numbers."

He also noted the unexpected take-charge attitude of young James Knight. Ignored in Akron, the *Herald*'s new secretary-treasurer was now freed of his elder brother's constant dominance and plunged into the business of reshaping the property. General manager Barry, in the meantime, followed his own instincts. "John, if I were easily discouraged I would say, 'Let it go!' But since this place is in such deplorable state, the success will be all the greater."

Jack Knight flew to Miami and was introduced to community leaders by Frank Shutts. The crowd included such *Herald* satraps as elderly Judge Frank B. Stoneman, longtime editor in chief. Shrewdly, Knight would keep Stoneman until his death four years later, when his ashes would be mixed reverently into the concrete of a new Herald building. Also in attendance was bluff, handsome Dan Mahoney, a political wheeler-dealer, publisher of the rival *Miami Daily News,* and son-in-law of its owner, former Ohio governor Cox. Knight rose to speak with a friendly glance at Mahoney. "I would like not to inherit any of the animosities of the past. What's gone is gone. We'll have ours eventually. No forthright newspaper can succeed without having people condemn it."

Except for Barry's business housecleaning, Knight held to the old Springfield lessons, avoiding abrupt editorial change. Readers expecting upheaval found gradual development instead. The drab single-column headlines of the Shutts era remained for the present, as did the sometimes inane jottings of columnist H. Bond Bliss.

Random Thoughts. Special Weeks. The past one has been a humdinger. Foreign trade. Cotton. Poetry and Debts. At least these are official. Probably others are crowded into it. Such as Tip Your Hat Week. Brush Your Nails. Spinach. Hogwash. And Why Write Week. That's right, why write? Because!

But behind the scenes, a new broom was sweeping. This was most evident to Alabama-born managing editor Ellis Hollums, a *Herald* employee since 1922. Under Frank B. Shutts, Hollums had functioned as a political pipeliner and manipulator with friends in local high places. It was Hollums's job to know which skeletons rattled in Miami political closets and to exert pressures accordingly. Both the *Herald* and the *News* had long functioned this way, inspiring local wags to call the former Big Tammany and the latter Little Tammany. "I need at least a year," Knight told McDowell, "to find out what Hollums knows about Miami." There began a spirited exchange of memos between publisher and managing editor. These were often voluminous things, Hollums crowding thoughts, routine decisions, trivia, and insight into single-spaced typed pages; Knight replying with crisp, often numbered paragraphs on subjects ranging from details of layout and new feature acquisitions to terse expressions of journalistic philosophy. Subordinate that he was, Hollums displayed a canny ability to adjust:

> *Oct. 22, 1937*
> *Dear Jack: Mr. Shutts telephoned me this morning and said, "Tom Grady has been our friend for many years and, while I know new people own the* Herald, *I still think we ought to take care of our friends." I replied that I have nothing to do with editorial policy and would not presume to establish one without consulting you.*

> *Oct. 26, 1937*
> *Dear Ellis: I hate to prate about the ideals of journalism, but you and I know from experience that there*

are several ways of running a newspaper. My way is to tell all the news, be fair to all parties concerned and pull no punches. It is the only formula by which a newspaper can become great, or a great newspaper can maintain reader confidence.

Oct. 28, 1937
Dear Jack: We are toying with the so-called women's page in an effort to brighten it. We might consider shifting some features elsewhere for decent makeup.

Oct. 30, 1937
Dear Ellis: 1. Try to display more Page One art. 2. Put more emphasis on local news, with one or two interesting feature stories each day. 3. How are you coming along with developing a more intimate treatment of society news? 4. I would like to see the comics next to the last page of the paper, where they belong. 5. Are you planning to present both sides of the bus franchise controversy? Please don't hesitate to write to me frankly at any time.

Hollums would maintain his memo-writing pace with an intriguing blend of business detail, gossip, and chitchat.

ITEM—*Ballinger called, wanting to know if the Florida Power and Light Company and various utilities were still sacred cows. I replied by letter that we have no relation with FP&L, the railroads or anybody else; that your policy on news is to treat everyone objectively, and that editorially we have no alliances.*
ITEM—*Eddie Rubin, the much-arrested jeweler, came into our newsroom about 1 o'clock this morning plastered and began cursing at reporter Steve Trumbull, who finally threw him down the stairs. Rubin left, shouting that he would have warrants out this morning. It is 1 p.m. now. No sign of the warrants.*
ITEM—*Frank (Red) Squires, formerly with Annen-*

berg's Tribune, *is circulating the story that Annenberg secretly owns the* Herald *and that you are on a salary of $100,000 a year. He made the statement in the presence of myself and several others recently, but nobody believed him. He was tight.*

In Akron, the rival *Times-Press* could no longer take the strain. Knight's spending to improve the *Beacon Journal* contrasted sharply with the harsh cutbacks at the *Times-Press.* It had been a long and bitter competition, with a chronic local economic slump tipping the balance. Rubber plants were moving out of Akron to areas having a friendlier labor climate. Declining jobs and payrolls eroded the base for newspaper advertising and circulation. It became evident that one newspaper would have to fold. Knight grimly rejected proposals that he sell out to the *Times-Press* owners, Scripps-Howard. In the haggling, he dealt directly with Roy Howard, an old friend. They came down to a price difference of $50,000. Knight said, "Let's flip for it." Howard agreed, and produced a fifty-cent piece. Knight flipped, and won. On August 28, 1938, he absorbed his competitors, giving them a 30 percent nonvoting interest in the *Beacon Journal.* Roy Howard would recall long afterward: "It was bad enough dropping fifty thousand dollars to Knight on a coin flip, the sonofabitch forgot to return my half-dollar." For Scripps-Howard, however, it was to be a worthy transaction. Thirty years later, Knight Newspapers would buy back the *Beacon Journal* shares for $8.5 million in cash.

With a population of 250,000, Akron, Ohio, was suddenly the nation's largest city having only one newspaper. Knight gave orders to move the *Beacon Journal* into the five-year-old Times-Press building, the towered gray structure of sculpted slab granite dominating a dreary hillside stretch of East Exchange Street. He geared the six-day *Beacon Journal* for a Sunday edition, and a boost in circulation from the current seventy-two thousand to ninety thousand or more. His exultation, however, went strangely flat. "We are now solely responsible for printing and distributing information in this city," he told *Beacon Journal* editors. "And that, gentlemen, is sobering."

Akron worried. "No one questions Mr. Knight's integrity and

ability," said radio's anonymous Voice of Labor, "and yet we regret the passing of the *Times-Press*. A tremendous power for good or evil has been placed in Jack Knight's hands." Militant unionists saw it as part of a plot to smash organized labor. Merchants feared skyrocketing advertising rates. Pressure groups— manufacturers, doctors, lawyers, preachers, crusaders for this cause and that—worried that their special interests would suffer. Readers fretted over the fate of favorite comics, features, and columnists.

Knight would reflect on all this years later. "This was no ordinary community, no peaceful, placid residential town. This was Akron, vital and turbulent, composed of bitter factions and widely conflicting interests, a city of strong men with strong convictions."

He pledged a *Beacon Journal* that would be politically independent and as proof resigned his membership on the Summit County Republican Executive Committee. He promised a newspaper open to all points of view. He added a full page of former *Times-Press* comics, bought another press association wire service, established more outlying Ohio news bureaus. He exhorted the staff to avoid complacency. "When you're the only newspaper in town, the chief threat to good journalism is overconfidence. In fact, we've got to work even harder."

Skeptics were unconvinced. When a citizens' group vowed to create another newspaper, Knight offered to contribute surplus equipment from the *Times-Press*. There were no takers.

He was the favored son, outgoing and handsome, a natural athlete, good at boxing, football, and golf. At age fifteen, John Shively Knight, Jr., spent his summers at camp, on the golf links at Portage Country Club, and in a part-time job at the *Beacon Journal*. School terms were spent at private Western Reserve Academy in nearby Hudson, Ohio. It was a campus of ivy-covered colonial brick buildings, green fields, and stately elm trees, serving sons of the well-to-do. His Uncle Jim had preceded him there. It was generally thought that the boy would follow his father and uncle into business. To Jack Knight's vexation, however, Johnny was an indifferent student.

No one in the family knew about the pistol. It was a small .22

caliber model, bought by mail order. On a Saturday in February 1938, Johnny stuck the loaded gun into his pants pocket and went with other students to a movie in the school gymnasium. During the movie, for some unexplained reason, the gun went off. Eighteen-year-old upperclassman Arthur Saalfield was struck in the leg and taken to a hospital, where the bullet was removed without complication. Johnny confessed privately to faculty members, but other students were not told the miscreant's identity. A sheriff's deputy, summoned to investigate, did not file a report. On Sunday morning, nevertheless, Akron read a full account of the incident in the *Times-Press:* STUDENT EXPELLED FOR HAVING GUN . . . JOHN KNIGHT JR. OUSTED AT ACADEMY.

Repentant Johnny Knight wrote to his parents in Miami: "This has changed the whole slant of my life. I know you will never look at me again, but I have learned my biggest lesson. Mark my words, I will pay you back for all you've done for me." He signed the letter, "Very sincerely yours."

The following day, a Monday, the *Beacon Journal* carried a single paragraph on an inside page saying the wounded student was in good condition. "Young Saalfield was slightly injured in the leg at Western Reserve Academy when a toy mail order pistol accidentally discharged, the pistol having been in the possession of a 15-year-old classmate." John S. Knight, Jr., was not named.

A few days later John H. Barry quietly arranged for his enrollment in Akron's Buchtel High School.

Miami was, in the words of *Herald* editor John Pennekamp, "a strange frontier." It was actually two cities in one. The mainland city was heavily populated by southern crackers from North Florida and Georgia who called it "Miamuh" and held to the insular ways of small-town society and politics. Across the bay lay glittering Miami Beach, a city dredged from sand by such plungers as Carl G. Fisher, a millionaire promoter from Indiana. Miami Beach attracted a human potpourri, from the rich and highborn to film stars, hustlers, hookers, and racketeers. By the late 1930s Collins Avenue in season was bumper-to-bumper with Rolls-Royces, Packards, and Pierce-Arrows. A shadowy S & G rackets syndicate, established by local gambling satraps in 1944 to coordinate south Florida illicit bookmaking operations, ran the town, collecting extortion fees from businessmen (cost to open a cigar stand: $5,000), conducting open bookmaking, and having its own representative on the city council. Mainland Miami, too, stuck to a policy of ignoring gambling, prostitution, and corruption in the name of tourism.

Into Jack Knight's office there strode Miami city commissioner John W. DuBose, a lawyer and old-line politician. "What do we have to do at City Hall to get right with you, Mr. Knight?" DuBose asked. The publisher fixed him with a bland stare. "Nothing, except be good public servants."

When DuBose left, Knight dashed off a memo.

> *Dear Ellis: It seems to me that the* Herald *should wage an even stronger campaign against what City Hall is doing. I base this on several points. 1. A higher budget, apparently without justification at a time when favored jobholders are receiving sizable pay increases. 2. The sordid system of political reward currently in vogue. 3. Strong evidence that commissioners will not give the city manager a free hand and are selfishly determined to stick by the old spoils system at any cost. I would keep at them relentlessly until we find some way to bring good government to Miami. What do you think?*
>
> *J.S.K.*

When John S. Knight was in his second year of ownership of the *Miami Herald* he reviewed the pluses and minuses.

On the business side, Barry was doing a splendid job. Advertising showed big gains; circulation was up by fourteen thousand copies per day. Jim Knight was bringing order to the mechanical departments and talking about technical innovations. But Knight was less than happy with the newsroom. He had promoted veteran John Pennekamp to managing editor and Hollums to executive editor, but incompetents remained and the staff did not seem to grasp essentials. There were too many typographical errors. Page makeup would be good one day, unbelievably cluttered the next. The society pages were dull and lifeless, the columns lacking sparkle. He found himself writing lengthy critiques to Hollums on fundamentals ("The society makeup on Saturday was very poor, uninteresting throughout. It seems that we go from one extreme to another . . ."). There was no continuity of style in the use of pictures. He wanted to add a weekend rotogravure section, but had no one in Miami capable of putting it together. The *Herald* obviously needed a stronger hand, someone to shake the ashes.

In Akron, he summoned to his office the *Beacon Journal*'s hulking Sunday editor, Maidenburg. The man filled the room with his six-foot, four-inch presence.

"Ben, how would you like to go to Miami?"

"That's fine with me."

"When can you be there?"

"Monday morning, bright and early."

"Good. I'll raise your salary to eighty-five dollars a week."

Knight turned to his typewriter and tapped out a note to Hollums.

I am sending B. M. Maidenburg to Miami. You will find him to be an excellent newspaper man. It is my hope that you and Pennekamp will give him the utmost cooperation. Please show this letter to Pennekamp so there may be no misunderstanding between us. If I have not made myself perfectly clear, the telephone is available for your use. Sincerely yours . . .

Memos from Hollums to JSK:

ITEM—*Rumor mongers are spreading a story that you are in the process of swapping the* Herald *for the* Brooklyn Eagle. *Haven't been able to run down the sources, but it's pretty well all over town.*

ITEM—*The local union of radio entertainers advised us yesterday they are filing a complaint against one of the local stations. The station owner called Pennekamp last night threatening to sue if we published the story, saying:* "I am damned tired of the Miami Herald *kicking me around." Pennekamp told him he*

was being ridiculous and said goodnight. We're print-
ing the story.

ITEM—Fritz Gordon, local attorney, has a cordial
political dislike for Dan Mahoney of the News. *Gordon*
showed up at the Royal Palm Club last night carrying
a tiny goat. He set the goat in the middle of Mahoney's
table and said, "Dan, the Herald's *been getting your*
goat ever since Jack Knight came to town. Here's another
one." Dan's face turned fiery red. Then Gordon picked
up his goat and walked out.

Some locals were nettled by the new political and social independence of the *Herald.* To the traditionally conservative regular columnists, Knight added such names as Walter Winchell, Westbrook Pegler, Heywood Broun, and Eleanor Roosevelt. Colonel Shutts, whose $12,000 yearly fee carried with it the title of consultant, called on the publisher. "Mr. Knight, my friends at the Surf Club don't like some of the changes you're making." Knight offered a frosty smile. "Colonel Shutts, I'm not publishing a newspaper for the Surf Club."

He expected staff members to follow a code of ethics, and set the tone himself. Thus, a souvenir firm received a package in the mail and a note on *Herald* stationery: "I am returning the desk set sent to me the other day, as it is against my policy to accept any Christmas gifts from commercial firms. Sincerely, John S. Knight." When the manager of a Miami Beach restaurant insisted there would be no check for Mr. and Mrs. Knight's dinner, the publisher said, "That's up to you. If I can't pay, I won't come back." The check was produced.

Not everyone followed the policy. Nightclub waiters continued to despise amusement critic Bob Fredericks, who demanded front-row seats and the most expensive steaks but always left without paying or leaving a tip. Fearing Fredericks's wrath in print, they made no complaint. He never knew that every steak brought to his table had been spat on.

Journalistic leeches galled Knight. In Miami, he found that sportswriters were on the payroll of the Hialeah racecourse, receiving cash for stories favorable to the track. The custom became the topic of a signed Knight column.

Free meals, free drinks, trips to Cuba, "publicity" jobs and other manifestations of life on the cuff have been accepted for so long among Miami journalists that mere mention of the fact produces bored expressions of mock surprise. But the public has a right to look to newspapers as protectors of its interest. That interest cannot be guarded when reporters receive this sort of outside compensation. No man can serve two masters.

The *Herald* began to show fresh journalistic vigor. Stories became bigger, coverage broader.

Bryan C. Hanks, president of Florida Power and Light Company, walked into Knight's office to report that he had been approached by a City of Miami rate consultant offering to settle a long-standing rate controversy if FP&L would pay $250,000. Hanks intended to reply in a paid advertisement. "I'm not about to pay a bribe," he told Knight. The publisher helped him to write a strong ad, headlined I WON'T PAY A BRIBE! It went to the *Herald* and the *News* on the same day. Reporters dug into the mess. The *Herald,* handling the matter as part of a long-running controversy, gave it routine coverage. The *Miami News* plastered the story across page 1, accompanied by a scathing editorial and cartoon depicting Corruption in the form of an octopus with tentacles strangling City Hall. Several city officials were indicted and two tried but acquitted. The *News's* aggressive coverage won a Pulitzer Prize, the first for a Miami newspaper. Subsequently, R. R. Williams and Commissioners DuBose and Ralph Ferguson were thrown out of office in a recall election. Jack Knight exulted in a personal editorial. "Their municipal government riddled for years with incompetency and graft, Miami's voters finally have risen up in wrath. . . ."

Raw milk triggered an uproar. When *Herald* writer Marion Shutts Stevens, daughter of Colonel Frank Shutts, was stricken with undulant fever after drinking unpasteurized milk in a Miami restaurant, the Health Department confirmed that Dade County had one thousand such cases yearly. The *Herald* urged the City Commission to ban raw milk for human consumption. At stormy public hearings, a leading farmer-physician extolled the virtues of untreated milk. The issue was put to a public vote, which went narrowly against compulsory pasteurizing. The *Herald* effort succeeded anyway, as consumers refused to buy raw milk, forcing dairies to pasteurize. Undulant fever disappeared.

For all its human diversity, the *Herald* newsroom had never seen anything like Maidenburg. Loud and profane, his white body burned beet-red from outings at the beach, Jack Knight's 250-pound "Big Boy," as he was called, slouched in the newsroom's fetid heat stripped to the waist and dripping sweat, his great head permanently wreathed in a cloud of cigarette smoke. A glutton for work, he was on the job six days a week from ten in the morning until late at night. From Sunday editor he was nominally promoted to news editor, but actually ran everything. He bossed subordinates with tyrannical fury, delighted in practical jokes, and erupted in boisterous guffaws when inflicting discomfort, "Haw, haw, haw!" A Maidenburg paper clip, fired from a rubber band, would strike its sedentary target, producing a howl of protest. "Haw, haw, haw!" Woe unto the preoccupied scrivener who sat down in his chair without checking first, for it might be freshly dashed with ice water. "Haw, haw, haw!" Reporter Nixon Smiley was so angered by the ice water gag that he hurled his chair across the room at Maidenburg, but missed.

Pennekamp, nominally the big man's superior, was so cowed that he gave the new man virtual autonomy with power to hire and fire. Maidenburg's gruff voice barked constantly across the newsroom. To a hapless reporter: "Goddam it, how could you write such a stupid piece as this?" To arts writer Henry Cavendish, whose pieces ran to ponderous lengths: "Look at this! Where in hell do you think we can put this much copy?" Cavendish quit. To the staff, payday became a nervous ordeal; one never knew when he might receive not one envelope but two, the second containing his severance pay. Rough as Maidenburg's methods were, they got results. Copy tightened and brightened. Headlines improved. So did spelling and layout. There were inner strains. Maidenburg found Ellis Hollums not to his liking. Personality clashes were part of the newspaper business—Maidenburg himself was widely disliked and knew it—but in the managing editor's case, he sensed something deeper. For one thing, Hollums seemed to live incredibly well on a newspaperman's wages, with a nice home at a very good address. No mention was made of this in Maidenburg's frequent telephone talks with Jack Knight in Akron. The boss was pleased with the way things were going; if there were executive problems, he did not discuss them with his news editor.

The Hollums matter came to the surface in an unexpected way.

Weekend local stories were important and usually planned in advance. Maidenburg liked to have a strong lead article for Sunday's edition. While thumbing through a magazine, he came upon a brief item of interest. The Justice Department was sending a team to Miami to investigate widespread illicit gambling. Maidenburg sensed the irony of it. Nobody enjoyed the dice more than John S. Knight. When in Miami, the boss was a familiar figure at the illegal casinos. No matter. Maidenburg summoned to his desk Steve Trumbull, a former Chicago reporter and one of the *Herald*'s best. "See what you can make of this, Steve." Trumbull tore out the magazine clipping and stuffed it into his pocket.

It was not a great investigative effort. So wide open was gambling that all one had to do was drive around the city and report what he saw. Trumbull's familiarity was such that he could name all the kingpins of local casinos, *bolita,* and bookmaking. His lengthy, colorful piece, ready in three days, gave the *Herald* a front-page strip story for Sunday, keyed to the federal strike force.

On Monday morning Maidenburg was confronted by an enraged Ellis Hollums, shouting, "I want to know how that gambling story originated." Maidenburg told him.

"Well, I don't know how you do things in Akron," Hollums said, "but this is Miami. We're a tourist town. Tourists want gambling. They want to have a good time and a little excitement. A story like this reflects badly on the *Herald,* the community, everybody. . . ."

Hollums stormed into his glassed office and slammed the door. Maidenburg went back to his work. An hour later his telephone rang. It was Miami police chief Leslie Quigg, a drawling

Georgian whose image of an effective policeman was a hulking heavyweight, good with his fists.

"They tell me you're the editor who put Trumbull onto that story," Quigg said. "I want to talk with you."

"Sure," Maidenburg replied. "Come on up."

"Not in the office. I'll meet you at your apartment at two o'clock."

Maidenburg went to meet the chief. Barely had they walked into his parlor when Quigg began lecturing him about the gambling article. "Young man, don't you know who's in thick with gambling in this town?"

"No," Maidenburg said. "Who?"

"Your own damned editor, that's who. Ellis Hollums!"

Thirty minutes later, Maidenburg was on the telephone with Jack Knight in Akron.

"What do you want to do about it?" Knight asked quietly.

"I don't know, Mr. Knight. It's your paper. I can't do anything myself."

"Well, fire him."

"Fire Hollums?"

"Yes."

"Hell, I can't fire Hollums. He's my boss!"

Knight grunted. "Let's give this some thought, then call me back on another phone. Don't call from the office."

Maidenburg turned over the dilemma in his mind. An hour later, he called Akron again.

"All right, what shall we do?" Knight said.

"I think it's time for Mr. Hollums to retire," Maidenburg said.

He never found out precisely how Hollums was persuaded to step down gracefully. After all, the man had done nothing illegal and could have challenged the police chief's allegations. Was the persuader Blake McDowell, the artful all-purpose lawyer? Or John H. Barry, the tough business manager for whom no chore was too unpleasant? Or Jack Knight himself, who for all his strong purpose hated personally firing anyone? Whatever the mechanics, a few weeks later Ellis Hollums was feted with a retirement party in the *Herald* newsroom. He was presented with a portable typewriter and given a pat on the back, and he departed.

In his "Editor's Notebook" column, John S. Knight wrote, "Some of us have boys who one day may decide to take a whirl at this newspaper business. We would like to be able to tell them that it is not a racket.

"Some of our newspaper offices need a strong arm and a good broom."

THE FREE PRESS

Summer 1939: For Americans it was a strange interlude of rising promise and dark portent. The outlook depended on whether one's perspective was focused on home or abroad. To John S. Knight it was the best of times. At forty-four, he was independent and outspoken and was making a name for himself in national publishing. Men of substance sought his ear. At a New York publisher's convention, writer Ward Morehouse found him in the crowded bar of the Waldorf-Astoria. "A mixer," he wrote of Knight in *Editor & Publisher,* "a man who talks straight at you; probably as interesting a newspaper personality as you could find."

Morehouse's article gave vent to a range of Knight comments. On his successes in Akron and Miami: "We're individualists. I take full responsibility for editorial content and policies." On his newspaper management philosophy: "We don't practice chain journalism. We try to run progressive, independent news-papers." On himself: "I like fun. I like to live, to do things, to get around. I like bridge and dice and conversation and golf."

The writer quoted an assessment of Knight by fellow Ohio publisher Paul Bellamy of the *Cleveland Plain Dealer.* "Jack Knight's position in Akron is a tough one," Bellamy said. "Akron is a one-industry town, rubber. The high men of rubber are tough babies. During the last major strike, Jack stood up in his boots and called down both sides. He stood for sanity and reason and got away with it."

Among those who took a more than passing interest in the article was eighty-one-year-old Edward Douglas Stair, publisher of the *Detroit* [Michigan] *Free Press.* Stair was looking for a suc-cessor and felt that John S. Knight just might be the man.

White-haired, secretive, and aloof, E. D. Stair had owned and operated the morning *Free Press* for more than three decades, extolling "American individualism, American courage, American initiative, American thrift and American industry." It was the oldest paper in Michigan. Stair personally had coined the masthead slogan, "On Guard for Over a Century."

Skeptics saw the old man as primarily guarding the status quo. The paper served as mouthpiece for Detroit's conservative Gold Coast crowd. His personal foibles were legion. He opposed municipal zoning as an infringement on personal property rights. He vowed to shut down the *Free Press* rather than allow his workers to organize into labor unions. He disliked night baseball because it drew patrons away from theaters, in which he held a large financial interest. He disliked airplanes for the noise they made flying over his house in fashionable Grosse Pointe. He disapproved of unfavorable weather reports that might prevent shoppers from patronizing advertisers' stores. At editorial meet-ings his word was law. "Yes, sir!" chorused his editorial writers. "Yes, Mr. Stair!" He kept a blacklist of people who were not to be mentioned favorably in the *Free Press,* including Franklin Delano Roosevelt. His idiosyncrasies could be costly. Once, miffed to find his way to the elevator blocked by a mob of people waiting to buy classified advertising, he called the police to clear his lobby. *Free Press* classified business nosedived. The paper's circulation of 293,000 trailed those of its two Detroit rivals, the afternoon *News* and the *Times.*

Stair and his editors had grown old. It was time for new blood to take over the paper, preferably that of a young man whose ideas, if not patterned after his own, at least were acceptable. He valued political conservatism and editorial independence. He was not interested in selling to a large chain such as Hearst or Scripps-Howard. This man Knight showed promise. And the more Stair studied his subject, the more intrigued he became.

Knight's now-weekly "Notebook" columns offered insight into the man. He espoused a work-ethic conservatism similar to Stair's. Wrote the Akron / Miami publisher:

> We were taught that if we worked hard, developed our minds and tried to be decent citizens, there was a chance of getting somewhere. Today, this type of good citizen is the target of demagogues. The employer is pilloried as a "labor hater," a labor leader of force and principle is a "dictator," and any potential candidate who has more than the price of a filing fee is derided as a "rich man."

Knight attended President Roosevelt's periodic meetings with publishers at the White House and acknowledged the personal charm of FDR, but he took a dim view of administration spending. "What are we doing to avert the day when we must choose between national bankruptcy and starting the printing presses? The answer is, absolutely nothing." He could write with sensitivity about the new movie *Goodbye, Mr. Chips,* admitting that it moved him to tears. "I wonder if there really are people left in the world like old Chips. There are perplexing intervals in life when one would like to turn to him for kindly philosophy, but I'm afraid he disappeared with the coming of the streamlined age." Knight had spirited exchanges with skeptics of his own hometown. Rubber factories were abandoning Akron for better labor climates in the South and West. Rumor circulated that Knight's newspaper dealings elsewhere portended his own departure. The publisher bristled in print, "My family and I believe in Akron. We're not quitters."

E. D. Stair invited him to Detroit for a chat.

The man who walked into Stair's office seemed dressed for a banker's convention. Knight's gray suit of finest English wool was accented by a snowy white shirt, gold cuff links, dark tie, highly polished shoes. His thin hair was combed straight back from a broad forehead. Clean-cut features were dominated by steely gray eyes. Knight was accompanied by a quiet man of middle age whom he introduced as John H. Barry, his business manager.

Matters quickly came to cases. "We're getting old," Stair said. "The paper isn't performing as it should." He was thinking of selling, to the right person at the right price. The old man looked sharply at his visitor. "They tell me you're not the man your father was."

Knight smiled. "I plead guilty to that. I am certainly not the man my father was. But I may have attributes that you would wish to consider. . . ."

They looked over the plant, the newsroom, the shop, the newsprint storage areas, the loading dock where trucks awaited the next edition. Out beyond the neo-Gothic tower of the *Free Press*, Detroit was a sprawling, smoggy industrial metropolis hugging the sluggish big river that bore its name, a busy waterway linking Lakes Erie and Huron. From the waterfront, with its massive bridge over to Ontario, one watched the ponderous passage of red-dusted ore boats, carrying iron ore from the mines of Lake Superior south toward the steel mills of Pittsburgh and northern Ohio. It was a vastly different city from Akron or Miami, a city of hard edges and deep ferment, where people and newspapers battled against intense competition. Among the masses drawn to Detroit's factories were hundreds of thousands of blacks, living in steamy ghettos. It was a town of easy virtue and sudden violence; a tough union town, with no guarantee of a friendly shop.

Could Jack Knight take on Detroit?

John H. Barry was eager to bring in McDowell and start dickering on price. Stair wanted $3.2 million. They would try to bring him down. Nonetheless, the offer was enormously attractive. That afternoon Jack and Beryl Knight visited Stair and his wife at Grosse Pointe and played bridge. Returning to Akron the next day, Knight pondered what he knew about Stair and the *Free Press.*

The Detroit publisher had been born poor in Morenci, Michigan, quit school at age fourteen; and started a hometown weekly newspaper, which failed. Loading a secondhand press onto a horse-drawn wagon, he and his brother trekked 125 miles to Maple City, Michigan, to start again. This second venture, the *Maple City Dispatch,* made money. From such beginnings Stair developed a rugged philosophy: "There's not much difference between success and failure. Most men fail by just a little bit, when another ounce of steam would have meant success."

E. D. Stair bought and sold newspapers, built up a chain of 158 live theaters, and invested in Detroit real estate, business, and banking. By the age of forty-six he was worth $10 million. He bought the *Detroit Journal* and then, in 1917, took control of the *Free Press.*

The *Free Press* had a legacy of rugged independence since its founding in 1831, as the weekly *Democratic Free Press and Michigan Intelligencer,* when Detroit was a muddy river town of twenty-five hundred. Its first editor, John P. Sheldon, once spent nine days in jail as publisher of the weekly *Detroit Gazette* for printing articles critical of the Michigan Supreme Court. When Sheldon's health failed, the *Free Press* was taken over by his nephew, Sheldon McKnight, who sold it a year later after killing a man in a barroom brawl.

In the 1850s the *Free Press* passed into the hands of stormy eccentric Wilbur Fiske Storey. Intolerant and brilliant, Storey favored, among other things, slavery. He changed the paper into a scandal sheet featuring juicy exposés of evil (SHOCKING DE-PRAVITY! HORRORS OF THE OPIUM DEN!), then sold it for a big profit and went to Chicago. After his death in 1884, a biographer would write, "Storey specialized in gratifying the base instincts of the mob." But he also left a paper with a strong financial base.

In the 1870s control of the *Free Press* fell to William Quinby, a genial idealist who brought it into the technological revolution of the telegraph, web press, typesetting machine, stereotyping, halftone engraving, long-distance telephone, and typewriter.

The paper experienced enormous expansion, publishing a weekly national mail edition of 200,000 circulation, the first homemaker's section in the United States, and a weekly London edition overseas. In time, however, spiraling debts forced the aging Quinby to sell, and in an emotional farewell speech to colleagues he declared, "The noblest profession on earth is that of editor. I say to you, as St. Paul said to Timothy, 'Oh, Timothy, keep that which is committed to thy trust.'"

E. D. Stair's trust, if rigidly personal, was steady. "The *Free Press,*" he insisted, "places principle above personalities." He stood foursquare against Franklin D. Roosevelt, labor unions, and U.S. involvement in World War II. The *Free Press* developed new editors and writers. A team of five reporters won its first Pulitzer Prize in 1932 for, of all things, their sixty-five-hundred-word coverage of a gigantic American Legion parade. Beefy editorial columnist Malcolm Bingay became the most locally identifiable staff member, but the most famous nationally was Edgar A. Guest, reporter and poet. From 1898 until his death in 1959, Guest wrote fifteen hundred verses for the *Free Press* and numerous books. Poetic purists winced, but the public doted on his homespun style.

Now the *Free Press* was about to make another big change.

Things were coming together rapidly. Knight liked to have his options in order. He disliked muddled thinking. He was a maker of lists, a refiner of discussion, a dealer in specifics. In this spirit, he sat down in January 1940 and took stock in a letter to J. H. Barry. "Discussion of the purchase of the *Detroit Free Press* brings up a number of situations which I believe should be studied carefully," he began. The *Miami Herald* had exceeded all their expectations. The debt was down to $900,000, profits steady. They would need a new press and a new building, costing perhaps $1 million, but the *Herald* would be able to finance the entire project by early summer. In Akron, the *Beacon Journal* continued its money-making ways. "To me, personally, it means a great deal in the pride that comes with publishing an interesting, progressive and honest newspaper." He urged that news, pictures, and features never run less than 125 columns.

He turned to Detroit. "The *Free Press* represents an unusual opportunity." But was it their opportunity, or someone else's? The paper had prestige. Its purchase would add to the Knight laurels. Terms seemed favorable. Cost cutting could increase the net yield. "This paper could be a good earner." The problem was Sunday competition. Detroit had three Sunday papers, and the *Free Press* ran a poor third. They would have to spend heavily to promote sales. For now, they needed very complete data just to decide on buying it, and that meant cost breakdowns for wire services, features, printing, circulation, personnel, everything. "In no other way can we arrive at an accurate estimate of potential earnings. . . ."

War rumbled beyond the seas. In Europe, China, and Southeast Asia, dusty legions marched through the smoke palls of blasted cities. At home, the daily headlines were of war and potential American involvement. Knight wanted no part of it. He worried about White House policies that set the nation drifting into alliances. He saw no cause to stake American lives on German rearmament or, on the other side of the world, Japan's march on China. Were they destined for a grim repeat of 1917? "Today, 22 years later," he warned, "the United States again faces being drawn into foreign conflict. To what purpose? Is it our duty to police the world?"

It was the same course that his father had taken. Knight now appreciated his father more and more. An editor who spoke his mind lived on the bull's-eye of public opinion. But his pacifism had complex roots, and was not wholly a legacy from C. L. Knight. In Akron, surrounded by the domestic gentility of her home, her flowers, and her books, there lived another whose passion for peace was equally strong: his mother, Clara. They walked together in the evening light, she small and frail and holding softly to his arm. They talked of the news from Europe, and of William L. Shirer's radio interview of a German U-boat captain. She wondered whether America could really remain neutral. Jack told her that he doubted it. She sighed. "Life goes by so swiftly. The days pass, and we don't do the things we planned. . . . One has a queer, unnatural feeling nowadays. Living through one war was enough, I think."

New Year's Day passed, and it was the winter of 1940.

Beryl continued to charm E. D. Stair with bridge games at Grosse Pointe. "He's like an old Roman," she said, "always demanding his way." Negotiations over the *Free Press* dragged on. As usual Blake McDowell carried the brunt of things, sorting out details, developing points of discussion, studying the newspaper plant, personnel, and inner works.

In Miami, Jack Knight engaged in unexpected conflict with J. Edgar Hoover. The FBI chief, an annual winter visitor to south Florida, was making headlines deploring the concentration of gangsters and racketeers in Miami, their presence condoned by local powers-that-be. Knight saw it as Hoover's grandstanding. "Is there any good reason why a growing city should continually be pilloried?" he editorialized. "Let the FBI sweep out the public and private crooks and their work will get no louder applause than in Miami." The flurry quieted. *Herald* circulation surged by twenty thousand copies per day over the same month a year earlier. South Florida boomed, with celebrities to match. Walter Winchell made his weekly radio broadcast from a glassed booth off the *Herald* City Room, taking many of his "scoops" from the Associated Press wire. Big egos could be a pain. Winchell groused about the editing of his column in the *Herald*. "Is he getting touchy on us?" Knight mused. Winchell retaliated by reporting rumors of the proposed *Free Press* sale.

Knight bided his time with Stair, leaving details to McDowell and Barry. The price for the *Free Press* did not suit him. In March he and Beryl drove to the old publisher's winter mansion at Palm Beach for a talk. Stair stood firm; he wanted $3.2 million, not a penny less. Knight wrote to McDowell in Akron. "This will have to be negotiated. As I see it, this is a question of whether we want to make the move. If not, negotiations should be terminated."

Stair's standoff with the Guild was nettlesome. The union had won its organizing vote over his opposition. Tempers seethed. "The thing has been badly botched," Knight complained. "A situation is in the making that could tumble down on our heads." The comment would prove grimly prophetic, for in future years labor turmoil would plague the *Free Press* with tiresome regularity.

Stair refused to yield on his price. As matters developed, however, this did not really matter. Final details were resolved in a brief conversation.

"How do you plan to pay for this newspaper?" Stair wanted to know.

Knight replied that he would borrow the money from the Chemical National Bank of New York.

"Why don't you let me lend it to you?" Stair said.

Knight nodded brusquely. "Very well."

Thus, he was virtually handed one of the nation's major newspapers, in the fourth-largest city in the United States.

On April 30, 1940, Knight wrote a check for $100,000 and signed promissory notes for $3.1 million. He then called a staff meeting and announced, "I didn't buy a newspaper; I bought a staff."

The employees applauded.

It was quickly evident that things would be different.

An editor, Charlie Haun, had charge of a story unflattering to the paper's biggest advertiser. Haun walked into the new publisher's office and showed him the article. "I don't know what to do with it, Mr. Knight."

Knight looked at him levelly. "You're the editor."

Haun beamed. "I'll run it."

An editorial statement appeared on page 1: "Under the new ownership, the *Detroit Free Press* will be politically independent in its editorial policy. It will always be operated on behalf of the general public, uncontrolled by any group, faction or selfish interest and dedicated solely to the public service. . . ."

For all the fine verbiage, it was no simple matter stepping into a new role in Detroit. Unlike Miami, a town constantly changing, Detroit was set in its population and preferences. *Free Press* readership was solid, if not dominant. Still adhering to the old Springfield lessons, Knight made changes gradually. He resolved to stay with flamboyant Malcolm Bingay as chief editorialist. Despite maverick ways and a fondness for the bottle, Bingay could be flexible. Journalism's mavericks had their place, Knight knew. "You never have trouble with routine people." The editorialist, in turn, wrote glowingly of the new boss in his popular "Good Morning" column: "Detroit, I am sure, is going to like him tremendously. Jack Knight is what the old town has needed for a long time." It was the first of many gushing accolades by Bingay, whose expressed adoration of Knight was to verge on the sycophantic.

Knight hired a car for a whirlwind tour of Detroit, including the slums. He invited to lunch an astonished R. I. Thomas, boss of the United Auto Workers union. He asked community leaders what they thought of the *Free Press*. When two leading merchants complained of too much horse-racing news and not enough baseball, Knight shook his head. "I don't agree with you, gentlemen. There were fifteen thousand people at the racetrack yesterday and only three thousand at the ballpark." In the office, he designated John H. Barry as the *Free Press* business manager, with complete charge of commercial operations. He added new columnists to offset Stair's traditional conservatism, Eleanor Roosevelt and Drew Pearson. He bought a new comic strip, *Smilin' Jack.* To institute gradual changes in editing and layout, he put in a call to Maidenburg in Miami. "Ben, I need a Sunday editor in Detroit." Maidenburg replied, "I'm on my way." He startled Guild organizers by walking in and introducing himself at a bargaining session, something E. D. Stair would never do.

With clinical intensity, Knight studied his newly adopted city. Depression and labor wars had taken a heavy toll. Auto industry payrolls lagged. Ten percent of the 1.8 million population of Detroit was on relief. And yet economic signs pointed to a comeback. Bank deposits were high, department store sales were up, building permits were soaring, and military spending fueled an industrial resurgence. A war would bring boom times. "Detroit," Knight wrote in the "Notebook," "does things on a Gargantuan scale."

The power structure opened its doors, welcoming the Knights into homes, private clubs, and intimate dinner parties. ("She is from Chicago, you know. A Zoller. Quite wealthy.") There were invitations to golf, to luncheon clubs, to tea. Downtown, he spoke his mind to civic groups. "In our news columns, we believe in facts, aggressiveness and giving both sides a hearing. We think of our editorial page as a public defender and a builder of causes."

He was now the publisher of a metropolitan paper with a weekday circulation of 322,683 and 301,788 on Sundays. Such success had a rejuvenating effect.

But the nation drifted toward the maelstrom.

fortune seemed a little more evenhanded in its treatment of John S. Knight. He grew closer to his brother and son. The few honors that he had not already won as a journalist and a human rights advocate were heaped on his shoulders.

Then, on Aug. 8, 1974, his wife of 42 years died after a long illness. And there was more to come.

The news of the death of John S. Knight Jr. in Germany was kept from Johnny's wife, the former Dorothy Wells of Columbus, Ga., until after the birth on April 13 — about two weeks later — of a boy who was named John S. Knight III.

Knight. Through the medium of the Editor's Notebook they discussed the campus violence of the '60s and the course of the Vietnam War. They exchanged letters frequently, played golf together and talked on the phone.

Paul Janensch, managing editor of the Daily News, said of young John, "He was really a charming guy. He knew who he was. He knew he was an heir to a fortune and to a key job in the organization if he earned it. But he didn't take himself too seriously."

It was obvious that John S. Knight hoped through his grandson to see that

John S. Knight III and lives, I can't think of down. So I am not myself guilty.

"I am not going to her me," he told Thor start a new life."

He returned to Flo after his grandson's nounced he would ma beth) Augustus. They 1976, in the chapel of Sea at Bal Harbour Lifestyle editor of the

8

THE GATHERING FURIES

latter cum laude in 1968 with a degree in history, then went on to study philosophy, politics and economics at Oxford University in England, where he earned a master of arts degree, with honors, in June 1970.

During high school and college he worked summer vacations at several Knight papers, including the Beacon Journal.

His first full-time newspaper job came at the Detroit Free Press in 1970. He gained experience in the circulation

center of Philadelphia, John S. Knight III was stabbed to death during a robbery by three men. There were homosexual overtones.

At the time, his grandfather was visiting at the home of Mr. and Mrs. Edwin C. Whiteheads of Greenwich, Conn. Mrs. Whiteheads is a daughter of the then Betty Augustus, widow of Cleveland millionaire Ellsworth H. Augustus. Knight and Mrs. Augustus had known each other for 35 years though a mutual interest in thoroughbreds and horse racing.

Mrs. Knight died while watching the R the LaGorce Island ho

WHEN HE STEPP torial chairman of Kn 1976, his title became Knight-Ridder and the His decision to qui by Thomas and others "The trouble wit Knight's position," The only that they stay on to hat the business can't

Disaster was afoot. The thing was so palpable you could smell it on the spring air. In his "Editor's Notebook" of May 11, 1941, John S. Knight assailed the man whom he regarded as prime architect of the inevitable, Franklin D. Roosevelt. "It won't be long now. The Great White Father has turned loose his pack of howling medicine men to beat the drums and lead the dance of death."

The publisher considered war unthinkable. He saw no alternative but rigid neutrality. Looking back years later, isolationism would seem utterly naïve in the face of Hitler's madness, but in these waning months of peace the idea of being drawn into a European bloodbath still was bitterly opposed by many Americans, including Knight.

Until now the nation had been too preoccupied with domestic problems to become alarmed by events abroad. In a Detroit movie theater, Ben Maidenburg watched news films of the bombing of Shanghai, never dreaming that he would one day go into combat against the Japanese.

Conservatives worried about where the president really stood. Editorial critiques of his judgment in foreign affairs spurred administration pledges of U.S. neutrality. By early 1939, however, events steadily worsened. Hitler had marched into Czechoslovakia and unleashed aggressive tirades on overseas radio. Roosevelt warned, "War is a contagion. World lawlessness is spreading." Charles A. Lindbergh visited Nazi Germany and came home declaring that America should "resist the propaganda that our frontiers lie in Europe." Critics labeled him a Hitler-lover. "What luck it is," Lindbergh said, "to find myself opposing my country's entrance into a war I don't believe in."

Knight was of a similar mind, scoffing at the notion that war would make the world safe for democracy. "England and France are democracies, having universal suffrage and representative government. Externally, however, they are vast imperialisms governing masses of subject people." Many readers were outraged. An Ohio matron called him an "isolationist nincompoop."

Summer came. Americans crowded the New York World's Fair. Kate Smith sang "When the Moon Comes Over the Mountain," awash in sentiments of home and hearthside. Italy marched into tiny Albania. Roosevelt urged lifting curbs on U.S. arms sales abroad. Knight's old political ally, Senator William Borah, led the isolationists' movement in Congress, declaring, "All this hysteria is manufactured and artificial." Knight told his readers, "America is being finessed into trouble."

In September, German panzers overran Poland in eleven days. Congress debated selling U.S. arms to all comers, Axis powers included. Knight had reservations. "There can be no guarantee against our joining the European holocaust except an aroused public opinion and our iron determination to stay out." Britain and France mobilized. Finland lost its bloody little war with Russia. Stalemate set in. Borah called it "the phoney war."

On Christmas Eve 1939, with the children at home in Akron, Knight pondered the uncertain future of a generation that included his eldest son John, Jr., aged sixteen. "The youths of many nations are again pawns for greed and ambition. There is no Christian spirit among nations at war. It is a struggle without hope, a conflict without principle. . . ."

The logic of things, he believed, had become unbelievably tangled.

In Miami that winter, an elderly European visitor came to his office seeking editorial support for Polish and Finnish war relief. Peevishly, Knight asked how the *Herald* could support relief abroad when Miami's own Community Chest had fallen short of its goal. "We have an old saying, 'Charity begins at home.'"

"No one is starving in this country, Mr. Knight. In Europe, civilization is tottering."

Knight flared. Wars, he argued, were struggles for trade supremacy. This one had been dictated at Versailles in 1919 by ruthless old men. The Poles were victims of their own duplicity. "We strive to keep our people neutral."

The visitor picked up his hat, bowed, and departed. Knight watched him go, conscious that it was a strategic withdrawal, not retreat.

Thursday had become his day of trial. Wherever he happened to be, in Akron or Miami or Detroit, this day brought the weekly chore behind closed doors, writing the column. It meant no telephone calls, no visitors. Stolidly, sometimes angrily, he banged away at the old typewriter, crossing out errors, reworking the copy in pencil, typing it again. He envied people who wrote smoothly or, as Bingay did in Detroit, with flowing power. He struggled more than he flowed.

By summer 1940, peace was but a ravaged memory. Nazi legions invaded France and the Low Countries. The British retreated from Dunkirk. Germans goosestepped into Paris. Britain endured the Blitz. Young Nazis mustered at channel ports for invasion, singing "Wir fahren gegen England" ("We're sailing against England"). The voice of Winston Churchill hurled defiance over the airwaves.

For the neutralist, these were arduous times. Nazi brutalities revolted civilized man. American sentiment swung heavily pro-

British. The split between interventionists and isolationists widened. Knight saw the rise of an old, familiar dilemma. "Why is it that in times of great national stress, tolerance and understanding fly out the window?"

By now he shared the prevailing British sympathy. Still, he felt America manipulated. "It is natural that we be excited about preparedness. But this doesn't mean that we forfeit the right to express opinion . . . that anyone who disagrees should be denounced as a Nazi sympathizer."

The mail poured in, pro and con.

And then the 1940 presidential campaign opened, with the meteoric rise of a former Akron lawyer, Wendell L. Willkie.

He was a tousle-haired maverick, plain in manner and tastes as befitting one born and reared in small-town Indiana. He lived modestly with his wife and son, never owned a car, cared nothing for society or golf, and yet adored public acclaim. He had a boyish frankness but gave no quarter when championing causes in which he believed. This beguiling combination vaulted him into national politics.

Knight had met Willkie in 1920, an obscure young lawyer in the legal department of Akron's Firestone plant. Eager to make a name, Willkie became a civic activist and public speaker. He sought C. L. Knight's help to break the influence of the Ku Klux Klan in Akron schools, engineering the defeat of Klan-backed candidates for the school board. A Democrat, Willkie became a delegate to the national convention. In 1929 he was offered a partnership with a major New York firm of lawyers specializing in electric utility cases. He and Jack Knight happened to ride the same train out of Akron. "I don't like leaving Akron," Willkie said. "I can't imagine living in New York."

Four years later, at age forty, Willkie was president of the billion-dollar Commonwealth and Southern Corporation, a giant holding company resisting forced sale of private utilities to the federal Tennessee Valley Authority. He developed an intense distrust for Roosevelt, telling Knight, "The man has no compunctions."

Knight shared Willkie's antipathy. As a member of the Protestant establishment, it galled him to hear FDR deride "economic royalists" and "gentlemen in well-stocked clubs." The publisher noted that the president was no stranger to private wealth or well-stocked clubs. Knight chafed over New Deal spending and labor philosophy. The latter was taking a heavy toll of Akron. The Wagner Act, he complained, "is framed to guarantee collective bargaining rights of labor but does nothing to impose equal responsibility."

The neutrality fight slopped over into party politics. A thousand Dartmouth students sent a telegram to Roosevelt: KEEP US OUT OF WAR. Churchill's name was booed at isolation rallies. In opposition, Knight's journalistic idol, William Allen White, formed a liberal Committee to Defend America by Aiding the Allies.

Willkie wrote a provocative article for *Fortune* urging an end to the "attitude of hatred" toward business. Conservatives applauded. When he quit the Democratic party and registered Republican, admirers formed Willkie for President groups with plans to pack the summer GOP convention. Republican intellectuals were enthralled. Knight himself hailed the lawyer as "intelligent, vocal and forthright," but concluded that in a convention dominated by the Old Guard, Willkie wouldn't have a chance.

Philadelphia sweltered in June heat. Knight mingled with Republican politicians and delegates in straw hats and sweat-splotched seersucker suits. He dined with party leaders. But the atmosphere was depressingly familiar. "The same old faces are here that have been in evidence at every Republican convention since the postwar era. . . . They cling pathetically to the old order."

Willkie's groundswell strengthened. Street crowds mobbed the new idol. Reporters clamored. The candidate, flushed and exuberant, told Knight, "I'm going to be nominated!" The publisher's skepticism remained. "Nothing counts but delegate strength," he wrote. And these delegates had been pledged since spring, mainly to Ohio senator Robert A. Taft.

No one was prepared for the shocker.

In the galleries, every spectator under forty wore a Willkie button. As one young businessman exulted, "Willkie represents youth and success." A chant began, "We want Willkie!" Balloting deadlocked as neither of the GOP frontrunners—Taft and New York prosecutor Thomas E. Dewey—would yield. "We want Willkie!" Delegates began to waiver. At the sixth ballot, they broke. The result was broadcast to a stunned America, listening on radio: "Ladies and gentlemen, the Republican nominee for President of the United States, the Honorable . . . Wendell L. Willkie!"

Columnist Knight ate crow. "Poor prophet as I am, the Willkie nomination is the most heartening in the political history of our times. He will stage a spectacular campaign."

Wrong again.

In the months to follow, Willkie's campaign turned out to be noisy but ill-starred as he hurled down his gravel-voiced challenge: "The President has courted a war for which this country is hopelessly unprepared." He barnstormed 18,500 miles in fifty-one days. The effort was muddled and confused. In midcampaign the candidate lost his voice and was barely able to croak "No . . . indispensable man." By September even Knight saw the cause as lost. "Mr. Willkie is a victim of world events beyond his control."

Roosevelt won a third term by polling 26 million popular votes to Willkie's 22 million. Columnist Knight reflected on a system in which ideas clashed without bloodshed. "As Americans, we are still able to shake hands when the fight is over."

FDR moved resolutely ahead. In December, he told the American people, "We must be the arsenal of democracy." In January, he launched the Lend-Lease Act to supply the Allies on credit. By summer 1941, U.S. troops occupied Greenland and American ships were exchanging shots with German U-boats. In October, the destroyer USS *Kearny* was torpedoed, with two Americans dead and eleven missing—the nation's first combat fatalities.

Five years later, chastened by personal anguish, Knight would reflect on his isolationism and acknowledge the terrible price paid by the young for the shortsightedness of their elders. "Had those of my generation foreseen the consequences, much of this insane tragedy and colossal suffering might have been averted. But we were blinded in pursuit of our own selfish aims, and failed miserably."

For Knight, the year 1941 opened in caustic debate with author Philip Wylie, who bristled at his suggestion that American security did not necessarily hinge on England's survival and the nation should stay clear of the shooting war.

WYLIE: "If America is not ready to sacrifice every man and every dollar to defeat Hitler, then our day, too, is coming. If England falls, America will be Nazi in five years."

KNIGHT: "We are already engaged in the war. And Mr. Wylie should be very happy."

He was angry and frustrated. He continued to feel that Americans were being deceived. In February he wrote: "This is not OUR war and it never was. This is not a war to save democracy, it is a war to decide who shall hold the balance of power in Europe."

Hollywood joined the propaganda blitz. Audiences hissed as Edward G. Robinson played a Nazi spy. They wept over the syrupy, war-ravaged romance of Humphrey Bogart and Ingrid Bergman in *Casablanca*. Grumbled "The Editor's Notebook," "It is difficult to see a movie without having one's intelligence insulted by propaganda."

On June 22, Hitler invaded Russia.

Isolationism was a hopeless cause. Even Wendell Willkie returned from a fact-finding trip to England urging "all aid short of war." Knight snorted in disgust. "Mr. Willkie has sold the Republicans down the river." They were, he acknowledged wearily, at the threshold of war "—one that will revolutionize the social, economic and financial structure of this republic."

Like his father before him, John S. Knight reached the limit of his resistance. In an editorial in all three newspapers, he pledged total support to the president, but with a note of reservation. "If our republic is to endure, there must always be room for free expression and constructive criticism."

The clock ran out on December 7, 1941, as Japanese warplanes swooped over Pearl Harbor. In the devastated aftermath, Knight expressed the American dismay: "How did it happen that we were taken so completely by surprise?"

Four decades later, the question would continue to haunt survivors.

fortune seemed a little more evenhanded in its treatment of John S. Knight. He grew closer to his brother and son. The few honors that he had not already won as a journalist and a human rights advocate were heaped on his shoulders.

Then, on Aug. 8, 1974, his wife of 42 years died after a long illness. And there was more to come.

The news of the death of John S. Knight Jr. in Germany was kept from Johnny's wife, the former Dorothy Wells of Columbus, Ga., until after the birth on April 13 — about two weeks later — of a boy who was named John S. Knight III.

Knight. Through the medium of the Editor's Notebook they discussed the campus violence of the '60s and the course of the Vietnam War. They exchanged letters frequently, played golf together and talked ...

Pa... Ja...sch, managing editor of the Da... said of young John, "He was really ... arming guy. He knew who he was ... knew he was an heir to a fortune and to a key job in the organization if he earned it. But he didn't take himself too seriously."

It was obvious that John S. Knight hoped through his grandson to see that

John S. Knight III and ...lives, I can't think of change. I can't think down. So I am not ...yself guilty.

"I am not going to ...uer me," he told Thom to start a new life."

He returned to Fl ...ter his grandson's ...nounced he would ma ...beth) Augustus. They 1976, in the chapel of Sea at Bal Harbour Lifestyle editor of the

THE WORLD TURNED UPSIDE DOWN

...phy, politics and economics at Oxford University in England, where he earned a master of arts degree, with honors, in June 1970.

During high school and college he worked summer vacations at several Knight papers, including the Beacon Journal.

His first full-time newspaper job came at the Detroit Free Press in 1970. He gained experience in the circulation

overtones.

At the time, his grandfather was visiting at the home of Mr. and Mrs. Edwin C. Whiteheads of Greenwich, Conn. Mrs. Whiteheads is a daughter of the then Betty Augustus, widow of Cleveland millionaire Ellsworth H. Augustus. Knight and Mrs. Augustus had known each other for 35 years though a mutual interest in thoroughbreds and horse racing.

WHEN HE STEPP ...torial chairman of Kni 1976, his title became Knight-Ridder and the His decision to qui ...oy Thomas and others ...night's position," Tho ...ly that they stay on to ...hat the business can't

The battle was no longer in some distant place beyond the seas, unfelt and unseen. War came to south Florida's doorstep with fires in the night and glistening black German U-boats surfacing from the heaving Atlantic, guns blazing. Grisly leavings, once human, washed onto Miami Beach with the morning tides. The lights of the city glowed at night, silhouetting slow-moving target freighters. Stunned tourists stood on the hot sands, so recently given to good times, peering expectantly seaward. Rumors of Nazi saboteurs' landing from submarines abounded. A distant muffled boom signaled another torpedo hit. Smoke columns smeared the blue subtropic sky, and here and there a burning hulk drifted northward on the Gulf Stream. Oil-drenched survivors were plucked from the coastal Atlantic by civilian yachtsmen in their private boats. "The vastness, scope and horror of this war," observed John S. Knight, "cannot be measured by any other conflict in the history of the world."

Horrors that were the talk of Miami bars and barbershops got scant notice in the press. Wartime security muzzled the news; reportorial enterprise was thwarted by common consent. Knight chafed, torn between duty and frustration. How much of this journalistic silence was vital to the war effort and how much of it bureaucratic nonsense? Self-censorship, the wartime credo to which they all subscribed, was the more galling for government bungling. The *Sturtevant* story was a case in point. The *Miami Herald*'s Key West correspondent filed copy on the submarine sinking of the destroyer USS *Sturtevant* even before the navy's press section in Washington knew about it. Government censors moved with such maddening slowness that the story wasn't cleared until the following afternoon, to be grabbed off by the rival *Miami News*. Navy bigwigs had no sense of journalistic competition. Knight expressed his dismay in a letter to chief U.S. censor Byron Price. "We have no quarrel about withholding information in wartime, but it hardly seems fair to release to the afternoon newspapers a story that broke on morning time."

In Washington, Price read the Knight letter with special interest. In peacetime the censor had been an Associated Press executive. A thoughtful and fair-minded man, he was given the impossible task of placing wartime restrictions on the world's most open society. He was well aware of Knight's disdain for arbitrary censorship. The publisher wielded heavy clout among U.S. newspapermen. Price toyed with an idea. He could use a man like Knight in government service. A top aide, N. V. Carlson, agreed. American censorship badly needed top-level contact with the British in London, someone with entry at Cabinet level and higher. "Whereas the British have established very effective liaison here in Washington, we have not done so in London simply because we have no one there with knowledge or ability," Carlson noted. "Mr. Knight in all likelihood could be that man."

In late summer Knight went to Washington for a convention of U.S. editors. He found a sweltering city, packed with bureaucrats, office workers, and military personnel in every kind of uniform. Wartime agencies overflowed temporary wooden buildings erected on the Capitol Mall.

Stimulated, Knight shouldered into hotel lobbies and bars where frantic surface gaiety overlay the hard realities of war. But even now the old ideological debates persisted. Conservatives brooded on the triumph of Roosevelt liberalism in a nation at war, convinced that sinister forces, given respectability by the alliance with Russia, plotted to communize the nation. "Mark my words, Jack, the communal termites are going in for postwar planning on a grand scale. We're all too damn busy to notice them."

American newspapers, in the meantime, were beset with problems, from censorship and newsprint shortage to critical loss of personnel. Aging Eugene Meyer of *The Washington Post* looked dourly ahead. "Knight, things will get a lot worse before they get better." Some small-town publishers worried that they might have to close up shop.

Knight was not prepared for Byron Price's invitation to lunch. The censorship chief dispensed with preliminaries. "Jack, I've got a proposition. You might be able to contribute a real service to the war effort."

They talked for two hours.

It was a bizarre kind of activity, a polite spying between the best of friends, America and Britain. At the luncheon meeting and in a follow-up letter from the censorship chief, Knight gained uncomfortable insight about the extent to which citizen privacy was routinely invaded under conditions of total war.

Voluntary suppression of news by press and radio was but a small part of the process, Price later wrote him.

> *This office is censoring communications entering and leaving the country by mail, cable, radio, radiotelephone, land wire and other means, including press dispatches. We engage in this work 14,000 people who have access daily to about a million pieces of mail and 70,000 cable and radio messages. From this we collect a great deal of information indicating subversive activities and violation of wartime regulations, which we turn over to the appropriate government agencies.*

The British maintained a similar kind of effort, with stations around the free world. Three U.S. naval officers had charge of American censorship in London, but none held sufficient rank to admit him to the highest social and governmental levels. "We need someone with force of character to maintain friendly relations at the top, Jack, someone who can make sure we're fully advised of what the British are doing. . . ."

Knight did not reply immediately. He needed time to think. Given the psychological climate of the times, it was a chance to become involved in the war effort, and this he welcomed. At the same time, he had no desire to be a government functionary, working the other side, so to speak. Hadn't his father demonstrated the pitfalls of that course? Jack Knight was independent, an unyielding advocate of the free press, standing on the principle that newspapers were monitors of government, not participants. On the other hand, this was total war; many dictates of peacetime were temporarily shelved. He sensed, moreover, that while serving in the murky political environs of London, he could break logjams of wartime bureaucracy committed not to freedom of information but to its denial, regardless of necessity. In the name of patriotism and security, petty tyrannies sprouted everywhere, and woe betide the war correspondent trying to report legitimate news over the entrenched objections of small-minded authoritarians. Knight pondered. And the more he pondered, the more he was inclined to accept.

War dominated everything. To have older sons meant to bear the risk of unspeakable sacrifice. Jack and Beryl, accompanied by his mother, Clara, traveled to Culver Military Academy to visit Johnny, Jr., a senior about to graduate with an army commission. The boy had grown into a strapping, personable young man. They watched as six hundred cadets paraded and demonstrated field tactics. Clara Knight was especially moved. She wrote in her diary, "The fact that Johnny is one of them gives me a heavy heart. I dread to think of what the future holds for him and the others." The date was June 7, 1942.

Johnny announced that he intended to volunteer for the army paratroops.

As was his custom each spring, Knight wrote an "Editor's

Notebook" column addressed to young people completing high school and college. Typically it was a message of challenge and hope. But now things were different. Uncertainty weighed upon them all. At his typewriter in Detroit, Knight tried to apply logic to a world turned upside down. "There is nothing to be gained by harping on the virtues of work, thrift and ambition. There is only one issue, to fight and live as free men. There are no niceties to the game. To lose is unthinkable."

Detroit was committed to war production. On crowded streets around the *Free Press,* off-duty factory workers jostled for living space with teenage zoot suiters, roving young hoodlums armed with brass knuckles and switchblades, office workers, uniformed men on military leave, the full human tide of a multiethnic nation. The city's smog rose from factories running day and night, producing materials for war. In Akron, too, the rubber industry boomed for the same purpose. And Miami, land of sunshine and tourists, was turning into a military cantonment as hordes of troops poured in for training.

Knight was part of all this, and yet detached, a recorder and analyzer of events but not an instigator of them. He was forty-seven years old, fit and trim, rich and moderately famous with many social acquaintances and newspapers flourishing in three cities. And yet, deep down, he felt a dark foreboding. "The winning of this war will entail countless sacrifices," he wrote, "but no price is too high to pay."

That phrase would come back to haunt him.

For the newspapers, war or no war, the objective was still good journalism. This meant hiring talented men and women. A newspaper's success began with its editors; Knight expected them to be people of strength and character. He endorsed publisher David Stern's view that "sooner or later an editor who is insincere reveals himself, and the public senses insincerity with an intuition as quick and canny as a child's."

A newspaper had to profit, Knight insisted; without profit there was no independence. The newspaper also was a curious combination of elements—a craft, a calling, a business, a production plant. It demanded the services of writers, photographers, artists, and editors, and these were creative, sometimes eccentric people difficult to fathom. But one also needed salesmen, accountants, laborers, foremen, truck drivers, production engineers, people to deal with personnel, circulation, advertising. And then to put it all together and give it direction, one needed the talents of individuals whose role could be the most complex of all, the management executives. A business rose and fell with its management; the more multifaceted the enterprise, the more demanding their task. As Knight newspapers expanded, so did the need for such people. A publisher could extend himself only so far.

All three newspapers faced personnel shortages as men entered the armed services. Detroit demanded Jack Knight's time as the venerable *Free Press* adapted to its new regime, war prosperity brought fresh tides of humanity into the city, and there were portents of trouble. Akron, too, was in a war boom, but the *Beacon Journal* could handle it. Miami was more complex and worrisome. Newsprint rationing was in the works. Brother Jim Knight wrote letters warning of an impending shortage of paper. The city was becoming a military cantonment, with fancy hotels converting into barracks and golf courses into drill fields. They all bought newspapers, creating a strange dilemma. What would be a windfall in peacetime was a liability under the tight newsprint rationing of war, for rationing made scant allowance for booming circulation. The paper used what it was allotted. Period.

The *Herald* suffered further from a serious gap in editorial management. Ellis Hollums was gone. John Pennekamp, a good man, had his limits. Jim Knight had no experience in news and editorials, and, besides, his gifts were vitally needed in business and production.

Knight selected key people by instinct. In future years, the newspapers would have an elaborate personnel and management recruitment system complete with in-depth testing, headed by a graduate psychologist. But now, the publisher picked his key people in the same way that C. L. Knight had, by looking a man in the eye, weighing his strengths, getting a gut feeling for his potential, and taking a chance.

In Akron, Knight received a phone call from Louis B. Selzer, editor of Scripps-Howard's *Cleveland Press*. A bright executive of the chain, Lee Hills, was looking for change. At age thirty-six, the man was not likely to be drafted soon. Selzer spoke glowingly of Hills. "Jack, I told him the only man he should work for is you."

It was Sunday morning when Hills arrived at the house on Portage Path. Knight found him a quietly personable executive with mental toughness and energy, immaculately dressed. As they talked, Hills recounted a personal background that reinforced the publisher's surface impressions.

He had been a newspaperman since age fourteen, when he had gone to work for a weekly paper in Price, Utah, sweeping floors, writing school news, selling ads, and helping out in the printshop. He had worked his way through high school, taking typing and shorthand, and attended Brigham Young University and the University of Missouri. Out of money in 1929, Hills quit college and got a job as a reporter and copyreader on the *Oklahoma City Times.* By 1932 he had moved to the *Oklahoma City News,* covering local and state government, courts, and the state legislature.

Seeing that most reporters achieved little advancement for lack of education, Hills enrolled in night school in Oklahoma City and took a law degree. Scripps-Howard then transferred him to the *Cleveland* [Ohio] *Press,* where he rose to news editor. There followed a succession of executive jobs on the *Indianapolis Times,* the *Oklahoma City News,* the *Memphis Press-Scimitar.* In summer 1942 he returned to Cleveland to await another assignment, but immediate prospects were not bright. Hills wanted out of Cleveland.

It was a restless ambition that Knight valued. Equally impressed was Beryl, who drew her husband aside and whispered, "Don't let that young man get away." Knight remained noncommittal. The best job he could offer was that of city editor in Miami.

"I'll take it," Hills said.

When the new man arrived in the newsroom of the *Miami Herald* a few days later, the temporary city editor offered his chair. "Don't get up," Hills said pleasantly. "I want to get acquainted with the staff first."

He had already advanced beyond the scope of the job.

As months went by, it became clear in the *Herald* newsroom that whatever his title, Lee Hills was boss. The new man had his hands full. Personnel depleted rapidly as each week meant the loss to military service of another editor, writer, or photographer. To fill vacancies, Hills recruited people he knew from other papers around the country, advertised in trade magazines, hired more and more women. Gradually things stabilized, but talent was spotty. Hills began putting his own style on page formats and typefaces, mindful that a sharp and critical eye scanned his work daily in the publisher's offices at Akron, Detroit, Miami.

Initially, the advisories came in curt little notes.

Dec. 24, 1942
Memo to Hills: I thought your news play on the Ricken-
backer story was weak. . . . There should have been better
tie-in on Page One with the opening of Tropical Park.
The News *handled it somewhat better. . . . I still have*
not had an answer to my question about why the Boston
nightclub fire was so underplayed. JSK

Dec. 31, 1942
Memo to Hills: I think Loftus should write his racetrack
stories in the same manner you would expect them to be
handled by a reporter on the city side. For instance, the
amount of the mutuel play and attendance should ap-
pear near the top. Kindly see that he conforms. JSK

For Hills, the *Herald*'s failure on the disastrous fire in Boston's Coconut Grove nightclub was a sore point. It had happened after his second month on the job. The *Herald*'s Sunday paper was engaged in rugged competition against the *News.* At one o'clock on that Sunday morning, November 29, Hills had gone wearily home to bed after another long day, leaving copy desk slotman Charlie Ward to put the final edition to bed. He was unaware of a standing *Herald* rule that no major change could be made in the final edition without joint approval by the composing room chief and the circulation manager. The rule had been invoked by Jim Knight to prevent costly disruptions in the final press run, causing late deliveries. When Hills picked up his doorstep copies of both the *Sunday Herald* and the *News* at daybreak, he was aghast. Spread across the *News* front page was an eight-column headline, 212 DEAD, HUNDREDS INJURED, AS FIRE, PANIC SWEEP BOSTON NIGHTCLUB. As the nightclub was engulfed in flames, patrons were stampeded, trampled, and burned to death when their bodies jammed shut vital exit doors that opened inward. It was the most spectacular news event since Pearl Harbor. The *Herald*'s final edition did not carry a word.

An hour later, Hills was angrily confronting his slotman.

"But, Lee," sputtered Ward, "there was nothing we could do. . . ."

Hills took his protest to James Knight: "If you're going to have the composing room and circulation department make the editorial decisions, then you don't need me as an editor. I think it's a hell of a way to run a newspaper."

Knight heard him out and nodded. "I think so too." The standing order was cancelled. A full report went to Jack Knight in Akron. Two days later, a telegram landed on Hills's desk: ORANGE BOWL COVERAGE BEST IN YEARS. CONGRATULATIONS TO ALL. JSK. No mention of the fire incident.

Hills had weathered his first Miami storm.

There would be others.

Be it Miami, Akron, or Detroit, running newspapers Knight's way took the measure of an executive. Key personalities differed widely. But there was opportunity to flourish if one applied himself.

John H. Barry, now business manager of the *Detroit Free Press*, was a fastidious man and staunch Catholic who went to church every day, danced the rumba for relaxation, and had a passion for the cold disciplines of ledger sheets and accounting tables. He worked sixteen-hour days but expected everyone else to finish in eight. He saw the making of money as one of man's high callings, even though his specialty was making it for others. His expertise earned him $100,000 per year, a fortune in these 1940s. His position in the Knight organization was unassailable, and he defended it with vigor. A confrontation with Jack Knight himself was the talk of the *Free Press*.

One of Barry's advertising salesmen sold a full-page ad promoting a dealer in smut books. The risqué titles stirred a furor as conservative subscribers protested that they were "pornographic" and "irreverent." When some of Jack Knight's society friends complained, the publisher ordered the ad salesman fired. John H. Barry refused, reminding his employer that he, as business manager, was in charge of advertising. "Jack, you cannot fire anyone in the business office. The man stays." Knight backed down.

The Knight formula of aggressive news coverage, local editorial control, slick layout, and expanded features was working well at the *Free Press.* Although the publisher himself remained Republican and, on many issues, personally conservative, editorialists such as the flamboyant Malcolm Bingay were not wedded to that point of view. Labor, so despised by the paper in the bygone Stair era, found a friendlier *Free Press* under Knight. So did minorities. When white laborers at the Packard plant struck in spring 1943, protesting forced race mixing of workers, the *Free Press* thundered back: "Discrimination against Negroes challenges the sincerity of our beliefs in Christianity and in Jefferson's declaration that all men are created equal. . . . The issue is moral. The virus of racial bias must be exorcised."

Detroiters bought the *Free Press.* In less than three years under Knight, circulation surged by nearly 100,000. Even more surprising was the financial wizardry of business manager Barry. With rigorous disciplines on spending, already he was paying off the paper's $3.2 million debt. Not everyone was impressed by the feat. Wartime excess profits taxes were extracting huge sums from successful businesses. James Knight argued for plowing *Free Press* profits into newspaper promotion and increased home circulation, thereby avoiding excess profits and postponing the payoff of debt. Barry refused to yield. The issue was to simmer between the two for life. Jack Knight did not interfere. Strong individuals, he knew, were not always going to be friends.

Detroit was a pressure cooker. Since Pearl Harbor, 350,000 people had poured into the city looking for defense jobs. Housing was characterized by desperate shortage. Racial tempers ran hot. On a humid Sunday in June, the angry buildup broke. Black and white mobs raged in Paradise Valley and along Woodward Avenue. Troops arrived with fixed bayonets. Rioting left 34 dead, 675 injured, 1,890 jailed, and $2 million in property damage. Covering it all was a struggle, but the *Free Press* managed. Manpower was always critically short, always in turnover. As Charlie Haun, a wartime city desk man, would recall years later, "I wonder how we ever put out a newspaper. I came to work one day and eight people arrived, and I didn't know any of them. Two weeks later they were all gone."

And suddenly, even the boss joined the exodus.

John S. Knight accepted Byron Price's job offer in London.

It was one of those grinding dilemmas, in which you were damned if you did and damned if you didn't. Somehow, Jim Knight and Lee Hills would have to find a way out.

The *Miami Herald*'s newsprint shortage was becoming acute. First, they had been ordered to cut back paper consumption by 10 percent. The *Herald* could live with that reasonably well. But no one had anticipated south Florida's becoming a huge military training camp, flooded with 150,000 serviceman and their families, with a corresponding surge in the local economy. By November 1943, newspaper advertising soared, circulation steadily increased, and both the *Herald* and the *News* were in trouble, their newsprint ration for the balance of the year all but exhausted. Appeals to Washington for more newsprint were rejected. Jim Knight bore the bleak tidings to Hills: To survive December, they would have to cut back the daily paper by a dozen pages on weekdays and three dozen on Sundays.

Something had to go—advertising, news, or both.

Hills was a newsman, and his priorities put news first. An informed public was vital, especially in wartime. He presented Knight with the hardest kind of proposal: strip the paper of display advertising during December, allocate a single page in which advertisers could briefly summarize their goods and services without charge, confine classified ads to bare necessities such as housing and jobs, and eliminate circulation beyond the *Herald*'s immediate territory. It was, Hills reasoned, a patriotic imperative. "Let's continue full war coverage and give people information they need."

James Knight pondered. Such a move would mean heavy losses in revenue, advertising contracts, and long-term circulation. The weight of decision fell upon his thirty-four-year-old shoulders. "All right," he said, "we'll do it."

Miami was shocked when the trimmed-down paper

emerged stripped of ads. The *News,* by contrast, took the opposite tack, packing in advertising and drastically curtailing news pages. As weeks passed, the *Herald* absorbed a financial drubbing. John S. Knight, now in London, expressed skepticism in private letters to Jack Barry in Detroit: "It's probably a good thing for brother Jim. Maybe he will get over some of that smug optimism that he enjoys so much." In Miami, however, a curious thing happened. The crisis became a turning point in the long, hard-fought competition with the *News.* Public approval skyrocketed and, when the newsprint shortage passed, so did *Herald*'s loss of circulation. After that, the afternoon *News* was never again in serious contention.

Diary of Clara S. Knight, Akron, Ohio, autumn 1943:

> I have spent a nostalgic evening listening to music on the radio. Memories crowd me. The announcer said the program was being broadcast to our soldiers and I felt that I was with them, for just a little while. I can't bear to think of young Johnny going off to war. It is with me all the time.

The place was a battleground. The extent of war's devastation astonished him. From a small airplane provided by Lord Beaverbrook, Jack Knight looked down on a London ravaged by three years of intermittent bombings. Whole blocks lay in fire-blackened rubble. Down close, he already knew, some mountains of debris still gave off odors of unreclaimed bodies.

In the late summer and fall of 1943, air raids differed from the massed tactics of the earlier Blitz. No longer did the Luftwaffe send bombers over in waves. Now the Germans came singly or in small groups from varying directions to drop their bombs and veer away to airdromes in occupied France. "Scalded Cat" raiders, the British press called them. The attacks were noisy, a din of bomb hits, antiaircraft fire, and wailing ambulances and fire engines. Friendly flak, raining back down, caused injuries and deaths.

Knight was impressed by the spirit of the British people. His old isolationist hostilities gave way to a rising affection. He praised them in a July radio interview with broadcaster Morgan Beatty, beamed from London to the States. "I should have thought that after 203 weeks of war the English people would be harassed and worn. But every person I meet generates an unyielding optimism."

Knight's dual role as American government representative and newspaper publisher gave him broad social and professional contacts. He dined with Churchill, Eisenhower, and U.S. ambassador Joseph Kennedy. He dealt with the brilliant, red-haired Brendan Bracken, British information chief, whose aloof manner infuriated correspondents. He came to know such diverse figures as Foreign Minister Anthony Eden, the cool aristocrat suffering from a severe duodenal ulcer, and Herbert Morrison, minister of home defense, son of a policeman and a housemaid. He encountered the grim, bull-throated Ernest Bevin, Churchill's wartime minister of labor, who reminded him of John L. Lewis but without the latter's colorful command of classical literature.

Knight was drawn to Lord Beaverbrook, the crusty Max Aitken, multimillionaire publisher of the *London Daily Express,* who had worked miracles promoting aircraft production for the Battle of Britain. The son of a Scots-Canadian Presbyterian minister in Ontario, Canada, Aitken had worked his way through law school selling newspapers and made his first million before emigrating to England at age thirty.

At dinner with several publishers, the press lord gave Knight a whimsical smile. "The code of the journalist should be written on the heart. Don't you agree, Jack? And first, he should be true to himself. The man who is not true to himself is no journalist." To keep his wits sharp, Beaverbrook was fond of engaging in street debates, taking on all comers. When Labour rowdies tried to shout him down in a London park, he retorted archly: "You deny free speech with such regularity that the result will be the annihilation of the very political party that you stand for."

Censorship, by comparison, was a dull bureaucratic business. Knight's role was policy, not detail, so he was constantly having meetings and dictating memos. If the work was less than the exotic intrigue depicted by Byron Price, he did find himself in a position to reduce needless artificial barriers to reporting war news. The typical civilian or military bureaucrat, given a choice of disclosure or nondisclosure, usually chose secrecy. Frustrated correspondents found that a word from Knight could work wonders.

London teemed with humanity. Piccadilly was a swarm of uniforms—British, America, Free French, Polish, Czech, Belgian, Norwegian, Dutch, Chinese—and nearly as many women wore them as did men. Military police patrolled in pairs. Knight's prudish eye was offended by the multitude of street prostitutes, "Piccadilly Commandos," they were called, who paid off supposedly incorruptible British bobbies for the privilege of plying their trade. "A shocking condition," he wrote. "This would not be tolerated back home for very long." He seemed unaware that the world's oldest profession also flourished in Akron, Detroit, and Miami.

One lived with harsh reminders of war. An attractive young secretary in Knight's censorship office learned that her husband, a British soldier, was in a Nazi prison camp, his leg amputated by German doctors. Knight offered her the day off. "It's not necessary, sir," she said stoically. "We all do our bit." A few nights later, he went home after an air raid to find all the windows of his West End apartment smashed by antiaircraft fragments. Soon afterward, while driving in the city, he and a friend came upon a freshly bombed apartment block. Rescue workers searched the rubble by torchlight, drawing out bodies. The warden shook his head wearily. "We've got a good two hundred dead in there, sir. They didn't have much chance, poor sods."

Despite the horrors, he found himself enormously stimulated. The city was filled with things to do. "Hardly a day passes that I don't run into some old friend of mine," he wrote to Jack Barry in Detroit. "There are more shows playing here than in New York." In October, correspondents celebrated his birthday with a party. Composer Irving Berlin played "Happy Birthday" on the piano.

Barry sent him chatty weekly letters from Detroit. During August, the manager reported that profit at the *Free Press* had increased by a stunning 29.3 percent, netting $1.3 million for the year thus far. Final payment of the debt to Stair was made on November 2, a feat that Knight properly termed phenomenal. Barry was flushed with his success: "We must have some new objectives, John, and it's up to you to say what they are." Knight urged the manager to be on the alert for attractive newspaper buying opportunities. Should they try for the *New York Sun*? By the year's end, profit at the *Free Press* alone exceeded $2 million and the three papers combined netted $3.8 million. Barry told his employer: "Our financial standing is so secure that you can expand in any way you desire." As January rolled past, Knight informed Barry that he was thinking of expanding to at least six papers after the war. "I have never thought more about the future than now."

"Everyone in England is fed up with the war, but it has been going on for so long that life under restriction is accepted without complaint," he wrote in the "Notebook." "Unlike us, the British have learned to be patient." Meat was in short supply. Starchy vegetables prevailed in the daily diet. The egg ration was one per month. Oranges were scarce, because German agents in Portugal had planted time bombs in citrus cargoes bound for England. The blackout was in force every night, and everybody carried a small pocket flashlight. "Theaters and movies are packed. The air raid signal might flash during a performance but seldom does anyone leave his seat. Outside, the sky resembles the Fourth of July as raiding planes drop flares."

But this had become very much a two-way war. The RAF went out over the rooftops of London at night, bound for Germany and flying low to evade German detection as long as possible. Their departures brought Londoners running out of pubs and houses, to cheer and wave.

> American airmen see the terrific destruction of German industrial centers. They show you pictures of Hamburg, Wuppertal, Essen and other cities, being systematically destroyed. The constant day and night bombing seems too horrible for people to endure. But the fact is, human beings have an amazing capacity to suffer. The Germans are no different. Their morale will stand a lot of stretching before it breaks. . . .

By winter 1944, England was a gigantic staging ground for the invasion of Europe, the most open secret of the war. More than 150 U.S. correspondents were assigned. Knight, in constant talks with Allied censors and members of Eisenhower's staff, urged positive thinking about news. "When the invasion begins, our objective should be maximum free flow of information consistent with military security. Let's direct our energies toward releasing news, not bottling it up unnecessarily."

He had planned to return home after six months, but remained in London at Byron Price's request. Lengthy association with military men, bureaucrats, and politicians gave him a sense of nagging unease. His attitude toward news differed so sharply from theirs that he seemed constantly at odds with men obsessed with secrecy. He expressed his views at a meeting of the English-Speaking Union at Manchester, urging that uncensored news be assured worldwide as a condition of peace. "Be it in England, America, Germany or the Soviet Union, the right of worldwide news agencies to gather and report honest, unbiased and truthful news must be protected." Audience response was lukewarm.

By spring, Knight felt he had done his best and it was time to go home. He flew back to Washington in time for the American Society of Newspaper Editors annual convention, and was elected the organization's president. His acceptance speech reflected deep concern for the future.

> The very idea of censorship is repugnant to every good newspaperman. In war, security is paramount. But when peace returns, worldwide freedom of information is essential to preserving the very things for which we are fighting.
> The people are entitled to the truth.

THE DAILY NEWS

The possibility was enormous. He had toyed privately with the idea even before going to England. In London there had been pipedream talks with portly editing genius Basil ("Stuffy") Walters—"two-drink" conversations, they called them—while speculating on areas in which to expand the Knight enterprise. But this, Chicago, was one of those ambitions one nourishes gingerly, knowing the prospects are remote. And yet here was newspaper broker Smith Davis back again, exuding excitement. Jack Knight's several chairs of professional life weren't even warm again, and Davis was urging him to go out and buy the *Chicago Daily News*!

"It's the opportunity of a lifetime, Jack. This is going to be a gold rush."

Knight shook his head in wonder. The papers in Akron, Detroit, and Miami all needed his attention. He was getting reacquainted with his family. He had just been elected president of the American Society of Newspaper Editors. His secretary was awash in speaking and dining invitations. "Smitty, I've got my hands full."

Davis persisted. "It's one of the hottest newspaper properties ever put on the block."

Events involving the *Daily News* had indeed shaken the journalistic order of things. On April 28, 1944, while Knight was still in England, the paper's owner Frank Knox had died, leaving control to a group of three executors including the widow. Aside from his role as publisher of the *Daily News*, Knox had been Alf Landon's vice presidential running mate in 1936 and served as Roosevelt's wartime secretary of the navy. Knight knew him well.

"Under terms of the will, the executors don't have to sell to the highest bidder," Smith Davis was saying. "Their priority is to find a publisher qualified to carry on the *Daily News*'s character and traditions. Jack, they would like for you to submit a bid."

"Did they tell you that?"

"Yes."

Knight's interest quickened.

Quietly, he decided to go to Chicago to pay a courtesy call on the man who dominated journalism in the Windy City, Colonel Robert Rutherford McCormick, publisher of the *Chicago Tribune*. It would be a way of testing the potential opposition. But the trip also would give him a chance to look at the city from the perspective of one thinking about competing there.

He found the view awe-inspiring. Chicago was a vast reach of smoke-belching metropolis, sprawled back onto the prairies from Lake Michigan. Summers were steamy, fetid, choked with traffic and mingled odors of riverfront and stockyards. Winters brought the north winds howling down, etching in ice the skyscrapers, lakefront mansions, elevated trains, and dark slums. The city was a vast human Babel, home to more Poles than Warsaw, more blacks than some countries in Africa, and the third largest municipal German population on earth.

And yet, curiously, man flourished. War had brought $1.3 billion in expansion to its industrial plants. Four out of ten Chicagoans worked in manufacturing. It was a place of musicians, artists, poets. Architect Frank Lloyd Wright was inspired by its urban dynamics. Poet Vachel Lindsay had wandered those teeming streets chanting verses. Novelist Theodore Dreiser had worked as a bill collector and remembered, years later, "It sang, I thought, and in spite of what I deemed my various troubles, I sang with it. Chicago was so young, so blithe, so new." Racketeer Al Capone once wielded more power than the mayor.

Chicago.

"Queen and guttersnipe of cities," trilled an English tourist, "cynosure and cesspool of the world."

The newspapers reflected Chicago, fighting bitterly for readers. Blood had flowed in wars over street sales. Legions of strange and brilliant characters gave Chicago journalism a cant of freewheeling irreverence. In lofty eminence atop the *Chicago Tribune,* Colonel McCormick ruled as self-anointed lord, his tempers causing politicians to pale and tremble. McCormick was so conservative that he once ordered an aide to remove a star from the giant American flag in his marbled lobby, symbolically casting out the state of Rhode Island for "packing" its Supreme Court with Democrats. Having second thoughts, he ordered the star replaced, but not before the rival *Chicago Times* had photographed the forty-seven-star flag and gleefully gone to press with the story. The *Tribune,* dominating the city with daily circulation of 964,778, suffered the abrasive competition of Hearst's *Herald-American* (484,870), Frank Knox's *Daily News* (426,644), the tabloid *Times* (425,672), and Marshall Field, Jr.'s, *Sun* (329,441). The *Daily News* mercilessly lampooned McCormick's military pretensions with a cartoon character called "Colonel McCosmic."

Knight broached the purpose of his visit in McCormick's private sanctum as they faced each other across a massive desk.

"I've been invited to bid on the *Daily News.* I'm here to ask if you have any objections."

"I have no objections, Mr. Knight. But frankly, I don't think it's much of a newspaper."

"That's beside the point."

"Perhaps."

True to Smith Davis's expectations, the sale attracted a score of bidders. Executors included Annie Reid Knox, Chicago banker Holman Pettigrew, and attorney Laird Bell. Some bidders represented unsavory interests; some were front men for mystery investors. Strong legitimate proposals were offered by the Ridder brothers, owners of newspapers in New York, Duluth, and St. Paul; the Snyders, publishers of the *Gary* [Indiana] *Post-Tribune,* and a group of executives of the *Daily News* itself. The latter were sentimental favorites of executors Bell and Annie Knox.

For data and analysis, Knight again looked to McDowell and John H. Barry. But now he also drew upon the newest major addition to Knight Newspapers management, portly, chain-smoking Basil Walters, whose very presence was partly hinged to the *Daily News* possibilities. Jim Knight and Lee Hills came from Miami to take part in discussions. "We're spread thinly already," Knight said. "The question is, is it feasible?" Walters, hired in February 1944 as Knight Newspapers executive editor, offered a blunt assessment of the *Daily News*'s editorial condition: "Distinguished, but dull."

Distinguished, yes. The paper was steeped in traditions. Melville E. Stone had founded it in 1875 with $5,000 in borrowed money. Four years earlier, the great Chicago fire had laid waste to 17,450 dwellings and left three hundred dead. As poet John Greenleaf Whittier would write, "Men clasped each other's hands and said, 'The City of the West is dead!' " The *Daily News* became part of Chicago's rebirth—a paper in which, by order of founder Stone, "nothing should be printed which a worthy young gentlewoman could not read aloud in the presence of mixed company."

Stone foundered and sold out in 1876, eventually to organize the Associated Press. During the next half-century, new owner Victor F. Lawson brought the *Daily News* newspaper greatness, a Chicago-style mix of brains, brawn, and literary style, and the newsroom would be peopled by the likes of Eugene Field, Finley Peter Dunne, humorist George Ade, Howard Vincent O'Brien, and Sydney Harris. The raffish Ben Hecht would suggest that managing editor Henry Justin Smith hire a new reporter, explaining, "He writes good poetry." And so Carl Sandburg was hired to cover news and do movie reviews, while mainly writing poetry and finishing his monumental biography of Lincoln. Writer John Gunther joined the *Daily News* as a Phi Beta Kappa graduate of the University of Chicago, wound up in Vienna, and ultimately became a best-selling author.

As the twentieth century advanced, foreign correspondents became the stars. *Daily News* reporters covered every important world event from trench fighting in World War I to the rise of Nazi Germany and combat in World War II. Bureaus were staffed in London, Berlin, Stockholm, Paris, Moscow, Rome, Istanbul, Peking. Eyewitness accounts could test the reader's stomach, as in Edgar Snow's report from embattled Shanghai, where "the smell of smoking flesh slapped against the steel sides of a bombed troop train." By 1944, the foreign bureaus were sacrosanct, their copy pouring over incoming wires and published in endless columns, uncut and unedited. Stuffy Walters, an editor with a passion for terse journalism, now perused the gray pages with disdain. "What this paper needs is an editor who can cut." The notion struck *Daily News* partisans as sacrilege.

The paper's financial affairs were as complex as its traditions. McDowell chafed over preliminary figures.

> *They claim combined assets of $24.2 million, including the building. The paper this year will gross $11 million, with a net income of $720,000. Ownership is largely between the Knox estate and a holding company, Daneco. Mrs. Knox has a majority interest in Daneco. There is substantial debt to be assumed, nearly $11 million in all. I expect we can reduce this by refinancing. For control, I think you're looking at a cash outlay of $2 million or more, depending on how the bidding goes. . . .*

McDowell was not pleased. Matters could easily get out of hand.

The rival *Daily News* executive group selected Chicago attorney Adlai Stevenson as their legal representative. If their effort to take control succeeded, Stevenson was to become publisher, Paul Scott Mowrer would continue as editor, and Arthur E. Hall would be general manager.

Each bidder was interviewed by the trustees. Knight's outspoken style during a two-hour session put him at an immediate disadvantage.

"Mr. Knight, what do you think of the way my late husband ran the *Daily News*?" Annie Knox asked.

"I don't much like the way he ran it, Mrs. Knox. But then, I don't think the head of a newspaper should be in politics."

The others pressed him to elaborate.

"I have no political connection," he said. "Newspapers and politics don't go together. I want to be objective." Despite his Republicanism, he went on, Knight Newspapers were nonpartisan; the *Detroit Free Press* had backed a Democrat for the U.S. Senate, the *Akron Beacon Journal* a Democrat for governor of Ohio.

"Mr. Knight, don't you think the *Daily News* should be owned by Chicagoans?" executor Bell asked.

"I think it should, provided they're qualified."

"Would you move to Chicago?"

"Akron is my home. I intend to keep it that way."

Bidding intensified. The employee group ran into trouble. Adlai Stevenson was an intensely cautious man with little feel for newspaper economics. He was hesitant when bidding opened at $12 a share. Other bidders offered varying amounts, but competition quickly narrowed to the employee group and Knight. The executors had divided preferences: Bell favored the Stevenson group; Pettibone was for Knight; Mrs. Knox was uncommitted. Knight bid $13 a share. Adlai Stevenson agonized. Arthur E. Hall, *Daily News* general manager, pleaded. "Adlai, a dollar a share isn't going to make that much difference." Stevenson relented. It was Knight's turn again.

"Fourteen dollars."

Others took the bid to $15. This would set the cash requirement at $2.2 million.

Mrs. Knox pledged to vote for Stevenson's *Daily News* executives if they met the $15 high bid. The lawyer was aghast. "The paper is not worth fifteen dollars a share," he protested. Stevenson personally controlled $750,000 in investor funds. He abruptly reduced that by half. The executive group found itself $1 million short.

Arthur Hall went to Marshall Field, publisher of the *Chicago Sun,* a tenant in the Daily News building. Field granted him a $1 million loan at 2 percent interest. Unable to believe his good fortune, Hall called Stevenson. "Adlai, we've got a deal. We can close this right now!"

Stevenson's reply was a hoarse whisper. "Art, we shouldn't do this." The shaken Stevenson arrived at Marshall Field's office to announce that he would have nothing more to do with the transaction.

Knight had won the day. But now he also began to look askance at the price, his views colored by the cautious McDowell. "The cost is out of line with what we paid for the *Herald* and the *Free Press,"* McDowell said. "It hurts me to pay more than something is worth." Knight withdrew, with a note to executor Holman Pettibone: "I am sorry we were unable to get together on price." He flew back to Detroit, holed up in his office at the *Free Press,* and refused to accept phone calls from Chicago. Thus, he gave himself time to review. There were more brainstorming sessions with Barry, McDowell, Walters, Jim Knight, and Lee Hills. Knight had strong support from a Chicago civic group, including jeweler Gordon Lang, an old friend. It was Lang who got through to him by phone. The executors were in a bind because the favored Stevenson group was no longer in contention and the other bidders lacked stature. Knight must conclude a deal. "It's washed up," he said. "The executors want too much money." With Lang as intermediary, long-distance bargaining opened between Detroit and Chicago. Another ten days passed before Knight finally came to terms.

On October 19, one week prior to his fiftieth birthday, he wrote a check for $2,151,537.88 and took control of the *Chicago Daily News* at just under $15 a share.

The ink had not dried before word of Knight's coup reverberated in the newsroom at 400 West Madison. Managing editor Lloyd Lewis, a Knight admirer, decided to have some sport with the staff. There arrived at his office a well-dressed, baldish man with the manner of a sophisticate. Whispers circulated that this was John S. Knight himself. While editors and reporters bent to their work, Lewis ushered the stranger about, pointing out the copy desk, sports department, photo desk, city desk. Tension mounted as the visitor offered suggestions on how the office might be rearranged and peered over editors' shoulders, making sounds of disapproval. When the two men emerged from an inspection of the men's restroom, a hush fell over the staff as the visitor loudly remarked, "If the Guild wants pay toilets, we'll put in pay toilets. I've found that they pay well on my other papers." Then, with a flourish and a handshake, he was gone.

Lewis let all this stew for a while before announcing that his visitor had not been John S. Knight but longtime personal friend Marc Connelly, the playwright.

When the real Jack Knight arrived, one of his first acts was to call a staff meeting. "In my humble opinion the day of the dull, stodgy newspaper is nearing an end," he said. "Popular newspapers will have the call, and by 'popular' I am not implying that they have to be cheap or sensational." He also declared an end to the *Daily News*'s feud with Colonel McCormick, saying he had bought a newspaper, not a war. "I am confident to let God and Colonel McCormick fight it out for supremacy."

Then he announced that Stuffy Walters would become executive editor of the *Chicago Daily News.*

Carl Sandburg refused to darken the door. The poet, long departed from the reporting staff, plainly disliked Knight's way of running newspapers. Later, when his worst fears seemed justified, Sandburg would grumble, "John Knight has committed so many little sins that they amount to one very big one."

Paul Mowrer quit as executive editor three days after Knight took over, ending forty years as a *Daily News* editor, writer, and Pulitzer Prize–winning foreign correspondent. News of the changeover found veteran political reporter Edwin A. Lahey on the road, covering Thomas E. Dewey's presidential campaign. Lahey was famed for his Irish wit, noble drinking, and journalistic ability. To a friend, he muttered, "I've always loved the *Daily News,* and that's my mistake. Loving a newspaper is like loving a whore." He took a pull from his flask and vowed to have a confrontation with this man Knight. A few weeks later, he did. And got a raise.

Knight and Stuffy Walters stood in the plaza of the Daily News building eyeing the elaborate bubbling fountain. "When we pay off the mortgage," Walters said, "I'll take a bath in that fountain." Knight chuckled. "When we pay off the mortgage, you'll have whiskers down to here."

They were both wrong.

Life was suddenly a footrace. In a single stroke, Knight's newspaper holdings had burgeoned into an empire. But he also had a family to think about, and that meant spending weekends at home in Akron. Home, of course, was his father's expansive house on Portage Path with its climbing vines and spreading maples, the wide staircase, chandeliered hallway, and downstairs cellar bar where they served martinis to guests. Home was Beryl, chic and trim, a striking woman who managed to wear the style and colors that offset her white hair. Beryl's daughter, Rita, now eighteen, had inherited her mother's beauty and was doing well at Ogontz School, but Jack worried about her footloose social life. The new generation, jitterbugging and going steady, jarred his paternal sensibilities. It took old Akron boyhood friends like Harold Graves to remind him of his own adventuresome teen years, with schoolboy hayrides and double dates, and the morning he came to class at Central High in white tie and tails. "You had your good times, Jack."

The boys were usually away—Landon, at twenty, a student at Ohio State University; Frank, sixteen, at Culver Military Academy; and Johnny, twenty-one, now married and a paratrooper lieutenant stationed in Tennessee. Jack kept their pictures on his bedside nightstand and maintained with each an infrequent correspondence. It vexed him that no son seemed able to meet his standards of excellence in school. Landon fought physical handicaps, hauling his body around by wheelchair, crutches, and braces. There were depths of anger in the boy; although some friends insisted Landon was potentially the brightest of the lot, the relationship between perfectionist father and physically afflicted son was strained. Frank was a quiet, gentle sort, not unlike his grandmother, but sickly. It was Johnny who bore the standard. Although an indifferent student, he seemed to be maturing in army life.

After the shooting scrape at Western Reserve, they had finally enrolled Johnny at Culver Military Academy in Indiana. The colonel, George Miller, had been disappointed in his performance: "John has a great deal of difficulty paying attention. He continually misses important class instruction." Jack had urged Miller to bear down: "Johnny simply must learn how to concentrate and I would put it to him until he does." After Johnny gained his army commission in June 1942, Jack wrote him fatherly advice. "Once in the Army, you do as they tell you and there isn't much argument about it."

Even before the *Daily News* purchase, Knight had lived on rigorous schedules. Carrying his bulging brown briefcase, each Monday morning he took the 11:27 flight from Akron to Detroit, where he spent the week supervising the *Free Press* and living in an apartment nearby. He kept in touch with Akron and Miami by telephone, telegram, and mail. As president of the American Society of Newspaper Editors, he made frequent trips to New York and Washington. His social and business connections were constantly expanding.

As boss of the *Daily News,* he moved with Beryl to Chicago to be in the center of things full time.

Quipped *Time*: "The headquarters of Knight Newspapers is in Jack Knight's brown briefcase."

Basil Leon Walters was nearly as round as he was tall, a moon-faced extrovert who smoked thick cigars and exuded surplus energy. At fifty he was five months older than his new boss and widely acknowledged as the leading apostle of a journalistic style which, although still unique in 1944, within a few years would set the trend for virtually every major American newspaper. He had a passion for crisp writing, short sentences, and snappy page layouts that commanded the reader's attention. "If it clicks, use it," he declared. "It's no sin to be interesting." He had been called Stuffy since boyhood, when his adroit fielding in sandlot baseball reminded spectators of John Phelan ("Stuffy") McInnis, the great Boston Red Sox outfielder of the 1920s. The nickname suited the adult Walters's physique.

Knight was drawn to Walters for a very basic reason: the man's creativity sold newspapers. Intellectual purists might shudder, but for eye appeal and reader impact, Walters was your man. Indiana born and educated, he had started overturning traditions in the early 1930s as managing editor at the Cowles brothers' *Des Moines Register.* There, Walters had been fascinated by reading studies at Drake University by Dr. Herman Strang, the psychologist, and newspaper analyst George Gallup. The latter, later to gain fame for his Gallup Poll, theorized that the public actually read very little of a daily paper, regardless of what editors thought. Reader interest was hampered by lifeless layout and dull, wordy writing. To illustrate the point, Strang set up a hidden camera to photograph readers' eye movements. The camera revealed that the typical reader "shopped" a page for material, skipping most of it. The studies would become the basis of a book, *The Psychology of Seeing.*

Walters was so impressed that he applied the findings to new ways of editing and writing for the *Register.* In 1937, John Cowles sent him to Minneapolis as editor of the *Star,* a run-down paper struggling against two dominant competitors. Walters promptly gave priority to local human interest, including lost-dog stories on page 1. He exhorted reporters, "Tell your story; don't write it." To demonstrate the power of the spoken word, he had a hidden stenographer take down verbatim his casual conversations with reporters and then read them back, out loud. He pushed for slick layout and shrewd use of pictures. Results were astounding. Within two years the *Star*'s circulation boomed from 90,000 to 135,000 to lead the rival *Journal* and *Tribune.* By 1941 it had absorbed both papers. Two years later, when Knight was in England, Walters was part of a group of American editors sent over to plan press coverage of the coming Allied invasion of Europe.

Jack Knight had known Walters for many years, writing in a 1939 "Editor's Notebook": "Dr. George Gallup says the *Minneapolis Star* is 10 years ahead of the times in news technique. Managing editor Stuffy Walters admits he 'has something' at the *Star,* doesn't quite know what it is but intends to stick to the formula as long as circulation keeps growing." By 1940, Walters was discussing his theories with Neiman Fellows at Harvard, using such erudite concepts as *reader pulling units* (RPUs): "A good newspaper should have enough RPUs on every page to make the reader want to examine the paper from front to back every day." The *Star,* analysts found, was designed as a page 1 newspaper all the way through. The novelty appealed to young journalists unfettered by traditions. "In Minneapolis," Walters advised them, "I refused to listen to traditional newspapermen."

In England, Knight and Walters had visited London papers, which provided strong, concise wartime news coverage in four- and six-page editions. The fat man's fame had preceded him. Knight was surprised to learn that the great editor Arthur Christiansen, of Lord Beaverbrook's *Daily Express,* subscribed to both the Des Moines and Minneapolis newspapers. Over drinks at Knight's London hotel, Walters and his future employer speculated about what could be done if they had control of a major U.S. newspaper such as the *Chicago Daily News.* Walters was disenchanted with Minneapolis and spoke wistfully of retiring to a dairy farm. Knight was so impressed with the man that he wrote about him to Jack Barry in Detroit: "Walters and I see eye to eye on the editorial side of a newspaper. He makes no pretensions to being a deep thinker, but he does know what gets readers and keeps them interested." On his return to the States, Walters sent Knight a note: "I have just about concluded that being on your team would be more exciting than being a dairy farmer." Five months later, Knight hired him at the then-enormous salary of $50,000 per year.

The Sunday *Detroit Free Press* had served as a testing ground. Walters rode the streetcar to work from his house in Grosse Pointe and watched as commuting readers skipped the front page and turned to inside pages of special, if nonnewsworthy, interest. Working with *Free Press* subeditor Bill Coughlin, he contrived a Sunday formula of topics. Survival articles had strong appeal. Health stories could deal with everything from typists' hangnail to control of blood pressure. People wanted to know how to get a job, how to impress the boss, how to develop money-making ideas. Sunday's *Free Press* geared up for feature articles about fire peril in autumn, ice storms in winter, dangerous swimming in summer, home safety, and ways to lose weight and attract the opposite sex. Reporters wrote about social skill, profiled interesting people, and probed the mysteries of hope, the supernatural, dreams, and religion. Within nine months, Walters had made a profound impact on Detroit's Sunday reading. And by then he was commuting by plane to Chicago for four-day weekly stints on the *Daily News*.

The word was *brevity*.

Hence, a lead weather story in the *Chicago Daily News*, front page:

> Cloudy Monday—rain Tuesday.
> That's the weather forecast Chicago faces as it bails out after its wettest weekend in 69 years.
> The city is still partly paralyzed.
> The rain started at 4:30 P.M. Saturday.
> By Sunday morning even the skyscrapers had wet feet. . . .

The Knight era thus came to the *Daily News*. It meant bright writing, snazzy pictures, ruthless cutting of once-imperishable copy from the foreign bureaus. Even columnists were no longer sacred; a column running full length today might be chopped to four paragraphs tomorrow, or not appear at all. It depended on whether Stuffy deemed it worth the space.

Old-timers groaned. "They're putting bobby sox on the Madonna."

It was Knight's doing. Stuffy was the instrument of John S. Knight's policies. When someone lamented the demise of the long gray columns from the foreign bureaus, complaining that the *Daily News* no longer attempted to inform its reading public, Knight snapped, "A paper has got to be read before it informs anybody."

These were times of competitive rough-and-tumble. At Hearst's *Herald-American,* former marine captain Louis Ruppel had taken charge as executive editor by telling his staff, "What I want around here is lots of sock!" Over at the tabloid *Times,* publisher Richard Finnegan sensed an opportunity to forge ahead of the *Daily News.* And Marshall Field's *Sun* was, in the words of one staff man, "at last beginning to act and look like a

Chicago paper." As for the *Tribune*'s durable Colonel McCormick, he had nothing but disdain for the lot of them. All this inspired *Collier's* to comment gleefully, "Every newspaperman in Chicago looks for an outbreak of the exciting journalism for which the city has always been famous."

At the *Daily News,* another veteran of the foreign service resigned in disgust. There were those, however, who relished the new scheme of things. Groused reporter Ed Lahey, no lover of foreign bureau favoritism, "The only way you could get a local story into this paper was cable it from Paris." Business manager Arthur Hall urged Walters to speed up the process. "Stuffy, the *Times* cheers every funeral procession. They say, 'There goes another *Daily News* reader.' " Walters obliged. The dictum went out that no sentence should have more than fourteen words, no lead paragraph more than two sentences. Typography underwent dramatic change. Uppercase Gothic headlines gave way to caps and lowercase. Walters larded the paper with white space, as at Minneapolis; varied type fonts in the same story; dropped in asterisks to separate paragraphs. Wags joked: "Whatever happened to Stuffy Walters?" "Oh, he's growing asterisks on a farm in Chicago." What the staff did not know was that much of the layout had been assembled in mockups the previous summer in Detroit, ostensibly for the *Free Press.*

Knight, meanwhile, drummed at the fundamental challenge to newspaper editors. "Your first duty is to the citizen who buys the newspaper in the belief that it has character and stability, and does not yield to the pressures of merchant, banker, politician or labor union."

As a Chicago publisher, he was a rising new star in the business. But there were those who took a skeptical view. In a two-part profile in *PM Magazine,* "The Man Who Bought the *Chicago Daily News,*" in November 1944, writer Kenneth Stewart observed, "Admirers of Knight talk glowingly of his courage, his honesty and his vision. I found him one of the frankest men I'd ever met. Yet in nothing he said or has written did I find ringing evidence of challenging, tradition-breaking philosophy. To the contrary, those who would preserve the status quo have little to fear from Knight or his papers."

The *Saturday Evening Post* sent writer Jack Alexander to

profile the new man in Chicago. In his article, "Up From Akron," August 18, 1945, Alexander wrote, "The parallels between scientific crapshooting and newspaper ownership are not dwelt upon in colleges of journalism; but Knight, who never attended one anyway, has applied crapshooting principles to publishing with high success."

Jack Knight was on a high roll in business.

In personal life, however, events were about to take another hellish turn.

fortune seemed a little more evenhanded in its treatment of John S. Knight. He grew closer to his brother and son. The few honors that he had not already won as a journalist and a human rights advocate were heaped on his shoulders.

Then, on Aug. 8, 1974, his wife of 42 years died after a long illness. And there was more to come.

The news of the death of John S. Knight Jr. in Germany was kept from Johnny's wife, the former Dorothy Wells of Columbus, Ga., until after the birth on April 13 — about two weeks later — of a boy who was named John S. Knight III.

Knight. Through the medium of the Editor's Notebook they discussed the campus violence of the '60s and the course of the Vietnam War. They exchanged letters frequently, played golf together and talk...

Pa... Jan...ch, managing editor of the D... New... said of young John, "He... was r... y a ...rming guy. He knew who, he ... He ... w he was an heir to a fortune and to a key job in the organization if he earned it. But he didn't take himself too seriously."

It was obvious that John S. Knight hoped through his grandson to see that...

John S. Knight III and ...lives. I can't think of ...change. I can't think ...down. So I am not ...yself guilty.

"I am not ...oing to ...er me," he ...ld Tho... start a new ...life."

He returne... to Flo...ler his gr...dson's ...nounced he would m...1976, in the chapel of ...Sea at Bal Harbou...Lifestyle editor of the...

A CALL TO ARMS

latter cum laude in 1968 with a degree in history, then went on to study philosophy, politics and economics at Oxford University in England, where he earned a master of arts degree, with honors, in June 1970.

During high school and college he worked summer vacations at several Knight papers, including the Beacon Journal.

His first full-time newspaper job came at the Detroit Free Press in 1970. He gained experience in the circulation

center of Philadelphia. John S. Knight III was stabbed to death during a robbery by three men. There were homosexual overtones.

At the time, his grandfather was visiting at the home of Mr. and Mrs. Edwin C. Whiteheads of Greenwich, Conn. Mrs. Whiteheads is a daughter of the then Betty Augustus, widow of Cleveland millionaire Ellsworth H. Augustus. Knight and Mrs. Augustus had known each other for 35 years though a mutual interest in thoroughbreds and horse racing.

Mrs. Knight died ...while watching the R...he LaGorce Island ho...

WHEN HE STEPP...torial chairman of Kni...1976, his title became ...Knight-Ridder and the ...His decision to qui...y Thomas and others...."The trouble wi...night's position," Th...ly that they stay on t...hat the business can't

He had difficulty demonstrating affection. With the children he was always supportive but never really close. It was a matter of temperament and emotional reserve. It applied even to Johnny, the eldest son, who was in his mind when he wrote such column thoughts as "Some of us have children who, we hope, will follow us in this business. . . ." His ambitions for the boy were tempered by disappointment, but Jack Knight loved him deeply nonetheless.

As a cadet at Culver, Johnny had made up in athletics what he lacked as a student, excelling in boxing and cross-country running. He spent summer vacations working in Harold Graves's Akron lumberyard, relishing the hard physical labor. When Johnny entered the army in the spring of 1942, he drew paternal praise. By the following December, as he went through paratrooper school at Fort Benning, Georgia, his father lectured him by letter about catching a cold. "It won't do you any good to be in the parachute division unless your health is A-1." When Johnny switched to the glider troops at Fort Bragg, North Carolina, the letter from Akron was less than enthusiastic. "The work you are doing in gliders sounds interesting but I do not think I would pick that branch of service," wrote the veteran of World War I observation planes. But he also had a word for Johnny about Landon: "His school work has been exceedingly poor and I am afraid I cannot give you an optimistic story of his progress. Why don't you write him a letter to pep him up?"

Romance came unexpectedly to Lieutenant Johnny Knight. He fell in love with pretty Dorothy Elizabeth Worth, daughter of a car salesman in Columbus, Georgia, near Fort Benning. They married without consent of his parents. Beryl disapproved.

By June 1944, Johnny and Dorothy were in Tullahoma, Tennessee, where he trained with an artillery battery. When Jack Knight returned from England, the young couple visited him in Akron. Afterward, Knight wrote them a warm, fatherly letter. He was cheered by the fact that son Frank, now at Culver, had been promoted to the rank of cadet first sergeant and Landon had buckled down to produce unexpectedly good grades at Ohio State. Johnny replied with advice for his father. "Reward Landon well for those good marks, Dad, and show him that by a little honest work he will reap a fine crop." The young lieutenant closed his letter with an appeal. "I hope with all my heart that you do like Dorothy, for I know, down deep, that no finer person ever walked this earth. She is making me very happy." He signed it, "Your loving son and daughter. . . ."

He was twenty-one years old and preparing to go overseas.

Chicago was demanding, tumultuous, a hardball league of metropolitan journalism. As boss of the *Daily News,* John S. Knight had been catapulted into the first rank of U.S. publishers. His name, photograph, and words were widely published. Interviewing journalists found him stimulating and unpredictable. He, in turn, relished the give-and-take of spirited discussion.

On politics:

Q. Mr. Knight, how would you define your political preferences?

A. I believe in the two-party system, that parties will seek better candidates if they think newspaper support will be for the man, not necessarily the party. My policy is anti-machine. My father was against the machines too, but he loved politics as a game. He sometimes said, "Vote her straight." But I never do. I can't follow a party line. I have to make my own judgments. I'm for the man who does a creditable job, regardless of party.

On labor:

Q. You have been highly critical of organized labor's striking against defense industries. Labor relations tend to be strained in Akron and Detroit, where you have newspapers. What is your position generally on unions?

A. I don't choose certain cities for their labor climate and I don't run away from hot spots, either. I've been goddamned by both labor and capital. We neither appease nor flail our enemies. I can't honestly say that I have any love for the Guild, but I have always negotiated in good faith.

On press freedom:

Q. You have expressed criticism of your own colleagues in American publishing, warning that their ambivalence endangers the free press. Just what are you driving at there?

A. I get disgusted with men who go to editorial conventions and orate about freedom of the press when they don't use what freedom they've already got. They are generally frightened, timid rabbits when real questions of press freedom arise.

He maintained a strange ambiguity when it came to Franklin D. Roosevelt. But then, the president's magnetism was phenomenal. With a raffish grin, a backward toss of the head, and a cheery wave, FDR took the masses in his grasp and held them. Chicago was a Roosevelt town, America a Roosevelt nation. Demand for wartime continuity of leadership had won him a third term and seemed certain to win a fourth. By autumn 1944, Roosevelt was the master politician of U.S. history, his power impressing even such perennial critics as Knight: "Let us give full credit for the reforms and social gains of Roosevelt's administration. Radical as they seem, they are now fully accepted by Republicans and Democrats alike."

The characterization "fully accepted" was not wholly accurate. Hard-shell conservatives still found the New Deal an abomination. And so to the GOP forefront there now stepped New York governor Thomas E. Dewey, earnest, forthright former district attorney. Knight was a Dewey admirer but knew that, like Willkie's, his timing was off. Who could quarrel with Roosevelt's wartime performance? Still, he gave Dewey what support he could, arguing, "The administration suffers from hardening of the arteries, its bureaucrats bickering like small boys, all wanting to be pitcher."

There was more to it, beneath the surface. The sixty-two-year-old president was a doomed man. Navy doctors secretly found him suffering from high blood pressure, severe angina, and chronic bronchitis. The press knew. But FDR's health remained a taboo issue. Editorialists tiptoed around the subject as if it were a live bomb. "Let's not be squeamish," the *New York Sun* commented squeamishly, "six presidents have died in office."

Knight, whose newspapers a generation later would break such stories as vice presidential candidate Thomas Eagleton's history of mental treatments, also refused to raise an alarm about the threat of Roosevelt's dying. This was 1944, and the nation was in all-out war. Like the others, he did not seem to want to think about succession to the presidency, specifically that Roosevelt's vice presidential running mate, former Missouri senator Harry Truman, was a compromise nominee, virtually unknown. Truman himself had been shocked to be selected, gasping, "My God!"

The Dewey campaign lurched ahead, a tempest in a teapot. Knight blasted the pro-Roosevelt press for characterizing his mustachioed champion as "an intellectual and physical midget." He called Dewey's critics a Smear Brigade. "What really irks them is the fact that the man is so thoroughly efficient. The very qualities they find objectionable commend Dewey to me." So it went, an exercise in nonissues and evasions.

Wendell Willkie, weary, disconsolate, rejected by his party in the primaries, died on October 8 of three massive heart attacks. A month later Roosevelt steamrollered over Dewey with an electoral vote margin of 432 to 99.

Overseas, Allied armies drove deep into France. Second Lieutenant John S. Knight, Jr., went into combat with the 17th Airborne Division, leading a small reconnaissance unit in search of enemy strongpoints ahead of the main body of paratroopers. They moved toward the Ardennes forest against stiffening German resistance.

Dorothy was four months pregnant and living back with her parents in Columbus, Georgia. Jack Knight expressed his delight and promised to write to her more frequently.

With Johnny in the thick of things, Knight's view of the war took a more abrasive edge. It was as if the conflict had become intensely personal. If one could not fight with bullets he lashed out with words. His own past moralizing about tolerance seemed momentarily forgotten. Readers of the "Notebook" were startled when he lambasted columnist-socialite Elsa Maxwell for throwing a lavish Hollywood party to celebrate the liberation of France: "My stomach turned when Hollywood's pampered aristocracy gathered . . . at the very moment when thousands of American boys were being killed to make the world safe for Elsa and the rest of us dangerless patriots of the home front."

Miss Maxwell retorted in print that John S. Knight ought to have his head examined.

In the Ardennes, German Tiger tanks came clanking, trailed by gray legions of the SS. As the 17th Airborne dug into defense perimeters, its recon units roamed the icy outlands by Jeep and foot patrol. The leading companies took positions along the Ahr River, a meandering black ribbon of water cutting through snowy fields and woodlands. Lieutenant Knight trimmed his recon force to a dozen men in three Jeeps, mounted with .50 caliber machine guns. The unit worked under divisional staff and had wide freedom of movement. The overall reconnaissance commander, Lieutenant Colonel Lyle McAlister, had promoted Knight to first lieutenant in December and considered the rank well merited. The young officer was an individualist to whom a commander could give general outlines of a task and know that Knight would find his own way to carry it out.

Johnny's letters from France reached his father in Chicago. The "Notebook" took an even tougher tone. Units in frontline combat were short of supplies and ammunition. German tanks were superior, badly outgunning the Americans. At home, industrial absenteeism reached an all-time high, unionists balked at a proposal to conscript men to work, racetracks set new attendance records, and nightclubs flourished.

"We might be fooling ourselves," observed the "Notebook,"

> but we're not kidding the men in France. I would like to quote one paragraph from a letter I've received as this is being written. "Tell me, Dad, why are the people at home led to believe the war is almost won? Maybe this latest Kraut offensive will wake up a few of them." It is difficult to answer a letter like that. You see, the kids have our number.

Frequently the recon force roamed beyond the river to capture German stragglers and gather intelligence on enemy strength. Private First Class Earl Holcomb, twenty-one, was just a year younger than his quiet young commander. Later, Holcomb would recall this dangerous period of combat. "He never told us to go where he wouldn't go himself. When you went out on a job with Lieutenant Knight you knew that he would lead and you would follow."

On January 21, the 101st Airborne Division was starting to break out of Bastogne, a few miles away. Lieutenant Knight chafed for action. He loaded his Jeeps with gas, ammunition, and his twelve men and took off down the road. They drove through three German-held villages in Belgium, attacked the town of Hautbellain near Bastogne, and, in a fierce firefight, routed a garrison of sixty Germans. Knight then withdrew without losing a man.

The feat won him a Bronze Star for valor. On March 3, Knight wrote to his son: "I am terribly proud of you."

March 29, 1945: Miami was hot, sunny, and dry. Three days earlier, one of those insane glitches had permeated the nation's news wires, setting off a wild rumor. The International News Service in Washington had sent out a distorted report that the White House was ready to announce victory in Europe. As the story swept the nation, the *Chicago Herald-American* splashed red ink across its front page: FDR—STAND BY FOR VICTORY. Hearst's *Detroit Times* put out an extra. Radio's Blue Network announced a newsflash. Telephones were madly ringing. At the *Miami Herald,* however, veteran telegraph editor Charlie Ward advised caution. "Those Hearst guys have a way of going out on a limb."

False alarm.

Now it was Thursday, "Notebook" day. Knight closeted himself away for the weekly writing chore. He had reason to feel good. In Georgia, Dorothy was due to give birth within a month. Knight would be a grandfather at age fifty.

The typewriter clattered. He wrote about the false alarm, and what a cruel hoax it was to a people at war. It demonstrated, he said, the news media's "grave responsibility to the American public, and particularly to the families and loved-ones of the men whose lives are in daily peril." He turned to a letter newly arrived from a combat medical doctor and typed excerpts from it into his column. The doctor had written:

In the dim light of a candle I thumb the emergency medical tags book. 1. Fracture, right femur and left forearm. 2. Penetrating wound, right frontal area. Shrapnel.

3. Perforating wound, abdomen. Machine gun bullet. 4. Compound fracture of left femur and right lower leg. 5. Traumatic amputation of left leg by artillery shell.

I have just added a few words to tag No. 5. "Died in the aid station." The soldier was only 20 years old. His body now lies covered with a blanket on the cold, damp ground behind this building. I know exactly why he died. Yesterday when I visited the medical supply depot and handed my requisition to the sergeant, he said, "I'm sorry, Captain, there is no more plasma."

That boy died because I didn't have the plasma to save him.

And yet Americans at home were living in unbelievable luxury.

Knight finished the column in an angry mood.

He hoped it would make his readers angry too.

On that same day, March 29, First Lieutenant John S. Knight, Jr., took four of his troopers in a single Jeep to reconnoiter the right flank of 17th Airborne's approach to Münster, at the time the Westphalian capital. After passing unhindered through the village of Haltern, they continued eastward toward another small town, Hullern. Knight, in steel helmet and combat gear and cradling a tommy gun, rode in the front seat beside the driver.

For days enemy resistance had been fading away as the Allies continued their push into the German homeland. Village after village had fallen without a shot, their western approaches pocked with abandoned defense trenches and foxholes. The Russians were said to be seven miles from Berlin, and the greening spring air bore the scent of victory. So decimated was the Reich's defense that many of its troops consisted of old men and boys of the Volkssturm, Hitler's last-ditch civilian home guard. Now Hullern lay dead ahead, its quaint, picturebook houses looming up in front of the American patrol. The only fortifications to be seen in the overgrown terrain were a few empty holes. The driver glanced at Lieutenant Knight, who waved him ahead.

And then gunfire ripped into the Jeep from all sides.

It was Private First Class Earl Holcomb who told the story two days later. He was a lean, gangly youth with an old man's eyes. In a slow West Virginia drawl, he spoke to B. J. McQuaid, a combat correspondent for the *Chicago Daily News* advancing with the 17th Airborne Division.

> We never had a chance. It looked like any other abandoned Volkssturm position. They'd camouflaged a series of deep-dug trenches and foxholes alongside the road there, in an ambush. They let us get past their first positions, and then opened up from all sides. They threw everything at us, including anti-tank stuff, which was firing tree bursts into the branches right over us where we hit the ditches on either side of the road. The ditches were shallow and gave us no protection. I saw that we were going to be wiped out, but Lieutenant Knight was firing his tommy gun back at them and so the rest of us fought back as well as we could, but they were dug in. The fight lasted about five minutes.

A German hand grenade plopped out of the underbrush and exploded near Holcomb, raising a cloud of thick smoke. The soldier scrambled up from his ditch, sprinted across the road, and ducked behind the houses. He then made his way across a railroad embankment and walked two miles back to the American lines.

McQuaid also interviewed Knight's fellow officer and friend, First Lieutenant Denis J. Jones, aged twenty-three, who arrived at the village an hour later. In one of the houses Jones found a German officer dying of bullet wounds from an American tommy gun. He then went to the scene of the ambush to help recover the American bodies.

In Miami, correspondent McQuaid's message arrived by cable in the early afternoon of Monday, April 2. John S. Knight was away from his office. An editor took the message downstairs to James Knight, who spread it onto his desk:

KNIGHT, JR. KILLED THREE DAYS AGO WHILE HEROICALLY LEADING HIS RECONNAISSANCE SQUAD INTO A GERMAN-HELD TOWN. THE BODY WAS RECOVERED BY HIS COMRADES WHEN THE TOWN WAS SUBSE-

QUENTLY CAPTURED. I AM WRITING THE STORY AND
GIVING FULL DETAILS AND WILL REQUEST THE CENSORS
TO FORWARD IT TO SHAEF, PARIS, TO EXPEDITE ITS RE-
LEASE, WHICH NORMALLY TAKES TEN DAYS OR MORE.
THE TOWN IN WHICH KNIGHT WAS KILLED WAS HULL-
ERN ON THE RIGHT FLANK OF OUR MÜNSTER DRIVE. HIS
RECONNAISSANCE JEEP WAS AMBUSHED BY A STRONG
GERMAN FORCE WITH MACHINE GUNS AND ANTI-TANK
GUNS. THREE OF HIS FOUR ENLISTED MEN WERE KILLED
WITH HIM. SIGNED MCQUAID, APRIL 2, MÜNSTER.

James Knight found his brother midway through a golf game
with three friends at Miami Beach. James handed over the message and they stood awkwardly while it was read. The face of Jack
Knight turned to stone. The men murmured their condolences
and made as if to break up the game. Knight handed the message
back to his brother and said, "Let's finish the round."

Knight would remember years afterward: "Suddenly I had
a terrible need to hit something. The golf ball would suffice."

He was off his stroke at first, but by intense concentration
managed to settle down and finished only four points off his
normal score.

They did not notify Dorothy immediately. Pulling strings in
Washington, Jack Knight managed to delay the War Department's official telegram to the widow. Not for two weeks was she
to be told, after her baby was born in Georgia.

The publisher now spent virtually all of his daylight hours on
the golf course. He did not go to the office except to write the
"Notebook." But there was much to write. On April 12, at Warm
Springs, Georgia, Franklin D. Roosevelt died. Knight went back
to the typewriter to remind his readers that man is neither im-
mortal nor indispensable. "In a land as great as ours, no one man
was ever intended to preside over our destinies in perpetuity."
It was the future that mattered, not the past, and the future now
rested in the hands of a new president, Harry S Truman.

"Civilization," wrote the "Notebook" columnist, "can never
again withstand the ravages of another world war."

Dorothy gave birth to a boy.
They named him John Shively Knight III.

Whatever the circumstance, it was grist for the mill, the stuff of processing. Every story was a thing to be dispassionately gathered, written, edited, given a headline, sent to the printers. It was the same even when a man wrote about the loss of a son. It would be the same if the story were reporting the end of the world. Write it. Edit it. Process it.

"Johnny is gone," he wrote.

> The lovable kid . . . sleeps in Germany because of the senseless ambitions of a demented paranoiac; because in the last 30 years the "statesmen" of Europe have repeatedly sacrificed principle to power politics; because those of us who fought the last time failed to insure a lasting peace. . . . It is difficult not to be embittered. The sympathetic words we have spoken to others now are like ashes in the mouth.

Writing it was a catharsis of sorts, a means of expression. But even in the writing, Knight seemed to keep his distance, keep his aloofness. And so the writing had a stilted, impersonal cast, almost as if he were discussing someone else's loss. There were those who wondered about this, and always would wonder. What really went on inside the man? How could he keep so much pain bottled up and under control? He could express compassion over the tragedies of others, was known even to shed tears. But rarely for himself. Not in public, at any rate. It had been so with Katie's death. Now it was with Johnny's. Did his emotions ever break out and spill over, even in dark of night with nobody to hear, nobody to see? Or did he dare to risk venting grief even then, on the chance that once he started he could never stop; that if ever he gave way, it would be too much to bear?

The tragedy of war was immeasurable. But at least the war dead died for a cause.

The tragedy of the Johnnies, and all the other young men who have died, is that they had no chance at life. Their chance is denied them forever, so that you and I can continue to have security and freedom from fear. We must pledge to them never again to shirk the task of achieving a peaceful world. The test will come when the parades are over and the bands stop playing.

Johnny is gone.

We have covenant with the dead.

fortune seemed a little more evenhanded in its treatment of John S. Knight. He grew closer to his brother and son. The few honors that he had not already won as a journalist and a human rights advocate were heaped on his shoulders.

Then, on Aug. 8, 1974, his wife of 42 years died after a long illness. And there was more to come.

The news of the death of John S. Knight Jr. in Germany was kept from Johnny's wife, the former Dorothy Wells of Columbus, Ga., until after the birth on April 13 — about two weeks later — of a boy who was named John S. Knight III.

Knight. Through the medium of the Editor's Notebook they discussed the campus violence of the '60s and the course of the Vietnam War. They exchanged letters frequently, played golf together and talked often.

Janensch, managing editor of the Daily News said of young John. "He was really a charming guy. He knew who he was. He knew he was an heir to a fortune and to a key job in the organization if he earned it. But he didn't take himself too seriously."

It was obvious that John S. Knight hoped through his grandson to see that name kept in lights on the marquee

John S. Knight III and lives. I can't think of change. I can't think of down. So I am not myself guilty.

"I am not going to let her me," he told Thor to start a new life."

He returned to Florida after his grandson's announced he would make Elizabeth) Augustus. They 1976, in the chapel of Sea at Bal Harbour. Lifestyle editor of the

DESTINY'S CHILDREN

latter cum laude in 1968 with a degree in history, then went on to study philosophy, politics and economics at Oxford University in England, where he earned a master of arts degree, with honors, in June 1970.

During high school and college he worked summer vacations at several Knight papers, including the Beacon Journal.

His first full-time newspaper job came at the Detroit Free Press in 1970. He gained experience in the circulation

center of Philadelphia, John S. Knight III was stabbed to death during a robbery by three men. There were homosexual overtones.

At the time, his grandfather was visiting at the home of Mr. and Mrs. Edwin C. Whiteheads of Greenwich, Conn. Mrs. Whiteheads is a daughter of the then Betty Augustus, widow of Cleveland millionaire Ellsworth H. Augustus. Knight and Mrs. Augustus had known each other for 35 years though a mutual interest in thoroughbreds and horse racing.

Mrs. Knight died while watching the Ro the LaGorce Island ho

WHEN HE STEPP torial chairman of Kni 1976, his title became Knight-Ridder and the

His decision to qui by Thomas and others "The trouble wit Knight's position," Tho ly that they stay on to hat the business can't

Six weeks. That was the difference between life and death. Germany surrendered six weeks after the killing of Johnny Knight, Jr. Had he held on, had he survived the war, many elements of the future undoubtedly would have followed different courses, perhaps the directions of the Knight enterprises themselves and the lives and fortunes involved. Even the fate of Johnny's own son now hung in the balance. Thus chance abruptly altered the complex chain of human events.

As before, John S. Knight put his life back together and looked outward. Letters of condolence poured in, many of them from other parents of war dead. Wrote F. F. Paul, Sr., of Chicago, "As fathers, we at least have the pride of being blessed with sons such as these." It was small consolation. Doggedly, Knight went through the stacks, writing personal replies to each one. To Second Lieutenant John D. Bonner of San Pedro, California: "I fully expected that Johnny would get back safely." To J. W. Thomas of Akron: "I am doing my best to move forward."

On May 7 he listened to the radio as the new president announced the surrender of Germany, his twangy Missouri accent a startling contrast to the patrician voice of FDR: "The Allied armies, through sacrifice and devotion and God's help ..." It was Harry S Truman's sixty-first birthday. Knight felt good about the man, and said so; for all the former senator's political ties to the old Pendergast machine in Kansas City, "no shade of suspicion was ever attached to his name." The following month he visited Truman in the White House and came away impressed. "I predict that he will be no one's man but his own."

Jack and Beryl spent the summer in Chicago and Detroit. At the *Daily News,* Stuffy Walters's brand of journalism continued to pay off in rising circulation. At the *Free Press,* big stories that kept Knight's pulse pounding and his attention fixed were breaking. A *Free Press* exposé of huge payoffs in the Michigan Legislature at Lansing, growing out of a Knight tip, brought corruption indictments against twenty elected lawmakers and prison terms for three members of the infamous Purple Gang in the murder of a key prosecution witness. Pulitzer Prizes to reporter Ken McCormick and the *Free Press* were the first for a Knight newspaper.

Knight hailed the triumph.

> *True journalism—and I emphasize that word "true"—is the lamplight of our modern society. Without it, the lamps are turned down and we revert back to the Dark Ages. The modern newspaper is the means by which the whole human race, if but allowed the opportunity, may acquire knowledge and gain wisdom. It is the beacon light of this new experiment we call democracy.*

The war dragged on. American and Japanese troops fought hand-to-hand on Okinawa while kamikaze planes launched suicide assaults upon the U.S. fleet. A vast army of men and weapons mustered in the Philippines for a planned invasion of Japan. Knight, as president of the American Society of Newspaper Editors, was invited to Washington to meet with Army Chief of Staff

George C. Marshall. With Germany conquered, the British seemed to think the war was won, but they were needed in the Pacific. Would Knight help to apply pressure? He dispatched a letter to Lord Beaverbrook, citing rising anti-British feeling among Americans who felt they were bearing the brunt of war in the Far East. Replying on behalf of the Churchill government, Beaverbrook declared, "We shall put forth our full strength against Japan."

Knight and two fellow publishers, John Cowles of the *Minneapolis Star-Journal* and Julius Ochs of *The New York Times,* set out to visit major command operations in the Pacific. They arrived in Honolulu on August 2, unaware that two mystery bombs were being flown from the secret atomic development site at Los Alamos, New Mexico, to the Pacific island of Tinian. An ultimatum by President Truman, warning of the "utter destruction" of Japan unless they unconditionally surrendered, was running out of time. On the morning of August 6, as Knight boarded a military transport to Guam, a B-29 Superfortress was flying from Tinian to Hiroshima bearing a single bomb having the destructive power of 20,000 tons of TNT. By the time Knight's plane landed, four square miles of the Japanese city were vaporized, 60,175 were dead or missing, and man suddenly possessed the technology to destroy his planet. On August 9, a second atomic bomb was dropped on Nagasaki.

Civilized man was stunned. The *Beacon Journal* ran black headlines: ATOM BOMB SPRAYS DEATH ON JAPAN. The *Detroit Free Press* announced: ATOMS SMASH JAPAN. In the Pacific, Knight was aghast that the affable man whom he had visited so recently had harbored, even then, such a horrendous secret.

A week later, Knight bounced in a Jeep across the battle-torn terrain of Okinawa in the company of General James Doolittle. They talked of the dramatic turn of events. Conventional weapons, God knows, were ruinous enough. In a dispatch to his newspapers, Knight would describe Okinawa in the wake of battle. "The hills and valleys are littered with burned-out tanks, trucks and debris of all kinds." He accompanied a patrol seeking holdout Japanese soldiers, the Seventh Division troopers armed with tommy guns, rifles, and grenades. No enemy troops were found. He stood at the mass graves of Americans who had died in the fierce fighting for the island, thinking of another fresh grave on the other side of the world. And he talked with Japanese war prisoners, who impressed him as "men of pride and confidence, not the beaten, whining weaklings we have read about. It will take a strong hand to enforce the peace in Japan."

News of the Japanese surrender came as he flew to Manila. Like Okinawa, the Philippine's capital had been bombed and shelled mercilessly. Somberly, he picked through the ruin of the fortress of Corregidor, jotting in his notebook: "In the mountain passageway where General Wainwright had his hospital one can see the bones and rotting bodies of countless Japanese soldiers." His mood quickly lifted, however, with an invitation to lunch with General Douglas MacArthur and his wife.

Knight seemed overwhelmed by the MacArthur presence, his writing afterward gushing hero worship. "The general carries his years with a zest that would do credit to a man of 50. His hair is black, his face imperturbably strong. In conversation he never leaves you in doubt as to what he means. . . . One realizes that he is talking to one of the greatest heroes and strategists of all times." Knight spent three hours with MacArthur, so enthralled that he seemed to forget that this was the same general who had driven penniless veterans of the Bonus March from Washington with bayonets and tear gas in 1932, an act that C. L. Knight had deemed reprehensible. Strategist that he was, MacArthur took Knight for a ride through Manila in his staff car, starred pennants flying. It was enough to take a publisher's breath away. "Little children on the sidewalks stood erect and saluted. It is a tremendous thrill to see a military man so universally respected."

After Manila, Knight made a quick, grim visit to the battle-field of Iwo Jima, where Japanese survivors were still holed up in caves. Then he flew to Tokyo for the formal surrender and on September 2 was one of the first American postwar visitors to check into Tokyo's Imperial Hotel. A solitary walk through the devastated city affected him deeply. "An air of depression permeates this scorched and burned-out place of death. You try to evaluate the meaning of the word 'civilization' as you gaze over miles of ruin and destruction. . . ."

On September 3, 1945, as morning sunlight struck fire to Tokyo Bay, Knight occupied a box seat on a sixteen-gun turret of the battleship *Missouri,* eyewitness to the surrender of Japan. In describing the event he teamed with correspondent William McGaffin of the *Chicago Daily News* under a joint byline.

The gleaming deck of the battleship was resplendent with wartime commanders. At the stroke of 8 A.M., the white-uniformed band of the *Missouri* struck up the "Star Spangled Banner" and the British anthem, "God Save the King." MacArthur was dressed in freshly-starched khaki trousers and shirt without a tie or decorations. He stepped to the microphone and began a short address, reading from a manuscript that trembled in his hands. . . .

The war was over. It had claimed the lives of 54 million people on earth, including John Shively Knight, Jr., aged twenty-two. For those who survived, life would never be the same again.

Peace: Suburban Akron basked in the loveliest summer in years. Tea roses bloomed in front yards. The hills were clothed in rich grass. Nature filled the humid air with scents.

The nation turned to the future. Troopships came steaming home. Returning servicemen embraced their families at docksides and train stations. It was a time of rich emotions and new beginnings. But overseas, war had left devastation. Europe lay prostrate, her great cities in ruin and millions facing starvation. Many metropolitan areas in Japan were firebombed wastes and the masses lacked homes and jobs, their culture caught between the ancient known and the frightening new. The rubble of Hiroshima was terrible testimony to the dawn of the nuclear age.

For free men, this was the tomorrow so ardently awaited.

Jack Knight drove to the auditorium of the University of Akron, mounted the stage, and looked out on his student audience. How young they were, how eager; destiny's children, not much younger than Johnny had been. Theirs was the job of putting it all back together again. So he spoke of the challenge of peace, to produce life of quality in a complex and ravaged world. "Cast aside the view that your country has no more frontiers. Remarkable advances in science, invention and research will change completely our living standards, even now the most advanced on earth."

But these things did not just happen, he warned. Cultural and technological advancements were the fruits of individual enterprise. Private, personal achievement was the essence of productivity. He spoke his beliefs. He had been conditioned by private enterprise and profit. Without profit, the American Dream could not exist. "Beware creeping socialism. The spirit of individual risk must not die. Security is for the old and should be shunned by the young."

They had just come through a terrible war, an orgy of hate, rending asunder the veil of civilization: manners, order, tolerance. He remembered his walk through the rubble of Tokyo. Spiritual values needed rebirth. He was no preacher, but "we must make our choice between corroding cynicism and practical idealism. We must achieve understanding among diverse people. We must concede the right of others to differ."

It was a strong, liberal speech. He left with the students' applause ringing in his ears.

The newspapers flourished.

In Detroit the morning *Free Press* circulated more than 400,000 papers daily by Christmas 1945, gaining a slender lead over both the afternoon *News* and the *Times*. But competition was rough and getting rougher. Knight's editors pitched for strong features. A popular new column on postwar veterans' affairs drew twenty-four hundred letters a week. In one column, a Detroit woman asked for advice on how to keep her husband in the army. "My daughter and I live much better on the allotment, and he's such a pest when he is home."

In Chicago, Stuffy Walters intensified his crusade for clear writing and short sentences. Walters clearly relished working for Knight; theirs was a partnership committed to excellence, and the editor had freedom to exercise his gifts. Walters saw Knight as breaking fresh ground in American journalism, in style and vigor, in quest of fairness and accuracy, in fostering an attitude of independence and courage: "Get the truth," Knight told his people, "and print it." It was a far cry from the kind of toadying, special-interest journalism still widely practiced in America.

In the meantime, Walters's rule of brevity was tacked to the newsroom bulletin board: SHORT LEADS AND SHORT SENTENCES. NO LEAD IS TO BE MORE THAN THREE TYPEWRITTEN LINES, TWO IF POSSIBLE. The fat man continued to deplore the reading skill of the average adult. To belabor the point further, he singled out the most erudite member of the *Chicago Daily News* staff, columnist and Yale graduate Howard Vincent, and announced, "Vince, you're going to take a reading test."

The results were startling. Motion pictures of Vincent's eye movements showed that instead of sweeping across a printed page, they skipped words and darted back frequently to catch meaning. He was long on fixation, short on concentration. He scored 70 percent in comprehending the central thought of a sentence but only 50 percent when quizzed on details and 42 percent on integration of ideas.

Stuffy Walters exulted.

By October 1945, one year after Knight's takeover, *Daily News* circulation zoomed to 479,000, up 45,000 per day. In the battle of Chicago newspapers, the *News* passed Hearst's *American* and placed second only to the *Tribune.*

Jack Knight's enthusiasm was guarded, however. No matter how readable Stuffy made the paper, it had a fatal fault. The *Daily News* lacked a Sunday edition. Without that, they could never meet McCormick's *Tribune* head-to-head.

In Miami, Lee Hills returned from duty as a war correspondent in Europe and resumed his work as managing editor of the *Herald.* He functioned well with James Knight, who ran business and production with a shrewd eye for efficiency. Staff members trickling back from military service found the morning *Herald* dominating the afternoon *Miami News* and steadily increasing sales. The plant included a new business office and expanded production facilities.

South Florida's economy was surging, its seasonal tourism augmented by inpouring veterans; introduced to Miami as trainees in wartime, they now returned as permanent residents.

Not all the influx was welcome, for it also included a postwar tide of civilian hoodlums from Chicago, Cleveland, New York, New Jersey, Detroit, and Philadelphia. Miami was neutral turf to warring gangs. The underworld economy thrived on the numbers racket, prostitution, bookmaking, casino gambling, loan-sharking, and encroachment on otherwise legitimate business, all with the tacit support of police and public officials.

Knowing this was one thing but proving it another. If cleanup were to come, the *Herald* would have to be a catalyst. Hills began to exchange information with northern newspapers and law enforcement agencies on known criminals. Data included individual records and mug shots. This he filed along with information on each hoodlum's south Florida activities and his address in the Miami area. The *Herald* also began reporting routinely such tidbits as the opening of illicit gambling houses. Operators were outraged. Politicians charged that the practice was hurting tourism. Sporadic arrests achieved little: the accused could bank on being sprung by local judges on technical faults in affidavits, indictments, and warrants.

Hills's private information bank grew. It was not material that he could immediately publish, for unindicted criminals enjoyed the same protection from libel as did honest folk. An editor could only prepare, and bide his time.

Hard-nosed journalism had its pitfalls. Two judges blocked efforts of a cleanup-minded county prosecutor to shut down gambling clubs; another scrapped, as improperly drawn, eight rape indictments. A *Herald* editorial by the erudite Arthur Griffith, who had attended Oxford and the Sorbonne, declared that the courts belonged to the people, not to wrongdoers. When judges "recognize and accept, even go out and find, every possible technicality . . . to protect the defendant, to block, thwart, hinder, embarrass and nullify prosecution, then the people's rights are jeopardized and the basic reason for courts stultified." The ease with which accused criminals were getting off, he added, had people wondering whether the courts had become "refuges for lawbreakers." The editorial was accompanied by a cartoon depicting a judge dismissing a defendant, while a dismayed citizen protested, "But Judge!"

This was strong stuff. Judges Marshall C. Wiseheart and Paul D. Barns cited the *Herald,* and editorial chief John Pennekamp, for contempt of court, charging that the editorials interfered with the administration of justice. The stunned editor wanted to fight. "If you're sure you are right," Knight told him, "then go ahead."

Pennekamp was fined $250 and the paper $1,000. An appeal to the Florida Supreme Court was rejected. State justices saw the editorials as "an open effort to use the power of the press to destroy without reason the reputation of judges and the competence of courts." The *Herald* took Pennekamp's case to the United States Supreme Court.

On June 3, 1946, seven months after the original citations, the Justices threw out the contempt convictions and redefined the rights of citizens to a free press as well as an independent judiciary. The dual nature of the question was powerfully expressed by Justice Felix Frankfurter:

> Without a free press there can be no free society. Freedom of the press, however, is not an end in itself but a means to the end of a free society. The independence of the judiciary is no less a means to the end of a free society, and the proper functioning of an independent judiciary puts freedom of the press in its proper perspective.
>
> Criticism must not feel cramped, even criticism of the administration of criminal justice. . . .

Knight congratulated his stubborn Miami editor.

It was a landmark victory.

The war had exacted an unbelievable cost from mankind. In the aftermath, men turned to the business of restoring balance. It was a precarious and stormy effort. Knight's reporters and editors dealt with labor disputes, shortages, violence, inflation, and the throes of peacetime conversion in industry, politics, and human society.

In Washington, dapper Harry S Truman was out of the White House for morning walks at 7:00 A.M. each day, leading a pack of hard-breathing newsmen at 120 steps per minute. The Missourian had met the Russians at Potsdam in 1945 and returned saying, "Force is the only thing they understand." Eighty-seven percent of Americans approved of the way he handled the presidency, including Jack Knight. But the honeymoon would not last.

Strikes proliferated in textiles, lumber, steel, automobiles, railroads, oil. John L. Lewis's coal miners threatened to shut the nation down.

Republicans had won control of both houses of Congress, with navy veteran Richard M. Nixon a new congressman from California and Joe McCarthy, a small-time judge, noncombat marine veteran, and whiskey drinker, representing Wisconsin in the Senate. Boston Democrat John F. Kennedy took a seat in Congress, as did Texan Lyndon B. Johnson.

American traitors were selling atom bomb secrets to the Russians.

Writer H. G. Wells predicted on his deathbed that man would soon be extinct.

In May 1946, Lewis's 400,000 miners left the pits in twenty-one states. The *Chicago Daily News*'s Ed Lahey saw the union boss as agitating for creation of a $64 million welfare and pension fund. In the "Notebook," Jack Knight roasted the mineworkers' chief. "The country fumes while a vain and pompous labor leader renders it paralyzed in order to enhance his personal prestige."

Readers gave a mixed response.

"Clean out the crooks, Communists and gangsters," an angry Fort Lauderdale, Florida, woman wrote to Knight. "Make unions respectable again." From Miami Beach, a physician took the humanitarian view: "Miners never won anything without a struggle. Even if Lewis's welfare fund brings in five times its goal, it will not eradicate generations of evil."

Brash Harry Truman faced down Lewis. The mine boss capitulated.

In San Francisco, international delegates gathered to inaugurate the United Nations. The wartime Soviet-American alliance was dead.

It was the press's job to sift complex issues.

There was a growing sophistication in American society. By mid-1948 America had 172,000 television sets. Married veterans crowded college campuses. The Kinsey Report found that a woman became pregnant every seven minutes. Worried population planners predicted a boom in teenagers by the 1960s. Winston Churchill warned that war-ravaged Europe was "a rubbish heap, a charnel house, a breeding ground of pestilence and hate." Harry Truman called for massive U.S. aid to stem Soviet expansion there, inspiring the Marshall Plan for European reconstruction. Conservatives decried it as a multibillion-dollar American giveaway, and John Knight became progressively hostile to the Democrat administration. When Truman appealed for "human resources," Knight editorially shrugged: "A dull effort by a commonplace man."

For all the complexities, basic journalistic principles were unchanged. The times demanded best efforts of newspaper writers and editors. The publisher expressed his thoughts in a wide-reaching memorandum addressed to A. T. Burch, associate editor of the *Chicago Daily News,* but applying to all editorial pages of Knight newspapers:

> *It is primarily our duty to inform, rather than instruct.*
>
> *I am not implying that we should be without positive opinions, because it is our duty to cause people to think and very often this can best be accomplished by stating our views so cogently that no reader can possibly be in doubt as to our position.*
>
> *Nevertheless, I like the phrase which precedes our editorials, "As We See It—." By its use, we indicate that we do have definite views on the subjects of the day but are not completely obsessed with a sense of our own infallibility.*
>
> *It is unnecessary, I know, to remind you that we must be scrupulously fair to all sides in the presentation of our editorial policies. This does not mean the dilution of our opinions but rather that our editorials must be based on facts that are well documented.*
>
> *Above all, avoid the use of watered-down, please-everybody editorials which might be better consigned to the waste basket. There is no room on our editorial page for verbose essays which come to no very firm conclusion.*
>
> *Remember at all times that you can have full free-*

*dom to approach every subject with an open mind.
We are not obligated to any political party or special
interest.*

*The Chicago Daily News has long been renowned
for unbiased, factual reporting and the independence of
its editorial page. Let us adhere to that tradition and
improve it, if we can, with simple and pungent writing.*

Being human, however, the staff always had room for error.
And Knight and his editorialists were about to commit a monumental one. For looming just ahead was the presidential election
campaign of 1948.

The columnist-publisher was in Philadelphia's sweltering
convention hall in June when the Republicans again picked
Thomas E. Dewey as their standard-bearer. Confidence surged.
This time the dapper New Yorker with the toothbrush mustache
was not dealing with a Franklin D. Roosevelt; he was out to
unseat the Missouri pip-squeak Harry S Truman, a man untested
in a presidential race. Jack Knight, backer of losers in every
White House campaign since Alf Landon, licked his political
chops. "Truman's mediocrity can hardly survive the people's
verdict in November."

Like many pundits, Knight anticipated a lopsided race, with
Truman badly outclassed. The man was a terrible speech reader;
only when he threw away the script and spoke his mind did he
move audiences. He was heckled at party rallies, was ignored by
southern Democrats, and had a threadbare campaign treasury.
One had to dig behind the scenes of American life, among farm-
ers, unionists, blacks, and the elderly, to find Truman's core of
voting strength. He was despised in country clubs and board-
rooms, a feeling that was mutual. "The reactionary of today is a
shrewd man," Truman responded, "with a calculating machine
where his heart ought to be." Dewey, on the other hand, had
mellifluous delivery and exuded confidence in public. Only privately was it perceived that he lacked warmth, had a bank clerk's
mind, and was so short that he wore elevator shoes. "You have
to know Dewey well," observed a critic, "to really dislike him."
Opinion polls, including Gallup and Roper, wrote off Truman
nonetheless. Dewey, supremely confident, avoided controversy,

campaigning for unity, better water, faith. Truman stuck doggedly to gut issues—housing, wages, crops, medical care for the elderly. Crowd partisans shouted, "Give 'em hell, Harry!" to which he replied, "I'm a' doin' it!"

On Sunday before the election, John S. Knight's "Notebook" delivered a mighty pitch for the GOP candidate. "A vote for Dewey is a vote for integrity in government and housecleaning in Washington. A vote for Truman is a vote to continue the blundering, inept policies of a small-time politician who got into the White House by accident and never quite measured up to the job." Even though Knight perceived this as the public's mood, ironically it was not the consensus in his own home. His wife Beryl regarded Dewey as a cold fish and made it clear that she was betting on Truman, telling her dismayed husband, "You can't elect Charlie Chaplin President of the United States."

For all the vaunted local editorial autonomy on Knight newspapers, editors accepted the "Notebook" as holy writ. Their editorial pages in Akron, Miami, Detroit, and Chicago joined the majority of papers across the nation in supporting Dewey. Truman made sport of his handicap. "Everybody's against me," he chuckled, "except the people."

The situation was prime for historic gaffes.

In Chicago, McCormick's *Tribune* went to press at 7:45 P.M. on election day with a bulldog edition for street sales. The news editor faced a tricky task, writing an attention-grabbing front-page headline when the votes weren't even counted. Boldly, he jotted the words, DEWEY BEATS TRUMAN. The headline went to press in huge black type.

On the editorial page of the *Detroit Free Press,* chief editorialist Malcolm Bingay's enthusiasm for Dewey was absolute, in keeping with his blind devotion to Jack Knight. On this election eve, Bingay prepared a morning-after lead editorial that threw caution to the winds and bade farewell to Harry Truman, "a game little fellow who never sought the presidency and was lost in it, but who went down fighting with all he had." In order to assure a proper transition of power, the editorialist urged Truman to replace Secretary of State Marshall with Dewey's adviser for foreign affairs, John Foster Dulles. "True, this is asking a good deal of Mr. Truman, but these are times which ask a great deal of all Americans." Having written, Bingay went off to a party to celebrate Dewey's victory.

By 10:30 P.M., Harry S Truman had a commanding lead. Editors on the night shift worried about the *Free Press* editorial. Only Bingay could change it. Unable to find him immediately, they called Knight in Akron. "It's up to Bing," Knight said. They finally tracked down the editor, well into his cups. "Bing, the returns show Truman is ahead," said managing editor Dale Stafford, who disliked Bingay. "The numbers suggest he might win." Bingay scoffed. Later, he sauntered into the newsroom to say, "What's this about Truman winning?" He was shown the headline for the next edition, keyed to the president's surprising show of strength. The editorialist tossed several coins onto the desk. "I'll bet that and more that Dewey wins." It was the last they saw of him that night. The editorial ran in all editions, unchanged.

Truman was reelected by a smashing 304 electoral votes to Dewey's 189 and Dixiecrat Strom Thurmond's 38. The Democrats triumphed in both houses of Congress.

American journalism was stunned. Editorialized a humbled *Washington Post:* "Mr. President, we are ready to eat crow whenever you are ready to serve it." Pollster Gallup, when asked what had happened, replied simply, "I don't know."

Knight was defensive. "Harry S Truman painted the Republicans as princes of privilege and himself as the true friend of the little guy. The strategy paid off."

And there were endless letters to write:

> *Dear Mr. Liebling:*
> *Our editorials, which you cite as horrible examples of pre-election myopia, were written and published without consulting me, because our editors are under no compulsion to ask this advice. They are omniscient men, unfettered.*
> *But, my God, what they did to me in Detroit!*

Still, one could not mince words and be effective. In local governments, reform was in the air. Citizens were tired of being fleeced by corrupt politicians. The regime of Chicago mayor Edward J. Kelly was shaken by scandals of gambling payoffs linking police, politicians, and gangsters. Unsolved murders stacked up in the police files. Liquor licenses were the stuff of political barter. "It is a rank, rotten story of maladministration, corrupt influences and favors exchanged for campaign funds," Knight protested. "It is a story of civic inertia and easy conscience."

Chicago voters would start breaking Kelly's grip in the next election.

Knight spoke on active citizenship to a real estate convention in Akron. "No city is ever any better than the caliber of its local government. Your elected representatives at all levels are no better or worse than you deserve. It is depressing to hear citizens say they're too busy for politics and then express disgust at the outcome of an election. Just who is supposed to make that fight for them?" The realtors applauded politely. He was given a certificate of appreciation for the speech. He was not invited back.

Strikes rumbled in the newspaper industry. Miami newspapers had long been unionized by printers, pressmen, mailers, and engravers. There had never been a strike. The *Miami Herald* got its first whiff of trouble on January 5, 1947, when pressmen unexpectedly went "out to lunch" and didn't come back for three days. James L. Knight arranged for an abbreviated paper to be printed outside the *Herald* plant. Then he and managing editor Hills, aware that this was just the beginning, quietly started planning ahead.

The new federal Taft-Hartley Act made unions liable for production losses from wildcat strikes and secondary boycotts. It allowed states to ban closed shops, which hired only union labor. It required labor leaders to file financial reports and sign anti-Communist affidavits.

Union chieftains were outraged. Especially bitter was Woodruff Randolph, president of the printers' International Typographical Union (ITU). Closed shops had given the ITU virtual control of major U.S. newspaper production, locking them into archaic, labor-intensive methods and work rules despite soaring costs. Randolph marshaled his printers for an all-out fight to overturn Taft-Hartley. As prime battleground he picked Chicago, where the ITU's contract with six daily newspapers—including

Knight's *Daily News*—was about to expire. As contract talks stalled, publishers braced for a strike.

Knight talked strategy with McCormick of the *Tribune.* The ITU was pushing for a closed shop in Chicago, he told the colonel. "We've urged them to sign a legal contract and leave the Taft-Hartley issue to the courts. They reject us flatly, saying, 'Do it our way or else.' " Strike or no strike, he intended to publish the *Daily News.* Even now, Knight's production manager, C. E. Woodward, was installing electric Varitype machines and tele-typesetters, with typists to operate them. Such equipment provided cheaper, faster printing through photoengraving. An expert teletypesetter operator could punch out lines of type twice as fast as the union Linotype operator on his big, awkward machine.

McCormick approved. "You handle the strike, Knight. I'm going on a trip to Japan."

ITU printers walked out in November 1947. Every Chicago paper continued to publish. The strike would drag on for twenty-two months and end in a union defeat, as other unions—pressmen, stereotypers, and photoengravers—negotiated new contracts and continued to cross the printers' picket lines. Years later Knight would boast, "We made our greatest circulation and advertising gains during that strike."

The Chicago walkout was a year old when fresh trouble developed in Miami. At the *Herald,* composing room workers walked out as part of a union effort to pressure Chicago publishers by moving against other newspapers they owned. The Miami work stoppage came two days before Christmas, as employees picked up their annual bonus checks. Some printers got their bonuses and went out to the picket line. James Knight was furious. "That's the last Christmas bonus we'll ever pay."

But this time, the *Herald* was ready. Off-duty personnel were called in; employees'. wives enlisted to answer telephones, read proof, and help out as volunteers. Workmen moved in tele-typesetting machines, operated by young women who had been training for months. Editors and reporters doubled as printers in the composing room. As an added safeguard, the *Miami News*—as yet unstruck—began setting *Herald* type, with the cooperation of its union printers. The newspapers' chief negotiator notified the ITU that its contracts with both the *Herald* and the *News* were now regarded as terminated.

A week later, printers struck the *Miami News.* James Knight led a group of his workers into the *News* composing room to help a competitor in distress. It quickly became clear that both papers could function without union printers. *Herald* strikers were invited to return to work at their old pay scales, but few did. Local youths were hired and trained as printers. As weeks went by, the mood became progressively more ugly. Roughnecks arrived in Miami from Chicago and Detroit to harass nonstriking workers. Tires were slashed, paint splashed on automobiles, late-driving employees followed home, stink bombs set off on private property. There were scuffles and fistfights.

Inside the *Herald* plant, tension ran high. One day reporter Jack Anderson heard a disturbance outside editor Pennekamp's office. He arrived in time to see James Knight arguing with a pressman. "The next thing I knew, they were throwing fists at each other," Anderson recalled years afterward. People finally broke up the fight and Knight went down the stairs with his shirt in shreds. In northern cities, tourists were startled to see union pickets at airports displaying placards reading, STAY AWAY FROM MIAMI, FLORIDA—SCAB CITY OF THE USA.

Stress wore on individuals. On nights when he worked at the *Herald* until 3:00 A.M., electrician Lloyd McAvoy walked to his car carrying a loaded pistol. He was not accosted.

Shortly after 6:00 P.M. on October 1, 1949, engraver Charles King discovered a trash bin on fire on the fourth floor of the *Herald*'s newsprint warehouse building, which contained more than six thousand rolls of newsprint weighing fifteen hundred pounds apiece. Fire quickly spread to the giant paper rolls. Smoke and heat hampered firefighters' efforts. Newsprint rolls soaked up water like giant sponges until their swollen masses filled the entire upper floors. A fire chief summoned electrician McAvoy to the roof. "Mac, we can't get light below. Water's shorting out the system. Can you cut the hot wires loose at the panel?" McAvoy donned an oxygen mask, groped down a smoke-filled stairwell, and cut away the live wires. He came out just as his oxygen tank emptied. In the reel room below, James Knight and press chief Chick Hopkins struggled to salvage heavy paper rolls, manhandling them on rolling dollies in six inches of water while a group of union pressmen idly watched. "You want to help me get this stuff out and save your jobs?" Knight shouted. The pressmen ignored him.

Extinguishing the blaze took thirty hours. Scores of fire-fighters suffered from smoke inhalation, fatigue, and injuries. The fire destroyed two thousand tons of newsprint and resulted in $600,000 in losses. Arson was suspected, but not proved.

Strike violence at the *Miami Herald* would continue sporadically for another two and a half years, until new composing room workers won an injunction in Circuit Court against union harassment. A judge found the union guilty of intimidation. Pickets continued to walk while the issue was fought through legal appeals. Finally, five years after it all began, the last picket vanished.

fortune seemed a little more evenhanded in its treatment of John S. Knight. He grew closer to his brother and son. The few honors that he had not already won as a journalist and a human rights advocate were heaped on his shoulders.

Then, on Aug. 8, 1974, his wife of 42 years died after a long illness. And there was more to come.

The news of the death of John S. Knight Jr. in Germany was kept from Johnny's wife, the former Dorothy Wells of Columbus, Ga., until after the birth on April 13 — about two weeks later — of a boy who was named John S. Knight III.

Knight. Through the medium of the Editor's Notebook they discussed the campus violence of the '60s and the course of the Vietnam War. They exchanged letters frequently, played golf together and tal... or

P... Jane...n, managing editor of the D...y New... id of young John, "He... was ...ly a cha...ing guy. He knew who... he ... ...w he was an heir to a fortune and to a key job in the organization if he earned it. But he didn't take himself too seriously."

It was obvious that John S. Knight hoped through his grandson to see that name kept by lights on, the campuses...

John S. Knight III and lives. I can't think of down. So I am not myself guilty.

"I am not going to ...er me," he told Thoi start a new life."

He returned to Flo... ter his grandson's ... nounced he would ma... beth) Augustus. They 1976, in the chapel of Sea at Bal Harbour Lifestyle editor of the

A WORLD DIVIDED

...pare for Harvard. He graduated from the latter cum laude in 1968 with a degree in history, then went on to study philosophy, politics and economics at Oxford University in England, where he earned a master of arts degree, with honors, in June 1970.

During high school and college he worked summer vacations at several Knight papers, including the Beacon Journal.

His first full-time newspaper job came at the Detroit Free Press in 1970. He gained experience in the circulation

center of Philadelphia, John S. Knight III was stabbed to death during a robbery by three men. There were homosexual overtones.

At the time, his grandfather was visiting at the home of Mr. and Mrs. Edwin C. Whiteheads of Greenwich, Conn. Mrs. Whiteheads is a daughter of the then Betty Augustus, widow of Cleveland millionaire Ellsworth H. Augustus. Knight and Mrs. Augustus had known each other for 35 years though a mutual interest in thoroughbreds and horse racing.

Mrs. Knight died ti while watching the R the LaGorce Island ho

WHEN HE STEPP

torial chairman of Kni 1976, his title became Knight-Ridder and the His decision to qui by Thomas and others "The trouble wit night's position." Tho oly that they stay on to hat the business can't

The day was gloomy and cool. Clouds scudded in gray ranks above the Brandenburg Gate, its gigantic, bullet-pocked columns rising over a divided Berlin. Five years after war's end, the former capital of Hitler's Germany was still a sprawl of ruin, divided between East and West by barbed wire and rifle-toting sentries. Most of the 3.5 million residents lived in cellars, cold-water walkups, and rabbit warrens of bombed-out desolation.

John S. Knight showed his press credentials to a grim-faced Communist guard and walked eastward through the Brandenburg Gate and along the crowded Unter den Linden. Behind him, on this Whitsuntide holiday, West Berlin was a study in contrasts. While crowds thronged the free city's biggest event of the holiday, a showing of new cars, Allied tanks lined the eastern frontier, guns pointed at the Soviet Zone. The show of force was a response to rumors of trouble as Communist East Berlin staged a parade of 500,000 Communist German Youth. Knight walked into Russian-controlled territory, sensing the guns aimed at his back.

There were remarkable differences between the halves of this divided city. West Berlin's people were much better housed and fed, their reconstruction advancing. In the eastern sector, one saw the dreary faces of people still living in a massive untended rubble.

As Knight watched, drums and bugles echoed down Potsdamer Platz. Blue-uniformed youths paraded in densely packed ranks, bearing massed flags, placards, and propaganda posters. Loudspeakers played martial music and marchers chanted in English, "Americans go home!" Huge street banners proclaimed the solidarity of the Communist state.

For six hours, as the day's chill deepened, the marchers marched and the drums drummed. The spectacle drew power from its very tedium. At last the final ranks passed. Knight trudged back into West Berlin, where Beryl waited at their hotel. He cabled a report to the Knight newspapers back home: NO ONE WHO WITNESSED THIS COULD BE CONVINCED THAT WE WERE NOT AT WAR WITH RUSSIA, EXCEPT THAT NEITHER SIDE WAS SHOOTING.

The date was May 29, 1950. On the other side of the world, nine Soviet-equipped divisions of the North Korean Army poised secretly along the Thirty-eighth Parallel, ready to open fire.

For Jack and Beryl Knight, the Berlin visit was the high point of a European trip rich with nostalgia. He had taken a forced holiday while they made the Atlantic crossing in six days aboard the liner *Queen Elizabeth,* luxuriating in deck chairs and dining in black-tie splendor. All this, Knight reflected, was a far cry from his miserable first Atlantic crossing on the World War I troop ship *Megantic.*

England had changed dramatically since the war. Surprisingly few physical scars remained. He scribbled notes for a column. "London in spring is always beautiful, but I have never seen the flowers in such profusion." At Oxford, he and Beryl lunched with a young Rhodes Scholar from Chicago who talked glowingly of the way the university developed one's ability to think for himself. Knight was impressed, convinced that Oxford was far superior to the assembly-line atmosphere of most American colleges. He thought of his grandson, John Shively Knight III, a six-year-old entering elementary school in Columbus, Georgia.

London was theaters, nightclubs, and social events. Lord Beaverbrook gave a dinner for the Knights, attended by assorted lights of the British press. They also were guests at the Pilgrims Dinner honoring U.S. Secretary of State Dean Acheson. From Britain, they flew to Paris and stayed in a hotel overlooking the Place de la Concorde. Knight found Paris "still fantastically beautiful with its great boulevards, spacious parks and monuments to the days of France's greatest glory." Among French intellectuals, however, he heard disturbing expressions of neutralism in the struggle between East and West. If anything, the worldly French perceived American politicians as being more warlike than the wily Stalin. "Somewhere along the line," he concluded, "our own propaganda has failed." But the French could take vicissitudes in stride. As a newfound Parisian acquaintance expressed it, "Enjoy the day, enjoy the hour."

Knight returned to the United States nagged by the memory of the marching masses in East Berlin. Events seemed to generate successive shock waves. In his writing, he soberly took stock.

China had fallen to the Communists. The Russians had exploded their atomic bomb. Paranoia was rampant in Washington, with right wingers charging that the American government was riddled with traitors and spies. Young Richard Nixon was making a name for himself prosecuting former State Department functionary Alger Hiss for giving national secrets to the Communists in the late 1930s. And the dour senator from Wisconsin, Republican Joe McCarthy, hogged the limelight with his hunt for subversives, waving mysterious papers as "evidence" and muttering darkly, "The Democratic label is now the property of men and women who have . . . bent to the whispered pleas of traitors."

Knight had not been well. A bladder infection had caused considerable discomfort the previous year. Doctors took him off acid foods, coffee, and booze. He missed his dry martinis, but enjoyed practicing self-control and confided to Stuffy Walters in January,

"I'm still off the alcohol and might continue the treatment all winter." His abstinence extended through spring.

The newspapers thrived, with Chicago as the centerpiece. *Time* announced: "Barely five years and four months after Knight added the slipping *Daily News* to his thriving chain, it paid off nearly $8.7 million of its $12.5 million mortgage, had a commanding lead over Hearst's rival *Chicago American* and hoped shortly to become Chicago's biggest afternoon paper." The reason, *Time* went on, "is what Knight's *News* was giving Chicago—fresh, warm-hearted, local-angled stories, sometimes crusading, almost always lively."

Not everyone agreed with this glowing assessment. At a cocktail party in London, *Daily News* bureau chief William McGaffin met a U.S. envoy on his way to a new post in Yugoslavia. The man launched into a bitter critique of changes in the paper. "The *Chicago Daily News* had the best foreign service in the world until that man took over."

Knight's management style had a flair all its own. He preferred a light touch. When a Miami advertising customer called him in Akron complaining of churlish treatment at the hands of *Herald* ad manager John T. Watters, Knight demanded an explanation. Watters's reply came a few days later.

> *Dear Jack:*
> *Following is the gist of a telephone conversation between me, as JTW, and the customer, Mr. Swigert, as recorded by my secretary on an extension phone:*
> *JTW: Mr. Swigert, I understand you called Mr. Knight and told him that I told you to jump in the lake. When did I say that?*
> *SWIGERT: Well, you practically said that.*
> *JTW: What do you mean?*
> *SWIGERT: I didn't tell him you said exactly that. I said you practically told me to jump in the lake.*
> *JTW: Well, exactly what did I say that made you think I practically told you to jump in the lake?*
> *SWIGERT: You said you wouldn't guarantee me position on an ad.*
> *JTW: I said I couldn't guarantee position on an ad.*

SWIGERT: Well, I have heard I can't get anywhere with you so there's no use arguing.

JTW: Where did you hear that?

SWIGERT: I've heard it from various people. . . . Will you give me the position I want for my ad Sunday?

JTW: I'm sorry, but I cannot guarantee a position.

SWIGERT: There's no use arguing then. Goodbye.

JTW: Goodbye.

Rest assured, Mr. Knight, there has been no change in my handling of advertisers since you purchased the Herald.

Sincerely yours, John T. Watters.

Dear John:

Thank you for your letter. I am glad to be reassured.

J.S.K.

The fact was, he loved the newspaper world. It was less than a religion but more than a craft. Someone had asked that if, given a second chance, he would live it as a newspaperman. Knight replied, "I was born to journalism and had no other course." This wasn't totally accurate. Many publishers inherited newspapers and devoted their energies to business, and it made little difference to them whether the business involved newspapers or dry goods. Knight, on the other hand, devoted himself to news and editorials with aggressive energy. It was, he believed, a thing of instinct. One did not learn true journalism from books, and yet learning, in its broadest sense, was essential.

Just what made a journalist, anyhow?

"The newspaper is something apart from law or business or engineering," he said.

It is more of an art. City editors don't like that terminology but they have nothing to offer in its place. The basic principle is this: Unless a man has that indefinable *something,* that sixth sense we call a "nose for news," it is stupid for him to be in the craft. . . . Some of the most highly educated men and women, with many earned degrees, have failed on newspapers because they lacked a sense of news values and public psychology. And I have known people who were almost illiterate become great reporters and editors. This sets journalism apart as something peculiar unto itself.

As for his own place in the scheme of things: "A man can no more change his nature than can the eel which beats its way out to the great Sargasso Sea. All I know is that this is the only profession in which I am truly happy."

By May 1949, he was fifty-four years old, secretly wearing a harness against a weakness of the back, his hair thinning and a characteristic glint in his eye. The back harness gave him a military posture. He dressed with great care, kept a closetful of suits made by a Detroit tailor, but possessed few leisure clothes. He was fussy about his weight and tempered a fondness for martinis with those periods of abstinence. Even at home, he usually wore a necktie.

He maintained his passion for golf, playing with cold intensity to win; read a dozen newspapers each day; and dominated social gatherings with a broad knowledge of public affairs. Employees of the *Akron Beacon Journal* periodically honored him with office parties, at which he also dominated dice games. As *Beacon Journal* columnist Ken Nichols later put it, "Jack always won because he had all the money."

He kept homes in Akron and Miami, apartments in Chicago and Detroit. Married life with Beryl seemed to suit him well; she was socially strong, if tightly organized. "When you had cocktails before dinner with the Knights," Stella Hall would remember long afterward, "you felt that she was looking at her watch."

He enjoyed writing his column, for it gave him prestige, recognition, and a creative reward. He relished doing exciting things and hobnobbing with famous people. He enjoyed being the boss, for it gave him independence and power. He enjoyed being a multifaceted man in a world of specialists, for it stretched his talents. He was reporter, editor, publisher, businessman. And he enjoyed speaking his own perceptions, even when at variance from the crowd.

Thus, to a group of union printers in Akron, he dealt with the subject of restrictive contracts and work rules that increased costs and reduced production, driving many newspapers into bankruptcy. The thirty-six-hour workweek, he warned, had little meaning in a shut-down plant. To advertising executives, he deplored the popular practice of condemning the capitalist system, which provided such abundance for all; advertising prided itself. in motivating people but failed to sell the very concept on which it survived. To youth, so often captive of fashion and peer pressures, he drummed for self-reliance.

But his judgment was not unerring.

On a fine summer day he was back in Paris, city of light and enlightenment, to speak to the World Brotherhood Organization under the auspices of the American Conference of Christians and Jews. Earlier, President Truman had made the featured address, calling for "a world rule of decency and brotherhood." Knight, facing the multiracial audience, took a different tack. Merely changing laws, he said, didn't make people love each other.

"Frequently our idealism falls short of the mark because it takes too little account of the realities we are compelled to face. Progress . . . consists of a series of steps, often slow and painful." To this conference pushing for change, the publisher deplored "well-meaning but arbitrary methods of those who would administer tolerance by compulsion."

A heavy silence descended over the hall. He forged ahead.

"The impatient among us will cry out that this approach is too slow. But I do not happen to believe that intolerance can be purged from man's soul by forcing him to swallow legal capsules compounded in a political laboratory."

The applause was perfunctory. The program chairman thanked him for coming; he had given them another aspect to consider. "I guarantee you one thing, Mr. Knight. We listened."

These were tumultuous times. Russia had the atom bomb. Spy scandals were widespread. Executive Order 9835 urged Americans to snoop on potential traitors. The FBI watched "disloyal and subversive persons," maintaining ten thousand full field investigations and opening files on millions of people. Whispered allegations could cost a suspect his job, his friends, his way of life. Regional loyalty boards wielded power to decide guilt or innocence, the accused often powerless to protest lest a hearing betray "national security." Public librarians were intimidated by American Legionnaires, the Sons and Daughters of the American Revolution, the Minute Men. In Bartlesville, Oklahoma, librarian Ruth Brown was fired because she gave shelf space to the *New Republic, The Nation, Soviet Russia Today,* and other publications deemed offensive to patriotic watchdog groups. There were those who advocated press censorship "to protect America against its enemies."

The trends left him deeply troubled. When the University of Missouri awarded Knight its Honor Medal for distinguished service to journalism, he warned in his acceptance speech of the issues at stake for a nation torn between liberty and patriotism in the atomic age.

> The American press is your last bulwark of freedom. Unlike radio and television, it is not subject to government license. The printed media alone can and does resist growing encroachments of government upon individual rights. It is a free press. Disagree with it if you will, indict it for its sins, but never let its voice be stilled. For on the day the press comes under government control, your freedom will perish forever.

As a public man, he had star quality. "Wherever Jack Knight sat," an editor would recall long afterward, "was the head of the table." In personal and family life, however, his performance was not always so glowing.

Neither his sons nor his brother James were especially close. Knight seemed to set unrealistic expectations for them, as if forgetting his own lackluster career in college. He held associates in higher esteem than male relatives, and in the family it was the females to whom he expressed warmth. One can only surmise reasons. The old competitive instinct, so magnified in the relationship with his own father, certainly could be daunting. In any event, he demonstrated affection more readily toward his mother and Beryl and stepdaughter, Rita, now the wife of a young Chicago physician. Landon, twenty-six, and Frank, twenty-two, were regarded with a kind of courteous detachment.

Charles Landon Knight II was bright and outspoken. Gossips remarked that his affliction added to the paternal strains. His mobility was dependent on a wheelchair and metal crutches. School life had been difficult. At the private Hun prep school in Princeton, he had been needled by instructors for lateness to class, caused by his having to make his way up and down steps on crutches. Later, Landon had struggled through courses at the University of New Mexico and Ohio State University but did not graduate. Aggressive of manner and sometimes ill-tempered when he drank, he had worked at various editing and writing jobs in Michigan and New York. By spring 1950, he was at his father's *Free Press* in Detroit.

For all Jack Knight's ability to inspire affection from men who worked for him—*Free Press* editor Malcolm Bingay gushed in a memorandum: "God was good to me when He ordained that you were to take over the *Free-Press*"—communication with his sons often became the task of trusted subordinates. Stuffy Walters went to Detroit, spent time with Landon, and gave Jack a favorable report: "I have the feeling that Lanny is becoming more mature. He is doing better work, is not drinking heavily and has joined the Lions Club. If the trend continues, you will have the satisfaction of seeing a son pass from the follies of youth into solid adulthood." The perceptive Walters offered a thoughtful footnote. "Lanny adores you, Jack. Don't ever forget that."

The younger son, Frank McLain Knight, was quiet, unassuming, and well liked. Frank had done well at Culver Military Academy, where despite persistent but ill-defined health problems he won varsity letters in football and boxing, became first sergeant of the cadet corps, and was editor of the student magazine. He then attended Cornell University, like his father, but was adversely affected by the cold weather and transferred to the University of Miami.

Frank's physical problems stemmed from childhood. Landon could remember his younger brother's once losing his balance for no apparent reason and almost falling as they tossed a football. Now, in the early 1950s, Frank complained of chest pains and shortness of breath. Doctors found irregularities in his heartbeat but advised no specific treatment, concluding, "Mr.

Knight should live a normal life but avoid physical exhaustion and exposure."

Jack Knight's attention, meanwhile, focused on the continued rush of outward events.

For all the talk about a free and independent press, the notion was far from sacrosanct. The shocking truth was that there were many, even in the profession, willing to barter it away. This galling revelation brought the *Chicago Daily News* another Pulitzer Prize, shared by staff reporter George Theim and reporter Roy J. Harris of the *St. Louis Post-Dispatch*. They found that more than fifty editors and publishers of Illinois newspapers accepted state payoffs exceeding $480,000 during the administration of Governor Dwight H. Green. The newsmen's function: "To print canned editorials and news stories lauding accomplishments of the Republican state administration."

Barely had the dust settled on the press payoffs scandal when calamity struck in the Far East. On June 25, 1950, the 120,000-man North Korean Army attacked South Korea across the Thirty-eighth Parallel, overwhelming the defenders. President Truman ordered U.S. naval and air support, but in four days half the South Koreans were killed or wounded. Truman ordered in U.S. ground troops, outnumbered twenty to one and armed with surplus World War II weapons. America had been caught napping again.

For the first, and last, time in his life, Knight now endorsed American involvement in a bloody foreign conflict. Remembering the grim realities of the East Berlin Communist parade, he declared, "It is vital that Russian aggression be stopped."

The long hot summer filled with sweat and blood.

The hoodlums knew he loved to gamble. They had watched him for years in the Miami casinos, attired in tuxedo and surrounded by his fancy friends, coolly shooting craps and playing cards. And who occupied a box seat at Hialeah racetrack when the Thoroughbreds ran? John Shively Knight, of course.

There was no justification for his participation in the casino games. Their very existence violated Florida law. They flaunted the standards of community propriety that his *Miami Herald* advocated. Editors and reporters were painfully aware of the contradiction, but Jack Knight was Jack Knight and could do as he pleased. And it pleased him to taste the high life, even if his losses helped to fatten the coffers of organized crime. Gambling was an adventure, albeit calculated; when he gambled, a man and the dice could seek their own destinies, with fate the final arbiter. It was, in a mixed-up world of rules and pressures to conform, a pleasant nonconformity, with manly appeal. Besides, in Miami the powers-that-be condoned such pleasures in the name of tourism, the industry that fed and clothed them and added substance to their bank accounts.

But Knight's nights at the tables were numbered. His own *Miami Herald* turned up the burners of reform, drawing Senator Estes Kefauver's Senate Crime Committee to Miami to expose and shut down the local rackets. Ironically, it was a move instigated by Lee Hills and James L. Knight. But publisher Jack came quickly to the focus.

YOU'VE SHOT IT ALL, KNIGHT! headlined the *Morning Mail*, a local newspaper sprung up suddenly in defense of casinos and their mob operators.

"Knight shoots a thousand dollars in a crap game, but says it's wrong for Joe Blow to play pennies. . . . He will find that those who use men as pawns in any gamble eventually wind up with the stick man saying, 'Seven the devil. Next shooter.' "

The critique had been published in February. Now it was July and the weather, like the heat on the mob, had turned torrid. In the steamy courtroom of Miami's Federal Building, Smilin' Jimmy Sullivan, a former traffic cop elected Dade County sheriff on personal popularity, sat in the witness chair before the Senate Kefauver Committee, sweating and talking. The sweat was caused by the failure of the building's air-conditioning; the talk was Sullivan's admission that he had banked $70,000 in four years on an annual salary of $10,000. At the same time, the Miami Beach–based S & G rackets syndicate had done $160 million in illegal offtrack bookmaking, casino gambling flourished, and south Florida was infested with hoodlums whose connections were said to reach to the governor's office in Tallahassee.

Managing editor Hills's methodical collection of file data on crime had finally exploded into a national exposé. But it was a long time in preparation. Hills had set up a voluntary information exchange on known rackets figures with fourteen U.S. newspapers, ranging from Chicago and Detroit to Minneapolis, New Orleans, New York, and San Francisco. When a gangland figure bought a home in south Florida, Hills noted the address, dispatched a photographer to take pictures, and put it into the file along with other pertinent information.

To break the initial exposé, former FBI agent Virgil W. Peterson, director of the Chicago Crime Commission, went to Miami in July 1948 to address a newly formed citizens' anticrime group.

For two hours, Peterson detailed for a standing-room-only audience the realities of gangster rule, drawing on his own background and Hills's *Herald* files and naming names for the benefit of the press: "Joe Massei, prominent racketeer from Detroit with a record of charges of robbery and murder, is a resident of Miami Beach. . . . Tony Accardo, frequently mentioned as the top ranking member of the Capone Gang, is a part-time resident of Miami. . . ." The *Herald* packed its next day's paper with Hills's file material about gangsters—their crimes, their fancy life-styles, their mansions, and boats. Item: "A few miles north of Miami, in Broward County, lie the rich gambling fields controlled by Frank Costello, underworld lord of the United States." Item: "Martin Leo Accardo, hoodlum and felon, lives in a $46,000 two-story house in Coral Gables. . . ." In months to follow, the *Herald* carried a regular picture feature, "Know Your Neighbor," featuring photographs and local home addresses of hoodlums.

Long-slumbering Miami awoke with a start. Already, James L. Knight and others were organizing a Crime Commission, headed by former FBI agent Dan Sullivan. As gangland exposés spread to cooperating newspaper cities, the stage was set for a full-scale investigation by Estes Kefauver's Senate Crime Committee. Hills invited the Tennessean to launch his effort in Miami, followed by hearings in New York and Washington. The notoriety would catapult Kefauver into national politics as the vice presidential candidate with Adlai Stevenson six years later.

Knight received thinly veiled threats from the mob. One hint of danger came from a casino manager. "He was alarmed for my safety," Knight told Hills. "He said, 'These guys don't fool.' "

Knight refused to worry. "If they do anything to me, it will do them more harm than good." Verbal potshots came from varied quarters. There was a thin line between the publisher's personal gaming zest and his newspapers' antigambling crusades. Rumbled *Miami Life:* "John S. Knight is a cynical hypocrite. Back when gambling ran wide open in this county, he was in the Brook Club so often that people thought he ran the place." In Detroit, a circuit judge criticized the *Free Press* for publishing horse-racing results. "Free advertising for bookmakers," the judge called it. Knight replied that he had no intentions of banning legal racing news. "We can't reform the betting instinct by pretending that racing doesn't exist."

Florida governor Fuller Warren smarted from *Herald* reports that a dog track owner had given $154,000 to his campaign fund. The governor, though never personally implicated, blasted "the villainous *Miami Herald*" in a Miami speech. The startled crowd applauded as Warren assailed John S. Knight as "power-hungry and profit-grabbing," accepting paid advertising from gambling casinos even while crusading to shut them down. Mindful that the nation seethed with fear of Communist subversives, the canny Warren went on: "John S. Knight is no Communist, but he is using a Communist tactic in his vilification of public officials. I say it's un-American and undemocratic. If John S. Knight wants political power, let him run for office."

The speech was reported in the *Herald* without editorial comment. But finally, for the first time since Miami's incorporation in 1896 as a rowdy railroad and tourism town, the dice stopped their public rattle and vice retreated into the shadows—bridled and officially condemned, if not eliminated. The *Miami Herald* was awarded the Pulitzer Prize for public service.

As the year ended, managing editor Hills received a note from his boss: "I am in need of help. . . ." Dale Stafford had quit as managing editor of the *Free Press.* Would Hills take charge in Detroit while continuing as executive editor of the *Herald*? There was a tremendous job of work to be done, but the salary would be ample.

Politics! Like his father before him, Knight loved the game. And although his journalistic code forbade seeking office or taking an official party role, being a reporter and analyzer had its unique excitements. The press expressed editorial preferences and thereby influenced events. As publisher and weekly columnist for four metropolitan newspapers, Knight enjoyed a widening prestige extending to the White House itself. And that, of course, was the ultimate arena of politics, the ultimate prize. Now, amid deepening national troubles, his quarrels with the Truman administration became increasingly bitter. Change at the top, he believed, was long overdue.

Korea was the cutting edge. Knight's *Chicago Daily News* correspondent Keyes Beech had brought home the horrors of that conflict, describing the marines' terrible retreat from the Chosin Reservoir, carrying their dead and wounded and fighting off hordes of attacking Chinese at fifteen degrees below zero. "Trial by blood and ice," Beech called it. The Chinese conducted their war from Manchurian sanctuaries safe from retaliatory attack, and General Douglas MacArthur's pleas for presidential authority to bomb beyond the Yalu River went unheeded. In Washington, Knight perceived Truman as trying to silence the press in the name of national security. "If the press is muzzled, only the American people will be deceived." He lambasted "political mountebanks and self-seekers" around Truman and urged relentless public inquiry "until we root out every chiseling stinker having a grip on a government job."

Shades of C. L.

The publisher's ire soared when Truman fired MacArthur on April 11, 1951. He hurried to Washington to record the scene as the old soldier came home to a hero's welcome. Knight sat in the press gallery wiping his eyes as MacArthur made his theatrical farewell speech to Congress: "Old soldiers never die, they just . . . fade . . . away."

"Living or dead," Knight wrote, "the footprints of such men are stamped upon the sands of time."

Three months later, Dwight D. Eisenhower's name headed the list of likely GOP candidates for the White House. Knight was jubilant. "Quite plainly, he is the people's choice." But the wartime Allied commander was also an enigma; he stood for everything, and nothing; claimed no political party, no overriding creed beyond duty. Eisenhower simply came across as good and decent. For most Americans it was enough. Knight flew to Paris for a two-hour interview, which was not substantive. "The general seemed almost naïve when it came to politics," he reported. But in July 1952, even before the balloting, Ike was the overwhelming choice of the Republican National Convention in Chicago. The only question was his choice of running mate.

To Jack Knight, prowling delegate meeting rooms and caucuses, the answer was merely an exercise in logic. GOP strategists wanted as vice president a conservative newcomer and forceful speaker who would be tough on "subversives." The name was on the lips of every reporter there, but nobody could spell it out. Publisher Knight needed no quotable source and was answerable to no skeptical editor. Despite his past errors of prophecy, from Alf Landon to Dewey and Truman, he took another plunge for the front pages of his newspapers. "General Eisenhower will be the next Republican nominee for President, with Richard Nixon as his running mate. . . ." Three days later the convention made it official, Ike and Nixon.

Knight denied suggestions that he had inside information. No one looked into his past record of prediction failures. The coup became a permanent fixture of his official biography, attesting to reportorial brilliance. In November, the Ike-Nixon ticket swept to victory over Democrats Adlai Stevenson and Senator John Sparkman.

For the first time since the administration of Herbert Hoover, a man of Knight's own party occupied the Oval Office.

The key men ran things. That was the secret. You surrounded yourself with good people, gave them scope to operate and a sense of belonging, and, in time, they built your fortune for you. And he had them, in Barry, McDowell, Stuffy Walters, Hills, Jim Knight. Their individual strengths were in business, or production, or finance, or the newsroom. Hills's talents seemed all-encompassing. Their loyalties were as distinctive as their talents. Second-echelon management came and went, but change was rare at the top. It was a combination of attractions. Men of journalistic integrity liked the principles under which the Knights operated. They perceived the company as expanding, with ample room for personal growth. They had freedom to make decisions and carry them out. They were well paid. In years to come, Hills, especially, would be courted heavily for top management of the *New York Herald Tribune,* virtually able to name his salary, but turned it down.

Barry was the veteran: fussy, fastidious John H. Barry, with his immaculate desk and passion for positive numbers, a miracle worker of profit and loss. Then there was Blake McDowell, the lawyer, breezy and folksy and shrewd, the best bargainer Knight had ever known. McDowell's brain sopped up data like a sponge. Now, in January 1951, he was studying ways to assure them top-quality, affordable newsprint, a basic and expensive commodity. McDowell suggested that they invest directly in a Canadian plant rather than buy paper on the open market at a premium of $200,000 to $500,000 per year.

> The company I have in mind manufactures about 150,000 tons a year and has practically a new mill and plenty of groundwood and sulphite. My plan is for them to install a new newsprint machine costing $6 million and producing 60,000 tons. If Knight Newspapers' contract is for 10,000 tons of newsprint from the machine, we would purchase $1 million of the debenture bonds. . . .

McDowell was a human calculator.

As publisher, Knight expressed himself in different ways with different men. Stuffy Walters was a man of strong feelings and stubborn principle, who could quote verbatim John Stuart Mill's essay "On Liberty." His enthusiasm was boundless. "This is the Knight decade in journalism," Walters declared. The publisher freely exchanged ideas with him on the newspaper craft: "I see a fallacy in following the opinion line of some columnists. They are often chosen instruments through which propaganda is spread by bureaucrats, and thus become captive to the very system they create to produce exclusives." And: "Regarding your misgivings about D. N., I agree that he is not as productive as other writers on the Foreign Staff. He is given to moody spells, brooding about the state of the world. What we need are reporters, not statesmen." And: "Merchants today are looking for ways to sell their products through intelligent use of all media. It is up to us to keep up with the times and make radical changes in technique if necessary."

Knight encouraged experimentation. At one point, he thought that the recipes of the *Chicago Daily News* food editor ought to be double-checked in a test kitchen. The *Detroit Free Press* had had such a facility many years earlier, before Knight came on the scene. "A very simple kitchen, with good but not elaborate equipment, could be located in a room near the cooking editor's desk," he told Walters. "When it's time to test a recipe, the cooking editor could step into the kitchen and do the job. The food could go to the office cafeteria." The idea went nowhere.

Malcolm Bingay, editorial chief of the *Free Press,* continued to lavish praise on his boss. "I thought of you the other night when reading an essay by Hugh Walpole, in which he had this sentence: 'He was a courtly gentleman, and anybody who understands what this means needs no further explanatory matter.' It fits you, Jack. What the hell is the use of waiting for a chap to die before saying nice things about him?" With Bingay, Knight indulged in random observations. "Quite frankly I have difficulty in following these economists. They are academic in the extreme and I believe they duck realities." And: "I cannot agree with Mr. Pohek's conclusions that a good man has to 'butter up the boss' to hold his job. That is a completely old-fashioned idea." And: "Memorandum writing is a bad habit; they have a finality about them that is disconcerting."

In early 1950, Bingay was severely burned in an explosion. Dictating from his hospital bed, the editor described to Knight his ordeal. "I was so badly burned that all the skin had to be taken off my head and neck and both hands. . . . For days I smelled like an old burned shoe." He rallied. He returned to work. But complications dogged him. Less than three years later, Malcolm Bingay died.

Knight mourned.

"We have lost a gifted writer, and a friend."

The strikes in Chicago, Miami, and Detroit had inspired fresh ideas about newspaper production. Jack Knight recalled a conversation with Charles Kettering, inventive genius of General Motors. "Newspapers are always telling other people how to run their businesses but don't seem to know how to run their own," Kettering observed dryly. Knight asked what he meant. "Your production methods," the inventor said, "—you're using cams and gears that can turn only so fast and then fall apart. You should be using electricity."

It was true, of course. Newspapers were still locked into nineteenth-century technology. Few modern industries tolerated such inefficiency. In Miami, James Knight was thinking about new ways of doing things. With the most difficult union out of the picture, he saw an opportunity to revolutionize the composing room, typesetting, engraving—indeed, the entire field of processing words for the printing presses. Color, too, was coming into its own; as technology speeded processing, from camera click to printed news page, color pictures could be used on ever-tighter deadlines.

The *Herald* plant, however, was overrunning its space. It was impossible to expand presses for new color processes and increased circulation. If they were crowded now, what would things be like in the 1980s? Jim Knight began to envisage a new plant on a technical scale never before attempted by a newspaper.

Overall, it was a matter of vanity, thoroughly enjoyable. As publisher, writer, and tycoon, John S. Knight was a national figure. His name opened doors, and the limelight which his father had once accused him of coveting too much was his.

New York society writer Igor Cassini listed the publisher among his choices of society's "New 400." In Akron, stories and pictures about Knight and his family constantly appeared in the *Beacon Journal.* Merited or not, editors dutifully covered his speeches, his cultural and civic activities, his golf and social functions, his awards. Other papers of the group gave similar homage, though with more restraint.

By late August 1953, *Newsweek* was illuminating Knight business strengths. "Few major newspaper combines have grown so healthy so fast." Circulation of the *Detroit Free Press* had risen by 100,000, to 414,000, since Knight bought it in 1940. The

Chicago Daily News was roaring along at 560,000 per day, the *Akron Beacon Journal* at 150,000, the *Miami Herald* at 212,000. Each paper netted nearly $1 million a year. What was the secret of Knight's success?

"I'm trying to find people who're better newspapermen than I am," he said. "And I think I've got them."

14

THE POWER AND THE PRIZE

They were brothers, sharing bloodline and heritage, but their talents and personalities were remarkably dissimilar. The fifteen-year age difference was part of it; when James Knight entered first grade, his brother John was already a grown man. It was a psychological gap never to be bridged. Their relationship remained cordial but cool, in the manner of business associates. Their letters tended to be formal, often signed with titles. Jim Knight, having come into his own at Miami, still felt keenly his brother's dominance. It was a consciousness that would never leave him. Even in the closing years of life, he would recall his elder brother as having "a streak in him that most people failed to notice; Jack could be ornery as a goat."

James Landon Knight had never involved himself in writing or editing. His interest lay in what he termed the nuts and bolts of newspapers: production, technology, business, planning. In personality, he was a quiet, self-effacing man, more folksy than polished, with a passion for fishing and the out-of-doors. His favorite expression was "Shucks." For all this, business associates saw in him the same tough-minded perfectionism that characterized his brother, with the integrity to match.

John S. Knight arrived at the age of sixty baldish and stern-faced, with the trim build of an athlete and the style of an investment banker. To one profiler, he seemed "a man with ice water in his veins." Reporters for Knight newspapers tended to take a hard-nosed pride in their employer. "Like all publishers, he's an s.o.b.," said one, "but there's no s.o.b. in the business I'd rather work for." For one thing, in an era of dying newspapers the Knight group flourished. This satisfied the tough criteria of such veterans as *Chicago Daily News* Washington reporter Ed Lahey. "I only ask one thing of a publisher," said Lahey, "that he be solvent."

Knight's solvency was beyond dispute. Combined circulation of the four metropolitan newspapers exceeded 1.3 million. This was a 20 percent increase during the decade since the end of World War II, compared to 8.4 percent for all U.S. newspapers. In each of the four cities, circulation went up faster than did population. And while most of U.S. industry had cut back on investment in new plants and equipment, Knight was pumping $11.5 million into modernizing the newspaper plants at Akron, Miami, and Detroit. The Knight group's success was even more phenomenal considering its apparent structural looseness.

"Where is your central management?" an interviewer asked Knight.

"We don't have any," the publisher replied.

Such a seemingly flip philosophy made for bright copy but was far from accurate. Although Knight surrounded himself with smart men and gave them autonomy, the last word in decision making was his own. Nevertheless, he encouraged conflict of ideas and allowed his judgment to be overridden. "Anybody," he insisted, "can tell me anything." But telling could be easier than convincing. Jack had summarily rejected, for example, Jim's opposition to transferring Lee Hills from Miami to Detroit. And a new phase of Knight expansion was about to provide yet another test of wills between the brothers.

Jack Knight found stimulation amid the bright lights and famous names of Chicago, Washington, and New York. Jim's idea of relaxation was Roaring Gap, North Carolina, a rich man's resort of lovely summer hills and active, but small-town, society. Since the late 1930s, the younger Knight, his wife, Mary Ann, and their daughters had vacationed annually in the Carolinas. Never comfortable among big-city politicians and wheeler-dealers, Jim had an earthy nature that was more at home in the South. He was active in the Southern Newspaper Publishers Association and promoted the region's newsprint industry with plants in Tennessee, Alabama, and Texas. He helped to create the American Newspaper Publishers Association's Research Institute for study of new newspaper technology, a task that allowed him to rummage happily through other companies' back shops, pressrooms, and mailrooms.

One of James Knight's close friends was publisher Curtis B. Johnson of the *Charlotte* [North Carolina] *Observer.* In thirty-four years at the *Observer,* Johnson had built circulation from 19,000 to more than 130,000, making it the largest and most profitable paper in the Carolinas. After his death in 1950, ownership of the *Observer* became snarled in legalities of the will. Trustees hired as president and publisher a former New Orleans newspaperman, Ralph Nicholson, with Johnson's widow as board chairman. It was not a happy arrangement. Nicholson's political ultraconservatism drove the traditionally moderate *Observer* far to the right and strengthened its afternoon rival, the *News.* Staff members chafed. "The man was arrogant," columnist Kays Gary would recall long afterward. The legal conflict was resolved in 1953, with Nicholson ousted and Mrs. Johnson in charge. She began seeking a buyer for the 57½ percent ownership that she controlled, along with three of Curtis Johnson's nephews. Charlotte banker Carl McGraw, a friend and confidant, felt that the matter was clear-cut: what likelier prospect than Jim Knight, her late husband's old friend from Roaring Gap, a man who still said "Shucks."

Charlotte served one of the richest industrial belts in the South, the Piedmont. But when Jim broached the subject, Jack

Knight was unimpressed. The publisher knew little about Charlotte and saw scant prestige in small-town publishing. Besides, Mrs. Johnson's holdings represented only part of the property. "I am against any newspaper deal in the South where the other side holds a substantial minority interest. I can't see why we should do all the work and get less than 60 per cent of the return."

Jim Knight persisted. "I am certain that earnings could be increased to a $1 million gross in quick order and $1.5 million in five years." The younger Knight had an instinct for the jugular. He saw big, costly Detroit as plagued with problems. Deftly, he reminded Jack that older brothers were not necessarily omniscient. "I like this type of property better than any in Detroit. The earnings of these small units are terrific by comparison." Then he drove home his point. "If you are not inclined to go along, would you have any objections to my taking up the deal with a syndicate?"

Jack Knight, stung, instructed lawyer Blake McDowell and Lee Hills to try to buy the *Observer*. To his impertinent brother, the publisher made it clear that if they did succeed, he wanted no part in running the Charlotte paper: "It's your baby." Negotiations were intensive and secret, throwing off would-be competitors and keeping the selling factions fragmented. To maintain cover, Hills and McDowell took separate airline flights in and out of Charlotte. On December 29, 1954, it was announced that Knight Newspapers had bought the *Charlotte Observer* for $7 million.

McDowell's bargain price startled competitors. The paper's new president and publisher, moreover, was not to be the famed John S. Knight but his forty-five-year-old brother, James. In his statement, James Knight pledged that the *Observer* would serve as "an impartial portrayer of the news, a fearless interpreter of the moving events of our time, and a faithful, sincere and honest servant of the people."

Combined circulation of Knight Newspapers had just topped 1.5 million.

Lee Hills was forty-eight in 1955, an intense, quiet workaholic with a mind for myriad detail. Arch-competitor Dan Mahoney, longtime publisher of the *Miami Daily News,* had characterized him privately as "a cold fish." Veteran *Miami Herald* reporter Jack Anderson would recall years later, "I don't think I ever heard Lee Hills laugh out loud." No one questioned his abilities, however. Hills was highly organized; a meticulous keeper of files and shorthand notes; a crafter of strong, detailed correspondence; a painstaking assessor of human talent; a methodical planner.

As managing editor, Hills had carried the manpower-crippled *Herald* through its critical war years. His demand for good journalism, combined with a pugnacious spirit toward the rival afternoon *News,* was credited for the *Herald*'s circulation success. He displayed shrewd flexibility with people, whether handholding a brilliant woman news executive on the verge of mental breakdown, firing a drunken reporter who'd slept through a Key West hurricane, or brainpicking Ed Ball, crusty administrator of Florida's Alfred du Pont empire, on future economic opportunities in south Florida.

As early as 1946, Hills was looking for ways to better things for Knight newspapers and pondering future management needs. He saw this as a process of careful recruitment and training. "You can't build morale and organization by hiring an outsider for the top jobs. Mostly you have to promote from within. Over a period of years, our organization grows stronger or weaker depending on the caliber of people we get and develop with that potential."

Hills's loyalty to John S. Knight was absolute. The publisher, in turn, put a high premium on both loyalty and talent; he spoke of the "hard, slavish work" of management, and the scarcity of men and women who could handle it well. As executive editor of both the *Detroit Free Press* and the *Miami Herald,* with such sideline assignments as upgrading the *Charlotte Observer*'s content and news staff, Hills now labored under multiple pressures.

From the day of his arrival in Detroit in December 1951, it was clear to Hills that the *Free Press* suffered numerous ailments, ranging from weak circulation on home delivery routes to troublesome labor unions. Its circulation, 447,688, trailed that of the dominant *Detroit News* but led the *Times.* As circulation leader, the *News* took in about half of the newspaper advertising dollars in the Detroit market; the *Free Press*'s share was 23 percent.

For lack of aggressive promotion, morning home delivery of the *Free Press* was sharply limited, with sales concentrated in an early edition distributed the previous evening. Although midnight press runs gave the paper its freshest morning news, nearly half the daily circulation was home-delivered long before that. To complicate matters further, production equipment—press units, composing room, stereotyping machinery—was in a decrepit state, little improved since 1925 and incapable of handling an expanded circulation. The paper ran no color.

If it could take over the lead, the *Free Press* stood to gain millions of dollars in revenues.

Hills launched an intensive survey of plant and personnel and drafted a long-range plan that would virtually dismantle and reconstruct circulation, management, and equipment. Telephone solicitors were hired to drum up new readers. Opinion surveys tested the public's likes and dislikes. Pages took on crisper layouts, brighter features, and snappier photo displays. Job seekers got tougher scrutiny. A stream of densely packed memos from Hills to Knight spelled out successes, failures, and frustrations:

> *Dear Jack: I am taking the entire women's department to luncheon today to pep-talk them. The department has slipped from where it was some years ago. A great deal of the strained relations between editorial and advertising stems from them. . . . The photo department is headless. Our chief photographer has no faint concept of how to run the department. The picture editor is completely at sea most of the time, the picture handling more disorganized than if we had no picture editor. . . . I am going to have Cle Althaus [an expert in personnel recruitment and testing] interview a dozen or so of our key people. It may be quite revealing. I took the test myself to get some personal idea of its value. . . . Long-range prospects look better every day. The size of the*

circulation job to be done is almost monumental, but I
feel we're beginning to get our teeth into it. . . .

Knight approved major spending for new presses and stereotyping and composing room equipment. The *Free Press* published its first color picture, a duck dinner. New section fronts
displayed sports, women's news, business, local news. The paper
hawked itself with promotional slogans: EASY TO READ, EASY TO
FIND and YOU SEE THE FRIENDLY FREE PRESS EVERYWHERE. (A
wag, mindful that delivery boys were notoriously unable to
throw a *Free Press* onto the customer's front porch, added, "in
the Bushes, on the Roof, on the Grass.")

Detroit's newspaper circulation war became irrational. The
Free Press offered to donate Christmas cash to Detroit's Children's Hospital on behalf of each new subscriber. The *Detroit
News* questioned the "charity" of the arrangement. Jack Knight
flayed "blustering dog-in-the-manger tactics" by *News* president
Warren Booth. "We suggest that the hysterical Mr. Booth read
the Ten Commandments, generate a little more warmth in his
heart and stop acting like a sorehead." Booth retorted, "They
must be desperate over at the *Free Press.*"

But *Free Press* sales inched upward. In April 1955, circulation topped 500,000 to make it Detroit's leading paper.

Hills's personal tenacity had made it happen. He threw similar effort into covering a potentially explosive autoworkers' union
contract fight.

Fiery, Plato-quoting United Auto Workers chief Walter
Reuther was pushing for a guaranteed annual wage. Amid
threats of strike, labor-management talks began behind closed
doors and rumors swept a Detroit starved for hard news. Hills
dug into sources on both sides, spurred his staff for tips, and
started writing a special unsigned daily column, "A Look Behind
the UAW-Auto Curtain." It became a grueling business as he
combed the industry for information, literally living in his office
and sending out for meals. The result was an authoritative daily
offering of fact and insight. From blue-collar taverns to the executive cloisters of Grosse Pointe, "Behind the Curtain" became
the most widely read feature in the Motor City. Circulation rose
by another eleven thousand copies per day.

Hills predicted correctly that giant Ford Motor Company would settle with the union on a thorny question of unemployment benefits. Despite strong rumors that General Motors would balk, touching off a strike, "Behind the Curtain" predicted flatly that it would not happen. It didn't. The column was credited with helping to avert a major walkout.

Lee Hills was awarded his second Pulitzer Prize.

The focus was on Peron. Shrewdly he had captured the devotion of Argentina's masses, strutting and posturing in the manner of his long-dead idol, Italian dictator Benito Mussolini. Juan Domingo Peron stood at the peak of power and told his followers: "When a leader believes himself half a god, he is lost. And thus he signs his own death warrant." It would prove a grim prophecy.

There were those who doubted that John S. Knight would be allowed into Argentina. The publisher had become America's leading drumbeater for a free press in Latin America and staunchly defended Alberto Gainza Paz, the Argentine publisher who'd lost his newspaper, *La Prensa,* and fled to exile for resisting the power of Peron. Knight had written and spoken against corrupt and venal strongmen throughout the hemisphere who consolidated their power by throttling the press. And now Knight was en route to Brazil for a meeting of the Inter-American Press Association, with a scheduled overnight stop in Peron's capital city, Buenos Aires. Even the pilot of the Pan American Airways Clipper commented wryly, "How long do you plan to stay in Buenos Aires, Mr. Knight?"

Surprisingly, Knight and his party were whisked through customs in a dramatic demonstration of the caprice of dictators. For Peron, it was also a lapse of judgment. From Buenos Aires Knight cabled his impressions to 1.5 million weekly readers, describing life in a nation under the heel:

> Buenos Aires is one of the beautiful cities of the world. Only when one looks behind the façade does true understanding begin, and you feel the oppressive hand of the police state. . . . In personal conversations, people guardedly refer to President Peron as "Mr. P.," the "Big Brother" or simply "Mr. Big." Children are taught to

repeat at every lesson: "I love Eva, she is protecting us from above." History is rewritten. A whole new generation is never permitted to forget that Peron is the state. . . . Buenos Aires is a beautiful lady, with a broken heart.

Many Latin Americans knew Knight as publisher of the *Miami Herald*. From the Caribbean to Bogotá, Rio, Lima, and Buenos Aires, the *Herald* circulated a daily English-language Clipper Edition by air. The edition, an outgrowth of Miami's natural geographic and airline proximity to Latin America, had been created by Hills in January 1946. Twenty-five years later, the paper would circulate 11,000 copies daily (Monday through Saturday) and 16,500 on Sunday.

Knight's involvement with the Inter-American Press Association (IAPA) went back many years, but his fervor for hemispheric press freedom had been fired by the Gainza Paz case. The Argentine publisher, whom Knight knew through the IAPA, was cultured, bilingual, and conservative. In print, he called Peron "a monster." Abruptly, *La Prensa* was shut down. As president of the IAPA, Jack Knight dug into the affair and found numerous cases of Latin American newspapers' being suppressed or destroyed, their editors intimidated, arrested, or exiled. It happened not only in Argentina but also in Brazil, Bolivia, Ecuador, Cuba, Nicaragua.

Knight began speaking and writing about the threat to basic free expression in the hemisphere. It was a gut issue. As he declared in a speech in Rio de Janeiro, "The voices of freedom have been muted and a captive press crawls on its belly for the dubious privilege of earning a living by printing six to eight pages of innocuous pap."

The effort was not without successes. Reported Knight:

In the Argentine, David Michel Torino, editor of *El Transigente* of Salta, was only recently released after spending three years in jail on trumped-up charges. He credits the intervention of the IAPA for his freedom. Demetrio Canelas, editor of *Los Tiempos* of Cochabamba, Bolivia, was arrested and held incommunicado following riots and the destruction of his

Clara and C. L. Knight, c. 1900.

State champion football team, 1913.

Publisher Charles Landon Knight, c. 1920.

Army enlistee John S. Knight, 1917.

Katherine in her bridal gown,
November 21, 1921.

The young Akron editor, John S. Kni,
c. 1928.

John and Beryl Knight's children, 19
from left, John S. Knight, Jr.,
Landon, Rita, and Frank.

With Eleanor Roosevelt in Akron, 1937.

With Colonel Frank Shutts at the purchase of the Miami Herald, *1937.*

Knight with Frank Knox, left, publisher of the Chicago Daily News, *c. 1936. Knight would buy the paper after Knox's death.*

Second Lieutenant John S. Knight, J and his bride, Dorothy, Fort Bennin Georgia, 1942.

Frank Knight with nephew James Craig, Jr., 1949.

James L. Knight, c. 1945.

Knight is among the first Americans to sign in at Tokyo's Imperial Hotel at the end of World War II, 1945.

Harry Truman comes to the Herald. In background, George Beebe.

President Dwight D. Eisenhower, right, shares a joke.

A chat with John F. Kennedy four da[ys] before his assassination, November 1963.

The brothers Knight and the new building, April 1963.

John and Beryl Knight, 1961.

Lunch with the Duke of Windsor.

With close friend E. J. Thomas, right.

Lyndon and Lady Bird Johnson visit the Beacon Journal.

Knight as an election observer in Vietnam.

Writing the weekly "Notebook," 1965: "As a writer, I'm a bleeder."

With Thomas E. Dewey, August 1968.

Knight and family, October 1968: from left, Beryl; mother, Clara Knight; and son Landon.

Knight Newspapers goes public, 1969. Knight checks ticker tape with, from left, brother, James, and Lee Hills.

Flanked by his top men: from left, Alvah H. Chapman, Jr., brother, James, and Lee Hills, right.

With wife Betty at Hialeah racetrack, January 1976.

Knight and the author.

newspaper plant. He credits IAPA for saving his life. In Quito, Ecuador, *El Comercio,* edited by Jorge Mantilla Ortega, was closed by President Velasco Ibarra for refusing to let the government decide what should and what should not be printed. Editor Mantilla was jailed. He credits IAPA for the reappearance of *El Comercio* after a silence of 43 days.

"The threats to freedom of expression concern us all. To borrow a phrase, ideas can be dangerous but the suppression of ideas is fatal. Freedom is a dangerous way of life. But it is ours."

In September 1955, Juan Peron was toppled from power and journeyed into exile. His words came back to mock him, echoing through the marble palace from which he had ruled Argentina, "When a leader believes himself half god . . ."

One did not have to go abroad to find the free flow of ideas in jeopardy. In America, zealots sought to purge libraries, censor schoolbooks, label, blacklist, and condemn. Similar constraints would be placed on U.S. newspapers, Knight surmised, by those who disagreed with their editorial positions or sought press censorship in the name of "national security."

In Washington, the government search for Communists and fellow travelers expanded to the entertainment industry. Again, the accused were often condemned by innuendo and blacklisted from working without benefit of trial. President Eisenhower himself had difficulties with the concept; he had called the pursuit of Communists in government "a can of worms" and yet signed Executive Order 10450 banning from federal employment any person suspected of treachery, drunkenness, drug addiction, sexual deviance, mental illness, nudism, unsanitary habits, lying, or anything else deemed "inconsistent with national security." More than fourteen hundred federal employees lost their jobs in four months.

Much of this grew out of the anti-Communist hysteria generated by Senator Joseph McCarthy. By the mid-1950s even members of McCarthy's own party were having second thoughts. Ohio conservative Republican congressman George Bender flayed the senator's "witch-hunting, Star Chamber methods and denial of civil liberties." Former senator Harry P. Cain of Washington State quit as director of the Subversive Activities Control Board in 1954, charging that the nation had "gone too far; injustice was rampant, sickening."

John S. Knight was strangely ambivalent, as if torn between loyalty to a fellow Republican and reluctant repugnance. It was not the first time, nor the last, for the publisher to vacillate between his inbred conservatism and conscience. He wrote, at one point, that he agreed with McCarthy's objectives, but "the methods are wrong." Again he urged that the government "root out subversives but don't sacrifice democratic procedures"—whatever that meant. Then, as if to absolve McCarthy, he observed: "Joe didn't invent McCarthyism. Hatred is as old as mankind." And in an "Editor's Notebook" column of August 21, 1955, Knight praised the work of the House Committee on Un-American Activities investigating suspected Communists and fellow travelers in the entertainment industry. "We feel nothing but disgust and indignation over the refusal of actors to give satisfactory answers to questions put to them by the committee. It is their responsibility as citizens to speak up or be adjudged in their true colors as principals in the Communist conspiracy."

Again, this was wholly inconsistent with his stated convictions on freedom, including those of the press. Knight would never explain by what standard he interpreted an accused's silence as admission of guilt. Admirers of the publisher would defend him as often seeking to arouse readers by taking a controversial or provocative position. But one is left with troublesome questions: Was freedom merely the province of the press; did it not also pertain to private individuals? What about his speeches defending the right to dissent? And was the Fifth Amendment right against self-incrimination a mere trifle, to be discarded if one did not agree with another's politics? It was another seemingly random inconsistency of a man who seemed at times to stray from his own oft-quoted principles.

The late C. L. Knight, who had so angrily railed at "phony patriots" who besmirched as traitors antiwar dissidents and Americans of German descent, must have turned in his grave.

November 4, 1955: John H. Barry was dead.

A cold wind moaned down from Lake Erie and the northern Ohio high country to rattle the dreary factory windows of Akron. From his office on the third floor of the Beacon Journal building, Jack Knight, seemingly lost in thought, peered down the hill to Main Street, with its cheerless brick buildings and dingy bars. Out in the newsroom, editors were putting the finishing touches to Barry's obituary. The man whose financial genius had contributed immeasurably to building the Knight fortunes had succumbed at age eighty-two to recurrent heart trouble.

All his life Barry had worked hard, beginning as a young schoolteacher in Pennsylvania supporting three orphaned younger sisters. From this he had gained an intense humility. "I am," he would say, "as common as mud." He had taken a secretarial correspondence course, rising at four o'clock each morning to practice typing and shorthand, and won a job as secretary to a man whose profession was reviving ailing newspapers. Barry worked as business manager in Binghamton, New York, for seven years before going to Akron, where C. L. Knight needed a good manager. Through boom and bust, panics, depression, and two world wars, he had given the Knights sound business practices and shrewd dollar sense, finally retiring in 1952 from his position as general manager of the newspaper group. At his urging, C. L. Knight had once set up a $25,000 fund that someday would grow into the Knight Foundation, worth hundreds of millions of dollars. But most notably of all, Jack Barry had absolute integrity.

"Jack Barry was the cohesive force that drew together all elements of this organization," Jack Knight wrote. "He never wavered from the right as he saw it. . . ."

The funeral was at the Barry home in Akron, with the deceased on display in an open casket for mourners' farewells. The day turned sunny and fine. Maidenburg drove to the house with Knight. They walked from the car and up the front porch steps. Knight stopped, suddenly tightfaced.

"I'll wait for you here," he said.

"Aren't you going in?" Maidenburg asked.

"No."

"Why not?"

"I don't care to look at dead bodies."

He was still standing there when Maidenburg returned five minutes later.

They drove back to the *Beacon Journal* without speaking.

He was no stranger to threats. One could not speak his mind, in print or in person, without courting animosity. In letters and telephone calls he was called a fool, a jerk, a capitalist swine. If they weren't angry at something he wrote, it was at some unrelated story in the newspapers. He told of arriving at the *Herald* one day and being accosted by a distraught man waving a pistol and muttering, "I'm gonna kill you, sonofabitch." Knight replied coolly, "I'm not worth your going to the electric chair." The man blinked and lowered the gun. "You're right." He walked out.

But one never knew how serious a threat might be.

In December 1955, a crudely scrawled note arrived at Knight's winter home in Miami Beach. "Your family is in danger unless $600,000 is received by Extortioners, Inc. . . ." A hand-drawn map instructed the publisher to deposit the money on a garbage rack at a public housing project in Miami. An FBI agent posing as Knight delivered a fake payoff bundle and waited in hiding. A young man picked up the bundle and was arrested. He turned out to be the twenty-two-year-old mentally disturbed son of a local Baptist minister who lived nearby. "It just kept working in my head," he told a reporter. "I had to do it." A judge committed him to a mental hospital.

One year later, a mailed death threat to Knight charged that the *Miami Herald* had "stolen" the writer's thoughts and used them in editorials. This time the FBI arrested a twenty-nine-year-old jobless Sicilian from Miami. He, too, was committed. Soon, a telegram arrived from Akron: I HEAR SOMEONE HAS BEEN THREATENING YOUR LIFE. I'VE HAD THE SAME IDEA, WHEN YOU MISSED A TWO-FOOT PUTT. It was from Knight's friend Eddie Thomas.

Knight consolidated a growing company now being ranked with such "chain" newspaper operations as Scripps-Howard, Hearst, Gannett, Newhouse, and Cox. He disliked the term; a chain implied monolithic thinking and lockstep journalism. "Group" was more to his fancy. But obviously Knight Newspapers could no longer function from the depths of his brown briefcase. In July 1955, Knight brought together all the Knight executives, fifty of them now, in Akron to talk news, advertising, circulation, production, business management. "Newspapers have a tremendous obligation to provide truthful, objective news and vigorous editorial comment," he told them. They were beholden to no special interest or political faction, including bankers and moneylenders. "We must be constructive in purpose and dedicated to the public welfare."

The times were strange, in their way, but no less demanding of an enlightened and honest press. The "Eisenhower Siesta," as some would call these mid-1950s, filled with engrossing trivialities, rising prosperity, Cold War, and rampant materialism. Knight's Victorian morality was jolted as young Akron housewives, inspired by the Kinsey Report, chatted about sex at cocktail parties. In an obscure Kansas case, *Brown* v. *Board of Education,* the Supreme Court was about to outlaw racial segregation of public schools. Suburbs sprawled. Federal engineers planned a 41,000-mile interstate highway system. The nation's per capita birthrate approached that of India. Swivel-hipped teenage idol Elvis Presley whanged his guitar and assured the nation's mommies and daddies, "I don't do no dirty body movements."

The bloody "police action" in Korea had ended in a 1953 armistice, leaving 2 million dead, including 33,629 Americans. "We have paid a frightful price," Knight brooded, "and there are more sacrifices to come." Already he was warning of trouble in another part of Asia. The date was May 10, 1953. "People long subjected to colonialism and imperialism are demanding freedom," he wrote.

Shrewdly the Communists have traded on this. The French are in grave trouble in Indochina. Eventually a plea will be made for American troops. The Communist forces in Asia cannot be bought with dollars or driven permanently from the field. In the long run, the anti-Communist nations will not prevail. Like it or not, Asia is going back to the Asians. The white man is through.

As months passed in bitter fighting, the French gradually gave ground despite massive U.S. aid. Knight's "Editor's Notebook" drummed away, a lone voice against a rising American dilemma. February 21, 1954: "It is almost certain that at some stage France will pull out of Indochina. Are we prepared to cope with such a contingency? The answer is no." April 4, 1954: "Events in Asia may not be within our control. It is within our control to keep out of another fruitless, bloody war that neither side can win." April 11, 1954: "We are alarmingly close to another frustrating fringe war, following the pattern of gradual involvement that we have seen before." He sensed disarray around Eisenhower, expressed "shocking disappointment" at America's being sucked into the quagmire, enraged right-wing militants by declaring, "We should get over the silly notion that we can export democracy and capitalism like Coca-Cola." It pained him to be at odds with the Republican president—"a good and decent man"—but he pushed on.

And then the French went down in bloody defeat at Dien Bien Phu, leaving Indochina in a power vacuum.

The die was cast.

He liked Richard Nixon. The vice president had dark solitudes and strange quirks of personality, to be sure. Democrats especially despised him: "A man," said Adlai Stevenson, "of many masks." Even Eisenhower expressed private misgivings. In midsummer 1954, with the party convention barely six weeks away, a clutch of GOP functionaries tried to dump Nixon from the reelection ticket. Among those rising to his defense was John S. Knight.

For all Nixon's quirks—even the publisher's wife Beryl said, "There's something about the man I don't like"—Knight saw a basic quality that he valued in his own associates: loyalty. "Dick Nixon has been a trusted and faithful aide to the President," he insisted. "The Republicans are doing him a great injustice." It was time for the party to fish or cut bait. "Either he is of presidential caliber or he is not. . . . The Nixon problem is on the party's doorstep." The ouster effort collapsed. But seventeen years later the "Nixon problem" would still be there, and in the turmoil of

Watergate Knight would continue to be wrenched by the strange polarity of the man, standing no closer to the truth.

Most explosive of the nation's inner struggles was racial integration. Violent tensions gripped the South as white supremacists fought the black push for civil rights. In the heart of Dixie stood Knight's *Charlotte Observer* headed by tough-minded editor C. A. ("Pete") McKnight. On racial matters, McKnight vowed to report events impartially and make editorial comment without favor.

Debate further complicated emotion-charged issues. Among them was a legal tactic called *interposition*. This meant that a state could "interpose" its sovereign powers even to block federal law, thus maintaining racial segregation. McKnight argued editorially that interposition violated the U.S. Constitution's Fourteenth Amendment, which decreed that no state could abridge the constitutional rights of its citizens.

From his viewpoint in liberal Chicago and Detroit, Jack Knight backed the *Observer* editor. "The language is clear," he insisted, "and the Supreme Court's decision effectively bars any ideological secession from the union."

Some southern editors were in a frenzy. At Charleston, South Carolina, editor Tom Waring blasted "the carpetbagger press, meaning Northern ownership of newspapers in the South"—for example, the Knight-owned *Charlotte Observer* and *Miami Herald*. Knight bristled:

> My father was born at Milledgeville, Ga. My paternal forebears fought on the side of the Confederacy and had all of their worldly possessions destroyed by General Sherman in the sacking of Georgia. My daughter and grandson, John S. Knight III, are natives of Columbus, Ga. People like Tom Waring, who wrap themselves in the folds of the stars and bars, should put aside their venomous pens and join the Union.

In Charlotte, editor McKnight found sharp difference of opinion between the Knight brothers. His idea of moderation was at variance with that of his immediate boss, James Knight. When white readers accused the *Observer* of oversympathizing with the black cause, McKnight defended his policies in a letter to the younger Knight: "We have set forth, reasonably but forcefully, what I believe to be the only position a newspaper worth its salt could take. I do not propose to budge one inch from these principles simply because they might cost us a few subscribers."

Knight's reply from Miami was tart. "I am not as 'moderate' as either my older brother or yourself. I do . . . think it essential that we follow the dictates of the Supreme Court. But I think government is horribly stupid when it attempts to push the color line to attain some social and economic goals presently unobtainable except by martial law." Having spoken his mind, Knight made no attempt to tie his editor's hands. *Observer* coverage of civil rights continued as before.

In the ultimate order of Knight's life, it was the press that mattered. The press fueled and enriched, beguiled and fascinated him; it was the source of his strength and an outlet for his indignation; it even served as refuge when he needed refuge. There was nothing mightier in the democratic society than public opinion, and no diligence more vital than pursuing truth.

In Chicago, Pulitzer Prize–winning reporter George Theim, acting on a tip from Stuffy Walters, broke open the biggest swindle in Illinois history: an $800,000 milking of public funds by state auditor Orville Hodge. Theim's spadework ignited a massive investigation by the Chicago press, ending in Hodge's going to prison. Knight was exhilarated.

"The newspaper profession is . . . as fascinating today as when I pecked out my first story 40 years ago," he observed. But today's ideals were far loftier.

> The modern editor accepts as primary responsibility the presentation of truthful news. There can be little faith in a newspaper which distorts or tailors the news to fit its views. The effective newspaper also has a vigorous editorial policy, to stimulate thought on questions of the day, and should safeguard public interest with alert and intelligent reporting.
>
> It would be idle to pretend that every newspaper has measured up. Some editors are too lazy to let any-

thing but an H-bomb disturb their tranquility; others work for publishers who regard news as something to fill space not occupied by ads. Newspapers are continuously under criticism, and I have no quarrel with that. Journalism is not for Casper Milquetoasts. Politicians denounce the "one-party" press, readers denounce the newspaper in its own columns, merchants withdraw advertising, disgruntled pressure groups start boycotts, business leaders bridle over items not to their liking.

But the newspaper . . . is still our best protection against corruption, tyranny and injustice. Government needs an outside auditor, and this the press can do. As one reader summed up the Hodge case: "If we didn't have newspapers, those birds would steal ten times as much."

fortune seemed a little more evenhanded in its treatment of John S. Knight. He grew closer to his brother and son. The few honors that he had not already won as a journalist and a human rights advocate were heaped on his shoulders.

Then, on Aug. 8, 1974, his wife of 42 years died after a long illness. And there was more to come.

The news of the death of John S. Knight Jr. in Germany was kept from Johnny's wife, the former Dorothy Wells of Columbus, Ga., until after the birth on April 13 — about two weeks later — of a boy who was named John S. Knight III.

Knight. Through the medium of the Editor's Notebook they discussed the campus violence of the '60s and the course of the Vietnam War. They exchanged letters frequently, played golf together and talked for h

P J h, managing editor of the D y News id of young John, "He was ly a chan ing guy. He knew who he w w he was an heir to a fortune and to a key job in the organization if he earned it. But he didn't take himself too seriously."

It was obvious that John S. Knight hoped through his grandson to see that

John S. Knight III and lives, I can't think of down. So I am not myself guilty.

"I am not going to er me," he told Tho start a new life."

He returned to Fl er his gra son's nounced he would ma beth) Augustus. They 1976, in the chapel of Sea at Bal Harbour Lifestyle editor of the

15

FEAR NO EVIL

latter cum laude in 1968 with a degree in history, then went on to study philosophy, politics and economics at Oxford University in England, where he earned a master of arts degree, with honors, in June 1970.

During high school and college he worked summer vacations at several Knight papers, including the Beacon Journal.

His first full-time newspaper job came at the Detroit Free Press in 1970. He gained experience in the circulation

center of Philadelphia, John S. Knight III was stabbed to death during a robbery by three men. There were homosexual overtones.

At the time, his grandfather was visiting at the home of Mr. and Mrs. Edwin C. Whiteheads of Greenwich, Conn. Mrs. Whiteheads is a daughter of the then Betty Augustus, widow of Cleveland millionaire Ellsworth H. Augustus. Knight and Mrs. Augustus had known each other for 35 years though a mutual interest in thoroughbreds and horse racing.

Mrs. Knight died th while watching the R the LaGorce Island ho

WHEN HE STEPP torial chairman of Kni 1976, his title became Knight-Ridder and the His decision to qu y Thomas and others "The trouble wit night's position," Tho ily that they stay on to hat the business can't

He reached the age of thirty still unmarried and living in his parents' home, a quiet, bespectacled man, balding like his father. There was talk that he had loved a young woman in Toledo and wanted to marry her, but that his father disapproved and, heartbroken, he himself ended the relationship. Had he been someone else's son, Frank McLain Knight might have lived more independently, working as a middle-level manager or in some other line demanding loyalty and diligence, if not brilliance. As an heir to a giant of journalism, however, he was pressured to follow in his father's steps, and obediently he did so.

After graduation from the University of Miami in 1951, Frank spent a couple of years at the *Pontiac* [Michigan] *Press* before going to work for the *Beacon Journal* in Akron. His brother Landon had worked at the *Detroit Free Press,* run an unsuccessful race for Congress in Michigan, and joined *Life* as a subeditor in New York. Frank remained in Akron, where he was put into the learning grind as a reporter, classified ad salesman, and promotional man for the *Beacon Journal.* He served in outlying bureaus under the state desk. He did a turn in circulation, and when a carrier boy was sick and could not deliver his route, Frank did it for him. Then he sold display advertising. As *Beacon Journal* columnist Ken Nichols would write, "Nobody ever worked harder to belong to the profession in which his grandfather and father had distinguished themselves." By March 1958, Frank Knight was a director of Knight Newspapers and president of the Portage Newspaper Supply Company, a Knight subsidiary that sold printing supplies to the parent firm.

In the working world he was acutely mindful of his shortcomings, groaning, "Will I ever stop making mistakes?" An older staff member replied, "No. But never stop worrying about them."

Young Knight's health seemed to improve as he reached thirty. Lee Hills spent some time with him in Detroit and told Jack Knight, "Frank doesn't seem as preoccupied with illness as before." Hills took this as a good sign. That spring, however, Frank complained of headaches and dizzy spells and was taking heavy doses of aspirin. He walked into the office of *Beacon Journal* executive editor Ben Maidenburg carrying a jar of aspirin in one hand and a hard rubber ball in the other, which he constantly squeezed in order to improve his golf grip. "What the hell's the aspirin for?" Maidenburg wanted to know. Frank was vague. "A touch of the flu."

He was greatly concerned about his grandmother Clara, who in late winter was admitted to Akron City Hospital with a high fever. He visited her and wrote a lengthy letter to his parents in Miami. "Gran has a constant cough and looks extremely thin in her nightie, huddled among the covers in a large bed. Her mind is failing. She doesn't seem to know precisely where she is. But she continues to have spirit." As usual he had little to say about himself. "I'm still slaving away in national advertising and am now on the street selling space for a special automobile section." He hoped soon to spend some time training with a newspaper management firm in New York. The letter ran to four pages and was signed, "All my love, Frank."

Six mornings later, on March 9, 1958, executive editor Maidenburg received a frantic call from the housekeeper at the Knight home on Portage Path. "Frank is lying on the floor of his bedroom, unconscious. There's blood running from his mouth."

Maidenburg rushed to the house. The servants had lifted the unconscious Frank onto the bed, in his pajamas. Maidenburg took him by ambulance to Akron General Hospital and then notified Jack and Beryl Knight in Miami. Knight asked him to call Dr. Loyal Davis, a physician in Chicago. As the parents booked a flight to Akron, a hospital neurosurgeon inserted a needle into Frank's spine to assess pressure on the brain. Spinal fluid squirted out and hit the wall beside the patient's bed. The neurosurgeon was aghast.

"Why don't you operate and relieve the pressure?" Maidenburg asked.

The neurosurgeon shook his head. "I don't have authorization from the family."

Maidenburg held Frank's hand and talked to him. Occasionally there was light response—a squeeze of the fingers, a flicker of eyelids. By telephone, the Knights' Chicago physician suggested that an Akron doctor open the patient's skull to relieve pressure on the brain. The doctor said he could not do this without family approval. The Knights arrived at one o'clock the following morning and agreed to the procedure, and Frank was wheeled into surgery. After two hours, the surgeon emerged shaking his head. "There's nothing further that we can do tonight." The Knights went home to bed, planning to return early the next morning.

Frank Knight died before daybreak.

From Chicago three days later, Dr. Davis reviewed the strange case in a letter to Jack Knight. "The autopsy showed that Frank had a large, highly malignant tumor of the frontal portion of the right side of the brain. Undoubtedly, he had a series of convulsive seizures the night and morning preceding his admission to the hospital. The growth must have existed for some time."

The similarity to his mother's death thirty years before was obvious.

Again, a somber procession went to Rose Hill Cemetery. Ten

years earlier, they had brought Johnny Knight's remains back from Europe for burial in the family plot. Now it was Frank's coffin being lowered into the earth. A line of marble stones designated the graves of Charles Landon Knight, Katherine McLain Knight, John Shively Knight, Jr., and Frank McLain Knight. An unmarked grave beside C. L. contained the remains of a stillborn infant, unnamed, who would have been the first child of James and Mary Ann Knight.

They stood in a cold March wind as final rites were pronounced by the Reverend James Lichliter of St. Paul's Episcopal Church. "Yea, though I walk through the valley of the shadow of death, I shall fear no evil. . . ." The face of the principal mourner was a pale mask. When it was done, the crowd loaded into the cars for the return to Akron.

John S. Knight did not look back.

He did not write about Frank. Aside from obituary notices in the Knight Newspapers, and an *Akron Beacon Journal* editorial, the death was given scant notice. There was no weekly "Notebook" column the week of the funeral, and no explanation in print for the lapse. Only those close to the publisher knew his feelings. "It's a hard thing to take," he said bitterly to his Akron friend, Eddie Thomas. Then, with characteristic stoicism, he turned his mind outward.

His writing had changed in recent years. It revealed less of himself, dealing instead with national or international matters, particularly as they related to the presidency. His criticisms, however, had taken on a keener and more substantive edge. If Knight lacked the fiery flamboyance of his father, he was sounder in reportorial basics.

The range of public issues was enormous. For Americans, the times were strangely perplexing. Wages inched upward, but at the cost of creeping inflation. Peace persisted, but with constant anxiety about the Russians. People bought homes at a record pace, but amid rising concerns over an unprecedented baby boom. Racial violence racked Little Rock and Birmingham. Foreign affairs were shifty and volatile, with recurrent brushfire wars abroad.

Russian tanks rumbled in Budapest, sending a flood of Hungarian refugees to America. The Middle East was a tinderbox. For all its good intentions, American foreign aid also helped support President Diem's concentration camps in Vietnam and military dictatorships in Latin America. In Cuba, Fidel Castro trudged the hills with a ragtag rebel army, requesting U.S. financial aid to overthrow the Batista regime and being curtly refused.

Then, unexpectedly, Knight lost faith in Eisenhower. It had been gradual, surprising partisan friends. Disenchantment sprang from issues deep in the publisher's ideological makeup: welfare, weaponry, bloated bureaucracy, foreign policy, basic economics.

"I was surprised and disappointed," Knight wrote, "to have the President speak of budget cuts of $25 million to $150 million as 'foolish, piecemeal economy' and to brand such efforts by Congress as 'imbecile.' "

Knight Washington reporters Ed Lahey and David Kraslow undertook an itemized study of the Eisenhower budget, a massive tome of 1,249 densely packed pages. "They find it loaded with frills and boondoggles," Knight reported. "Is this good government?"

Time chortled that Knight's falling-out was "one of the most significant shifts in the U.S. press since the Truman era" and speculated that the rift was aimed at selling newspapers. Knight shot back, "I don't say something just because I think it's good for my newspapers." He tucked *Time*'s impertinence into his memory file.

And then a new nemesis rocketed into the heavens. On October 4, 1957, the Russians launched *Sputnik,* the world's first space satellite. While a shaken America gazed aloft, the alien light arced across the night sky, circling the Earth once every 96.2 minutes at eighteen thousand miles per hour. The word, in Russian, means "traveling companion."

Knight pondered its stunning impact. "The myth that the United States is world leader in every endeavor has collapsed."

His chance to get even with *Time* came sooner than expected. The newsmagazine reported that some newspapers were soft-pedaling the 1958 recession. Four of the alleged malefactors were Knight-owned. The "Notebook" grumbled, "Unlike [*Time*] editor Henry Luce, we try to mirror the world as it is and not as we should like it to be. But then, *Time* is not noted for fairness or accuracy."

Privately, he sought better ways to cope with life's hectic pace. He pored over Dr. Norman Vincent Peale's best-selling *The Power of Positive Thinking*, liking it so much that when Peale was in Miami to promote books, Knight invited him to lunch. But Knight had the impression of a man under enormous pressure from his own fame and spreading himself thinly. "Some men," he concluded, "write and speak too easily for their own good."

How did one handle the everyday rat race? For a man, Knight believed, it helped to live with the right woman. A marriage was more than a joining of sexes; it was also a combining of talents. He touched on this in a speech to a girls' preparatory school. "Today's woman is no longer the isolated homemaker of half a century ago. She has become deeply involved in the broader aspects of living."

Organizational pressures constricted him.

> The business or professional man cannot extend his imagination very far before it runs into the chain of command. He cannot hire and fire at will even if he is the big boss, because even the big boss becomes a creature of the company he creates. So the modern man is regimented, with mounds of paperwork, conferences, anxieties about personnel, government, labor unions and other often-mundane matters that give us premature heart attacks and galloping ulcers.

He made a bittersweet return to Culver Military Academy. The rolling Indiana hills were green, and the springtime setting—the lake, the meadows, the trees, parade grounds, and bridle paths—never more beautiful. It reminded him of his dead sons, Johnny and Frank. And he told the graduating cadets, "The competition that is open to the mind is as absorbing as athletics, and infinitely more important to a career."

The newspapers continued to prosper. Akron expanded its plant. In Charlotte, secret talks were under way to buy the *Observer*'s competitor, the *News*. The *Detroit Free Press* made money despite chronic labor unrest and strikes. In Miami, Jim Knight overrode his brother's doubts by planning the construction of a new *Herald* plant geared to the 1980s and costing $20 million. For the U.S. press generally, however, life was a struggle against spiraling costs, labor unrest, and stiffening advertising competition from television and radio. Southern publishers, meeting in Florida, weighed their business risks and heard Jack Knight express bluntly the rigors of the times: "Newspapers in competitive cities face the challenge of survival."

In the past decade, 217 U.S. papers had ceased to exist. Survivors were mainly in one-newspaper towns, or had joint ownership, or merged costly printing and business operations. In the 1,450 cities with daily newspapers, only 75 could claim local competition worthy of the name. Ninety-five chain operations now published some 500 newspapers from coast to coast, and the trend to chains continued to grow.

It took foresight and timing to prosper, and sometimes one had to make hard choices.

On January 5, 1959, nine months after Frank's death, John S. Knight sold the *Chicago Daily News* to Marshall Field, Jr., for $24 million.

The price was unprecedented in the industry. A typical peer reaction was that of *Life* publisher Andrew Heiskell: "Well, I'll be damned." In fifteen years, Knight had built the *Daily News* into a money-maker, its circulation peaking at 614,000 per day during 1957. Though sagging after that, business still netted a $1.2 million annual profit. On the surface, Knight implied that he had sold in hopes of slowing down a bit. "For the first time in years, I am acting for myself, thinking of myself. I want to take it a little easier." Some editorialists thought they saw deep personal influences. Said one close friend, "A lot of fight went out of Jack when Frank died." In reality, Knight's decision was rooted in business fundamentals; he had seen the *Daily News*'s strength slipping, with scant chance of recouping. It was all or nothing in Chicago. More than two years earlier, he had made a grab for the big prize and missed.

For all its jazzy layout, prizewinning reporting, and 40 percent circulation boost, the *Daily News* was an afternoon paper published six days a week in a world that favored morning papers with fat Sunday editions. A Sunday paper was vital if the *Daily News* were seriously to challenge the mighty *Tribune*.

Knight had seen his chance in 1956 with a possible takeover of the Hearst-owned *Chicago American*. After a feisty past of "slapdash and gin-soaked" journalism, as *Newsweek* termed it, the *American* had gone staidly respectable, and dull. It was losing $1 million a year. Knight offered to merge or buy. This led to secret talks with Hearst executives that went on for months. So close was a deal that Knight began receiving the *American*'s confidential weekly financial reports.

But others also coveted the *American*. Marshall Field, Jr., for example, was building a $21 million new plant for his *Sun-Times* tabloid, long printed under contract by the *Daily News*, with more than enough capacity to take on another paper. And then there was the *Tribune*, headed by a management triumvirate since the death of Colonel McCormick. Would the *Tribune* sit still while a dangerous competitor doubled his clout? By early October, unknown to Knight, details of his talks with the Hearst people were leaking to the *Tribune*.

The news came in a Saturday phone call from a financial insider. "The *American* has just been sold to the *Tribune*."

The price was close to $12 million, far more than Knight had offered and more than the paper was worth.

"Well, I guess that's it," Knight said bitterly.

In a single stroke, the *Tribune* had boomed its circulation control in Chicago from 951,000 newspapers per day and 1.2 million on Sundays to 1.4 million and 1.8 million. Field's *Sun-Times* published 562,000 daily and 630,000 Sundays; Knight's *Daily News* now averaged 575,000 per day.

Long afterward, Knight would recall the strange events that followed:

> In half an hour the phone rang and it was Marshall [Field], saying, "We've got to put our papers together and merge against this giant, the *Tribune* and the *American*." "Well," I said, "let's take things a little more slowly. I want to think this out."

Field became so distraught he was admitted to a hospital.

Knight wrote a "Notebook" column blasting the sudden transaction. "The spirit and principles of the late William Randolph Hearst were sacrificed on the altar of cold, hard cash." He did not mention his own failed attempt to take over the *American.*

The *Daily News* was now locked out, its main printing plant an aging hulk on the Chicago River with no room for expansion, and production overflow relegated to a new satellite plant on the South Side. Knight and his top men—Walters, Hills, his brother Jim, general manager Arthur Hall—saw the inevitable. "The future is limited." They offered to buy Marshall Field's *Sun-Times* for its Sunday market. Field declined, but countered that he might buy the *Daily News.* The more he thought about this, the more excited Field became.

At age forty-two he was the chunky, amiable great-grandson of the founder of the Marshall Field Chicago merchandising fortune. His late father, a strong political liberal, had founded the New York newspaper *PM* in 1940 as a voice for Roosevelt's New Deal and then established the *Chicago Sun* in opposition to the ultraconservative *Tribune.* By 1958, young Field was publisher of the tabloid *Sun-Times* and owner of Field Enterprises, including *Parade* magazine and World Book Encyclopedia, with an estimated worth of $150 million.

The *Daily News,* with its worldwide prestige, appealed to Field's vanity. As time passed, this attraction was reinforced by his spells of brooding over the new power of the *Tribune.* In an interview long afterward, Knight recalled the mercurial nature of the sale of the *Daily News:*

> Field was a manic depressive and there were times when he would call me up and say, "We're going to buy a paper in New York." Or, "We're going to buy a couple out in Honolulu." The next time I'd see him he would be very blue and depressed. So we finally got together and discussed the whole thing. In the library of my apartment in Chicago, he said, "Would you consider selling the *Chicago Daily News* to me?" I said yes, under certain conditions.

So we talked about that for about four hours and finally he said, "If you sell it to me, how much would you want for it?" I told him I wanted fifty dollars a share, cash, and there were about 481,000 shares, which came to around twenty-four million dollars. He said, "That's great. When do we do it?" No bargaining at all. I told him I could arrange the mechanics of it anytime, but he'd better talk to his bankers. Then he called me one day and said, "I hate to tell you this, but I don't have the money." I said, "That's too bad. Call me up when you get it." He said I was pretty blunt, and I said, "Well, I'm just telling you the truth; I don't want any slow notes from you or anybody else. When you get the money, and you want the paper, come and see me." So nothing happened for three or four months, and then I read in the *Tribune* that Field had sold *Parade* to Jock Whitney [John Hay Whitney, U.S. ambassador to the Court of St. James's and controlling owner of the *New York Herald Tribune*] for around ten million. We heard from him two days later. . . .

Secrecy prevailed. Lee Hills quietly made arrangements for the two men to meet and go over the fine points. Field wanted assurance that the existing *Daily News* staff would remain intact. Stuffy Walters chose to stay with the *Daily News*. At the Washington Bureau, veteran reporter Ed Lahey, a crusty, streetwise liberal whom Knight prized above all others, went to Knight Newspapers. Knight even agreed to make himself available for one year as a paid adviser. For this purpose, Field allowed him to keep his old office at the *Daily News*. Knight's share of the sale would be $18 million, with another $6 million going to minority stockholders.

At the closing, technicalities still dogged proceedings. As Knight would recall,

Field's lawyers began to argue about how this stock certificate wasn't dated properly, and so forth, and I said, "Marshall, if you want to kill the deal, this is the way to do it, but take your time." He got mad and went out and told his lawyers, "Damn you guys, you're about to screw up the deal. . . . Either get those certificates ready for me right away or you're fired." That's how worked up he was. Well, things were still stalled and it took time. The directors were sitting in the other room, and I had Jim Knight in there regaling them with stories about sailfishing and marlin fishing in Florida, and Jim had about run his string. But finally we cracked through and got it done and announced the sale to the directors. When it was over, I said, "Let's go to the Chicago Club and have drinks."

Nobody was against that.

Lee Hills, fifty-two, succeeded Walters as executive editor of Knight Newspapers.

The *Daily News* staff was shaken. "I have a choice today of leaving this space blank or writing about newspapers," columnist Jack Mabley wrote. "My thoughts are on nothing but newspapers." He closed the column with a lighthearted gripe about his battered old typewriter. The next day, Marshall Field, Jr., walked into the newsroom lugging a new typewriter and put it on Mabley's desk. Field pledged to keep the paper vigorous and strong. Morale turned up.

But the *Chicago Daily News* was doomed.

In North Carolina, Tom Robinson sorrowfully threw in the towel. His paper, the *Charlotte News,* had fought the good fight. But afternoon papers were losing ground everywhere and the rival morning *Observer* had proved a formidable competitor under the Knights. The *News* deserved better. Over the decades it had produced such talents as famed *Arkansas Gazette* editor Harry Ashmore, author Jack Cash, biographer Cameron Shipp, World War II humorist Marion Hargrove, historian Burke Davis, novelist Timothy Pridgen, and, of course, Pete McKnight, who had left the paper to direct the Southern Education Reporting Service on school integration before being hired by Lee Hills to edit the *Observer.* Matters had gone from bad to worse. Owner-publisher Thomas L. Robinson had been unable to interest financial backers. Dwindling revenues pushed the *News* toward bankruptcy, even though staffers cut costs and rationed long-distance telephone calls. Lamented Robinson, "I feel like a mother who has lost a child."

The *News* sale to the Knights on April 5, 1959, nevertheless shocked the town. Jack Knight was little known in Charlotte. As longtime *Observer* columnist Kays Gary would recall years later, "Jack was a stranger, and rather forbidding. When he came in for a visit you didn't rush to shake hands." Publisher Jim Knight was not around much either. Operating details fell to Pete McKnight and business manager J. E. ("Bill") Dowd. This is the way the Knights had planned it, and promised it to Charlotte: the *Observer* would be locally run, independent.

Although Jim Knight was now the real boss of both Charlotte papers, the national news media went to Jack for comment. "We could have taken a cynical position and let the *News* fold," he told them. "But I'm not a monopolist at heart, and it's better to have two contending voices."

It was made clear that the two papers would continue as competitors.

"The *News* has got to go it on muscle," James Knight said.

It was a strange order of existence. Few mortals managed to own even one newspaper, much less five. Rarer still was the publishing entrepreneur who said hello to one new, albeit shaky, acquisition and good-bye to an old and venerable one in the same year. But this is how it was with John S. Knight. His year as adviser to Marshall Field at the *Daily News*—an adviser never called on to advise—was ending. It was time to clean his desk, pack up his stuff, and clear out.

The two publishers continued to be friends. They had joined in a new venture called the Fourth Estate Stables, breeding and running racehorses. It was a gentleman's game, with profit potential. Knight bought four yearlings, and then he and Field acquired an Olympia colt. Some of the horses were shipped south for racing at Hialeah under the cerise and straw colors made famous by Field's late father, Marshall Field II, who had run Thoroughbreds for thirty years.

On a clear, crisp day in December 1959, Knight sat down for the last time at the *Daily News* to pound out a farewell column on his typewriter. "And so it's goodbye to an era," he wrote. "No more will the tireless Stuffy Walters be stopping by to compare notes. I shall miss the scholarly A. T. Burch, erudite Sydney Harris and explosive Jack Mabley. . . . Fifteen years of Chicago's lusty newspaper competition have left me with no visible personal scars. But in few other cities has the battle raged more fiercely. . . ."

James Knight's dream of a new newspaper plant in Miami was about to be realized. In an atmosphere of utmost secrecy, a local real estate broker dickered to buy ten prime acres of bayfront land. It was a complicated business, involving forty-two parcels and one crucial landowner who hated the *Herald* for its past exposés of his underworld connections. The broker, a man of persuasive guile, used the names of dummy buyers to hide the Knights' involvement. Plans for the plant itself called for high technology, based on a projected 1 million daily circulation of the *Herald* by the 1980s. The structure would be as big as the nearby Orange Bowl stadium, stretching along the bayfront six stories high, its seven giant presses totaling sixty-three units, the largest such new installation in history. Editorial rooms alone would cover a football field. Price estimates surged toward $30 million.

Jack Knight's fiscal prudence was jarred. "Jim, you've lost your sense of values. This could destroy us."

His brother stood firm. "You're wrong, Jack. This is the *Miami Herald* plant we're going to need in 1980, maybe even before. Let's build it!"

Grudgingly, Jack assented.

In the meantime, the *Herald* was beefing up its executive staff. In the newsroom there arrived such rising young talents as Allen Neuharth, who would become assistant executive editor of the *Detroit Free Press* and, ultimately, multimillionaire board chairman of Gannett Newspapers, and Derick Daniels, descendant of famed southern editor Josephus Daniels and a future president of *Playboy*. Soon to join the *Herald* were Don Shoemaker, a savvy southern newsman, as *Herald* editorial page editor; and Alvah H. Chapman, Jr., a newspaper management genius and former World War II bomber pilot from Columbus, Georgia. Chapman ultimately would lead Knight Newspapers during a booming era of coast-to-coast publishing, geared to the computer age.

Tall, lank George Beebe hovered at the phones, drumming his long fingers on the desk. At times like these, the managing editor of the *Herald* felt the burden of his job. Veteran reporter James Buchanan had been sent to Cuba to interview Miami adventurer Frank Austin Young, a fugitive fleeing a long sentence by a Fidel Castro revolutionary court, holed up and injured in a Havana hotel. Against Beebe's advice to abandon the mission, Buchanan had taken food and bandages to Young—and had been arrested by Castro militiamen. Beebe deemed Buchanan's judgment poor, for Castro now accused the reporter of trying to aid the escape. The regime intended to squeeze the situation, and the *Herald,* for all they were worth.

George Southworth, Latin American correspondent, had been on the scene. Now executive city editor John McMullan, a tough newsman with a law degree and a prosecutor's instincts, sent a confidential letter from Havana: "The Cubans have some damaging evidence against Buchanan, evidence which could well convict a man in U.S. courts. If he is released soon, it will happen only because of other than legal factors."

The *Herald* had retained a prominent Cuban attorney, but honest lawyers were on shaky ground with Castro. Buchanan was confined in a concrete blockhouse, guarded by trigger-happy rebels, amid fears that he would be transferred to the infamous Pinar del Rio prison. His wife was managing bravely in Miami. And Christmas was just around the corner.

The most persuasive voice Beebe had right now was that of John S. Knight.

The publisher had a passing acquaintance with Castro, who had addressed the American Society of Newspaper Editors the previous April. "Fidel Castro is appealing in appearance, manner and speech," Knight had written. "Few doubted his idealism and evident sincerity." In eight months, however, a chill had fallen over Havana and its relations with the United States. Now, on December 20, 1959, Knight's "Notebook" column consisted of an open letter to Castro demanding reporter Buchanan's immediate release. "The press of the free world has reason to be apprehensive. The press of Cuba itself is covered by a blanket of fear. Mr. Buchanan is an able and respected journalist. In no way can his activities be construed as 'giving aid to criminal elements,' as your government has charged."

Across the hemisphere, journalists remembered Knight's long campaign for press freedom and responded. Both the Inter-American Press Association, headed by publisher William Cowles, and the American Society of Newspaper Editors called for Buchanan's freedom. In Cuba itself, *Diario de la Marina* gave its editorial support. Publisher Jorge Zayas of *Avance,* himself the target of vicious attacks by government-controlled TV stations, made personal appeals to the regime. Cuban newsmen supporting Buchanan openly defied a new Castro law making them liable to imprisonment for up to eighteen years for publishing anything that "tends to limit the independence of the nation or provoke violation of laws."

Knight offered to go to Havana and talk with Castro face-to-face. The offer was ignored.

Two nights later, Buchanan was taken to Pinar del Rio prison for trial before a five-man revolutionary tribunal. He spoke limited Spanish, understood little that was going on, and protested in English, "I was never guilty of anything but being a newspaper reporter." Cuban lawyers Mario Lazo and Emilio Maza, heedless of their own danger, spoke passionately in his defense. Buchanan was found guilty of "counterrevolutionary activity" and sentenced to fourteen years at hard labor on the Isle of Pines. But the sentence was abruptly suspended and he was given twenty-four hours to leave the country.

In a wild midnight ride, Buchanan and McMullan rushed back to Havana to catch a plane out of Cuba. Their return to Miami on Christmas set off a celebration, with a banner hung in the *Herald* newsroom: WELCOME HOME, JAILBIRD.

Afterward, Jack Knight weighed the dark portent of future Cuban-American relations. He hoped that the press could still play a positive role. His offer to talk with Castro remained open. "We hold no bitterness. . . . It is far more important for a responsible press to seek understanding than to sit at a safe distance berating Castro for the indignities heaped upon a reporter who was merely doing his job. Let the effort be made. Perhaps newspapermen can succeed where the diplomats have failed."

Vain hope. In the years ahead, Fidel Castro would push the world to the brink of nuclear war and loose a deluge of political exiles on south Florida.

Miami would be changed for all time.

fortune seemed a little more evenhanded in its treatment of John S. Knight. He grew closer to his brother and son. The few honors that he had not already won as a journalist and a human rights advocate were heaped on his shoulders.

Then, on Aug. 8, 1974, his wife of 42 years died after a long illness. And there was more to come.

The news of the death of John S. Knight Jr. in Germany was kept from Johnny's wife, the former Dorothy Wells of Columbus, Ga., until after the birth on April 13 — about two weeks later — of a boy who was named John S. Knight III.

Knight. Through the medium of the Editor's Notebook they discussed the campus violence of the '60s and the course of the Vietnam War. They exchanged letters frequently, played golf together and talked for hours.

Paul Swensson, managing editor of the Daily News, said of young John, "He was really a charming guy. He knew who he was. He knew he was an heir to a fortune and to a key job in the organization if he earned it. But he didn't take himself too seriously."

It was obvious that John S. Knight hoped through his grandson to see that name kept in lights . . . .

John S. Knight III and lives, I can't think of down. So I am not myself guilty.

"I am not going to her me," he told Thor start a new life."

He returned to Flo for his grandson's . . 1976, in the chapel of Sea at Bal Harbour. Lifestyle editor of the . . .

THE DAYS
OF LIGHTNING

phy, politics and economics at Oxford University in England, where he earned a master of arts degree, with honors, in June 1970.

During high school and college he worked summer vacations at several Knight papers, including the Beacon Journal.

His first full-time newspaper job came at the Detroit Free Press in 1970. He gained experience in the circulation

by three men. There were homosexual overtones.

At the time, his grandfather was visiting at the home of Mr. and Mrs. Edwin C. Whiteheads of Greenwich, Conn. Mrs. Whiteheads is a daughter of the then Betty Augustus, widow of Cleveland millionaire Ellsworth H. Augustus. Knight and Mrs. Augustus had known each other for 35 years though a mutual interest in thoroughbreds and horse racing.

WHEN HE STEPP torial chairman of Kni 1976, his title became Knight-Ridder and the His decision to qui y Thomas and others <night's position," Tho oly that they stay on to hat the business can't

Although you have found me stubborn, exasperating, frequently wrong, unpredictably right, liberal, conservative, drastic and moderate, at least you have been reading me. And that is all I can expect.
—John S. Knight, letter to a reader, 1960s

It was a durable house on quiet, landscaped Sabal Palm Road in the exclusive walled neighborhood of Bay Point on Biscayne Bay. Steel beams at the corners of the house reinforced a basic construction of concrete block. So tight was the interior that virtually no sound could be heard from outside. Don Shoemaker, erudite, controversial editor of the *Miami Herald,* lived there with his wife, Lyal, and their ten-year-old daughter, Elizabeth. The child had a front room, facing the street.

With a habit of taking strong editorial stands on volatile community issues, including a current countywide bus strike marked by intense union activity and sporadic violence, editor Shoemaker kept his name and address out of the telephone book. But a home can be found easily by the diligent seeker. And so it was that unexpected visitors arrived at Sabal Palm Road at 2:00 A.M. on February 18, 1962, as the neighborhood slept.

These were turbulent times in Miami, a city where trouble never seemed to rest. In addition to the bus strike, with its bitter harangues and acts of sabotage, Cuban exiles hatched plot and counterplot against the Castro regime and each other, domestic political ferment constantly bubbled, and ideological fanatics spread hatred.

Among those who hated Shoemaker, or at least the newspaper he represented, was Donald Branch, a tall, twenty-six-year-old reader of water meters for the city. Branch was convinced that political liberals of the press—and he ranked Shoemaker and *Miami News* editor Bill Baggs among them—were part of the Communist conspiracy. He belonged to a small fanatical group calling themselves the Florida States Rights party, nicknamed Minute Men, who had targeted for assassination several local public figures. The plotters' vocal campaigns against liberals, blacks, and Jews had drawn from gentile Shoemaker a brief but biting editorial. Now, on this dark morning wrapped in silence, they planned to strike back.

A tall figure carrying a heavy object detached itself from the shadows of Sabal Palm Road and moved silently across the grass toward the Shoemaker house. Donald Branch stepped to the corner of the house, knelt down, and placed the object on the ground against the wall. He unrolled a length of fuse and lit it with the glowing end of a cigar. The fuse sputtered as he walked away and vanished into the trees.

Ten sticks of dynamite exploded, shattering the window of Elizabeth Shoemaker's room and showering glass and debris around her bed. The house's steel corner reinforcement deflected the full explosive force outward, however, caving in the wall of a home next door, slightly injuring two children sleeping there, and damaging three other houses nearby.

In their sound-dampened master bedroom Don and Lyal Shoemaker heard nothing until awakened by neighbors pounding on the front door. Shoemaker hurried into the shambles of his daughter's room breathing the stench of cordite. Elizabeth was terrified, but miraculously unhurt.

It was almost 2:30 A.M. Shoemaker picked up the telephone and dialed the *Herald* newsroom. Veteran news editor Charlie Ward answered. The final city edition was still running off the press. "Charlie, my house has been bombed. . . ." Ward stopped the presses long enough to insert a paragraph on page 1.

The following day, even as the mess was being swept up at Bay Point, Shoemaker put together an editorial statement.

> I am sorry for the misguided men who speak with dynamite in a dark forum of shadowy hate. They bring opprobrium on our community and discredit to our republic of laws. Neither the editor nor the newspaper proposes to play a martyr's role in a sick drama. The *Herald* has always tried to serve the public interest. I think it will always try to do so. We are not dismayed.

Nobody yet knew about Donald Branch and the Minute Men. Suspicion focused on the bus strikers, whose international union was bitterly resisting a county takeover of several heavily unionized private companies. On the Sunday following the bombing, Jack Knight focused his ire on George Meany, president of the AFL-CIO, and other prominent labor leaders who were gathered for their midwinter meeting at Miami Beach's posh Americana Hotel. Meany had made a speech charging Miami newspapers with biased antiunion coverage of the bus strike.

Knight retorted in print:

> No one questions Mr. Meany's right to intervene in a local labor situation. . . . So let no one challenge the *Miami Herald*'s right to lay the facts [of the strike] on the line. The persons who bombed Editor Don Shoemaker's residence under cover of night wasted powder. In the 25 years that I have been publisher of the *Miami Herald,* we have faced personal violence, threats of

death, boycotts and libel suits running into the millions. None of these tactics has ever made us crawl to safety. They will not succeed now.

It would be months before a German-born Miami police-man, infiltrating and wiretapping the Branch terrorist group in the guise of a neo-Nazi, broke open the conspiracy. Ultimately, a contrite Branch would plead guilty to the Shoemaker bombing and receive a twenty-year prison sentence.

Editor Shoemaker remained unflappable. "Donald Branch is more to be pitied than scorned," he editorialized. "He was a victim of bigotry and hatred quite as damaging to him as the bomb."

Young John S. Knight III was growing, bright and handsome, and showed a keen interest in the world around him. Jack Knight planned to take him out of what he regarded as the intellectual and cultural wasteland of Columbus, Georgia, and give him a first-class education in an eastern preparatory school. Over the years, in subtle and not-so-subtle ways, Knight had let his intentions be known.

Perhaps distance made the heart grow fonder, or he was inspired by the tragedy surrounding the boy's birth, but Knight doted uncharacteristically on Johnny III. Even back in May 1945, after his first visit to war widow Dorothy and her newborn in Georgia, the grandfather had written, "He is simply adorable. I was tempted to steal him." It was the first of what would become a steady output of notes spanning the next three decades, during which this complex grandson would give him pride, challenge, and, ultimately, black despair.

When the boy was four, Knight received a Father's Day card bearing Johnny's signature in uneven block letters and found the gesture significant. "He is beginning to scribble." That same year the grandfather urged Dorothy to join the local country club; he would pay the dues. "I think a membership would be most valuable to you both." By summer 1955, when the ten-year-old was still in grammar school, Knight was building an account for him in cash and stocks ("Dorothy, I am enclosing an additional 75 shares of City Auto Stamping Company"), offering to buy the mother a better house in Columbus and thinking about Johnny's high school education. "I have never discussed this with you, but I should like to send him to the best preparatory school in the East. With his good mind, it would be a shame not to have him take advantage of a superior education."

Dorothy Knight lived simply, with Johnny and her mother. She was strongly religious and felt at home in her native Columbus. She knew little of the sophisticated, power-wielding world of John S. Knight. She dreaded the notion of her handsome young son's leaving, to take up life at a strange preparatory school. But Jack Knight persisted. When he sent her an application form for the Lawrenceville Preparatory School in New Jersey, Dorothy put the form away in a drawer. Time went by. Now Johnny was finishing junior high. John S. Knight chided her for failing to send Johnny's application to Lawrenceville. "I hope this does not mean you have gone back on your promise to me. I have explained the reasons and there is no use repeating them here. May I hear from you? Love . . ."

Reluctantly, Dorothy Knight wrote to the school asking that a place be reserved for her son at the start of the fall term.

The decade had opened with soul-searching and high hopes.

"We need to face up to the fact that there are too many *Herald* haters and detractors, and that we give people too many reasons to be so," Lee Hills noted. "I sometimes wonder whether the average citizen respects the *Herald* for its aggressiveness or resents it for its self-righteousness."

It was an unusually frank letter to key editors. As executive editor of Knight Newspapers and the *Miami Herald,* Hills was treading sensitive ground. True, as Jack Knight said, any worthwhile newspaper made enemies, but it seemed to Hills that the *Herald* was disliked by too many of the wrong people. "I fear that some of our staff members are not constantly aware of the tremendous power of the paper to destroy the reputations of individuals, the happiness of a family, the progress of a business or industry, even the future of a politician who may be guilty merely of bad judgment. We should lead rather than bludgeon."

It had been a time, in Miami and America, of gathering

forces and fresh starts. Suburbia flourished. People were making money. Eight in ten homes had a TV set. Comedian Jack Paar kept the nation up late. Four black students quietly ordered coffee at an all-white lunch counter in Greensboro, North Carolina, and, when refused service, stayed all day. A "sit-in," they called it. The Cold War moved closer to home. Fidel Castro had brought Soviet jet bombers to within eight minutes of Florida, and an exile army was training secretly in Guatemala to invade the Cuban island. America still liked Ike, and Jack Knight had made peace with the administration; anyway, there would soon be a changing of the White House guard. Public opinion surveys ranked newspaper editors below dentists, but above undertakers.

Knight himself had opened the decade with a ripsnorting speech in Chicago to a convention of the members of the Inland Daily Press Association, touching on the subject closest to his heart: newspapers. If anything, he believed, the press suffered from too little aggressiveness, not too much. "Too many editorial pages are dull and uninspired and read as if the editor was more interested in wordage than wisdom and wallop."

Harry Truman chafed in retirement, building his library at Independence, Missouri, and taking vacations at his old tropical haunt in Key West. The former president was still his crusty self. In a speech at the University of Missouri, he waded in on the press, charging that it was dominated by profit-hungry publishers and really not very free. Hell, given a blue pencil and some copy, he could do as well or better. Knight responded by inviting Truman to visit the *Herald* next time he came to south Florida and spend some time on a desk. The doughty seventy-five-year-old obliged, strolling into the *Herald* one morning like a man ready to punch a time clock.

Trailed by editors and Secret Service men, Knight and the man he had once labeled "unfit for the White House" ambled through pressrooms and newsrooms, talking politics. "What do you think of young Jack Kennedy?" Knight asked. "I like him," Truman replied, "but I don't like his father. Never did, never will. . . ." The man who had once held the fate of the world in his hands sat down to edit some wire copy, read a few pages, doodled with pencil and paper, became bored, got up, and said, "That's your job, not mine."

Afterward, Knight would describe the incident warmly in his "Notebook," concluding: "It's a long way from Independence, Missouri, to the White House and then back to Independence, but Harry Truman has made the round trip unspoiled and unreconstructed."

Complex forces were at work. In ways both material and human, the *Herald* was retooling for the future. This meant change, and change was rarely easy. Most obvious was the change in hardware. On a steamy August day in 1960, the Knight brothers sank ceremonial shovels into the sandy soil of the Biscayne bayfront, breaking ground for the new Miami plant. Not so publicly apparent was the evolving change in management and style. Even as the spades flashed, inner conflicts were churning. Hills's scathing memo about the *Herald*'s community image had been inspired by an unusual editorial in a Knight-owned subsidiary paper, the *Times* of nearby Coral Gables, characterizing the big morning daily as being dictatorial and slanting the news. The *Times*'s editor, young Bill von Maurer, had taken to heart Knight's dictum of editorial independence.

Jack Knight was piqued. "I think it's a mistake for the *Times* to feud with the *Herald.*"

Hills felt that the source of criticism was beside the point; what mattered was that the *Miami Herald* was widely disliked, as reflected even in an editorial in a Knight-owned paper. Public response to a recent libel verdict—the paper's first such loss—was a case in point. "The most shocking thing about the verdict," said Hills, "was not that the jury socked us for $100,000, it was the gleeful reception that this unwarranted verdict got around town. The *Herald* has become a popular target."

Some of the paper's aggressive temperament was due to a man who combined the unique gifts of a great newspaperman with certain journalistic blind spots, *Herald* editor John Pennekamp.

Jack Knight harbored mixed feelings about his longtime Miami editorial chief. Straightforward, stubborn, unshakably honest, Pennekamp was a veteran of the Shutts era and had a broad knowledge of south Florida and its people and politics. But like many passionate reformers, he had an innate suspicion of politicians and public figures that often bordered on contempt. To Knight, this was a flaw; the truly effective editor functioned on all levels, not only as critic and—in Knight's words—"auditor" of government, but also as a civic activist capable of mingling with local movers and shakers. There existed a fine line between the aggressive editor and the town bully.

Postwar Miami had experienced massive changes, with Hills and Pennekamp in the forefront. Hills had restructured the paper and waged his Pulitzer Prize–winning cleanup of hoodlum elements. Pennekamp had pushed editorially for local governmental reform and environmental causes. To readers, Pennekamp's column, "Behind the Front Page," was the true voice of the *Herald*.

But the Knights believed that the newspaper was not doing enough to promote other worthwhile civic projects—reconstruction of downtown Miami, for example—and that Pennekamp's hostility toward business, the "Miami Club crowd," as he called it, was self-defeating. Jack Knight was thinking about infusing the *Herald* with new blood at the top.

And then Pennekamp and the paper were hit with a stormy libel suit.

The Dade County Grand Jury accused two local judges of mishandling receiverships, guardianships, curator appointments, and disbursement of lawyer fees and demanded that they resign. State Attorney George A. Brautigam, a political ultraconservative with gubernatorial ambitions, tried to suppress the grand jury report. The *Herald* published a scathing editorial, "Why Does State Attorney Muzzle the Grand Jury?" and recommended that Brautigam be removed from office. The state attorney sued the *Herald* for $2 million in damages.

Knight had considered the editorials too strong, but publicly backed Pennekamp. Brautigam's lawyer was the flamboyant self-styled "King of Torts," Melvin Belli. As the case came to trial, Belli called to the stand John S. Knight. A jubilant crowd overflowed the courtroom as Belli, nattily attired in an Italian silk suit and cowboy boots, fixed the publisher with a baleful stare.

"Now, Mr. Knight, tell us about the tricks in the newspaper business."

"We don't have any tricks, Mr. Belli."

"Well, tell us about the artifices and stratagems you employ."

"We don't employ artifices or stratagems," Knight replied, "but if you want to return to your first item—tricks—my impression is that I have found many more of these in your profession than in mine."

"Do you have reference to anyone in particular?"

"Yes."

"Who is it?"

Knight pointed at Belli. "You."

The courtroom roared. Judge William Herin banged his gavel and rebuked Knight. Belli faced the jury. "There sits the emperor who instructs the colonial governors on what to do. We are suing for two million dollars. Mr. Knight can afford this. When you go out, bring back the full verdict, the full two million dollars."

The jury awarded Brautigam $100,000. But it was to be a hollow victory. As the case wore into appeals—not until mid-1962 would it finally be resolved—Brautigam was voted out of office. His political future destroyed, he died of a heart attack.

Knight admitted that his blustery court performance had been a mistake. He gained a wary respect for Belli. "The greatest actor since Barrymore. And I should know. It cost us $100,000 for my seat in the witness chair."

July bore down on Los Angeles with prickly heat and smog as the Democrats gathered to nominate John F. Kennedy for president. The handsome New Englander had staked his claim with seven straight primary victories. The only matter still in doubt was his choice of running mate.

As usual, Knight was a member of the working press. He had covered every convention of both parties since 1920 and had a veteran's feel for a power struggle. Politics was theater, a world, as one future master of the game would characterize it, "of mirrors and blue smoke." Knight delighted in foraging behind the scenes. Besides, things were dull.

"The bands are playing, the banners flying and there is an air of contrived excitement," he told his readers. "Jack Kennedy has the prettiest girls in town. His prime opponent, Texas Sen. Lyndon B. Johnson, is fortified by enthusiastic partisans."

The nomination was Kennedy's in a walkaway. His followers were still celebrating when the young standard-bearer announced that his running mate would be Johnson. Party satraps were thunderstruck. As Senate majority leader, Johnson was already the second most powerful politician in Washington. Why would he seek the obscurity of the vice presidency? Knight had heard bizarre whispers. On July 15, he reported them in the Knight newspapers. The *Akron Beacon Journal* headlined it: DID JOHNSON FORCE KENNEDY TO TAKE HIM AS A PARTNER?

Knight described behind-the-scenes intrigue. Far from being a reluctant running mate, he insisted, Johnson had privately demanded a place on the Kennedy ticket and threatened a messy floor fight if rejected. "I deserve to be vice president and I intend to get it." Democratic chieftains, favoring Missouri senator Stuart Symington, had debated for hours before giving in. "Eventually," wrote Knight, "all agreed that they could not risk a fight with Johnson without endangering the party."

The Knight story provoked vigorous denials from both Kennedy and Johnson. In a memoir years afterward, *With Kennedy,* JFK's press secretary Pierre Salinger told of issuing such a flood of denials to other journalists that he succeeded in squelching the Knight report. He blamed the whole thing on "semantic misunderstanding," insisting that Johnson had threatened a floor fight to overcome labor opposition to his candidacy, not to demand the vice presidential nomination itself. Knight's erroneous information, Salinger went on, came from thirdhand reports, apparently relayed to the publisher by Governor James T. Blair of Missouri.

Knight stuck to his guns. "I caught a lot of hell," he later told Al Neuharth, then an assistant managing editor of the *Herald,* "but the basic facts are correct."

In November, Americans cast a record 69 million votes, electing Kennedy by a whisker over Richard M. Nixon. " 'Twas a victory," columnist Knight observed, "not a mandate." Two months later, Kennedy electrified the nation with his inaugural address. "Let the word go forth from this time and place, to friend and foe alike, that the torch has been passed to a new generation. . . ."

The thousand days of Camelot began.

Detroit continued to be torn by bitter newspaper competition.

For years a three-way battle for readers and advertisers had pitted the Knight-owned *Free Press* against its afternoon rivals, the *News* and the *Times.* The *News* had long dominated the field, with the *Free Press* running second and the *Times* trailing badly. In the decade since Hills's arrival as executive editor, the *Free Press* gradually closed the gap until it finally surpassed the *News* in March 1960. Much of this gain was at the expense of the Hearst-owned *Times,* which had lost $10 million in five years. The *Times* had tried desperately to recoup by coming out with a green-trimmed afternoon Family Edition.

Labor disputes did not help matters. All three papers were plagued with soaring overtime costs and union resistance to laborsaving technology. Five years earlier, a walkout of stereotypers, mailers, and printers—the first newspaper strike in Detroit history—had shut down all three papers for forty-seven days. Publishers grimly stood their ground. Basic issues ran deep; at stake was the very power of management to make its own decisions. That first 1955/56 strike cost Detroit merchants $35 million. By 1960, two more walkouts had occurred. Worse trouble loomed ahead.

By losing market dominance, the *News* stood to lose millions of dollars in advertising. *News* publisher Warren Booth heard rumors of a plan by the *Free Press* and the *Times* to join in a combined suburban circulation drive against him. Booth decided it was time to buy the sixty-year-old *Times* and put it out of business. Hearst management was willing. As secret talks began, word got back to Hills that the *News* intended to buy all the *Times* equipment, vehicles, presses, property, and circulation lists. But the paper's fourteen hundred employees were to be let go. By taking over the *Times*'s 375,000-reader subscriber lists, the new owners would reap a windfall.

Free Press executives began planning counterstrategy.

The *Times*'s popularity still hinged on the afternoon Family Edition, heavy on features. Hills decided simply to adopt the same format for a *Free Press* afternoon edition. The rival *News* would own the *Times* subscriber lists, but the *Free Press* could hire the defunct paper's circulation personnel.

Reliable information on the date of the *Times*'s demise was hard to come by. Rumors focused on the weekend of November 5–6. Hills confirmed this with an editor friend at *Newsweek,* which had scheduled an advance story. The *Times* takeover was set for the following Monday. The *Free Press* broke the story on Sunday night. Hills's final staff meeting ended at midnight, and he lay down on his office sofa to take a nap.

Across the city, employees of the *Detroit Times* began receiving midnight Western Union telegrams in their homes, informing them that they were fired. At 3:15 A.M., one of the stunned recipients called *Free Press* managing editor Frank Angelo.

Hills awoke and swung his feet off the couch.

"Let's go to work," he said.

Throughout Detroit, ringing telephones rousted from bed *Free Press* editors, reporters, printers, and truck drivers to launch the paper's first Family Edition. Everything but the masthead resembled the suddenly defunct *Times.* The surprise new *Free Press* edition started pouring off the presses shortly after noon, with a run of 250,000 copies and former *Times* circulation people waiting to deliver it free to former *Times* subscribers. In an editorial, Hills called it "a reflection of modern newspaper economics." The *Free Press* would operate for seven grueling months producing both a morning and an afternoon paper before discontinuing the Family Edition. By March 1961, *Free Press* daily circulation jumped by 73,000, to more than 573,500.

Hills, elated, pep-talked his troops. "Things are shaking down into a tough, wonderful fight."

Competition was waged on many levels. Fistfights broke out between rival newspaper street vendors. Ugly rumors from anonymous sources were planted like psychological land mines. Among the pernicious was a whisper that the *Free Press* was in financial straits and about to be sold. The idea was thought to be spread by union militants, but this was never proved. It popped up again one cold January evening in Cincinnati, Ohio. The local

Enquirer sent a routine inquiry to the Associated Press (AP), touching off a brief wire flurry.

DETROIT: ENQUIRER (AMS) SAYS THEY HEAR RUMOR FREE PRESS BEEN SOLD. ASKS CHECK PUBLISHER KNIGHT QUICKEST.

CINCINNATI, CLEVELAND: RE: SALE OF FREE PRESS, BEEN REPEATED SOME TIME. UNABLE REACH LOCAL EXECUTIVES. KNIGHT BELIEVED IN MIAMI. THIS RUMOR BEEN DENIED IN PAST. WE CHECKING FURTHER.—DETROIT AA8PES.

The AP's Detroit bureau found Lee Hills at home, then chattered out its conclusion.

CINCINNATI, CLEVELAND, COLUMBUS: ABSOLUTELY NOTHING TO YOUR REPORT OF FREE PRESS BEING SOLD.—DETROIT AA842PES.

United Press International (UPI) also made energetic inquiries.

AU / NS
PLS PAGE FRANK ANGELO, ME OF DU F-P ABT RUMORS F-P BN SOLD. HIS WIFE SAYS U MITE TRY ARCHIE'S WHERE HE HAD DINNER. SAPPEST TREATMENT PLS. RP / DU. RR705PMESTI / 8.

After getting denials from both Hills and Marshall Field, UPI also scotched the report.

Rarely were such wire advisories the stuff of news reports. This time, however, a news editor for Detroit's WXYZ radio and television saw a chance to liven up a dull night. The story went out over the air: "Rumors are flying from unconfirmed sources that the *Free Press,* Detroit's morning newspaper, will be sold. Lee Hills, executive editor of the *Free Press* and a vice president of Knight Newspapers, denies it vigorously but still rumors persist."

Hills was incensed. The following morning he wrote a full-page ad for all editions: "The *Detroit Free Press* is NOT for sale. Any such rumor is a lie. If any medium continues to spread it, this newspaper will sue." From Miami, Knight fired off a telegram of protest to the Associated Press. I MUST INSIST THAT YOU DISAVOW ALL RUMORS CONCERNING THE DETROIT FREE PRESS. . . .

The incident sputtered out.

Five months later, the *Free Press* was shut down by another strike, Detroit's seventh major newspaper walkout in as many years. *The New York Times*'s Arthur Krock saw the dilemma as "proof that any union can black out the press without the restraint of any law, without penalty for broken contracts and with much official tolerance of the violence it may commit. . . ."

Technology was wonderful.

It was the human element that galled.

The "Notebook" column was twenty-five years old. Jack Knight had launched it during the Depression, before the war, before TV or penicillin, before jet airliners or man-made objects in space, at a time when he himself had a keener edge of youth. Now he was sixty-seven. In his Akron office, surrounded by photographs and memorabilia, he again confronted the old stand-up typewriter to reflect on this thing that he did which was both chore and compulsion. "This column originated," he wrote, "out of the conviction that newspapers were becoming as impersonal as banks. . . . The author suffers from no delusion that he is a great writer. The overriding idea is to stimulate thought and not necessarily win agreement."

And yet he did enjoy molding opinion. Editors took the "Notebook"'s lead on major issues. As *Beacon Journal* editorial writer James Jackson would admit years afterward, "We looked to it for guidance." But writing the column, Knight reflected, also provided one with a unique identity. "Some years ago my old friend David Lawrence was talking about his newspaper column. 'How long do you intend to keep on writing?' I asked him. 'Why should I stop?' he replied. 'And that applies to you too. Did you ever stop to think that we would be nothing if we didn't write? No one would know us. . . .'"

Actually, he lived two lives. As Ed Lahey had once observed, "Journalism is both a business and a profession. . . . The first function of a newspaper is to survive and prosper." The business side was demanding. As the company grew, so did its scope of management. Knight recalled wistfully the days of his old brown briefcase. Now you could not even leave major overall decisions to individual business managers; a company executive committee oversaw things and smoothed out problems. God knew where it would lead. Someday, he supposed privately, they would go public, with listings on the stock exchange, reports to financial analysts, and all that. He disliked the idea.

Column writing was simpler, even if it was not always comfortable. One of Knight's perennial critics was Miami-based author Philip Wylie, who gleefully contended that the publisher had established a record for being wrong. Knight sniffed. "Phil is always unhappy about something, as the good ladies who attend his dolorous lectures will attest."

Twenty-five years, and there weren't many of his kind around anymore. "Grover Hall of the *Montgomery Advertiser* once called me as rare as the whooping crane. Incidentally, Grover doesn't think much of my column either."

In the journalist's workaday world, a worthy foe had importance too. A man was known for his enemies as well as his friends. As a foe of Teamsters Union boss Jimmy Hoffa, Knight felt himself in good company. Hoffa's rantings were grist for the columnist's mill, as when the unionist angrily protested a *Miami Herald* editorial correctly predicting his salary increase, a hike in union dues, and jurisdictional raids on other labor groups. "The pure rot, the garbage in this editorial!" bellowed Hoffa. "Let Mr. Knight write his stinking filth, we'll take the action we want!"

"And so they did," the "Notebook" mused. "And so they did."

The mail was never-ending.

A woman reader was miffed by a published interview with Walter Lippmann, recounting his conversation with Soviet premier Nikita Khrushchev. She felt that Lippmann's "defeatist" and "leftist" views had no place in a Knight newspaper. Knight replied mildly, "We published the interview because it was a fascinating discussion of pressing world problems."

Superpatriots galled him, waving the flag and suggesting darkly that anyone who disagreed with their views of the world were Kremlin dupes, or worse. Such prattle was nothing new; Knight remembered it from the 1920s and the early 1950s. "Those who prate of their own patriotism while seeing others as 'soft on communism' are unfair, uninformed and psychologically unhinged."

He was a man of the century, and experience had helped to shape his opinion. He had been a schoolboy during the presidency of Theodore Roosevelt, had heard the oratory of William Jennings Bryan, had marched against the kaiser. He danced the foxtrot, the lindy hop, and the two-step and still amazed party guests by standing on his head, given enough martinis. And for twenty-five years he had written "The Editor's Notebook."

"I was born to the craft. I love it."

Miami was a city in ferment.

By the tens of thousands, Cubans fled the Marxist regime of Fidel Castro, destination Miami. In cafés and storefront headquarters of exile groups, plots to exact vengeance and wrest back the homeland were hatched with an anger as scalding as the endless cups of *café Cubano.* On April 17, 1961, the CIA-trained liberation brigade blundered ashore at Cuba's Bay of Pigs. The operation quickly turned to fiasco as plans went awry and, in Washington, John F. Kennedy and his advisers—inheritors of this wild scheme from the Eisenhower administration—quickly lost heart.

For the *Herald,* covering the operation was a nightmare. Newcomer Larry Jinks, former city editor of the *Charlotte Observer,* ran the city desk and tried to bring order to a stream of CIA-fed distortions. Bedeviled by contradictions, Jinks inserted a box, headed WHICH SIDE DO YOU BELIEVE? on the front page, giving a capsule version of the rival victory claims. The affair ended in disaster for the exiled invaders, with 117 dead and 1,180 captured, many of them wounded.

Shouldering responsibility, Kennedy made a bellicose speech, heavy on Cold War rhetoric, to the American Society of Newspaper Editors. In the aftermath, Knight saw the affair as "a hard lesson for Kennedy. He is stronger now, more confident, wary of untested counselors." The statement was more wish than fact.

When Castro offered cynically to trade the invasion prisoners for five hundred tractors and other supplies, a prestigious Tractors for Freedom Committee formed, composed of such people as Eleanor Roosevelt and Milton Eisenhower. Knight brusquely declined an invitation to join, saying, "Any barter with Castro further demeans the prestige of our country." Released prisoners flew to Miami. In two decades, the Cuban exodus would become the largest ethnic inpouring experienced by a U.S. city in modern times.

More Cuban crises loomed. By fall 1962, reports that Soviet ships were unloading Soviet military and hardware in Cuba persisted. Knight saw a Soviet threat gathering. "The Cuban question must be met with force if force is required."

The showdown came abruptly. On Monday, October 22, a grim President Kennedy announced that Soviet missile sites were under construction in Cuba, threatening "nuclear strike capability against the Western Hemisphere." South Florida became an armed staging ground for Cuban invasion as Russian ships steamed toward a U.S. blockade and American nuclear bombers went aloft on red alert. Soviet premier Nikita Khrushchev backed down, called off his ships, and pledged to dismantle the missiles. Mankind stepped back from the brink and Kennedy's star soared. "The world," declared Knight, "applauds his leadership."

And yet the basic job, toppling Castro, remained undone. The thought nagged at him as Columbia University presented Knight its Maria Moore Cabot Award. "I am," he said, "most apprehensive."

Castro would remain entrenched, a constant reminder of the limits of national power in the nuclear age, well beyond John S. Knight's lifetime.

Knight's newsmen and executives were bright, energetic, positive. Talent excited him. One had to give talent latitude if it were to flourish, and only by flourishing did it build good newspapers. One thing led to another. James Knight would express the process in these terms:

It's simple. When we buy a newspaper, we spend money to improve the editorial product. That brings us more readers who read the paper more thoroughly, producing better results for advertisers. More revenue from added circulation and advertising produces better profit. And this we plow back into improving the editorial product still more.

Good newspapers meant good business.

All this had changed greatly in John S. Knight's time. The so-called good old days of journalism weren't good at all, he remarked. "The nation was dotted with publications in the form of newspapers representing political parties, railroads, banks, or purely personal prejudices of the owner without thought of public good. They were sorry examples of journalism as we know it today." Newsmen of that era seldom had much talent; they were abominable writers and worse managers of personnel. But this, too, was changing.

Within the Knight Newspapers one saw constant upward mobility as ambitious people pushed toward higher position. A newspaper staff, like a well-oiled machine, functioned best in harmony. But creative people could be difficult.

He put his thoughts into memos. To Al Neuharth at the *Detroit Free Press:*

> *Mark Ethridge is good and can be better. But his sulking is evidence of the immaturity I have sensed in personal contacts with him. . . . I agree with your recommendations concerning the "editorial board" and its operations. But the real need of the Free Press is not a "board" but an editor. The problem will not be solved until one person has final editorial authority and exercises it well. An editor must be big enough to be an editor.*

In Miami, Don Shoemaker showed spirit and class. He was a good social mixer, at ease at the Bath Club, the Surf Club, or the Miami Club. He held strong opinions on issues, did not hesitate to take an unpopular stand if he felt it was right, but could back off gracefully and recognize the basic realities of working for another man's newspaper. Knight enjoyed his company at the races. They would sometimes go to Hialeah in the afternoons; sit in Knight's clubhouse box, surrounded by Palm Beach socialites; and watch Editorialist or another of the Fourth Estate Stables horses run. Knight was always at his sartorial best, with knife-edge creases in his suits and a jaunty narrow-brimmed straw hat.

He bet the horses in $6 combinations and seemed to have a remarkable knack for it. As editor Shoemaker disgustedly tore up losing tickets, his employer would announce gleefully, "I've got another winner!" and head for the cashier's window. Shoemaker suspected, but never proved, that Knight often bought tickets on every horse in a race.

Miami and its unpredictable tempers took the measure of an editor. Shoemaker already had weathered noisy tussles over new county government, the bus strike, bitter factionalism between Cuban exiles. Economically, too, the place lived in delicate balance—a growing city hungry for jobs and industrial development, but set in a fragile subtropic environment.

When billionaire industrialist D. K. Ludwig proposed to build a huge oil refinery on the shores of Biscayne Bay a battle royal seemed certain. Environmentalists saw it as a threat to the mangrove-studded coastal waters. Developers, on the other hand, hailed Ludwig's plan for a "clean" refinery and new deep-water port. Shoemaker took the side of Ludwig and his promise of nonpolluting heavy industry and mass employment. Miami was a labor-surplus community. Minorities suffered. "The fact remains that we grind up people for lack of opportunity," the editor wrote. He believed that modern pollution controls could make it possible for heavy industry and environment to coexist. "Growth, like all aspects of life, is not without pain."

Jack Knight took this guardedly. Certainly he was all for free enterprise, and stood to be enriched personally by community growth, but other elements had to be weighed.

When an administrator of extensive private real estate holdings urged Knight's personal support of the refinery, the publisher replied: "We need more industrial payrolls. The question is, can this be built and operated without pollution. If so, are the Ludwig interests qualified to meet the high standards?"

Environmental protection had few organized advocates.

Traditionally Florida had given way to developers, with dire results. Some *Miami Herald* reporters, such as government writer Juanita Greene, were outraged by the refinery idea. Ludwig appealed personally for Knight's support, suggesting that he send a reporter to inspect a new "clean" oil refinery in Mississippi to prove that properly run modern refineries don't pollute. A reporter was sent, and found that what Ludwig said was true; however, around the nonpolluting refinery the town had sold out to other heavy industries that did pollute. Knight informed Ludwig that the *Herald* could not support a refinery in south Florida.

Shoemaker quietly accepted the decision. As he would recall years afterward, "We just never spoke of it again."

Ludwig canceled his project.

And so the interplay between publisher and editor was a subtle process, an understanding between gentlemen. Yet the editor, Knight insisted, must be strong.

> A successful newspaper is a reflection of its owner or editor. This is something more than dedication to printing unbiased news, giving voice to all points of view or the skillful assembling of interesting features and comics. The newspaper editor must also be the conscience of the community. . . . An editor should lead.

Not all editors and writers accepted Knight's judgment. When Washington correspondent David Kraslow revived the Bay of Pigs controversy in an interview with the president's brother Robert Kennedy nearly two years after the Cuban invasion debacle, Knight saw no purpose being served. "The President said he goofed," the publisher told his reporter, "so why do we keep on belaboring him?"

Retorted Kraslow, a gifted newsman who would one day become publisher of the competing *Miami Daily News:* "As a citizen and reporter, I have grown fond of a great tradition in this nation, that the governors must account to the governed for their deeds." There still had been no full accounting of the Cuban fiasco and the CIA's role in it. "We thrive to wash our linen in public," Kraslow went on. "If it happens to be dirty, all the more reason for a cleansing." The reporter would never get his full disclosure of the facts involved in the Bay of Pigs incident. But Knight, in disapproving, nonetheless admired his zeal, saying, "Always feel free to let me have your views, whether or not they agree with mine."

On April 14, 1963, Miami basked in bright sunshine under a crystalline blue sky. Overnight, the last trucks had deposited their loads and now the new Miami Herald building was officially open for business.

The thing was a massive hulk of marble, steel, block, glass, and stucco: six stories, stretching for a city block on Biscayne Bay. Its colors were an odd mixture of yellows, reds, off-whites, and grays, dominated by bright blue ventilated window shutters strangely resembling hundreds of eyelids in ordered rows. Critics pursed their lips. "The egg crate," sniffed *Newsweek*, "on Biscayne Bay."

Jim Knight's assistant, Alvah Chapman, had directed the move of the *Herald* from old plant to new while maintaining a full publishing schedule and without missing a beat. The paper even put out a special New Building Edition, rolled thick as a log and heaped with self-tribute. And then the Knights were in their glory, standing for hours in a reception line with their wives, shaking hands with ten thousand visitors. People gawked at the automated mailing room; the gang of Goss presses, big as an ocean liner, the fluorescent-lit newsroom the area of a football field. It was a glorious day, rich in the trappings of success.

Jack Knight rested from his handshaking in a splendid new fifth-floor office, decorated in fine woods and carpets with deep lounge chairs and banks of windows commanding the sunny panorama of the bay. The office had access via a small elevator with a phone, in case it got stuck. What more could a man wish for?

And yet, curiously, Knight's thinking turned backward, not forward. In a couple of paragraphs, his "Notebook" column brushed past the grand opening with its dignitaries and fuss. The week before, he had sorted through twenty-six years of desk clutter at the old Herald building. He wrote nostalgically about other desks he had cleaned out in places like Akron, Springfield, and Massillon, Ohio, and Chicago—eight of them, in all—since first going to work for the *Akron Beacon Journal* in the steamy prewar summer of 1914. And he remembered some of the hard lessons he'd learned, such as alienating the town of Springfield by publishing the Ku Klux Klan membership lists. "As old Ned Heiskell would say dutifully about his troubles many years later in Little Rock, we gained prestige but lost business."

Time marched on. Technology changed. Buildings changed. Names and faces changed. Human nature remained the same. "My first newspaper job dates back to June 15, 1914, and I have a nice, shiny watch to prove it. But years of experience aren't everything. The new breed of newspapermen have a lot on the ball. . . ."

There was menace in the air. Workmen suspended a giant banner across a hangar at Miami International Airport: WELCOME, MR. PRESIDENT. But the Cuban ferment remained strong. There were rumors of an assassination attempt. Security was doubled and redoubled. Rifle-toting police guarded bridges, expressways, rooftops. Plainclothesmen stalked the crowds. The Secret Service bodyguard had been reinforced. Along strategic routes, security men sat in unmarked cars, parked with motors running.

As the presidential jet, *Air Force One,* banked out of the afternoon sunshine a local high school band struck up a martial tune. Costumed middle-aged "Kennedy Girls" danced like cheerleaders in red, white, and blue. The Boeing 707 taxied to a stop and its door opened. A small crowd raised a cheer as the familiar trim figure descended the steps, waving, his hair ruffling in the breeze. Lee Hills greeted the president, and the group got into waiting limousines for the fast ride over the blue sweep of Biscayne Bay to the Americana Hotel in Bal Harbour. There, John F. Kennedy changed into a tuxedo and was greeted by 450 conventioneering members of the Inter-American Press Association.

The date was Monday, November 18, 1963. As always, this was a Kennedy of wit and charm. Jack Knight delighted in his company as they chatted at dinner, but thought the chief executive looked tired. Kennedy mentioned that he would be taking a swing into Texas later in the week.

Knight liked John Kennedy's style. He had known the patriarch Joseph Kennedy as ambassador to England during World

War II. He admired the son as a man of quick decision and brimming confidence, so impatient to get things done that he snapped his fingers as he talked, a man who dared surround himself with Rhodes scholars and esoteric thinkers. The Kennedy mystique had brought unprecedented excitement to the White House.

Still, the publisher kept his skepticism. Federal spending continued apace, and he wondered how in hell they would ever control it. For a column, he had obtained a list of random items from a new $14 billion package of federal research spending. It included $16,000 for a study of social behavior among termites, $7,000 for the psycholinguistic analysis of consonant clusters, $50,000 for correlates of persuasibility, and $17,000 for reclassification of earthworms. "No, I don't believe it either," Knight wrote with a sigh.

Other events during this administration, he noted, had moved at a blinding rush: the young president's confrontation with Khrushchev in Vienna; the Berlin Wall, rising like a concrete obscenity; black Americans' marching for equality; Martin Luther King, Jr.'s, preaching to 200,000 at the Washington Monument, "I have a dream"; the Soviets' launching the first man in space, to circle the globe at a stupefying eighteen thousand miles per hour. But most of all, Vietnam nagged at him. He saw Kennedy and the nation being drawn into the snakepit. "This incredible snafu is costing America $1.5 million a day. Haven't we been conned long enough?"

Readers were eager to lash out at the bearer of bad news, and Knight's darker commentaries drew their ire. R. W. Daugherty of Fort Lauderdale, Florida, called him "a meretricious mountebank, willing to compromise the truth when it suits your fancy." Lawrence Ferrera of Pompano Beach suggested the publisher would feel at home among "the irresponsible super-patriot lunatic fringe." He duly printed their comments in his column.

Latin America was producing some knotty problems for Kennedy. Hence, this quick trip to Miami Beach to address the Inter-American Press Association. Kennedy needed these men and women of the hemispheric press. If journalists could get along on no more than professional common interests, couldn't nations do as well? Knight himself touched on the point in welcoming remarks. "Why is it that newspaper people from all walks of life can unite in progress while diplomats produce continuing crises?"

Kennedy, youthful, beguiling, charmed them with his wit and warmth. Deftly, the president turned to the subject at hand: "For the United States, Latin America is the most important area in the world." Then, with a smile and a wave, he was gone. His motorcade sped back across the causeways in the darkness. Still in tuxedo, he pounded up the steps of *Air Force One.* The door slammed shut. The Boeing 707 hurtled down the runway and lifted into the soft subtropic night.

Security officers breathed easily again. The small army of police packed up its weapons and went home.

Three days later, John F. Kennedy was shot dead in Dallas.

America sat stunned and grieving before its TV sets, riveted by the seemingly endless funeral parade, the muffled drumbeats, the incessant clipclop of a black stallion's hooves, the wailing music of the Death March. With live broadcasting driving the event into the national consciousness, never before had there been such outpouring of grief.

"A tragedy beyond belief," John Knight wrote.

"The nation has suffered a fearsome loss."

17

"THE BEARING OF A GENTLEMAN"

Finally, when it came down to basics, it was the people who cared about you that mattered; family, friends, associates. But among all the people Jack Knight knew—newspaper folk, socialites, politicians, golfers, horsemen, lunchtime cronies at Akron's Mayflower Club—there was none so close as Edwin J. Thomas. This was a bluff, cordial man; stubbornly independent; forgiving of the human race for its cussedness and inconsistencies; and closer to Knight than any blood relative.

Their relationship had grown from deep roots in Akron, common status and values, and the mutual regard of two strong individuals. They played golf frequently, even though Knight could be irascible on a golf course—fiercely competitive, maddeningly precise about starting times, quick to criticize—and still managed to be friends. They socialized. They talked almost every day, by telephone if not in person, often long-distance.

Baldish and square-set, with bright crinkly eyes and pink cheeks, Eddie Thomas was four years younger than the publisher. Born to a blue-collar family in East Akron, he had delivered the old *Beacon* newspaper as a schoolboy. His life followed the pattern of the poor boy who gained wealth and power by his own abilities, going to work as a teenage clerk with Goodyear Tire and Rubber Company and rising to be chairman of the board before his retirement in 1964. Despite their wealth, Thomas and his wife, Mildred, lived in the same frame house in West Akron for over fifty years. Of Jack Knight, he would say approvingly, "Brilliant mind. You can always learn from the fellow."

It nettled him that the newspaperman, a methodical maker of lists and pursuer of squared business accounts, seemed careless about his personal spending money and kept a disorderly desk. Visiting Knight's Akron office, Thomas asked offhandedly, "Jack, how much have you got in your checking account?"

The publisher picked up the phone to his secretary. "Mrs. Brenner, how much is in my checking account?"

"A little over one million dollars, Mr. Knight," Lillian Brenner replied.

Thomas snorted. "Dummy. You don't draw a dime of interest on that. Why not keep what you need in there and invest the rest?"

Knight scowled. "I can't be bothered with those details."

The checking account remained unchanged.

On another office occasion, Thomas surveyed with distaste the newspaperman's desk with its litter of books, clippings, pencils, personal notes, a dirty ashtray, news articles. "How do you find anything?"

"I can find what I want."

"Sure. You depend on your secretary. One of these days, she won't be here and you'll be up the creek. Why don't you clean up this mess?"

Two weeks later, Knight called Thomas at home. "Come down to my office; I've got something to show you."

The place was shining, the books and papers in their places, desk cleaned and tidy. Knight beamed at his friend.

"What do you think?"

"Wonderful. I just hope it stays this way."

"It will," Knight assured him.

It didn't.

When friends began planning a celebration to mark John S. Knight's half-century in the newspaper business shortly after his seventieth birthday, Eddie Thomas was the natural point man. Four hundred turned out in Akron on November 16, 1964, to honor the publisher with speeches, a roast beef banquet, and a dance band.

He was at the peak of his career. Knight newspapers had won fourteen Pulitzer Prizes. He himself had collected enough awards and honorary degrees—three already as a Doctor of Laws—to stuff a closet. Now, in the tradition of the old-fashioned testimonial dinner, praise fell on him like rain, led by Thomas's own assessment. "John Knight is urbane, a man of learning and wit, of great charm and manner. He is no mean opponent, nor could anyone wish for a stauncher ally." Thomas saw his friend as a man stimulated by opposing views and a believer in his own adage, "There are no insuperable barriers to success."

Miami Herald editor Don Shoemaker timed a column for the event, saying of his boss, "He is independent to the point of unpredictability." "A newspaperman's newspaperman," chorused an editorial in the *Wilkes-Barre* [Pennsylvania] *Times-Leader.* From Washington there arrived a folded American flag that had flown over the White House and a handwritten message: "You have only one President and one editor. Be nice to him. Lyndon."

Knight rose to his feet. "We are so frequently misunderstood or misjudged," he said, "given too much credit for our accomplishments but only a limited understanding of our failures. . . ."

It was a lengthy speech, filled with remembrances of the turbulent decades through which he had passed, the people he had known, the lessons he had learned. "Our lives are enriched by the degree that we can purge ourselves of hatreds which consume . . . only our own minds and hearts. I am humbly grateful to bask for an evening in the warming rays of your friendship."

He doted on the boy, worried about his school performance, his interests. It was uncharacteristic of Knight, but there it was. At age nineteen, John S. Knight III began his final year at Lawrence-ville, with his grandfather's reading another report from the headmaster: "John has said to me that he is lazy. I think he needs self-confidence and should not be so angry with himself for re-ceiving a poor grade once in a while. The fact that he is learning is most important. He lets emotions get in the way of his work more often than he should."

Johnny suffered a torn ligament playing lacrosse, and Jack Knight called New York and Philadelphia to find the best ortho-pedic men obtainable. He was miffed when Dorothy chose a doctor in Columbus, Georgia, and wrote her a testy note: "It is useless to try to give advice because people seem to enjoy learn-ing the hard way." By spring 1963, Johnny was looking forward to finding a summer job. He went to work at the *Charlotte News* as a rookie reporter, getting his first byline on a story about widespread thefts of domestic pets. After a month, editor Brodie S. Griffith sent a complimentary note to Jack Knight. "Johnny shows self-reliance and the manners and bearing of a gentle-man."

Whatever he did in life, the grandson of John S. Knight seemed to be watched, graded, assessed.

One of the most perceptive analyses would come a year later from a former member of the Lawrenceville faculty, John J. Fatum, who had left the school to take a major's commission in the army. By then, the headmaster had noted traces of "arro-gance" in the young man's makeup. This troubled Fatum.

"Johnny has great drive, ambition and personal courage," the major insisted.

I was concerned about the opinion of arrogance. Why does the problem exist and what can each of us do to improve the situation? This has cropped up only since he left the influence of a down-to-earth mother.

You are a lucky man, Mr. Knight. Johnny worships the ground you walk on. I suggest that you take a posi-tive approach. Recognize his numerous academic, athletic and extracurricular accomplishments and tem-

*per constructive criticism by your faith in him as an in-
dividual.*

*Johnny has tremendous potential. He craves ap-
proval. If he can't draw strength and respect from us,
where is he to turn?*

It was a question that was to come back, years later, to haunt all
concerned.

The battle of Detroit went on. More strikes rocked the *Free
Press* and the *News,* and by mid-July 1964 the newspapers were
again shut down, this time by the pressmen and the Paper and
Plate Handlers' Union. It was a complicated business, as Lee
Hills explained to employees. "The *Free Press* and the
News have reached agreements with all the other newspaper
crafts. Between the two papers, we have settled 16 different con-
tracts. . . ."

Knight, though taking no part in collective bargaining, was
blunt-spoken about recalcitrant unions.

> The problem of every newspaper is to make enough
> money to put out a first-rate product and still stay in
> business. Modern equipment, efficiently utilized, could
> cut costs, improve earnings and stabilize the newspa-
> per's economic condition. And so it would were it not for
> . . . the unprogressive attitude of printing trades unions.
> They still cling to 1890s ideas in an age of space. The net
> effect of this backward thinking has been to wipe out the
> cost-saving efficiency of new methods and put more
> newspapers out of business.

Labor strategists attempted to pressure Knight in Detroit by
accusing him of union-busting in Miami. There, both the *Miami
Herald* and the Cox-owned *Miami Daily News* had defied work
stoppages to the point of ousting troublemaking unions from
their operations. As James L. Knight put it, "The unions eliminated themselves."

The *Miami Daily News,* publishing daily and Sunday, continued a chronic downslide. Owner James Cox, who did well in

Atlanta and Dayton, told Knight he had lost $25 million in ten years in Miami. To avoid collapse, Cox was eager to make a deal. If the *Herald* would take over the printing, circulation, advertising, and business operations under a contract arrangement, the *News* would scrap its Sunday paper. However, the *News* would remain separately owned and editorially independent. Such arrangements had become commonplace in U.S. cities. The Knights agreed.

The *News* abandoned its separate plant on the Miami River and moved its newsroom into the sixth floor of the new Herald building, as a tenant.

The *Herald* thus had the Miami Sunday market all to itself. Knight would contend in years to come that he himself had opposed the idea of keeping the *News* alive. "I thought it was a bad deal for us. But my brother, Jim, is a born monopolist. I said, 'Hell, they're starving to death now. . . .' We should have let them turn slowly in the wind."

For all the troubles in Miami and Detroit, Knight's *Beacon Journal* in Akron, a union shop since the nineteenth century, continued to operate remarkably free of strife. In reporting on the Detroit troubles, however, *Time* blamed "antiunion" sentiment among the publishers, especially John S. Knight. "It is Knight's avowed policy," *Time* told its readers, "to de-unionize his plants." Knight lashed back, calling the *Time* report "a mischievous melange of misusage and misinformation," adding that the magazine's editors seemed unaware that the Luce publications, including *Time*, were published in an open-shop plant. "Such venom-venting reportage is not unusual at *Time*. Facts mean nothing where editorial policy is involved. They call this 'keeping men informed.' I call it vicious distortion of the truth."

The presidential election campaign wore through the summer and into fall. The issues were not biting, not clear-cut, not even especially interesting.

Knight had never supported a Democrat for president. And yet this time, with the campaign's pitting Republican Barry Goldwater's often-puzzling rhetoric and militant conservatism against Lyndon B. Johnson's undisguised extension of the New

Deal—but with fiscally conservative undertones—Knight wrestled with the dimensions of his own position.

Democrat Johnson was not a towering intellect, but as a glad-handing politician he knew no peer. Press aide Bill Moyers described the phenomenon. "You can't understand the campaign if you haven't watched Johnson rise from the back seat of a car at dusk on a wide boulevard in Phoenix and bring the whole caravan to a screeching halt. How he took a bullhorn and verbally caressed six spectators on a street corner until he had them in the palm of his hand."

Wrote Republican John S. Knight in his "Notebook," "My judgment is that Johnson will be a strong president." It was not yet a direct endorsement, but it was the next best thing. Still, the formidable Texan wanted more.

Word filtered in from Washington that the president planned a whirlwind Ohio visit with a speech at the University of Akron. On the afternoon preceding his arrival, a Tuesday in October, the *Beacon Journal* editorially endorsed the Johnson-Humphrey ticket. On Wednesday, executive editor Ben Maidenburg had a strong hunch. He advised his boss not to go to lunch.

At 1:30 P.M., the city desk phone rang and a voice said, "This is the Akron White House."

"The Akron what?" said an assistant city editor.

"The president is on his way to the *Beacon Journal*. Would you please have your editor ready to meet him?"

Moments later the presidential motorcade arrived at the newspaper building, sirens wailing. Johnson pushed through the brass double doors and strode to the small lobby elevator trailed by his wife, Lady Bird, and Secret Service guards. A horde of White House press corps people went thundering up the marble steps to the third-floor newsroom.

Upstairs, a mob of *Beacon Journal* staff gathered, with more coming from the back shop. As the elevator door opened, the staff burst into applause. Johnson ambled around the newsroom, grinning and shaking hands. Then he held up his hand and the hubbub stilled. "I'm an hour late and a dollar short, but I do so much 'preciate the way you good citizens have received Miz Johnson and me."

Knight emerged to greet the president, shook hands, and escorted Johnson back to his corner office. The beginning of a Sunday "Notebook" column was in the publisher's typewriter.

"What are you writing?" Johnson asked.

"Just one man's opinion," said Knight.

"I hope it's favorable."

Maidenburg shooed out the staff and left the two men in private for a few minutes. When Knight and Johnson appeared again, the president carried a copy of the latest edition of the *Beacon Journal* under his arm. In the lobby, he handed Knight a gold LBJ lapel pin. Then he moved out, acknowledged the cheers of several hundred people gathered in the street, folded into his limousine, and was off.

He could be seen opening the paper and turning to the editorial page.

Jack Knight returned to his typewriter and wrote, "The overriding question is, which man would you rather see entrusted with the awesome decisions which come to the President's desk? My choice is Lyndon B. Johnson."

Nearly everybody else in a position to write agreed with him. But the Johnson groundswell at the *Beacon Journal* was not unanimous. Editorial writer Tom Horner saw things differently. A two-column, full-page advertisement stating his view, paid for by the Summit County Republican Executive Committee, was published in the paper on October 28. It began:

> I shall vote for Barry Goldwater.
>
> For the first time in the more than twenty-one years I have worked for the *Beacon Journal,* I am in disagreement with my boss over a major political endorsement. I find it difficult to disagree with Mr. Knight because I respect his judgment and recognize his ability to appraise the qualities of men.
>
> I also find myself a minority of one among my editorial colleagues.
>
> It is at Mr. Knight's suggestion that I write this.
>
> I believe that the election of Mr. Johnson will accelerate the already dangerous slide toward reduction

of the voice of the American people in their government. . . .

On election day, November 3, Johnson and Humphrey over-whelmed Barry Goldwater and Congressman William E. Miller, capturing 486 electoral votes to the Republicans' 52.

It was a kind of political gallows humor in the locker room of the Portage Club. "Hey Jack, you heard the one about the young lady who said, 'They warned me if I voted for Goldwater we'd be fighting a war in six months. I did. And we were.' Get it? Ha, ha."

Knight responded with a wintry smile.

Even as the new year opened, the trouble deepened. "South Vietnam continues to present an almost insoluble problem," he wrote. "We seem unable to decide whether we are there to save that unfortunate country or to serve our own interests."

There were many other issues, of course, and he explored them energetically. The press was filled with a daily diet of rape, murder, accident, international conflict, mental illness, juvenile delinquency, imbalance of trade, the United Nations, civil rights, the John Birch Society. Every writer wanted to be a pundit. "There is precious little in our newspapers to make a man laugh," Knight concluded. "And he wants to, you know." Briefly, then, he tried his hand at lightening the mood. "Two fleas stood at the bottom of a tall hill. One flea said to the other, 'Are you going to walk up, or wait for a dog?'

"Well, anyhow, it's short."

Some readers said that his weekly column was getting better. Criminal defense lawyers were not among them. The bar contended that the news media jeopardized the rights of accused persons to fair trial. Lawyers in Philadelphia favored denying newsmen access to police crime reports. Others sought to prohibit publication of a suspect's criminal record or descriptions of loot and weapons used in crimes. A former Supreme Court justice, Thomas D. McBride, told members of the Pennsylvania Bar: "Freedom of the press is the right to print, not to gather, news." Knight was outraged. Where the press was shackled, he insisted, the people were kept in ignorance; without newspapers, "the criminal scum and crooked officeholders would enjoy even greater freedom to rob, kill and loot the public treasury. It is the shady criminal lawyers, working in collusion with sleazy law enforcement officials, who make mockery of justice."

Whatever issue caught his momentary attention, his thoughts always returned to the crucial tragedy, Vietnam. He considered the president manipulated by war hawks. "Lyndon Johnson thrives on popularity, and too many people hope to use him for their own purposes." By February 1965, U.S. forces in Vietnam had grown to 23,000 men and U.S. cost to $2 million a day. By March this would double, by June redouble. Knight had been eleven years on the issue. Now, as the war gathered momentum, in 1965, his writing returned to it constantly:

> February 14—Our reasons for staying in Vietnam have never been explained to the American people.
>
> March 7—Now that President Johnson has decided to get tough in Vietnam, a good many "thought leaders" are cheering like mad for more blood and guts. This country has made a frightful mistake.
>
> April 4—Former Vice President Richard Nixon has said, "If the United States gives up on Vietnam, the Pacific will become a Red sea." This is nonsense. The tragedy of Vietnam is that we need never have become involved there in the first place.
>
> June 6—Each day's news is the same. More Americans are dying in jungle combat. Now that the light of truth finally pierces the fog of our misconceptions, we find ourselves committed to a bloody struggle.
>
> August 22—Our claim that we are in South Vietnam to maintain the freedom of the people is a dubious premise. We are there in our own self-interest, to arrest communism in Southeast Asia. . . .

Johnny graduated from Lawrenceville with excellent grades. Without doubt, he had talent. The question was, where would he go from here. Jack Knight was lukewarm about his own alma mater, Cornell. "An excellent university scholastically," he told the boy. "Whether you like the types you meet at Cornell is another question." The fact was, Johnny III preferred a school with higher status. Princeton and Yale both would admit him. His heart was set on Harvard, but Harvard put him on its waiting list.

The grandfather expressed his chagrin to friends. Grumbled Eddie Thomas, "Why should Harvard be so damned stupid and stuck up?" C. C. ("Gibby") Gibson, a Harvard graduate and Goodyear vice president, offered to intercede with a former classmate serving as assistant to Harvard president Nathan Marsh Pusey.

Months went by. Gibson was curious. "Well, what happened?"

"Oh," Knight said offhandedly, "he was accepted."

Grandfather and grandson differed on money.

Johnny professed to worry about finances. He felt obliged to his mother for her past sacrifices in getting him through secondary school. He told Knight he wanted to be financially independent and to make stock investments. It was all very idealistic. When he finished at Lawrenceville, Knight offered him $2,500 worth of stock as a present. But now he preferred cash. Knight gave him a check. "Thanks," Johnny said. "This will go a long way toward paying for my new car."

"What car?"

"I've ordered a Corvette."

"Rather expensive, don't you think?"

Johnny was adamant. Knight expressed his frustrations to Major Fatum. "I am not quite sure what kind of reception a freshman gets when he arrives on campus with a Corvette." A year later, Knight was still miffed. When Johnny called him long-distance, collect, he replied peevishly, "Anyone who can afford to drive a Corvette ought to be able to pay for a telephone call."

In summer 1965, Johnny Knight served as an intern reporter with the *Miami Herald.* He worked hard at being liked by older members of the staff. This was a larger and more sophisticated operation than the *Charlotte News* had been earlier. Johnny wrote to his grandfather:

> *Ever since I began working at the* Herald *I have felt a little inferior because those infernal IBM machines were whirring away downstairs, calculating how many lines I wrote, how many I should write in the future and,*

worst of all, paying me. So I have been spending after hours learning how to control them. Don't be upset if my salary is raised to the tenth power.

Harvard was to his liking. Deep into his second semester Johnny averaged three hours a night in the library and kept his grandfather informed by letter. His new history professor was Crane Brinton. "His lectures are interesting and amusing. Learning the history of the French Revolution under his tutelage should be quite an experience."

Torn between a trip to Europe and another summer on a newspaper, he sought Jack Knight's advice. Johnny knew that he was different from other hired hands and wondered whether it would be better to work on some other paper. "I believe that I would be much less favored and less partially evaluated. In Charlotte, I would have been naive not to notice the preferential treatment." The elder Knight suggested another summer at the *Miami Herald*. Johnny swallowed his disappointment. The tone of his letters seemed to seek approval and affection: "I was much impressed by the last two Notebooks. The one on Vietnam was one of the clearest statements on the subject that I have read, although I am in disagreement with your ultimate conclusion that the United States cannot win in Southeast Asia."

His grandfather's reply was a defensive rebuff. "I do not seek to win agreement but simply to be sufficiently provocative to create a climate for discussion."

It was the tone of a gruff old man impatient with schoolboy logic.

With advancing age, he was no less a hard man to know. There was always a distance between Knight and the rest of the world, including those with whom he worked. Columnist Polly Paffilas of the *Beacon Journal* found him intimidating. She would write years later:

One morning, tardy for work, I raced through the front door of the *Beacon Journal* carrying a paper cup full of hot coffee, skidded into the elevator—and into Mr.

Knight. He tipped his hat and intoned, "Good morning."

"Morning, sir. I'm a little late. I missed the bus," I
explained, as the leaking cup dripped coffee onto his
polished shoes. I wanted to die before the elevator
reached the third floor.

"You should get up earlier," he advised me. "Give
yourself plenty of time to get organized, like I do."

"Oh? How's that?"

"Well, the butler wakes me at seven o'clock. I
shower and get dressed. By this time the cook has breakfast prepared and Mrs. Knight and I sit down to a leisurely meal. At eight-fifty, the maid calls for my driver
and car and, you see, here I am. On time."

"Yes, sir."

After what seemed a week, the elevator door
opened on the newsroom floor. With an index finger,
Mr. Knight patted my hand (not the one holding the wet
coffee cup) and smiled. "Remember what I told you. Get
organized."

At the *Beacon Journal,* Knight had a reputation as a stickler for
reporting the news, even to the discomforture of his friends at
the Portage Country Club.

A local trial brought out untidy goings-on among some prominent Akronites. Knight strode over to the city desk, rubbing his
hands and chuckling over a phone conversation he had just had
with a country club member.

"Mrs. So-and-so is madder than hell," he announced. "She
said, 'Jack, I think it's disgraceful to put all those nasty things in
the paper. When are you going to stop printing those horrible
stories?'

"I told her, 'We'll stop printing those horrible stories when
people stop doing those horrible things.'"

In February 1965, Knight Newspapers acquired another southern property, the *Tallahassee Democrat.* It was a venerable
paper, founded in 1905 as the staunchly conservative voice of the

Florida state capital and controlled for thirty-six years by Colonel Lloyd C. Grissom and, after his death, by his widow.

Knight was unimpressed with the *Democrat*'s journalistic and editorial philosophy, which he regarded as behind the times. However, the potential for both the paper and its growing community was enormous. He was to have some lively exchanges with Malcolm Johnson, the *Democrat*'s longtime editor and an astute writer accustomed to doing things his own way.

The publisher himself harbored streaks of conservatism, of course, and had a Victorian distaste for gross language in print. After reading a batch of his newspapers one day, he sent out a memo to all editors. "For some time I have been concerned over the prevailing use of the word 'rape' in stories and headlines. It seems especially inappropriate since we have 'Newspapers in Classrooms' projects. How does one explain this word to a young child?"

In response, Malcolm Johnson sent him a tearsheet of an Ann Landers column containing the objectionable word. "Such stuff comes at us from all directions," Johnson complained. "We have to keep constantly alert for it."

Knight was unswayed. "Editors are supposed to edit. There is no reason to use what you consider to be objectionable material from any source."

Not long afterward, the *Miami Herald* came out with a jarring front-page story by two-time Pulitzer Prize–winning reporter Gene Miller. Local Circuit Judge Paul Baker charged that Florida's flamboyant Governor Claude Kirk tried to pressure him on a pending case. The judge quoted Kirk as saying, "They may impeach my ass, but you'll go down with me."

"New milestones in journalism," quipped a newsroom wag.

But from Akron there came a marked tearsheet and comment in Knight's bold red scribble: "A bit gamey, don't you think?"

One of the penalties of living long was seeing people die—friends, loved ones, people you admired.

He was stirred by the death in early 1965 of Winston Churchill, recalling in his "Notebook," "I first met Churchill in the grim days when London was under heavy attack from Nazi bombers." Knight had dined with the prime minister in the company of Lord Beaverbrook and Brendan Bracken.

Immediately after the war, in 1946, Churchill had visited Miami. At a Surf Club reception, Knight remembered, the British statesman was sipping a drink when a worshipful dowager fluttered to his side. "I wonder, Mr. Churchill, if I might have a hair from your head to preserve for posterity?" Churchill scowled, his nearly bald pate shining. "No, madame, you can see that I haven't a single hair to spare, not even for posterity." The lady retreated in confusion.

Churchill was entertained at a private dinner attended by Governor James Cox, owner of the *Miami Daily News*, along with Knight and others. Cox, who had been the unsuccessful Democratic presidential candidate in 1920, had a fondness for Britain's prewar prime minister Neville Chamberlain.

"During coffee and brandy," Knight recalled in his column,

> Governor Cox inadvertently addressed Churchill as "Chamberlain." Winston blinked, but said nothing. A little later, Cox said: "Now, Chamberlain, about that speech of yours . . ."
>
> The sentence was never finished. The object of Cox's blunder turned red in the face. "Damn it man, my name isn't Chamberlain. It's Churchill!" The governor became most apologetic, explaining that he had been talking earlier about Chamberlain and had only the highest regard for them both.
>
> "That may be," snapped Churchill, "but you had bloody well better decide which of your loves is present, sir."
>
> After a brief, deathly silence, Churchill's wife Clementine offered a light remark that got things back on track. Churchill and Governor Cox parted amicably.

Churchill's drinking capacity was legendary, Knight reflected. Field Marshal Montgomery had prided himself on being a total abstainer, remarking, "I don't use alcohol or tobacco, and I'm one hundred per cent efficient." To which Churchill tartly replied, "I use both, and my efficiency is two hundred per cent."

The column inspired a flood of Churchill stories from Knight's readers. Among them was one from Johnny at Harvard: "Lady Astor and Churchill were in the midst of one of their heated public debates. Lady Astor became so incensed that she blurted, 'If you were my husband, sir, I would poison your coffee.' Churchill straightened. 'If you were my wife, madame, I'd drink it!' "

But for Knight a worse blow was the death of his mother. Her health had deteriorated rapidly in recent years, necessitating the care of a housekeeper and three nurses. Their birthdays were only two days apart, and family and friends had celebrated her ninety-fourth and Jack's seventieth. A violinist from Clara Knight's favorite Italian restaurant in Akron played her favorites—selections from *The King and I* and *Moulin Rouge* and the song "La Vie en Rose." She listened quietly, petite and vulnerable, hands folded in her lap. As always, a small framed motto was close beside her chair. To Jack, it typified his mother's buoyant outlook: "Youth is not a time of life, it is a state of mind. . . . Whether seventy or sixteen, there is in every being's heart the love of wonder and the sweet amazement of the stars." And now, on November 13, 1965, Clara Knight was the subject of the lead editorial of the *Beacon Journal:* "We mourn the death of a gracious lady. . . ."

They gathered to memorialize her—Clara's sons and grandchildren and other relatives and friends—and then made the slow drive to Rose Hill Cemetery. Jack Knight remembered a poem by Charles Kingsley that had been his mother's favorite. He stood at Rose Hill, amid all those other dear names engraved upon the stones—Charles Landon Knight, Katherine McLain Knight, John Shively Knight, Jr., Frank McLain Knight—while the poem, "A Farewell," was read aloud: "Do noble things, not dream them, all day long; / And so make Life, Death, and that For Ever / One grand sweet song."

The newsmagazines: sprightly, caustic, often cruel, they made his blood boil. Previously, it had been *Time,* accusing him of antiunion sentiment during a *Free Press* strike that dragged on for 134 days. Now it was *Newsweek,* unleashing a piece headlined WHAT'S WRONG WITH THE PRESS? and answering the question in an article of barely cloaked editorializing, "It's fat but smug and, of all things, outdated."

In half a dozen pages the magazine flayed newspapers for falling behind the times, "technologically, as employers and— most damningly—in the professional tasks of writing and editing the news." It scoffed at their "familiar diet of police news, politics, puffery, such classic exposé targets as nursing homes, mental hospitals and welfare departments." The press had poor labor-management relations, *Newsweek* added, and most of the nation's 1,700 dailies suffered from Old Guard complacency, their management blind to the faults.

Jack Knight roared back, "Self-righteous screed!" and noted that *Newsweek*'s dim view of the press apparently was not shared by newspaper buyers, all 60.4 million of them. Technology? Newspapers spent hundreds of millions annually on research and equipment. Investigative reporting reached new heights every year. "This blanket indictment of the press is in itself shoddy journalism, because it simply isn't true." He widened his counter-attack.

> Both *Time* and *Newsweek* favor the rumor story, the one that can't quite be pinpointed or documented but yet contains enough shreds of truth to sound convincing. The editorial concept of these publications is to deni-grate, scorn and ridicule. All of this makes sprightly and interesting reading, but it is not responsible journalism.

Clara Knight's will provided some improved cash flow for her grandchildren and great-grandchildren. Both Johnny and Landon benefited from this, the former receiving proceeds from a trust fund.

In summer 1966, at age twenty-one, Johnny got his wish for a leisurely period of travel in Europe, including a quick visit to Oxford at his grandfather's suggestion. By September he was back at Harvard beginning his third year and thinking of financial stability. "I want above all to have complete financial independence." He was selling his Corvette with the intention of buying something more practical "now that the speed and flash have stopped flowing through my veins." What investment advice could his grandfather give him?

Knight was pleased by this apparent maturing. He sent his grandson a check for $2,295, the first installment under terms of Clara's will. Years before he had given Landon and Beryl's daughter, Rita, bank stocks and other securities from time to time, only to see them sell the investments to meet current expenses. "There are many excellent buys on the stock market today," Knight observed.

My theory on investments is that you buy good stocks and keep them. The history of good securities is they never miss dividends and always rise over a span of time. Avoid short-term transactions; you have plenty of time to let any securities you purchase grow with the country. This is the history of all successful investors with the exception of speculators who try to outguess the market, a difficult task at best.

By the following spring, Johnny saw the approach of another summer with mixed feelings. He was almost twenty-two and completing his third year at Harvard on the dean's list. It seemed that he had spent all his life in school, and most of the recent years working toward a career that others had chosen for him. Corporate people were always watching him, evaluating him, speculating on his future. But did he really wish to be a newspaperman, following his grandfather and great-grandfather and conforming to corporate regimentation, knowing that someday he might run the business? Steeped in classroom ideals, heavy on art and the humanities, at a time when college campuses were rebelling against traditional values and the Vietnam War, he expressed stirrings of independence.

Knight recognized the importance of what was happening and responded in kind, but from his own pragmatic perspective.

The question of a profession is indeed something to warrant a great deal of thought. I know that many young men have developed, as you put it, "a strong distaste for a regimented life, for a life oriented toward wealth and power." But many of them also enjoy both wealth and power while professing to be disturbed by them. As for corporate regimentation, business firms, including newspapers, are owned by shareholders who expect a profit. Such enterprises can't be run by disorganized individualists who disdain such mundane matters. Business requires a large measure of self-discipline. When I began, I also had reservations about working for my father. But I did it, and soon discovered how little I knew. A seven-day work week was not out of the ordinary as I tried to remedy my inadequacies. So don't get into business unless you have interest and enthusiasm and like the challenge.

fortune seemed a little more evenhanded in its treatment of John S. Knight. He grew closer to his brother and son. The few honors that he had not already won as a journalist and a human rights advocate were heaped on his shoulders.

Then, on Aug. 8, 1974, his wife of 42 years died after a long illness. And there was more to come.

The news of the death of John S. Knight Jr. in Germany was kept from Johnny's wife, the former Dorothy Wells of Columbus, Ga., until after the birth on April 13 — about two weeks later — of a boy who was named John S. Knight III.

Knight. Through the medium of the Editor's Notebook they discussed the campus violence of the '60s and the course of the Vietnam War. They exchanged letters frequently, played golf together and talked for hours.

Pa... J... n, managing editor of the D... N... said of young John, "He was r... he... ing guy. He knew who he ... he was an heir to a fortune and to a key job in the organization if he earned it. But he didn't take himself too seriously."

It was obvious that John S. Knight hoped through his grandson to see that...

John S. Knight III and lives, I can't think of change. I can't think of myself guilty.

"I am not going to start a new life."

He returned to Fl... down. So I am not ... nounced he would ma... beth) Augustus. They 1976, in the chapel of Sea at Bal Harbour Lifestyle editor of the ...

"AN AGE OF EXCESSES"

...pare for Harvard. He graduated from the latter cum laude in 1968 with a degree in history, then went on to study philosophy, politics and economics at Oxford University in England, where he earned a master of arts degree, with honors, in June 1970.

During high school and college he worked summer vacations at several Knight papers, including the Beacon Journal.

His first full-time newspaper job came at the Detroit Free Press in 1970. He gained experience in the circulation

center of Philadelphia, John S. Knight III was stabbed to death during a robbery by three men. There were homosexual overtones.

At the time, his grandfather was visiting at the home of Mr. and Mrs. Edwin C. Whiteheads of Greenwich, Conn. Mrs. Whiteheads is a daughter of the then Betty Augustus, widow of Cleveland millionaire Ellsworth H. Augustus. Knight and Mrs. Augustus had known each other for 35 years though a mutual interest in thoroughbreds and horse racing.

Mrs. Knight died ti... while watching the Ro... the LaGorce Island ho...

WHEN HE STEPP...

1976, his title became torial chairman of Kni... Knight-Ridder and the His decision to qui... by Thomas and others "The trouble wil... Knight's position," Tho... ly that they stay on to... hat the business can't...

The advancing years brought frustration. John S. Knight's hometown was dying at the heart, caught in the downwash of ruthless economics. The rubber plants had abandoned Akron's soaring costs and hostile unions, moving their blue-collar bonanzas to more hospitable economic climates of the South and West. Gone, now, the heady booms of old, the lovely money smell of burning rubber. Gone the Saturday night Main Street throngs with their silk shirts and whiskey breaths and ceaseless babble: gone back to West Virginia, or down to Memphis, or over to Pittsburgh, wherever a man could find work. The transformation was slow, spanning decades, but relentless.

In their place came a new kind of enterprise as local industry shifted from heavy production to high-tech research. Goodyear, for example, turned to aerospace technology. Well-paid white-collar scientists, researchers, and sales executives abandoned downtown for split-level homes and glass-walled office buildings in the suburbs. Incoming jet airliners bore flocks of black-suited sales executives from Japan and Europe and across the United States, toting briefcases and mohair overcoats, come to do high-tech business.

Downtown Akron was left a haunt of empty buildings and spreading blight. From his office window, Knight looked out on the crumbling hulk of the once-grand Mayflower Hotel, boarded up and deserted now, shelter for winos and drifters shambling the alleys. What could they do to reverse the trend? Surely private enterprise, Akron's creator, could now restore the city's dying heart? There was a flurry of meetings. Knight, Thomas, Walter Sammis, Ben Maidenburg, and others formed Citizens for Progress. They made speeches, reassuring each other. They sponsored luncheons. They persuaded leading local firms to take costly leases in a planned new complex of offices called Cascade Plaza and talked construction mogul John Galbreath into building it. The structures would be soaring and dramatic, on the site of the old Quaker Oats Mill, which had fallen into disuse with the defection of the oatmeal giant to Chicago.

Knight himself felt rejuvenated. There was nothing private enterprise could not achieve! On a sweltering August day in 1966, with the air conditioners gasping, he made a speech to launch the development phase of Cascade Plaza. The speech was heavy on boosterism. "The chief barriers to Akron's progress have been rugged individualism and lack of civic unity . . . magnificent development . . . rekindle the spirit and confidence . . ."

But one contrived spurt of reconstruction was not likely to bring downtown Akron back to life, and most people in Summit County knew it.

Knight kept to his customary hectic pace. From the Akron ceremony, he flew to Miami for a television interview with broadcaster Larry King on local station WTVJ. King, bespectacled and astute, was not one to tiptoe around controversy.

KING: How do you respond to this: That your *Miami Herald* is not a voice that tells the news but a paper that desires to make the news, to elect its people and to change to a form of government it likes?

KNIGHT: I think it's an unworthy assertion. . . . I feel that we should be for all things that are good for the community. But I'm not obligated to anyone, to any political party, to any bankers or politicians or leaders. I'm just Knight.

Q. How do you define, Mr. Knight, power as it relates to journalism?

A. That depends on the exercise of power. There's no question that politicians seek our endorsements. But I can't say that we've had any great score of wins. We win some, we lose some, and we all make mistakes. Our philosophy is to support the people we consider best qualified for public office.

Q. Why are newspapers decreasing around the country?

A. In a great many cities it's pure economics. They don't want to go out of business, nobody wants to sell to a competitor, and they don't like to give up the operation of the paper. But with increasing costs, there just aren't enough dollars for some of them to exist.

Q. What is your attitude toward trade unions?

A. Trade union leaders have been backward in their approach to technology. Automation is not new. Technical progress has been going on for a great many years. But suddenly, they see automation as a great evil.

Q. What has happened since you began writing in opposition to our position in Vietnam? Your views are quoted by people who walk on the street with signs. Have old friends turned on you in shock?

A. I don't have friends in the political sense. That is, I have no philosophical friends. Of course I have friends, and I might dine with them, but I've always tried to be fiercely independent. I study and analyze and try to write what I believe.

He had devised, through experience and thinking, his own philosophy about war and peace and the human condition. He had

had no love for Franklin D. Roosevelt, had abhorred the New Deal and all it stood for; yet an observation from Eleanor Roosevelt, in a letter to her husband written long ago, was among his keepsakes: "All human beings have needs and temptations and stresses," she had written. "Men and women who live together through long years get to know one another's failings; but they also come to know what is worthy of respect and admiration in those they live with, and in themselves."

He had met Mrs. Roosevelt only three times, and yet each was memorable. Now, on the day after Christmas 1966, he was the recipient of the Eleanor Roosevelt–Israel Humanities Award in the name of peace and brotherhood. He was extolled as "a man who lives by the values dear to people of all faiths." Knight had to admit, however, that this was often more goal than reality. "I have tried to substitute understanding for anger," he said, "to avoid prejudice, and to reason rather than insist." But these were demanding standards, and the search for truth never-ending. For example, in reporting a speech by Mrs. Roosevelt at Akron in 1937, he had drawn from her a gentle note of rebuke. "You are not telling all of the facts, any more perhaps than I covered every item," she had written. "But then when the time comes that nobody twists the facts, and when everyone has the space and time to cover every detail, then I suppose we will be less confused."

Communication was the essence of things, he now reminded his audience; people who could communicate had a way of resolving problems and even avoiding wars. For what was war but the ultimate breakdown in communication? "Conflict too often precedes communication rather than follows it. So it must be the job of thoughtful people to recognize that where there is room to talk, there is also room to avoid war as a substitute."

He turned seventy-three. By rights, a man should be taking his ease. Eddie Thomas was forever carping about this: "Damn it, you need to start pulling out, make room for younger men. Have you got your successor in mind?"

Knight was not overjoyed with the idea, but Thomas was right. The canny old Goodyear man had sound judgment. For this reason, and to break up the "compact majority" even within

Knight Newspapers, Knight decided to bring him on as a director of the company, the first outsider to become so involved.

Thomas did not leap at the invitation. "Jack, I respect you greatly but we don't always agree. Maybe we'd better leave things as they are."

"I want somebody from outside who'll speak his piece," Knight insisted.

"You might not like what I have to say."

"Maybe not."

Thomas accepted, provided that he could quit when he pleased. He started attending board meetings, sat in on discussions of company business, listened, said little. Finally, at a meeting in Miami, Chairman Knight turned to him. "Now that you've been around for a while, Eddie, what have you got to say about us?"

Thomas smiled ruefully. "If Goodyear operated its finances like you do, we'd have been out of business years ago." Eyebrows lifted around the room.

"You're so out-of-date I don't see how you get along at all," Thomas went on. "You need a full-time expert on financial affairs. Each newspaper handles its own earnings and bank deposits, but what's your overall cash estimate for the year ahead? Money in a company should all flow to one place; if you don't put it in central control, you're going to pay in the long run. You've gotten away with things so far because nothing has been too pressing."

"You don't think much of our methods, then?" Knight asked.

"You're not up-to-date, Jack."

"Are you finished?"

"No. You're also way behind in the way personnel is handled. Key management people should be trained, trained, and re-trained. Your hiring is haphazard. I don't see a lot of training to speak of, no planning about where your best people will go next and what you're going to build them into. It's a new ball game, Jack. Get somebody in here who knows finance, who knows personnel, put them in charge, let them organize."

"Is that all?"

"No. You've got a deficiency in selling. Our whole life at Goodyear was sales. If we lost a customer, we wanted to know why and what we had to do to keep him. You seem to have the attitude that people have got to read your newspapers. Well, they don't have to read them. I think you can do a better selling job, organize that end of it the same as you do anything else."

Knight smiled. "You certainly have been frank with us."

"You asked for my views."

Thomas was not exactly plowing new ground. Attention was already being given to restructuring company-level management. Professional personnel directors had been brought in at Detroit, Miami, and Charlotte. There were plans to hire on as a company consultant Byron Harless of Tampa, to set up strong recruitment, psychological testing, and leadership programs. Harless had developed his techniques as a wartime air corps psychologist putting together high-efficiency combat flight crews. Ironically, one of the rising young Knight executives, Alvah Chapman, Jr., had flown more than thirty combat missions as a bomber pilot over Europe. As general manager of the *Miami Herald,* Chapman had doubled the newspaper's business and demonstrated a strong grasp of finance.

Members of the executive committee privately applauded Thomas's audacity. As Lee Hills would recall years later, "Eddie egged Jack into modern management." Similarly, Thomas pressured Knight to relinquish authority gradually. "There comes a time," he insisted, "for old men to step down." And so at a 1967 spring board meeting in Miami, Knight handed over to brother Jim the titles of chairman and chief executive officer. Hills became company president and executive editor, while continuing as publisher of the *Detroit Free Press.* Chapman became vice president. Jack Knight, still the largest individual stockholder, kept the title of editorial chairman and chairman of the executive committee.

Knight Newspapers was drawing closer to the point of offering a public stock issue. The company was about to become big business. And John S. Knight's public notoriety was spreading more as a news analyst and editorialist than as a businessman.

The University of Arizona gave him its prestigious John Peter Zenger Award, named for the eighteenth-century American newspaperman tried for sedition in opposing governmental power and corruption. Zenger's exoneration, which followed a brilliant legal defense by Alexander Hamilton, had established truth as the historic test against libel. Knight titled his acceptance speech "To Speak One's Mind."

These were precarious times, he said. Americans were being deceived by their own government about the nation's entanglement in Southeast Asia. "The President forgets his responsibility to the people. It is one thing to hide vital facts which Hanoi, Peking or the Viet Cong don't know, and another thing entirely to misinform the public for no real security purpose." Newsmen daring to report truth about Vietnam courted disfavor from both the government of South Vietnam and the United States. And yet it behooved the press to report the developing crisis at all levels, Knight observed, and the task required continuing fortitude. He harked back to the words of political scientist and social philosopher Leo Rosten: "The purpose of life is not to be happy but to matter, to be productive . . . to have it make some difference that you lived at all." And so it had been with John Peter Zenger. "If not a happy man," Knight said, "at least he did matter. And it did make some difference that he lived at all."

Detroit festered in summer heat. Anger boiled in sprawling black neighborhoods where idle youths congregated on street corners, harangued by civil rights militants. Detroit's Mayor Cavanaugh spoke ominously of trouble. *Free Press* reporters wrote that ghetto stores charged higher prices for inferior goods than did similar businesses in white neighborhoods. Discontent built up like steam in a pressure cooker.

On July 23, 1967, rioting broke out and the first flaming Molotov cocktail smashed into a storefront. For days afterward, Detroit was a battleground of rushing street mobs, burning buildings and vehicles, riot-equipped police, national guardsmen, and sudden death. Forty-three people were killed.

The *Free Press* responded with daily and nightly coverage, capped with a detailed analysis of each death. One such probe, into the slaying of four alleged snipers at a motel, led to murder indictments against three policemen, but they were not convicted.

Feelings ran high on all sides. In Bogotá, Colombia, where he was spending part of his summer, John S. Knight III was less than impressed by what he read in the *Free Press*, especially in the initial days of trouble. In a letter to Lee Hills, he took to task an early editorial condemning the role of "hoodlums" in the riot. Young Knight noted irritably: " 'Hoodlums, whatever their color,' the editorial says, 'must be separated from society.' Unfortunately, the 'hoodlums' which this editorial so easily blames are already separated from society, and it is mandatory that we try to bring them back in, not further alienate them."

The assessment ran counter to the view of his grandfather, as expressed in a "Notebook" column. "Progress [in civil rights] is painfully slow," Jack Knight observed, "because the enormity of the task is overwhelming. A ghetto cannot be replaced overnight."

Ironically, the *Free Press* editorial arousing Johnny's ire had been written by the most politically liberal member of the staff, Mark Ethridge, Jr., recently returned from duty as a war correspondent in Vietnam. Ethridge's later analysis of conditions spawning the riots would acknowledge the alienation of street blacks, adding, "The frustrated and disenchanted must be given new hope."

In the mind of John S. Knight, the fires of Detroit and the fires of Vietnam burned from similar fuels, for this was a nation beset by both political and social turmoil. "We are living in an age of excesses. Hopefully, we shall find a better way." But not immediately, not without further agonies. The war, after all, served as a catalyst of violence. For the first time in history, all the bloody ugliness of battle came nightly to the nation's TV screens. By example it helped ignite the added tinderboxes of ideological conflict, race conflict, youthful rebellion, and defiance of middle-class values.

Vietnam was a crucible, and he beheld the nation tumbling headlong into it. And yet "The American government would smother the voices of dissent in the flag of patriotism." So Knight, an Ohio Republican, social peer of pillars of conservatism, defended the ragged hordes of dissent, the hordes who smoked pot, listened to outrageous rock music, and wore the flag sewn on their tattered jeans.

"Jack's gone daft," they murmured at the Portage Country Club, but not to his face, nor in the presence of Eddie Thomas.

And yet Knight himself had not changed. At heart he was still one of them, still bristling at those who twitted "economic royalists" and "bastions of privilege." Toward them, he maintained a strange duality of feelings, part love and part disgust. A quotation from *Esquire* struck his fancy, and he typed it off and stuck it in his files: "It is, in short, an impregnably self-confident Establishment, tolerant of wayward ideas because it is indifferent to them. It is supremely sure of its virtues."

His columns defended dissent. They consistently and passionately opposed the Vietnam War. Those sifting through his output found ten pieces of more than ordinary interest and six of exceptional merit. These six each addressed America's tragic floundering in the deepening quagmire of Southeast Asia. And certain sentences flamed with special indignation.

"Either our government has no well-defined policy," he wrote, "or it stands guilty of lying to the people, or both." And "If the young people of today are different from those of us who accepted World War I without question, it is because they dare to examine the causes of war and its morality." And "World opinion . . . is almost universally opposed to what we are doing. In the long run, the Asians will shape their own destiny." And "The American people, who read of bribery, corruption and graft in the Saigon regime, can't understand why our young men are sacrificed to keep unscrupulous South Vietnamese politicians in power."

In late August, Knight was one of twenty-three Americans appointed by President Johnson to observe the national elections in South Vietnam. Their purpose was to help ensure that the vote be free and unrigged. As appointees gathered at the White House, Knight, the only protester selected, asked Johnson's assurance that he be allowed to write what he pleased. "You have my word on it," the president replied.

In Vietnam, Knight sought out opponents of the existing military regime, including the editor of an opposition newspaper shut down by the Saigon government. Such talks enhanced the publisher's skepticism. On election day, he was assigned to the ancient capital city of Hue. He was impressed that 83 percent of the electorate turned out despite Viet Cong threats of violence. Rival Generals Thieu and Ky retained power, but with only 35 percent of the vote. Knight saw significantly heavy support for peace candidate Truong Dinh Dzu and concluded, "This may be indicative of the yearnings of the South Vietnamese to cease hostilities."

He found South Vietnam a strange world "—a land of contrasts, of many faiths and customs, a land of terror largely inhabited by gentle, peace-loving people." The beleaguered republic was no larger than the state of Washington, its climate ranging from subtropical jungle to cold highlands. Saigon, the capital, was teeming and shabby, its traffic horrendous, its masses inscrutable. He visited outlying villages and farm areas—80 percent of the people worked the land—and was intrigued by the layers of shadow government under which Vietnamese peasants accommodated both the American-backed power of Saigon and the more immediate authority of the Viet Cong. Visiting a combat unit of the U.S. 18th Infantry Division, Knight asked how long security would last when the troops pulled out. "Not more than one night," an officer replied tersely. "When we leave, the Viet Cong come back." For all his talks with smiling Vietnamese, Knight confessed that he had no idea what they really thought. "Nor does anyone else, including the Americans who profess to know them best. They are polite people with impenetrable minds."

On January 29, 1968, Walker Stone, editor in chief of Scripps-Howard Newspapers, wrote a letter to John Hohenberg, secretary of the Pulitzer Prize board at Columbia University. Stone had only a passing acquaintance with John Knight but knew Lee Hills well. As he had expressed his position to Hills: "I don't know why I should care. Jack Knight is no particular friend of mine, just another man in our business who has been polite to me. But I have a great respect for his persistence and skill in our craft. And I think, goddamnit, he should get recognition." Stone nominated Knight for the Pulitzer Prize.

It wasn't the first such nomination. Knight himself had always hungered for journalism's most prestigious award. In 1937, he had personally submitted the *Akron Beacon Journal*'s antivigilante editorials from the Goodyear strike, without success. In 1948, he had sent to publisher Joseph Pulitzer a lengthy signed editorial blasting the civic apathy of Akron citizens. Pulitzer turned it down as "twice too long" for consideration. In the early 1960s, Walker Stone had joined with Vermont Royster, longtime editor of *The Wall Street Journal,* in nominating Knight for editorial excellence, unsuccessfully. In 1966, it was four "Notebook" columns on freedom of dissent, entered by Robert Lasch, editor of the *Detroit Free Press* editorial page. No luck there, either.

Pulitzer board members had several misgivings. Columnist Knight, for example, was his own publisher. He had served on the Pulitzer advisory board, and that association smacked of conflicting interest. Moreover, his works were signed, but technically should have been entered as columns rather than editorials. The articles on dissent and Vietnam, however, had built up a kind of admiring groundswell. For example, syndicated columnist Sydney Harris of the *Chicago Daily News* told Knight, "Your stuff on Vietnam is among the best editorial opinion being written today. I wish I had some influence with the Pulitzer committee."

Monday, May 6, 1968, was a quiet news day in Akron. A budget line on the Associated Press wire gave notice the annual Pulitzer Prize awards would be announced in the early afternoon. At the *Beacon Journal,* publisher Ben Maidenburg made a mental note. He knew that his boss was nominated again. Maidenburg set a great deal of store on strong local news, a point that Jack Knight endorsed, if not as enthusiastically. "It is our obligation to print a lot of local news, and we do this very well," he mused, "—but sometimes, I must confess, to the point where I feel it is boring."

The publisher, at age seventy-four, continued to give editors great local autonomy and insisted on calling the company a group rather than a chain. The Knight news and business formula continued to succeed. The newspapers' combined daily circulation in Detroit, Miami, Charlotte, Akron, and Tallahassee now neared 1.5 million. The Knights also had interests in a TV station, three radio stations, and three Florida weekly papers. Gross revenues had soared to $123 million in 1967, with an $8 million net profit, despite another prolonged strike against the *Free Press.* There was persistent talk of going public, even though Knight openly disliked the idea. Being listed on the stock exchange meant that the company would have to answer to stock analysts and investors and commit itself to a policy of constant expansion. The alternative, however, to remain private and be eaten alive by taxes, did not leave much of a choice.

The news came over the AP wire in the early afternoon. Maidenburg let out a whoop and rushed into Knight's office trailed by two dozen staff members. "You've won it!" But it was more than just Knight's victory. For the first time in history newspapers under single ownership had carried off three prizes, the *Free Press* staff for its coverage of the Detroit riots and the *Charlotte Observer* for an editorial cartoon by Eugene Gray Payne. Knight himself had been selected, noted the Pulitzer board, for "clearness of style, moral purpose, sound reasoning and power to influence public opinion . . . due account being taken of the whole volume of the editorial writer's work."

The nation's press gave the event due notice. "Very encouraging to aging editors," editorialized the *Memphis Commercial Appeal*, "and to those youngsters who have overlooked the challenges lately." *Atlanta Constitution* editor Eugene Patterson offered a personal reflection about Knight: "We took a trip to Vietnam last fall; he thought I was a hawk and I thought he was a dove. Before long I stood corrected. Knight wanted the facts. He rose early, worked late and came home with the clear notion of what he had seen." *Time* called him "blunt, crusty, but never rash. As a man who does not hesitate to speak his mind, Knight has made it a firm policy to let others speak theirs."

A few days later, an interoffice memo arrived on Knight's desk from one of the *Beacon Journal* editors.

> *Dear Mr. Knight: "Crusty" appears in* Webster's Seventh New Collegiate Dictionary *as a synonym under the word "bluff." Other synonyms are "blunt," "brusque," "curt" and "gruff," all generally meaning "abrupt and unceremonious in speech and manner" but connoting good-nature. The word "crusty" specifically suggests "a harsh or surly manner sometimes concealing an inner kindness."*

FACING THE WRATH

He had been born and schooled in the Victorian age, to manners and scruples. During John S. Knight's youth, the wild fling was a hayride, a forbidden nip of his father's whiskey, or an all-night high school debutante ball ending with the boys' going to morning class still in their tuxedos. Parents were respected, if not always obeyed. Elders spoke of good children's being seen but not heard. There was a code of gentility one lived by. But now, in the latter half of the 1960s, the old rules were flung aside and youth had a culture and life-style all its own, one which he regarded as alien and dangerous.

The baby boom of the 1950s had done it; all those dire predictions came to pass, and Knight's generation found itself the elders in a society where every other American was under twenty-five, and 40 percent were under seventeen. A new materialism ran rampant as commerce catered to teenagers who spent $25 billion a year. Knight glowered over the pages of his own newspapers, discussing such formerly taboo, or unheard-of, subjects as teenage pregnancy, drugs, rock music, fads, and gossip. "We're more popular than Jesus!" declared Beatle John Lennon, and one had to admit that he was probably right. Crime exploded. The new drug cult spawned heroin, marijuana, and LSD. Concluded the aging publisher, "It's a subculture running amok."

Johnny III helped to give him a handle on reality. The boy was well-mannered, clean, and cut his hair. As far as Knight knew, he avoided illicit drugs. On a sunny day in June 1968, Knight watched his grandson take a degree with honors at Harvard University and was moved to tears. Beside him sat Johnny's mother, Dorothy, visibly ill at ease. "I felt sorry for your mother," he wrote to Johnny afterward. "I could see she didn't want to go." He gave the graduate a check for $5,000.

And then Johnny was off for two years of postgraduate study at Wadham College, Oxford. The decision was his own, postponing a career. "You must be somewhat disappointed," he wrote his grandfather, "but I believe I am doing the right thing." Johnny quickly plunged into the life of cultured privilege, traveling on the Continent, developing a taste for fine art, studying economics and the political dynamics of Western Europe. "I am no natural at economics and, though it hurts my pride to admit it, I have concluded that the only way I am going to gain competence is through very hard work."

At Oxford, young Knight's moods were cyclical, his joys tempered by occasional depression and stomach complaints. He confessed to being intimidated by the social whirl. At a party staged by U.S. ambassador Walter Annenberg, for which Jack had arranged his invitation, Johnny met Princess Margaret, Lord Snowden, dancer Rudolf Nureyev, actor Mel Ferrer, and others. "I was a bit nervous, confronted with so much nobility at once." Jack Knight, the doting elder, financed him with generous gifts of stock shares and cash, including income from a $200,000 certificate of deposit in Johnny's name.

For all his graces, JSK III could be self-centered and snobbish. Even before Oxford, this had grated notably on Beryl, whose outlook was now affected by the onset of emphysema. Interfamily relationships were delicate, as Knight once attempted to explain to his grandson. "It seems that when the three of us gather, the chemistry goes wrong." He assured Johnny that Beryl loved and admired him. "But there is always a great deal of conversation about Johnny and not much else of consequence. When she bridles at some assertion which she is unprepared to accept, I naturally throw in with her. As you know, she is not well and I'm afraid the generation gap is showing."

Despite the intellectual splendors of his new life, Johnny brooded about the future. When would he begin to use all this education? His grandfather offered reassurance, "I can understand your eagerness to enter the real world," Knight wrote.

But it is a different world than the one populated by academics. Tougher to survive in, more competitive, often frustrating, sometimes rewarding and above all demanding the power to concentrate on a given task. It is not the world in which I was raised, for it has changed. I try to adapt without compromising my principles, even though they might be strained a bit when expediency dictates. My rationalization has been that I could yield a little to gain a lot.

Never did Jack Knight so openly express his inner thoughts and affection with another male family member. Johnny III had become an object of personal pride and identification; their relationship was on a level never attained with his own father, his brother Jim, or his surviving son, Landon. Conversations with the latter could be difficult and quarrelsome. Eddie Thomas, who admired Landon's quick mind and determination to cope with his physical handicaps, said the father and son were too much alike. Landon often felt rebuffed. When his father did write to him, the letters were brief, sometimes with numbered paragraphs.

And so Knight relished being able to communicate with Johnny. He persuaded himself that it was a knack that enabled him to reach the minds of young people generally; that he could, as he put it, "bridge the generation gap without falling into the chasm." Never mind that he could not express warmth to his own son. Johnny reinforced the illusion. "There has never been any generation gap between us, Granddad, precisely because honesty, reason and affection have prevailed."

Fine words. And yet there were abrasions between grandfather and grandson as well. Widespread youthful resentment of adult authority irked Knight. When Johnny expressed admiration for some of the social rebels among his peers, his grandfather snapped back:

> *Revolting against adult authority is another indication of immaturity, particularly in business and industry. How in hell could we run a profitable business, and pay huge taxes, if our key people were running in separate directions and ignoring authority? You often refer to seeking my advice, but how can I advise anyone who has already made up his mind?*

He was especially miffed when Johnny challenged his own cherished opinions. If this was inconsistent with his oft-spoken avowal of free expression, Knight seemed not to notice. One of their tartest exchanges developed over a seemingly innocuous issue: foreign government and economics. These were matters on which the publisher considered himself a practical expert, and which Johnny studied in theory at Oxford. The young idealist expressed admiration for the nations of Norway, Denmark, and Sweden; their systems struck him as more humane, less conducive to crime, than U.S. capitalism with its harsh pockets of poverty in the midst of plenty. It was a European point of view, nurtured in social liberalism and reinforced by young intellectuals with whom he hobnobbed in London, Paris, and Stockholm.

Knight responded with a fistful of clippings critical of how those countries—Norway, Denmark, Sweden—lagged economically, with less labor efficiency and lower returns on investment capital. There was nothing wrong, huffed the multimillionaire publisher, with the free enterprise system. He was unprepared for his grandson's reply.

"Your attitude seems to be 'let them eat cake,' or 'let them find jobs, get an education, work for a living, be ambitious and prosper if they are able,' " wrote the twenty-five-year-old with cheeky disdain. "You say there is nothing wrong with our present system when 20 per cent of the blacks are unemployed in Detroit, not because they are unable to work but because undiluted capitalism demands high unemployment to curb inflation. I say that either you are insulated from the problem or unaware of the basic economics involved." No economic system, he acknowledged, could flourish without hard work. And problems were endemic to all. "But, my God, how can you look at the madness raging about you in the United States, much of it directly the result of 'the system,' and then gloat over the problems in other countries which are so much more progressive, humane and civilized that they defy comparison?"

Knight was furious. His reply was banged out on the old typewriter with such vigor that it became a mess of strikeovers and rare misspellings:

Your letter hit me like a punch in the gut. Not only because of its cavalier tone but in the revelation that after five years of Lawrenceville, four at Harvard and two at Oxford, you are still basicly ignorant about economics. . . .

It was the classic generational conflict of the times, youth versus age, education versus experience, youthful enthusiasm versus old, stiffnecked pride.

For you to allege that I am "insulated from the problem" and "do not understand the plight of the poor" is absurd. You never lived through a depression such as the early 1930s and can speak from no actual knowledge. . . .

And how many times was this being said, in bitter defense, by fathers and grandfathers across a nation torn and contentious? As he let it all out in a massive gulp of outrage, Knight displayed the depths of his own contempt for the state of the system of which he was a part.

> *We are actually an undisciplined nation with a rotten welfare system and a selfish and greedy attitude toward the national welfare aided and abetted by politicians. . . . I resent your placing me in the "let 'em eat cake" category. The businessmen I admire have done a hell of a lot more for this country and the world than the "I hate business" crowd. One day perhaps you should try your hand at attempting to understand where the money comes from to pay for both the good and the nonsensical programs imposed upon the working capitalist.*

Something between them had been torn, perhaps never again to be completely repaired.

And so it was in the family of America itself, from the calamitous disorders of Chicago, Watts, and the ghetto of the Bronx to the fateful fusillade of National Guard rifles, splashing blood onto the green campus of Ohio's own Kent State University.

Something had been torn.

Johnson's tragedy mirrored the tragedy of all. The lanky Texan with his oozing charm and vast ego had dragged the nation into the bloodbath of Vietnam and had himself become a casualty. The terrible political wounds began to hemorrhage in the spring primaries of 1968, where the president suffered badly at the hands of Robert F. Kennedy and even Hubert Humphrey. By March 31 the nation's mood was agonizingly clear. And so Johnson addressed the nation, looking haggard and gray. "I shall not seek, and I will not accept, the nomination of my party for another term as your president."

Knight was not surprised. He felt that he understood Lyndon Johnson. "He is heartsick. One doubts that he could have envisioned the divisions and hatreds which have developed over the war."

As if the presidential stepping-down were the opening of yet another gigantic American tragedy, there followed a period of bloody chaos during which one week seemed worse than the next.

On April 4, civil rights leader Martin Luther King, Jr., was shot by a sniper as he stood on the balcony of a Memphis motel. As the coffin was borne to its grave in Georgia, black America erupted in a paroxysm of violence: 168 cities burning from 2,600 fires, 55,000 troops mustered, 21,000 people injured. "His powerful, resonant oratory," Knight reflected, "stirred the emotions even as it presented the irrefutable logic of his cause." Two months later, in the predawn of June 5 at Los Angeles's Ambassador Hotel, presidential front-runner Robert Kennedy fell with a bullet in his brain. At Knight's home in Akron, the telephone rang at 4:00 A.M. with an unidentified, hysterical woman on the line. "Bobby Kennedy has been given last rites. You and your damn newspapers are to blame for this! I hate you!" He wondered: Was America going insane?

Turmoil was the setting for that summer's national political conventions. He was in Miami Beach as Republicans nominated Richard Nixon and Spiro Agnew and south Florida's first race riots exploded on the other side of Biscayne Bay. A month later, Chicago braced for a storm when the Democrats convened in the Amphitheater. Anticipating hordes of street demonstrators, Mayor Richard J. Daley marshaled 11,500 police backed by the National Guard. Knight's Chicago-bound flight circled over O'Hare Airport. "Our landing is delayed by military aircraft bringing in troops," the captain announced. "Thank you for your patience."

As the Democrats nominated Hubert Humphrey and his running mate, Maine senator Edmund Muskie, mob hysteria erupted outside the convention hall. Police charged, clubbing and hauling away bodies while TV cameras beamed the shambles to 90 million stunned American viewers. Knight worked as a reporter alongside such newsmen as Edwin Lahey, Robert Boyd, and James Batten of the newspapers' Washington Bureau. He interviewed young protesters in nearby Grant Park. "A firm but fair police policy could have controlled the crowd," he concluded. "If these kids came to the rally skeptical of government, they left it completely disillusioned."

Knight saw the ensuing presidential campaign as a tepid anticlimax. Nixon's running mate, Agnew, castigated Vietnam dissenters as "effete, impudent snobs." Humphrey came off as a decent man but lackluster candidate. The voters' third option, Alabama governor George Wallace, railed at "pointy-headed liberals." The affair ended predictably with Nixon's triumph in November.

Knight liked the man, personally and politically. They had golfed together, lunched together, socialized. Knight felt that the new president-elect had matured beyond the "Tricky Dick" of old, and was piqued when readers persisted in writing to him of their continued dislike.

He hoped they would give the new occupant of the White House every opportunity to succeed.

Peyton Anderson, president and publisher of the Macon, Georgia, morning *Telegraph* and afternoon *News,* pondered retirement at age sixty-five. He had no wish to be an absentee owner of these papers, nor of his weekly *Union-Recorder* at the town of Milledgeville, thirty miles from Macon, for fear that trustees eventually would simply sell them to the highest bidder. Anderson wanted the right people to take over the papers now. And he did not have to look far.

Among the most vigorous of southern publishers were the Knights, owners of papers in Charlotte, Tallahassee, and Miami. The Macon publisher was acquainted with both brothers, but especially James. The Knights had the added advantage of being virtually hometown boys, whose great-grandfather, state senator William Knight, had been a landowner at Milledgeville even before the War Between the States, and whose father, Charles Landon Knight, was born there.

Peyton Anderson contacted James L. Knight with a proposition. Would the Knights be interested in buying his Georgia newspapers?

The Fourth Estate Golf League was one of Jack Knight's creations. It gave him a chance to enjoy the company of his top executives on a golf course. On a sparkling Tuesday afternoon in

February, some of them gathered with the publisher at the Country Club of Miami. Notably absent were regular players James Knight and Alvah Chapman.

"They won't be with us today," Jack Knight said with an air of mystery.

Play progressed into the late afternoon. When they finished, Knight signaled his men to gather around and looked at his watch.

"Gentlemen, it's five o'clock. I have an announcement. Jim and Alvah are in Macon, Georgia, at this moment announcing our purchase of the *Telegraph* and the *News* there."

The statement set off a flurry of discussion. Advertising chief Howard Grothe made the comment that was on everyone's mind. "Jack, I'm surprised you're not up there too."

Knight smiled ruefully. "Howard, when you've played in the major league, you don't have much interest in the minors."

His tone dismissed the Macon deal as unimportant.

Reaction was quick and to the point.

The following morning, *Miami Herald* executives met with Alvah Chapman for management discussions. James Knight, president of the paper, rarely attended. This time, he made an appearance. Jack was not present.

"Jim has something to say," Chapman announced.

The usually affable younger Knight seemed to suppress an inner fury. "I understand my brother made some remarks yesterday that may require some response." Jim offered a brief review of the Macon purchase, which now gave Knight Newspapers the fifth-largest group circulation in the nation. He expressed confidence in the Macon market, insisting that it was a good purchase, at the right price, with room for growth.

Someone mentioned Jack's absence. Jim smiled without mirth. "In a few years, he will be taking credit for Macon just as he's taken credit for Charlotte."

The room became very still.

A few weeks later, on March 3, Jack Knight dashed off a note to his grandson. "Dear Johnny: We bought the two papers in Macon as part of our acquisition program. I was not personally enthusiastic. The newspapers are pretty bad but make good money. I feel sure that we can improve them, but slowly. Local people resent sudden change. . . ."

The idea of going public had been growing. Government policies virtually forced a profitable company to expand. Jack had previously expressed his vexations to Stuffy Walters. "Under our peculiar tax laws, which prevent the accumulation of 'excessive reserves,' a company which might wish to remain small has either to pay this money out in dividends or acquire another property. Thus, the small get bigger. Strange reasoning, isn't it?" He discussed the idea of a public stock issue with heads of several corporations and was referred to an expert adviser, Sidney Weinberg, partner in a New York securities firm. Knight liked Weinberg, a quiet, competent man of unquestioned integrity, and had confidence in his advice. But did they really wish to be committed to public ownership? To do so meant surrendering the confidentiality of a privately held company to the scrutiny of stock analysts, the Securities and Exchange Commission (SEC), stockholders, and their lawyers.

Other entrepreneurs encouraged the move, among them financier Louis E. Wolfson of Jacksonville. "Going public can give you access to public funds for expansion and mergers," Wolfson wrote.

It offers a wider distribution of your stock and wider ownership. But there are disadvantages. Lack of clearcut interpretations of SEC regulations can be costly and embarrassing. Stockholders can generate constant harassment. Many take the position that they not only direct the company but also rule your personal life. . . .

Blake McDowell's law partners began gathering heretofore private data on Knight's personal holdings for submission to the SEC—and the world at large—in a Prospectus and Registration Statement: "Your income during 1965 from Knight Newspapers, Inc., and subsidiaries was $202,884. . . . You own 1,509,000 shares of Knight Newspapers, Inc., common stock and 90,100 preferred shares. . . ."

There was the matter of commitment to growth. Could they achieve expansion and still keep things in bounds? There had been talk of acquiring a trucking firm, a shopping center, additional real estate. In the communications field, they had considered such acquisition possibilities as Grosset & Dunlap, the book publishing company, and the *St. Petersburg Times* newspaper. Neither came about. At Alvah Chapman's urging, they were persistently wooing J. Howard Creekmore, aging publisher of the *Houston Chronicle.* Creekmore was not interested in selling, but the fruitless effort would continue for seven years.

Jack pondered all this in a letter to his brother. Their goal, he felt, was not merely growth for growth's sake. "I think we have objectives other than simply trying to see how big we can become. . . . Sometimes the lure of bigness tends to make newspaper publishers forget their prime responsibilities."

In the meantime, one was pressured to keep abreast of the twists of strategy. He was constantly dictating notes to the executive committee, developing ideas for yet another meeting:

What criteria are used to determine price per share in new issue? What about timing of KNI issue? Outline stage by stage procedures. How many "outside" directors? We have only one, E. J. Thomas, at present. What about dividend policy? Annual reports—how simple, or elaborate? Quarterly reports? Meetings with security analysts? Where and when? Note: Copies of Stock Exchange guidance on insider's information. . . .

Still the public's questions poured in, and still Knight evaded direct comment.

Feb. 7, 1969

Dear Tom:

    In reply to your letter of Feb. 3, I have been instructed as follows: "We don't know. But even if we were going to, the SEC has strict limitations and our counsel advises us not to discuss it."

Best, JSK.

☐   ☐

Finally, on March 20, 1969, they filed with the Securities and Exchange Commission for a proposed offering of 950,000 shares of common stock in Knight Newspapers, Inc. The Knight family retained 58.8 percent of outstanding common. On April 22, KNI began selling on the New York Stock Exchange. Company president Lee Hills bought the first 100 shares at $36.25 per share.

For Knight Newspapers, a new era had begun.

The search for additional properties widened.

Walter Annenberg had made a success in business that would have done his father proud. A tribute to Moe, the hard-luck immigrant whose dreams of respectable empire had collapsed with prison and a slow death of cancer in the early 1940s, was inscribed on a plaque in Walter's twelfth-floor office at the *Philadelphia Inquirer:* CAUSE MY WORKS ON EARTH TO REFLECT HONOR ON MY FATHER'S MEMORY.

There were those who saw his works as too much of a good thing. By mid-1969, Walter Hubert Annenberg ruled a communications empire in Philadelphia, with control of both the morning *Inquirer* and the afternoon *Daily News,* the top-ranked AM-FM radio station, the magazine *TV Guide,* plus a local television station and two others in the Pennsylvania market. He commanded incredible power, was a confidant of presidents, and that spring had been appointed as Richard Nixon's businessman ambassador to Great Britain. He gave millions to civic causes and charity. For all this, he was a mystery to the public. His appointment to the Court of St. James's was buried on inside pages in his own newspapers. Some people considered him a benefactor, others a small-minded despot swift to exact vengeance against a foe. Annenberg took a harshly candid view of himself. "Without the *Inquirer,* I'd be just another millionaire."

But now his empire was besieged. In the wake of a bitter gubernatorial campaign in which Annenberg's newspapers had helped to defeat Democratic candidate Milton Shapp, the communications mogul was accused of monopolizing the news in Philadelphia. Shapp asked the Federal Communications Commission not to renew Annenberg's license for WFIL-TV, charging that his concentrated news media power "has been used to poison the political life of Pennsylvania and to attack the fabric of the democratic process." Annenberg decided to sell some media holdings, starting with the *Inquirer.* Besides, the paper was in a run-down condition and needed costly modernization.

First right of purchase went to John S. Knight.

Knight's interest in the *Inquirer* extended back many years. He had asked about the paper's availability after Moe Annenberg's death in the summer of 1942, but a Philadelphia financial adviser had informed him: "The son Walter, as sole executor and trustee, will carry on the business, which . . . definitely is not for sale." Walter Annenberg's commitment to Knight had been given years later, in a casual conversation at a Gridiron dinner in Washington, D.C. "I am obligated as a gentleman to keep my word," he confided to other prospective buyers. What he did not say was that his longtime editor, E. A. Dimitman, had urged him to sell to Knight, whose papers he regarded as superior.

Jack Knight was dubious. Both the *Inquirer* and the *Daily News* would need a great deal of work, investment, and personnel change. Some union contracts were due for renewal. The deal would require substantial indebtedness—Annenberg wanted $14 million in cash and would agree to hold $41 million in notes, pegged to the prime lending rate.

Talks dragged on into the fall. By October, Annenberg had assumed his ambassador's post in London. Lee Hills was sent there to complete negotiations. Annenberg agreed to serve as a consultant for fifteen years at a fee of $150,000 per year. "At this stage in my life," Annenberg told Hills, "the only thing that means anything to me is the character of the operations with which I am connected." Hills worked deftly at other points of agreement. Annenberg would have the title of editor and publisher emeritus, but without authority. It was a shrewd appeal to vanity, recognizing the emotional ties being severed from the paper once owned by his father. "Perfect," Annenberg said. "Eminently fair."

All members of the Knight executive committee except one voted to buy the Philadelphia newspapers.

John S. Knight voted no.

Knight Newspapers took charge of the *Philadelphia Inquirer* and the *Daily News* on New Year's Day 1970. *The New York Times* found the event significant.

To John Shively Knight, the individuality of his newspapers had been a passionate concern. Summing up his beliefs, he said, "Your first duty is to the citizen who buys your newspaper in the belief that it has character and stability. . . . There is no known substitute for integrity and character, no synthetic for guts."

Declared Walter Annenberg, "Mr. Knight and his organization have the character, the ability and the determination to carry on an impressive record of public service."

The honeymoon would not last.

The nation stewed and fermented.

Intellectually, Knight was torn between dissent as a right and mob violence as anarchy. Where did the one end and the other begin? He was in his seventy-fifth year. Many of his peers sat in nursing homes, worrying about bladder control. Knight still thrust himself into the middle of debate, telling an overflow student audience at Ohio University at Athens: "As a fervent advocate of free speech and the right to dissent, I confess my utter dismay over the lawlessness and breakdown of constituted authority on our college campuses." The Athens students treated him kindly, but with spirit. The follow-up question-and-answer session took longer than the speech.

He left the campus mentally refreshed.

A week later, three hundred students rioted at Athens, screaming obscenities, smashing windows, and firebombing.

The worst was Kent State. The memory of that terrible event of May 4, 1970, would lie like a raw wound on the national consciousness; Kent State, where nervous young Ohio National Guardsmen opened fire, spilling blood over the once-peaceful greensward and leaving four dead and nine wounded.

It wasn't even an activist campus, not like Berkeley or even Columbia. These Ohio students' idea of a wild weekend was football homecoming and a Friday night beer bash.

The *Akron Beacon Journal* assigned a task force of twenty-eight reporters and photographers, many of them barely out of college themselves, to cover the trouble. As the gunfire erupted from marching guardsmen, photographer Don Roese flung himself to the ground, cranking off pictures. Reporter Jeff Sallot grabbed a phone line and held it open for constant communication with the Akron newsroom. Reporter Bob Page collared a hospital emergency room physician to get the first identification of the four dead students.

Reporters and editors would spend many weeks in investigative follow-up, capped by the disclosure by fifty-three-year-old *Beacon Journal* reporter Ray Redmond of a secret government report: "The FBI has concluded that the campus shootings by the Ohio National Guard . . . was 'not necessary and not in order.'" Redman's story came from a memo in the civil rights division of the Justice Department.

FBI director J. Edgar Hoover was incensed.

"The FBI . . . did not make any conclusions in this case," he wrote to Knight. "The results of our inquiries into the Kent State matter were furnished to the Department of Justice without recommendation or conclusion." Knight acknowledged the inaccuracy of the word *concluded.* The reporter should have used *reported.* But he noted that Hoover did not deny the basic FBI findings and chided the director, "I am surprised at the hostile tone of your letter. There is no occasion to lecture the editor. We are quite as dedicated to the quest for truth as the FBI."

The FBI story triggered fierce controversy in that summer of 1970. Scores of Hoover admirers called and wrote to the newspaper protesting the disclosures. A typical response: "I question all of the *Beacon Journal*'s reporting on the Kent State tragedy." —L. D. L., Akron. On the other hand, reader Norma Alldredge wrote: "Your newspaper is a breath of fresh air each day. And that's pretty great."

One year later, the *Akron Beacon Journal* was awarded the Pulitzer Prize for its Kent State coverage. But there was no elation to it. An unsigned front-page editorial explored the terrible ironies that still haunted them.

We never thought to see the day when the *Beacon Journal* was sorry to win a Pulitzer Prize. We're seeing it today. Many of us wish that we could, instead, have won the prize for some other thing, some other year, without four young people dead and nine others wounded.

. . . We have been repeatedly and loudly accused of deliberate distortion. The only unbridgeable difference between us and the critics is this: We know how hard we were trying. Meanwhile, like Mark Twain's tarred and feathered character being ridden out of town on a rail, we appreciate the honor of the thing, but . . .

To the mind of John S. Knight, certain timeless truths had been reaffirmed. He expressed them in an address to three hundred members of the International Mailers Union in Akron.

The truly distinguished newspapers in this country are those which have dared to face public wrath and displeasure. Criticism rises in proportion to the amount of news read or heard that does not fit the public's preconceived ideas.

We must report the world as it is and not as we would like it to be.

He passed his seventy-sixth birthday at a pace that would exhaust men half his age. By some built-in mental flexibility, he managed to stay in touch with politics, domestic issues, his weekly column, editorial problems on various newspapers, the pressures of company expansion. To complicate matters, Beryl's health was failing. Chronic emphysema caused breathing difficulty and drained her of strength. They installed an oxygen tank in the house in Akron and had a doctor on call. She continued to smoke heavily and developed a hacking cough. The Knights socialized less. Jack traveled only when necessary for business and did much of his work from the *Beacon Journal* office. He made it a practice to be home every evening at five, so that he and Beryl could have cocktails before dinner. It became their private hour, intimate and pleasurable.

Among the few people in whom he confided was Stuffy Walters, now retired from the *Chicago Daily News* to a small editorial consulting business in Indiana. "I am doing my best to keep up the column writing," he told Walters, "but it is increasingly difficult due to the complexity of our business problems. Public ownership has certainly impinged on my time. Countless hours

are spent in meetings on matters that we used to handle infor-
mally." Wistfully, he wished they could get together for a two-
drink conversation, as in the old days. "It isn't as much fun any
more."

His letters and memos poured out at an astonishing rate.
The Knight company, he noted dryly, had become "the
greatest memo-writing organization since the palmy days of the
Pentagon."

The effort was paying off. Vice president Alvah Chapman
reported that the company markets in the decade had outpaced
U.S. business growth. Three southern markets—Miami, Tallahassee, and Charlotte—each had grown by 28 percent or more. The
company completed a $21 million plant expansion in Charlotte
and was installing $15 million worth of new presses in Philadel-
phia. But Knight was not sold on bureaucratic notions of progress. To a proposal that all top executives take aptitude tests, he
replied acidly, "My friends, you go right ahead with your tests but
I am not going to jeopardize *my* future."

He disliked the arrangement in Miami whereby the *Herald*
printed, circulated, sold advertising, and handled business and
accounting for the *Miami Daily News,* which was nonetheless
wholly owned by the Cox chain. To California publisher Virgil
Pinkley, Knight expressed some of his misgivings. "Will people
really believe that we do not own the *News?* We have been
completely frank in all our announcements but, as you know,
there are always the cynics and disbelievers." He felt that the
News was not nearly as good as it could be, especially since the
untimely death of its brilliant editor, Bill Baggs.

When a strong successor to Baggs was named, in the person
of Sylvan Meyer, Knight unexpectedly found himself in a spirited
exchange. *News* gossip columnist Herb Rau published a press
agent's item that Hialeah mayor Henry Milander, long a target
of *Herald* investigative reporters, had been seen occupying Jack
Knight's box seats at the racetrack. "Many eyebrows were
raised," Rau reported.

Knight protested to editor Meyer: "This 'item' by Herb Rau
is in keeping with his past record of nasty slurs. The story is
untrue, cannot be documented and seems intended only to em-

barrass me. If Rau wants to fight in the open, I will be glad to take him on."

It was Meyer's turn to bridle. "Rau says the item came through a Hialeah publicist. I have asked him henceforth to mention *Herald* people only in connection with some honor or if they are convicted in a court of law."

A man had to keep his sense of humor. When one of his own editors came out with a sentimental endorsement of Mother's Day, Knight ripped out the page, scrawled his sarcastic reaction in red pencil, and sent it off: "A noble stand, sir!"

There was no rest for the weary.

> *From JSK to the Executive Committee:*
> *Eugene Pulliam has related to me his position in a lengthy telephone conversation. He is generally opposed to public stock issues for newspapers. He fears that Newhouse or someone like him could buy in and prove to be troublesome.*
>
> *Pulliam personally owns 61 per cent of the voting stock in his newspapers, which can't be sold unless they go broke. His desire is to maintain strong newspapers with "sane editorial policies—neither right nor left." He says money is of no concern. My conclusion is that there is no present prospect of obtaining the Pulliam newspapers.*

The 1970s rolled along with continued social upheaval; rising concerns for clean air, water, and earth and human rights; and new challenges to business and government. In speeches and writings, Knight seemed to gain a keener edge of idealism, tempered by hard experience.

On pollution control:

> Entrepreneurs who pollute our clean air and water, put our parks to the bulldozer, build on our beaches and poison our waterways must be brought to book. But let the job be done without sacrificing free competition, which gives our nation its vitality.

On capitalism:

> By its generosity, America has sustained the leaky economics of countless nations. Ranting against big business may make extremists feel important, but what their theories would do to this country's economy is chilling to contemplate.

He found everything more complex. Even business was not simple anymore; every decision seemed to demand a consensus. At Knight Newspapers, just deciding the kind of people they wanted as company directors demanded a four-page analysis by Lee Hills, typed single-space. Did they want more outsiders—they now had three, E. J. Thomas, John Weinberg, and Peyton Anderson—or insiders? Did they want executives? Lawyers? Bankers? Educators? A rotating employee? Knight replied: "I prefer a top executive of a successful company. I think there is room for someone who has outside expertise. It is helpful to have directors who know their way around government, a combination businessman-lawyer. I am not impressed by bankers."

When you boiled it down, a company was composed of people, their strengths and weaknesses. He had been fortunate to attract and keep a staff having intense loyalty and talent. Hills, now president and executive editor, was Knight's idea of the perfect executive. On the thirtieth anniversary of Hills's hiring, Knight wrote a small testimonial: "No newspaperman whom I have known has so possessed the total sum of judgment, wisdom, energy, perseverance and genuine feel for people. . . ."

Johnny Knight III completed his studies at Oxford and went to work at the *Detroit Free Press.* Knight hoped this was the start of progressive training, preparing the young man for real leadership. Johnny expressed skepticism, however, about the future of publicly owned newspapers. What would happen when his grandfather, Uncle Jim, and others of the current hierarchy no longer guided the company's destiny?

His grandfather replied that no organization could live in the shadow of one man. Preparing for the future was an ongoing process. Things did not just fall into place.

I do not share your apprehension that the company may someday fall under control of market investors, bankers or business people having no real interest in good newspapering. . . . Professional management now realizes how imperative it is to have a great "product" —a term I detest—to sell. There will always be editors, managers and good production people to work together for the institution which is greater than any of them.

20

"THE MAN WHO CAME TO BREAKFAST"

As a citizen, I resent being asked to accept on faith the shabby tricks of gutter politics which are being masked in a deep and foreboding silence by those who govern my country.
—John S. Knight, "The Editor's Notebook," October 9, 1972

In the early days, when he had been a congressman or vice president or private citizen, it had been "Dick" and "Jack." Nixon would send chatty little notes referring to this Knight column or that, provided the article had been favorable. The practice continued, infrequently and with cordial detachment, into Richard M. Nixon's presidency.

There were occasional social events shared over the years— golf at Miami Beach or dinner in the company of other politicians—when he was vice president. Nixon had once made a big hit coming to Akron for the running of the All-American Soap

Box Derby. But then he had been second man in the Eisenhower administration. As president, Nixon came back to Akron for breakfast.

Knight had been his consistent supporter, even during the political vicissitudes of the 1950s when critics in and out of the Republican party dismissed him as "Tricky Dick." The publisher felt that politically Nixon deserved better. Knight Newspapers thus endorsed him for president against John F. Kennedy in 1960 and Hubert Humphrey in 1968. All this gave columnist Knight an entré rarely granted to other newsmen. And so it was that in August 1971, a "Notebook" column from Akron began:

> The President left our apartment and we had a good window view of the procession of bulletproof limousine and security cars moving slowly from our driveway. The telephone was ringing. Editors from Detroit and Miami wanted to know how soon my story of the presidential visit would be filed. Patiently I explained that since the President had been my guest, any comment from me would seem inappropriate. . . .

So there would be no earthshaking revelations, Knight insisted. After a lengthy private chat with one of the world's most powerful men, of a kind that would make any reporter drool, Knight kept mum. He gave his readers a humdrum account of what Richard M. Nixon ate (cantaloupe, poached eggs, bacon, English muffin) and the domestic hassles of having a president come calling.

> Mr. Nixon at first declined the jam. But then I reminded him that a faithful Republican lady in our apartment building had made it especially for him. "In that case," he said, "please pass the jam."

The idea for a breakfast chat had come from Nixon himself, a strange, self-isolating man looking for a friendly ear among journalists toward whom he was increasingly hostile. It did not occur to Knight to question Nixon's motives. Basking in sudden limelight, the publisher himself set the off-the-record ground rules. Such courtesy would have outraged him if extended by one of his reporters. Table talk touched on an array of meaty subjects such as China—Nixon would soon make his historic first visit to Peking—the Middle East, Berlin, domestic politics.

None of it made print.

> What did the President have to say? Other than the fact that we did not wholly agree on every subject, his views must remain undisclosed by me. The man who came to breakfast made no stipulations, but I must assume he was talking off the record.

Fiscal conservative Knight might have taken a different tack had he known that his guest was fast becoming the highest spender ever to occupy the Oval Office. The government was plowing $10 million into his vacation retreats alone. *Fortune* would tally up presidential household expenses of $100 million, including the cost of twenty-one presidential gardeners; seventy-five butlers, caretakers, cooks, and maids; three hundred guards; one hundred Secret Service agents; plus family and staff access to five Boeing 707s, eleven Lockheed Jetstars, and sixteen helicopters. The new uniforms of the White House guard would quicken the pulse of a potentate.

After the presidential visit, Knight continued to take it easy on Nixon in print. When an editor warned gently that his plaudits for administration policies in China and the Middle East, and even a soft touch on Vietnam, might be painting him into a corner, Knight replied, "If you will pardon my immodesty, I think I am wise enough to avoid such a mistake. When required, I can always make an end run."

On October 26, 1971, he passed his seventy-seventh birthday. He was not as fit as he would have liked to be, given an arthritic condition of the back and flutters of the heart. In light of the deference accorded him by friends and subordinates, he remembered a bit of doggerel by Finley Peter Dunne of the *Chicago Daily News:* "Many a man that cudden't direct ye to th' drug store on th' corner whin he was thirty will get a respectful hearin' whin age has further impaired his mind." But Knight was not alone in feeling the advance of age. Beryl unexpectedly was hospitalized with a broken hip.

Despite surgery, she remained in good spirits. At Thanksgiving, Johnny III came from Detroit to join them for dinner in her room at Akron City Hospital. They reminisced over previous Thanksgivings spent at the Chicago home of Beryl's sister and brother-in-law, Rita and Edwin Ford. Beryl laughed with friends who dropped by to wish her well, impressing Jack with her aplomb. "My own feelings are not as controlled," he admitted.

Beryl mended in time and went home in an ambulance to the care of her nurses and housekeeper. Christmas went by, and New Year's.

Then she fell again and broke the other hip.

Walter Annenberg was angry. He had heard unpleasant rumors that Jack Knight was telling friends he had made a bad deal in Philadelphia, paying $55 million for two papers worth $30 million at most; that the plants were in a decrepit state, the personnel inept and excessive, the equipment a disgrace. Annenberg considered such talk bad form; if the Knights had bought headaches, it was their own fault for not driving a harder bargain. He also found it hard to believe that Knight was outvoted by his own executive board. Annenberg did not do business that way. As he would tell his biographer, John Cooney, "Knight being outvoted by Lee Hills and the other stooges on his board is like the Ayatollah being outvoted by the mullahs."

But the former publisher's discontent sprang from other sources as well. His ego was chafed. The Knights were paying him $150,000 per year as an adviser but never asked him for advice. Worse, the *Inquirer* was undergoing a personnel blood-letting and editorial revolution at the hands of a new boss, John McMullan, whom many staff old-timers regarded with fear and trembling. The new Knight people, moreover, had little to say about the papers that was complimentary. As Annenberg put it, "They go around bragging about how great they are compared with the previous owner."

John McMullan was independent, combative, and stubborn. As vice president and executive editor of the *Inquirer,* he arrived from Miami with a reputation for bulldog tenacity and bore a strong physical resemblance to Henry Kissinger. Annenberg seethed when he heard about the man's assessment of the *Inquirer*'s news coverage as "a throwback, biased and ineffectual."

It was said that McMullan did not hesitate to challenge Jack Knight—or anyone else—if he thought he was right. A notable tiff with Knight had occurred in Miami a few years earlier when the publisher decided to settle a long-simmering libel suit stemming from a *Herald* probe into alleged rackets involvement in the operation of Miami Beach's swank Fontainebleau Hotel. In coming to terms with lawyers for hotel operator Ben Novack, Knight overrode the protests of editor McMullan and agreed to print a front-page box saying there was no evidence to substantiate the paper's earlier charges. Knight urged his tempestuous editor not to take the incident personally. Later, at a meeting of some twenty editors, McMullan publicly reproached his boss, declaring, "For us to come out in the *Herald* and say we had found no evidence was false. We found plenty of evidence, and presented it day after day. In a sense, this has renounced some of the principles that caused me to join this organization in the first place. . . ." It was heavy confrontation, with both men glaring. Afterward, Knight managed to bank the fires of indignation. When McMullan apologized privately for being so blunt, the old man said, "That's not important, John. What is important is what you think of me." McMullan would puzzle over the comment for years. Was John S. Knight acknowledging that he had knowingly compromised principle for other reasons, such as the gathering pressures of going public? McMullan never knew the answer.

By the time he arrived in Philadelphia, McMullan had a varied background in the Knight organization as *Miami Herald* city editor, assistant managing editor, executive editor, chief of the Knight Washington Bureau, and, briefly, assistant to Alvah Chapman. Such experience equipped him for the tough, unpopular task of whipping the *Inquirer* into shape. As one Philadelphia staff veteran would recall years later, "McMullan came in here like a bull."

For a newsman accustomed to Knight-style operations, lean and clean, the *Inquirer* was indeed a throwback. Old-timers who should have been long retired cluttered the payroll, drawing full wages though infrequently showing up for work. There were reporters having no talent for writing and writers who could not report, cartoonists who could not draw and employees holding strong private allegiances to local political machines. The word went out that those not giving their best efforts would not remain on the payroll. Institutional ancients found themselves replaced by eager young people, fresh out of college. In less than three years, McMullan replaced seventy reporters and editors and uprooted ten of the eleven department heads. Bitterness swept the Old Guard. In later years, McMullan insisted that he did not act cruelly. "I tried to be compassionate toward people who were totally unfit for the positions they held. I told our department heads, 'As long as someone is giving everything he's got to give, we'll keep him.'"

Younger staff people weren't all that comfortable either. Under a Guild contract clause, *Inquirer* reporters could demand their bylines stripped from stories that they found objectionably altered. Such requests proliferated under McMullan. There was a mood of dictatorial management. As one subeditor would remember it, "McMullan's great shortcoming was his belief that he could do everything better than everyone else. There were times when he'd get involved in a particular story and just overwhelm it."

Annenberg found added cause for rancor. The *Inquirer* had always been friendly with the police. Now, McMullan's reporters were digging deeper and their stories did not always glow with the usual tributes. When Police Commissioner Frank Rizzo decided to run for mayor, McMullan and another Knight editor, Creed Black, tried to talk him out of making the race, over lunch. Despite the old-style machine politics practiced by the commissioner, and serious allegations of Philadelphia police brutality, McMullan was personally fond of Rizzo and his Italian macho style.

Rizzo responded with monosyllabic intensity.

You fellas don't understand. I grew up here. I'm from South Philadelphia. I'm an Italian. My father was the first Italian sergeant on the force. You talk about discrimination against blacks today; there was discrimination against Italians back in my dad's day. He was the first one. I was the first Italian police captain. These things have great meaning. This is my city. I can do things for this city. I can make this city come alive. This oughta be a great city. . . .

There was a short pause. Then: "An' I gotta lot of scores to settle."

Rizzo won the mayor's race without *Inquirer* support.

As changes in the *Inquirer* threw out time-honored styles, McMullan and his superior, Hills, were prodded by little notes from Miami, Detroit, Akron:

Dear John: I have commented before about the Women's pages in the Philadelphia Inquirer. *In my judgment, there is too much emphasis on reforms. Readers are interested in people, as well as causes.*
—John S. Knight.

Dear Lee: I sent you a memo on the Philadelphia Inquirer *women's pages. No feel for the community, no good local comment, too much deemphasis on "society." But John is a hardheaded man, and sometimes about things he really doesn't understand.*
JSK.

It was not easy. It was not cheap. Among the major new costs was $15 million worth of modern presses.

Annenberg's name still rode the masthead as publisher emeritus. With the steady estrangement, however, he grew less happy with the arrangement. The last straw came with an editorial gaffe that McMullan failed to catch. The Sunday *Today* magazine, in a profile, repeated an old story that Moses Annenberg had once offered a local contractor $1 million to help keep him out of prison. The magazine had been printed in advance.

Managing editor John Gillen worried. "I hear Annenberg's raising hell." McMullan read the article and agreed that the item was unnecessary, but refused to kill the forthcoming magazine issue. The Annenberg anecdote was not something that hadn't been told before.

Alvah Chapman, now Knight Newspapers' executive vice president, felt that the magazine ought to be canceled. He and McMullan went to see Annenberg's first lieutenant, Joe First, who reiterated his employer's position: Kill the magazine; it wasn't worth it. Chapman agreed. The editor dug in his heels. There was a competitive spirit between him and Chapman. "I don't think this is your decision to make," McMullan said.

They conferred with Hills. Chapman was for killing the magazine. McMullan still disagreed. "That would make us the laughingstock of Philadelphia." He vowed to resign if the issue were forced.

The magazine ran, unchanged, in the Sunday editions.

Walter Annenberg severed all connections with the Philadelphia papers he had once owned, and his name was struck from the masthead.

At Akron, he still worked in the old office with its dark paneling and familiar clutter. His desk, attended by a couple of visitors' chairs, was flanked by windows overlooking a grimy downtown street corner. The windowless wall space was filled with photographs, framed awards, and keepsakes, the accumulated clutter of a social public man. Bookcases were crowded with books, catalogs, magazines, calendars, and more photographs. Behind and to the side of his desk were cardboard boxes stuffed with papers. A copy of the *Girl Scout Handbook* lay on a shelf.

The morning visitor was a young writer for the weekly magazine, *Cleveland.* Knight stood behind his desk, his eyes bearing a glint of challenge. "Well, why do you think you want to talk with me?"

The interviewer smiled. "Because you're a legend in your own time."

Knight waved him to a chair. "Sit down, then. I suppose we ought to get on with this."

The interview consumed an hour and a half. In that time, the writer noted, Knight lit and smoked seven cigarettes, interrupting his smoking only to have his picture taken and again to take a stick of gum. He fiddled constantly with four copy pencils on his desk, two black and two red.

"Where do you go from here personally, Mr. Knight? How much longer will you keep going with the newspapers?"

"Well, my wife is seriously ill, and has been for some years. I couldn't sit around somewhere and just play gin rummy, just fiddle. I try to keep current with everything. News fascinates me. When that first edition comes up, and it's still warm from the presses, I get a little glow out of it."

"Now there's this whole movement toward the New Journalism. How does that work, as far as your papers are concerned?"

"Some of it distresses me. I picked up the paper the other day and there was a story about some minor bureaucrat in Akron under fire. He was quoted as saying, 'That's a lot of bullshit.' We printed it that way. Is that New Journalism? I don't think it has a place in a newspaper of general circulation."

Talk turned to the quality of newspapers. Knight said there were many overlooked smaller papers of good quality. Some papers, on the other hand, had been owned by the same families for so long that they were operated primarily for profit, with no emphasis on journalistic excellence.

"Are you worried about that happening to your newspapers?"

"No, sir. We're a publicly owned company now. I believe in growth from within. We have some very bright, ambitious young people. We also have a vigorous acquisition program. A family paper gets down to the point where they've run out of heirs and if someone dies there is a huge estate tax to pay. People worry about how they're going to raise the money. Some of them come to us. We solve the problems by taking over the paper, provided it has good potential."

"Why do they come to you? Why are you so special?"

"Because they respect us. We think we have a very good organization. . . ."

"It's always the profit motive first?"

"I've argued this question with my editor's wife in Detroit. She said, 'You just think about profits.' Well, yes, I do think about them. Unless the newspaper is profitable, how the hell do you have any liberty? Without profits you're always at the mercy of the banks. You've either got to conduct a profitable newspaper or be subsidized, and no matter who does the subsidizing you're never again free. I'm free. Nobody puts pressure on me."

"That's important to you, isn't it? Being free."

"Very. I'm too old to change."

Growth had become policy. They were constantly scouting now for newspapers of promise. To help find new properties, they brought in from Columbia University big, breezy J. Montgomery Curtis, a man of vast newspaper contacts, and made him a corporate officer. They shopped for potential acquisitions in Houston, Cincinnati, Pittsburgh, Lexington, Louisville, Toledo, Jacksonville, St. Petersburg.

Knight's interest in racehorses often took him to Lexington, Kentucky. Despite the untimely death of his partner, Marshall Field, Jr., in Chicago, the Fourth Estate Stables had done well. A prize Thoroughbred, War Censor, had cost $21,000 as a colt and won $519,000 for Fourth Estate. But Knight's judgment was not infallible. He paid $20,000 for a yearling filly, Journalette, at the Keeneland sales in Lexington, then sold her for $45,000 as a three-year-old in foal. Her filly, Typecast, went on to win $535,000 in prize money, then was sold for $725,000. Knight didn't get a penny of Typecast's bonanza.

He loved Lexington and had many friends among horse owners and breeders. It was Monty Curtis who suggested that the *Lexington Herald* and *Leader* newspapers might be for sale. There followed a five-year effort, led by Knight, to persuade Virginia Stoll, widow of late owner John G. Stoll, and other key stockholders to sell.

To Executive Committee, Oct. 30, 1968: My friend in Lexington, George Swinebroad, attended a dinner where Virginia Stoll was present. He remarked, at my suggestion, "What's this I hear about you selling the Lexington papers?" She replied, "That's the craziest thing I ever heard. They'll never be sold while I'm here." George will keep me informed. JSK

May 22, 1972: I hear that Fred Wachs, publisher and driving force in Lexington, is very ill. Heart problems and other complications. Edward S. Dabney is board chairman of the bank and very close to the owners. . . . I believe the papers will be sold within a few years, and we should have a considerable interest. JSK

To Executive Committee, Aug. 1, 1972: One of the Stoll heirs expressed to me her interest in selling. Another heir is said to entertain similar ideas. George Swine-broad had another talk with Virginia Stoll, who reput-edly controls the stock. She repeated to him that the newspapers would not be sold in her lifetime. "We like the income." I called an attorney for the newspapers, asking what he knew about rumors of a sale. Virginia Stoll knows of my interest. I'll keep trying. JSK.

To Executive Committee, Aug. 23, 1972: I talked on the phone with Mr. John Stoll Lillard, an heir to the Stoll estate. He has heard of the various calls made upon members of the Stoll family. He says the overtures have been irritating to Mr. E. S. Dabney, who controls the Stoll trusts. He describes Mr. Dabney as wary, aloof and resentful of approaches from "outsiders." They don't really want to sell, but Mr. Dabney knows that someday it will happen. I understand they have been approached by the Detroit News *and Scripps-Howard. JSK.*

To Mr. E. S. Dabney, Lexington, Ky., Sept. 1, 1972: In-dividuals from your area have spoken to me about the possibility of acquiring the Lexington newspapers. I have expressed interest, but have no way of knowing what your disposition is. I would appreciate an opportunity to talk with you personally, possibly with two or three of my associates. May I hear from you at your pleasure? Sincerely, John S. Knight.

To Mr. John S. Knight, Sept. 11, 1972: Any advances to you were made wholly without authority from us. We are not now positioned to conclude a sale, even if it were advisable. However, since you are going to be here during the Keeneland meeting, we will be pleased for you to call on us. Sincerely, E. S. Dabney.

To Mr. E. S. Dabney, Oct. 26, 1972: Alvah Chapman and I deeply appreciated your courtesy in seeing us at your home. As I mentioned, it would be fairly simple for us to arrive at a negotiable offer if we had audits for the past five years, a list of non-operating assets—real estate, investments, cash value of life insurance—and a copy of your pension plan.

John S. Knight.

Time passed without further word from Dabney. In mid-January, Knight called the banker. He was noncommittal, remarking that they had been trying to come up with a sound estimate of the newspapers' worth and might be in a better position to talk in a few days.

"Can I be of any possible service to you, or come down and see you again?" Knight asked pleasantly.

"Not right now," Dabney said.

"I simply wanted you to know of our continued interest."

"I appreciate that very much indeed."

SUMMARY: I think there is real interest here, but I doubt that we are going to get any bargain. My gut feeling is that Mr. Dabney's consultant will point to present high prices for newspaper properties, and that there will be competition. So we may have to reach a little if we want the newspapers.

In late summer, things began to jell. The Knight brothers, Hills, and Alvah Chapman met with Dabney in Lexington. Jim Knight came away impressed, saying, "These horse and mule bankers are pretty clever. He is out for the big dollar."

Jack chuckled. "Confucius say, 'Man who tries to pluck top dollar sometimes falls out of tree.' "

There were other irons in the fire. On October 31, the Knights took possession of newspapers at Bradenton, Florida, and Columbus, Georgia, from the R. W. Page Corporation. The $26 million acquisition boosted daily combined circulation of Knight papers by another 86,000.

On October 31, they completed the purchase of the *Lexington Herald* and the *Leader* at a cost of $37 million, with combined morning and evening circulation of 99,000. "You have a bright future in Lexington," Dabney assured Jack Knight.

Knight Newspapers now published daily in nine U.S. cities.

On the morning of June 17, 1972, five men were arrested in a burglary at Democratic party headquarters in the Watergate office-apartment complex in Washington, D.C. In August 1974, a tearful Richard M. Nixon, accompanied by his family, boarded a helicopter on the White House lawn, flashed his two-handed *V* signal, and flew back to private life, the first U.S. president to resign. During the twenty months between, the nation underwent a historic internal upheaval. Its legal and legislative processes, spurred by a vigorous press and public opinion, toppled a president and emerged whole.

Knight's doubts had kindled even before Watergate and the 1972 election. He was increasingly disenchanted over Vietnam and nagging whispers of political manipulation and deceit. "Times change," he told his readers, "and perceptive men must change with them." But "I wish there were some way to escape the remainder of this dreary presidential campaign." He could not stomach the Democrats' standard-bearer, Senator George McGovern. As for Nixon, "in many respects the Nixon campaign is even more unpalatable."

Two weeks before the election, Knight's break with Nixon was complete. He found himself a man without a party. For the first time in his adult life he intended not to cast a presidential vote. "I cannot vote for George McGovern. But neither will I vote for President Nixon, because I am outraged by this administration's abdication of moral principles."

Strong Nixon supporters expressed outrage. In Indianapolis, an indignant Clem Keller threw down his newspaper in disgust and wrote a letter calling the publisher "an editorial and citizenship coward." In Philadelphia, Mrs. J. Herbert Kirby urged Knight to reconsider. "How can you say that you won't vote? Don't sit this one out."

There were, of course, many general election issues and contests. On November 7, Knight went to his precinct in Akron and, while a *Beacon Journal* photographer recorded the scene, stepped into a voting machine and cast his ballot.

He refused to say whether he actually voted for a presidential candidate.

The Watergate hearings dragged on. By February 1973, as the Justice Department, the Congress, and federal judge John Sirica drew an ever-tightening web, the burglary had burgeoned into a conspiracy of monumental scope. Still, there were those who blamed the news media. "What are you trying to do to our country?" Florida reader H. P. Lauritzen asked Knight. "You are destroying the President's effectiveness and creating worldwide disrespect!"

The House Judiciary Committee adopted three articles of impeachment.

Knight was seventy-nine years old. He had lived long and seen much. He had been a registered Republican all his life, and his heart and sentiments were in that party. Here, disgraced and unrepentant, stood a Republican president with whom he had had what was, for a politician, a close relationship. Regretfully, he saw that among the casualties of Watergate was the credibility of the press itself. With flagging spirits, columnist Knight addressed the issues during the steaming August of 1974:

> The conservatives, as they call themselves, ought to entertain some second thoughts about their denunciations of the free press in this country. It was the press which uncovered Watergate and exposed the arrogance of power within the White House itself. And yet there are

many people, otherwise thoughtful and intelligent, who have a hang-up on Nixon and the press. They believe, or profess to believe, that the newspapers and the networks are "out to get" Nixon, and that Watergate is "just politics." These conservatives see no guilt in subverting the Constitution or even flouting the laws of this country.

Many letter writers have favored putting shackles on the press by restricting its freedom. Is that what they really want in America?

May I say, to those who charge me with "betraying" the President or being intent upon "destroying" the country, that I have a substantial stake in America and wish to see the country governed by people of high competence and complete integrity, without regard to party affiliation.

I have long since given up on Richard Nixon. But on my country, no. . . . The present exercise of constitutional procedures will help insure the Republic's survival.

The colossal political bloodletting finally came to an end. The day arrived when, with a teary smile, Richard M. Nixon departed from Washington, leaving in charge his successor, Gerald Ford.

The man who had come to breakfast was gone.

"THE ONE CERTAINTY..."

The very idea of being ill repelled him. As a child he had written in his school copybook, "Without health, wealth is meaningless." Knight still seemed to put distance between himself and his son Landon's polio affliction, perhaps because this was his flesh and blood; yet he could shed tears over associates' misfortunes—severe surgery for Ben Maidenburg, the deaths of the first wives of Lee Hills and Don Shoemaker, the deaths a few years apart of John McMullan's two young adult daughters.

With advancing age, however, his own health problems multiplied. He had had hernia surgery, an arthritic condition of the back, a circulatory problem in his right leg, an attack of the gout. Recently his physician in Akron, Dr. Henry Kraus, had found evidence of cardiac insufficiency.

After his seventy-ninth birthday in autumn 1973, Knight complained of abdominal pain. Doctors diagnosed an appendix flare-up. He was admitted to Ford Hospital in Detroit, expecting to have the appendix removed. Lee Hills talked with him by telephone in his hospital room. "They don't know what it is. I'm convinced of that," Knight said bleakly. "They are going to explore. I'll go into surgery tomorrow morning."

The conversation ended. Hours later, he called Hills back. The operation was postponed. Preoperative checkups showed irregularities in his electrocardiogram (ECG). Knight was apprehensive. "I've been careful about everything. No smoking or drinking. It doesn't pay to live right."

Ford Hospital's medical chairman, Dr. Richmond Smith, talked with Hills. There were changes in the ECG, indicating minor heart damage. A cardiologist would assess it. They would know more later in the day. Smith's subsequent report was carefully worded. "We have delayed the elective appendectomy until the situation is completely stable."

Knight fretted over the disruption of his "Notebook" column. On Thanksgiving, just before entering the hospital, he had reflected on the thoughts of an old friend, James ("Scotty") Reston of *The New York Times:* "He has said that 'what America needs is more shortages. We need to cut down, slow up, stay home, run around the block, eat vegetable soup, call up old friends and read a book once in a while. Prosperity's what's been doing us in.' " It was, Knight observed, "a very basic line of thought for such a worldly man."

This would be his last writing for six months.

November ended with damp, chilly weather. In Detroit, watery sunlight fought a losing battle with the city's smog layer. In Ford Hospital, Dr. Smith gave Jack Knight the unpleasant news. "You have had a mild heart attack."

The handsome old face turned ashen.

The physician again spoke with Hills. "He feels trapped by circumstance. He resents it. He has taken great pride in his health and his abilities."

Hills arranged for Knight to move into a hospital suite. The patient's depression was palpable. "Dr. Keyes, the cardiologist, was in. He says all my signs are normal now. But I'll have to go on this way. It might be ten days or two weeks before they do more tests."

Beryl's illness worried him. He had made financial arrangements for her. Certainly there would be abundant income. But he seemed to forget how enormously wealthy he was. "Who will look after her interests?" It did not occur to him that Beryl might die first.

Hills tried to reassure him. Theirs was a bond of more than thirty years. Knight was a complex personality who kindled in other men a broad range of feeling, from dislike and fearful respect to paternal affection. Few of his associates could speak comfortably on a personal level such as this, man-to-man. Eddie Thomas was one exception, Hills another.

"You've had difficult personal problems, Jack, more than most men. You've handled them superbly. Most people are not blessed with such fortitude."

After being released from the hospital, Knight returned to Akron. A cold December knifed over the city. He fidgeted from inactivity. He wrote a brief explanation to readers, which appeared in all the Knight newspapers: "It is frustrating to hold firm and vigorous views on the issues of our times and yet be unable to set them forth in print. I hope that the Notebook can be resumed. . . ."

Vain hope. He underwent a heavy medical regimen, was ordered by his doctors to rest, relax, not exert himself. He moped around the Akron apartment, where Beryl's condition continued to deteriorate, and went off for treatment at Massachusetts General Hospital in Boston. There, the chief of general surgery was Dr. W. Gerald Austen, whose parents, the Arnsteins, had been the Knights' neighbors for many years on Portage Path.

The "Notebook" did not resume until May 12, 1974. The publisher, partially liberated from restrictions, pounded gleefully at the old manual typewriter.

> The urge to write has been coming on for some time. There have been long nights when I sat upright at three and four in the morning, muttering and reciting a great show of indignation over the crass stupidity of mankind. . . . Now I'm hooked. But the doctors advise against resuming my Sunday column on a regular basis. Occasional pieces yes, but only when I "feel up to it." Still,

one lacks confidence. As the punters at your favorite horse track would say, "Knight don't look too good in the first. He's been away from the track for a long time. Yeah, and he's got some age on him, too."

Editors sent him cheery notes of praise and congratulations. But he seemed to know, deep down, that it was no good.

Merger: the idea had floated around since three years before Knight Newspapers had gone public in 1969. Such a prospect was first broached in a private memo by a member of Sidney Weinberg's staff, Alan L. Stern:

> *Ed Hoffman of our buying department at Goldman, Sachs is the cousin of Herman H. Ridder, president of Ridder Publications. Through Ed I met with Mr. Ridder to discuss their plans. Mr. Ridder indicated that his first interest was merging with another large non-competitive newspaper chain. Specifically he mentioned Knight Newspapers. . . . We believe that Mr. Ridder would welcome a meeting with Mr. Knight to discuss such a consolidation.*

Weinberg dropped a note to Jack Knight. Did he have any interest? Knight said he would be happy to talk with the Ridders, but he felt that the real leader of the chain was not Herman but his brother, publisher Bernard H. Ridder, Jr., of St. Paul, Minnesota.

Eight years later, the suggestion would develop into the most lucrative merger in U.S. newspaper history.

The thriving Ridder operation had a colorful past. The clan's patriarch, the original Herman Ridder, had immigrated to the United States from Germany as a boy in 1848. As a man, he became involved in the Intertype business, producing typecasting equipment for newspapers. In 1892 Ridder acquired a small German-language newspaper, the *Staats,* in New York. With a growing tide of German immigrants arriving, the *Staats* prospered, as did a competing paper, the *Zeitung.* The two journals ultimately merged under Ridder ownership. By the mid-1920s the enterprise was in the hands of a new generation, brothers Bernard, Victor, and Joe Ridder. Circulation of the *New Yorker Staats-Zeitung* rose to 120,000. In 1926 they bought the venerable *New York Journal of Commerce,* which specialized in shipping news, and a year later expanded into the Middle West with the purchase of the *Dispatch* and *Pioneer Press* in St. Paul, Minnesota. In the early 1930s they picked up the competing *St. Paul Daily News,* which had been hard hit by the Depression, as well as 49½ percent voting stock interest in the *Seattle Times.* By 1933, they added the *Aberdeen* [South Dakota] *Daily News,* with a relative, Henry Schmitt, as publisher. Then came the *Grand Forks Herald* in 1935 and the *Duluth Herald Tribune* in 1936.

All this rapid growth, despite hard times, was rooted in basic economics. As Bernard H. Ridder, Jr., would recall years later, "The newspapers were a good investment. The family believed they would grow. Newspapers were the number one news media. Sheer power of the media meant that advertising revenue would continue to produce a profitable return."

The Ridders were frugal, energetic, and prolific producers of male heirs. Their newspaper operations prospered more from shrewd business operations than quality journalism. The papers varied in style and personality, depending on which Ridder happened to be in charge. Not all were idealistic about journalism or hesitated to suppress or color the news if it suited their purposes. Wheelhorse of the growing chain for many years was Victor. Driving, aggressive, and talented, Victor had operated the *Staats-Zeitung* during World War I. In later years, when the Ridder enterprises seemed to be expanding everywhere, Columbia University's J. Montgomery Curtis asked Victor why he was buying so many papers. The reply: "We are Catholics. We have many children and most of them turn out to be sons. We have to buy a newspaper for every son."

Among the strong personalities of the new generation was Bernard Ridder, Jr. Tall, handsome, and convivial, Bernard grew up with the advantages of wealth, became a champion squash player, and captained the squash team at Princeton. Graduating in 1938, he went to work for the *New York Journal of Commerce* at $15 a week, which he spent on squash rackets. His immediate interest was to become the New York State squash champion. It took marriage in 1938 to alter Bernie's priorities; he moved to the family paper at Aberdeen to work in the advertising department, and then to Duluth to begin learning general management.

With the outbreak of war, Bernie Ridder became a naval gunnery officer in combat in the Pacific. Then he was put in charge of navy journalists serving on ships throughout the Pacific war zone. Military life served him well, necessitating that he work closely with people. Discharged as a navy lieutenant, he would use the experience in later tough bargaining with newspaper unions in Duluth. "Military service gave me a better understanding of what makes people move and react," he would recall years later. "This was something I never learned in college."

Now the Ridders operated papers in New York, St. Paul, Duluth, and Aberdeen. With the decline of New York's German immigrant population, they sold the *Staats-Zeitung,* which was reduced from daily to weekly status. Bernie's father, Bernard H. Ridder, Sr., was active in St. Paul. He would live to be ninety-two. Two of his sons, Herman and Joseph, were in New York; a third, Daniel, was in St. Paul. With three such family branches producing male offspring, acquisitions continued. Ridders were to acquire whole or part interest in papers in San Jose, Pasadena, and Long Beach, California; Gary, Indiana; Wichita, Kansas; Boulder, Colorado; and Niles, Michigan.

Ridder strategy was practical. They bought papers in midsize, growing towns, preferably with circulations of 125,000 to 150,000. Gary, Indiana, a dying steel town, showed little promise of growth, but the price of the *Post-Tribune* was low. Bernard ran the St. Paul operation and represented the family in such industry groups as the Inland Daily Press Association, the Associated Press Board of Directors, and the Newspaper Bureau of Advertising. Herman died in 1969 and Bernard succeeded him as president of Ridder Publications.

It was in the industry groups that Bernard Ridder had come to know Jack Knight. Both served on the Associated Press board. Knight impressed Ridder as forceful and domineering, although they were not close friends. There were some similarities in the way each group did business, but the Knights put greater emphasis on editorial style. When word circulated that the *St. Louis*

Globe-Democrat was for sale, for example, the Ridders—Bernard, his brother Herman, and their aging father—went to the Missouri city, inspected the plant, and studied the paper's distribution problems, its business and union difficulties. After two days, they concluded that the paper was not a good buy. Later, Bernard found out that Knight also had taken a passing glance at the *Globe-Democrat.* At the next AP board meeting, he asked the publisher how he had gone about it. "Well, I called up the editor and we had a long talk," said Knight, "and I decided that that was not the way for us to go." It was a marked difference in style: on the one hand, a Ridder business and marketing study, on the other a Knight phone call to the editor. But where the *Globe-Democrat* was concerned, the two methods produced the same result.

For the Ridders, converting from private to public ownership had both business and domestic roots. Male members of the family received good salaries. On the other hand, females—wives, sisters, in-laws—drew only their dividends and had no ready market for their stock. Public ownership would provide such a market. Like the Knights, the Ridders also saw tax advantages. The family's decision to go public thus drew rare unanimity. But it also created new problems.

Ridders liked to do things their own way. As Bernard, Jr., would recall years afterward,

> Each family member ran his part of the operation like a duke in his private duchy. Each felt that he was his own boss. Even in public ownership, some were unwilling to give that up. And yet we all suddenly had a responsibility to people who invested in Ridder stock. Some of the practices that had existed before would have to be corrected. We would have to brush up our act.

It wasn't easy. The journalistic dynasty of immigrant Herman Ridder had produced some rugged individualists. Knight vice president J. Montgomery Curtis would touch on this in a quick study in 1974. The former director of the American Press Institute had found some Ridders, like Bernard, committed to operating objective newspapers. "His natural interests are in the Ridder management and business structures," Curtis reported. "But one of his longtime editors tells me that he never knew of a case when Bernie wanted news suppressed." Then there were the individualists like Joseph Ridder, who published the *San Jose Mercury-News.* Joe demonstrated scant interest in news and editorial functions and none in objectivity. Curtis quoted a conservative-minded longtime TV dealer in town: "The free press in San Jose is exactly what Joe Ridder says it is and no more. He prints what he wants printed to serve his interests and he will keep news out of the paper or distort news and editorial stuff which is not in his interest."

Merger, as concept and then as reality, took time to grow. As president, Bernard Ridder, Jr., thought deeply about the future of his company. The Knights were not the only fish in the sea; there were tentative talks with Gannett as well. Merger was a far-reaching step, joining two formerly independent companies; pooling management, assets, and style; surrendering individual initiative to the whole. For several years, then, the idea was put aside. Ridder went public in the same year as the Knights, 1969. Bernie Ridder received a letter from Lee Hills suggesting that they talk. Thus began the serious study.

Ridder thinkers, including financial vice president Ben Schneider, developed close rapport with Hills, Alvah Chapman, Curtis, and others. "Hills understood the Ridder family problems," Bernie Ridder would recall. "He was able to work them out." On the other hand, Ridder felt that Jack Knight was never wholly enthusiastic about merger, for much the same reasons that he disliked public ownership: merger was another step away from individually owned newspapers.

Some Knight hardliners, such as John McMullan, were already worried enough about corporate journalism, several steps removed from conglomerate journalism. They saw the editor's authority ultimately subjugated to the interests of directors, business managers, and stock analysts. In a letter to Jack Knight, McMullan pondered "the problem of thought control among a corporate group of newspapers. Increasing size imposes increasing responsibilities to preserve differences of opinion. We need to guard against group newspapers becoming group thinking."

Knight replied that he saw no such dangers; group operations could actually bring vast improvement to the press, given proper management. "We believe that we have improved every newspaper that we've acquired." In darker moods, however, Knight did not express such sunny optimism. In a moment of pique, he would be heard to grumble, "If I were a younger man, I'd lead a rebellion."

Merger offered benefits to both sides.

For the Knights, it meant a broader monetary base and earnings stability. By now Lee Hills was board chairman and Chapman president. As Chapman would recall years later, "We were looking for a way to become not only larger but also more geographically diversified." In five years as a public company, he noted, Knight earnings had tended to fluctuate with the fortunes of its three major classified advertising markets, Miami, Philadelphia, and Detroit. Chapman felt that the broader-based arrangement could overcome this. The Ridder balance sheet was excellent.

For the Ridders, merger offered linkup with one of the nation's most astutely managed operations and thus an even stronger market for the stock. It also could solve the potentially knotty problem of company leadership succession; by breaking up the family dynasty, it prevented future infighting for power. Bernard Ridder had been a unifying force for the three family factions, but rare was the individual who could navigate the tricky crosscurrents of intrafamily conflicts. Not all Ridders were pleased with the Knight financial condition, however, feeling that costs of buying the Philadelphia and Lexington papers had weakened them. Bernard Ridder saw this as vastly outweighed by Knight operational strengths. "Those people have a lot of editorial know-how," the Ridder president insisted. Some Ridder papers, he added delicately, needed all the help they could get. "The Knights can be a real plus for us." Two key family members, Eric Ridder, publisher of the *New York Journal of Commerce,* and Joseph, publisher of the *San Jose Mercury-News,* opposed the merger, but Bernie's brother Daniel, publisher of the *Long Beach Press-Telegram,* supported it. Daniel would later become a vice president of the merged company and member of the operating committee.

Negotiations in depth began in the early part of 1974 with a phone call from Chapman to Bernard Ridder, Jr. There followed a series of meetings aimed at unraveling the complex tangle of business and financial affairs. "We were merging," Chapman would reflect, "two styles of management and, to some extent, two publishing philosophies." But finally—and with surprising ease, considering the scope of the issues involved—it was done.

On July 10, 1974, leaders of the two companies met in Akron to announce agreement in principle to combine their operations into a group of thirty-five daily and twenty-three Sunday newspapers. In combined circulation—3.8 million on weekdays, including Saturdays, and 4.2 million on Sundays—Knight-Ridder would be the largest U.S. newspaper group at the time. The new company also would operate a national news and feature service, plus a commodity news service. It had a combined annual operating income in excess of $500 million, the bulk of this from advertising and circulation, and nearly eighteen thousand employees from coast to coast. Annual net income was a hefty $36 million. Lee Hills was named chairman and chief executive officer of Knight-Ridder Newspapers, Inc.; Bernard Ridder, Jr., vice chairman and chief of the operating committee; and Chapman, president. John S. Knight held a nominal title as editorial chairman and his brother James as chairman of the executive committee. Stockholders ratified the agreement on November 20 at meetings in New York and Miami.

Knights and Ridders: As separate entities, they had come a long way from C. L. Knight's feisty *Akron Beacon Journal* and Herman Ridder's *Staats-Zeitung.* But now it was a new game. Or was it? On the first day of combined business, December 2, 1974, Hills, Ridder, and Chapman put out a letter to employees defining basic objectives:

> *We believe that editorial quality and economic profitability are inseparable. We believe in change, and our ability to plan and master it. We believe in equality of opportunity. Our primary task . . . is to forge a new company which maintains a singleness of purpose*

while retaining individuality and difference. It will not be easy.

In Akron, Jack Knight read the statement and gave a knowing nod. Indeed, it would not be easy.

It never was.

Beryl had smoked heavily for many years and could not give up the habit, even with her life at stake. And so gradually emphysema robbed her of beauty, breath, and strength. Debilitating weakness was blamed for the falls that broke each hip and sent her to the hospital for surgery and recuperation. As illness sapped her, one was reminded of the draining of a beaker of fine wine. Thus three years of steadily worsening illness left Beryl Knight a wheezing invalid attended by nurses, dependent on oxygen, and so frail that merely walking from room to room was an ordeal. There was no question that she was terminally ill; Dr. Henry Kraus knew it, as did other physicians and attendants, and gently passed along the suggestion to her husband.

It had always been a close relationship between Beryl and Jack, but not without abrasions. Social acquaintances found little warmth in her. In times past there had been embarrassing little scenes between them in the presence of others, flare-ups more of mood than substance. With her final illness, however, all that passed. The hour they spent together each afternoon was the most important of her day, and one for which she regularly and meticulously prepared. Her stepdaughter-in-law, Cynthia Knight, the wife of Landon, would later depict these daily periods of companionship with Jack as Beryl's "last real contact with the life she had known."

The end came late on a Thursday evening in August. As she sank toward death, Jack spent part of the final vigil in the den of their Blair House apartment, waiting. And then Beryl died. She was eighty-one.

She was buried at Rose Hill, beside Johnny, Jr.

Her passing struck him like a blow. He had never felt so totally alone. He tried to cope, but the old protective instincts no longer seemed to function as before. Even work was not the palliative it had once been. "I am having a hard time adjusting to her death," he told Stuffy Walters. Time was conspiring against him; time conspired against them all.

There were those who could offer gentle support. Hills had lost his wife Eileen some years before, and then married Tina (Argentina Schifano Ramos), an Italian-American who was publisher of the newspaper *El Mundo* in San Juan, Puerto Rico. When Knight checked into Massachusetts General Hospital in October, finally having the appendix removed, Hills found him still trying to accept Beryl's loss. "Don't fight it," Hills said. "You're a guy who thinks that if something is wrong you should be able to fix it, or order somebody to fix it. Life doesn't work that way. The only thing that will help is time."

Still another problem now loomed for them all: Jack Knight's will. Preparing for death had never been among his priorities. He simply planned to leave his fortune to Beryl, John S. Knight III, and Landon; with smaller portions to Johnny's mother, Dorothy; Knight's stepdaughter, Rita, and her son, Robert Craig; and a bit to the latter's children. It did not concern him that such orthodox methods would create an enormous tax on the estate. Not that he lacked a practical alternative. A tax strategy was ready in the Knight Foundation. This was the outgrowth of a modest charitable account, the Charles Landon Knight Memorial Education Fund. Created in 1940 by Jack Barry, the fund had provided scholarship aid to deserving students—Barry was keen on developing young classical musicians and opera singers—through grants and no-interest loans. Small gifts had come over the years from the Knights or the various newspapers. The money went to musicians, medical students, teachers, librarians. As the federal tax bite on individuals increased, however, shrewd Blake McDowell saw potential for the fund to become a mechanism for holding Knight stock. In 1950, McDowell expanded it into the Knight Foundation, serving "charitable, religious, scientific, literary, general education and philanthropic purposes . . . for the benefit of the general public." The fund remained small until the death of Clara Knight in 1966, when her stocks gave it an infusion of $21 million in cash.

Still, the foundation was not one of Jack Knight's compelling interests. In part, he had been soured by tough congressional curbs on charitable tax strategies in the stringent Tax Reform Act of 1969. Knight was so frustrated by government meddling that he briefly considered abolishing the foundation altogether, grumbling, "To hell with it."

Stubborn pride was fraught with peril, however. His personal wealth put him in the 70 percent estate tax bracket. If he left $100 million to the heirs—his own rough estimate as the largest shareholder in Knight Newspapers, Inc.—then about $70 million would be owed in estate taxes. Some estimates of his worth ran to $200 million. To pay such taxes, a huge block of shares would have to be dumped on the market for public sale. In the best of times, such an offering could erode heavily the price of Knight stock and cripple the Ridder merger. And these were not the best of times. An explosive increase in world oil prices and the resultant deepening recession had sent the stock market tumbling. A stock sale of $70 million could liquidate half the Knight company.

Knight's poor health brought the problem into critical focus. His wife had left $1.9 million to her sister, the children and grandchildren, and a residue to the Knight Foundation. Hills, as board chairman and chief executive officer of Knight Newspapers, approached the main problem delicately, asking Knight whether he had considered the Knight Foundation in his estate plans.

"I have no interest in the foundation," Knight said. "I'm not going to leave it anything."

Hills quietly persisted. The foundation, properly funded and managed, could become enormously important in the cause of better journalism, community improvement, the arts, health care, and education, he said. Knight had given money to Cornell University and the Chicago Hospital and personally helped to finance college educations for some deserving young people. Did he consider leaving anything for other charitable causes?

"No. And I don't intend to."

He was peevish and out of sorts. There was a lot more to life, Knight reasoned, than money. What had money brought him? "Lee, I'm not having any fun with the newspapers any more. People aren't following my thinking or my advice." He was still unhappy with the business arrangement to print and distribute the *Miami Daily News.* The memory of the Philadelphia purchases rankled him. "I had ten reasons for not buying Philadelphia. At our final meeting in Cleveland, I called Jim Knight outside and told him it was not too late to stop it. Jim brushed me off, saying we could do it." He was unhappy about bowing out of the company and having little voice in management. He picked at personalities, including that of Mark Ethridge, Jr., the bright young former editor of the editorial page in Detroit, now moved to Akron as executive editor of the *Beacon Journal*. But he had to admit that the *Beacon Journal* was looking better. "Maybe," he said grudgingly, "I just want to run everything."

And so the issue lurked like a specter. "Your illnesses are not unknown, Jack," Hills remarked. "You are the largest, and Jim the second largest, of the stockholders. Suppose an analyst asks, 'What about this?' That's a sticky question. How do you think we ought to respond?" Wills were not sacrosanct, he reminded Knight. One lawsuit could tie up a will for years, and the executors—bankers, most likely—would wind up in control of the company, voting the Knight shares.

The point was well made. "Bankers," Jack Knight muttered, "might not be the best custodians of newspapers."

Hills nodded. "Some bankers might not be in tune with your ideas of what newspapers ought to be."

In early October 1974, Knight told Hills that he intended to review his will with a lawyer friend in Cleveland. The board chairman dropped him a brief follow-up note:

> *If a large public offering of our stock became necessary in this worst money market in modern times, it might have a bad effect on the company and on the shareholders for a long time to come. I know you have thought about this and doubtless have the best advice available on how to deal with the radically changing situation. Because of the responsibility you entrusted in me as head of our company, I thought I should mention it.*

Hills's point struck home.

Abruptly, Knight's will underwent radical change. He asked Hills to go to Cleveland and look over the new version. "I want to make certain it avoids the dangers we were talking about." It did. The new will provided for the heirs by means of trust funds and left virtually everything else to the Knight Foundation.

Ben Maidenburg had been running the foundation part-time while also serving as publisher of the *Beacon Journal.* By 1975, however, assets had mushroomed to $23 million and the workload vastly increased as more and larger grants went into various communities served by Knight Newspapers. Former Goodyear executive C. C. Gibson was hired as full-time foundation president.

It was to become a job of remarkable expansion. By 1986, with the final settlement of Knight's estate, assets would mushroom to more than $400 million, and the foundation would be the twentieth-largest in the nation.

His return to writing in spring 1974 had been a bittersweet experience. His health problems, the need for constant medication, and, of course, Beryl's illness had sapped the vigor of his mind. He brooded about the sorry state to which the world had descended and government's encroachment on business. Today's businessman lived in an insane world of official paperwork. "Some of our agencies are bureaucrated to the point of absurdity. The owners of a business enjoy few freedoms; many of them have been preempted by regulatory agencies. . . . Can capitalism survive?" In private conversation he would grumble, "There's nothing free about free enterprise." His essays continued through the summer, but spasmodically. And then they stopped again.

The fall and winter passed, and he did not write. At the urging of Dr. Gerald Austen, he went down to Miami for the cold weather months and spent them in the house on La Gorce Island. He walked or rode his bicycle for a mile a day and was proud of the effort. Before the appendectomy, he had had to subsist on a heavy diet of Jell-O, which he despised. At least now he could eat again. He relished the exercise of self-control, despite being eighty years old and feeling that time was passing in a mighty rush. He would drop in to the newsroom of the *Miami Herald* and know almost nobody: all the faces were strange, and the people terribly young. "I've quit smoking," he told one of the few older reporters whom he still knew. "I've quit drinking. I haven't written anything in months. There isn't much left, is there?"

Spring approached, renewing his vigor. He felt like resuming the column, physically if not mentally. Mentally he was fearful of making a hash of it. The opportunity came with a visit by the new president, Gerald Ford, to south Florida and an invitation to breakfast. They were longtime acquaintances from the Detroit days. Knight's ensuing column on March 2, 1975, was his first in seven months. "Breakfasting with presidents," he began, "is one of my favorite pursuits. . . . Gerald R. Ford, President, looked and acted much the same as did Jerry Ford, representative from Michigan's Fifth Congressional District 20 years before. He is still the friendly Jerry Ford, no frills or pretensions."

Knight's admirers were pleased to have him back in the papers. There was a rush of congratulatory mail. A week later he came up with another 750-word discussion of Ford's talk about renewing trade relations with Castro. How soon America forgot the bloody works of the tyrant! "Are we influenced more by money than principle?" Miami's rabidly anti-Castro Cuban exiles cheered him. Knight was mentally refreshed, but physically worn out. His heart seemed to begrudge any extra effort. He took pills to thin his blood and pills against angina attacks and taped nitroglycerin to his chest to keep the pains manageable.

Deep down, he was frightened.

He was not really prepared for the column's ending. After writing two thousand "Notebooks" in thirty-nine years, it was not the final column that he would consciously choose to write. He sat down as usual on a Thursday in Miami and pecked it out on the old Underwood, giving Ford a little hell for refusing to veto a $22 billion tax-cut bill stage-managed by the Democrats for the next election. "The President should have bitten the bullet. Now is the time to take a stand for sanity in fiscal affairs. . . ."

The date was March 30, 1975.

Suddenly he didn't have the heart to do it anymore.

Knight went back to Akron. He spent time at the *Beacon Journal* and lunched with old friends at the Mayflower Club. He had dinners with Stella Hall, whose late husband, Bill, had written the company's insurance. He also strengthened a social relationship with Betty Augustus, widow of Cleveland industrialist Ellsworth Augustus. But even among friends, he was frequently out of sorts and unpleasantly critical of people. At Knight-Ridder board meetings it was difficult to contain his bad moods. Despite the deference they gave him, the meetings reminded him that others now ran things. He had words with Clark Clifford, the handsome Washington, D.C., lawyer and former secretary of defense who had been the Ridder family's longtime legal adviser. Clifford had joined the board with the merger. Eddie Thomas was forever telling Knight to behave himself, but understood better after seeing all the medicine vials on his dresser in the Blair House apartment. "Do you take all this stuff?" Thomas asked. "No wonder you feel rotten."

Knight could not express out loud what was on his mind. How did one speak of the ending of life? And so on June 4, 1975, he sat down and typed a letter to Dr. Kraus, his physician in Akron. It was a letter of instructions, for the guidance of his family, physician, lawyer, clergyman, or for any medical facility that might be charged with his care: a letter about death, and dying.

> *Death is as much a reality as birth, growth, maturity and old age. It is the one certainty of life. Let this statement stand as an expression of my wishes, while I am still of sound mind.*
>
> *If the situation should arise in which there is no reasonable expectation of my recovery from physical or mental disability, I request that I be allowed to die and not be kept alive by artificial means or "heroic measures."*
>
> *I do not fear death itself as much as the indignities of deterioration, dependence and hopeless pain. . . .*

He signed with his characteristic, forward-thrusting scrawl, "John S. Knight."

There was a tremor in the writing.

Age and infirmity slowed a man's steps but did not temper his beliefs. Knight at eighty surrendered no convictions and neither did he lose his zest for the spirited interview. Writers, students, and compilers of records still visited, with their tape recorders and notebooks, to talk about his life and thought. If his remarks were not always what they wanted to hear, then so be it; he had been schooled in hard practicality, and the new shape of things did not inspire him.

"I do not believe in schools of journalism," he grumbled to one such interviewer. "I think you ought to give a man a good liberal arts education with the accent on languages and history, geography and some finance."

Knight worried about the lot of the entrepreneur in a time of progressive government meddling, union intransigence, and an economy heavily dependent on public payrolls.

I've always been an optimist about this country on the theory that we've lived through various economic and social changes and wars, and we've persevered and emerged stronger. And yet few people understand today how the system is supposed to work. Somebody asked me the other day, "What would you do if you were starting out again, fresh?" I said I wouldn't go into business. He said, "What would you like to be?" And I said, "Well, if I were as good-looking, I'd like to be a Clark Clifford, who advises his clients, charges them outrageous fees and plays golf two day a week."

fortune seemed a little more evenhanded in its treatment of John S. Knight. He grew closer to his brother and son. The few honors that he had not already won as a journalist and a human rights advocate were heaped on his shoulders.

Then, on Aug. 8, 1974, his wife of 42 years died after a long illness. And there was more to come.

The news of the death of John S. Knight Jr. in Germany was kept from Johnny's wife, the former Dorothy Wells of Columbus, Ga., until after the birth on April 13 — about two weeks later — of a boy who was named John S. Knight III.

Knight. Through the medium of the Editor's Notebook they discussed the campus violence of the '60s and the course of the Vietnam War. They exchanged letters frequently, played golf together and ta...

Pau... Janens..., managing editor of the D...y New... said of young John. "He was really a ...ing guy. He knew who... he was an heir to a fortune and to a key job in the organization if he earned it. But he didn't take himself too seriously."

It was obvious that John S. Knight hoped through his grandson to see that...

John S. Knight III and lives, I can't think o... down. So I am not m...yself guilty.

"I am not going to ...her me," he told Thoi... start a new life."

He returned to Fl...ter his grandson's ... ...ounced he would ma... beth) Augustus. They 1976, in the chapel of Sea at Bal Harbour Lifestyle editor of the...

"A YOUNG MAN BLESSED"

...pare for Harvard. He graduated from the latter cum laude in 1968 with a degree in history, then went on to study philosophy, politics and economics at Oxford University in England, where he earned a master of arts degree, with honors, in June 1970.

During high school and college he worked summer vacations at several Knight papers, including the Beacon Journal.

His first full-time newspaper job came at the Detroit Free Press in 1970. He gained experience in the circulation

center of Philadelphia, John S. Knight III was stabbed to death during a robbery by three men. There were homosexual overtones.

At the time, his grandfather was visiting at the home of Mr. and Mrs. Edwin C. Whiteheads of Greenwich, Conn. Mrs. Whiteheads is a daughter of the then Betty Augustus, widow of Cleveland millionaire Ellsworth H. Augustus. Knight and Mrs. Augustus had known each other for 35 years though a mutual interest in thoroughbreds and horse racing.

Mrs. Knight died t... while watching the R... the LaGorce Island ho...

WHEN HE STEPP...torial chairman of Kni... 1976, his title became Knight-Ridder and the His decision to qui... ...y Thomas and others "The trouble wit... ⟨night's position," The ...ly that they stay on t... hat the business can't

At age thirty, John S. Knight III had matured into a muscular, handsome man of wealth, living the bachelor life with a taste for fine furnishings, good wines, and works of art. If he lacked for anything, it was not money. His great-grandmother Clara and grandfather John Shively Knight had assured that he would be well fixed. His personality was low-key and gracious. He demonstrated a strong desire to be liked, especially among colleagues of the Knight newspapers. His social life ranged from the posh environs of Grosse Pointe, where he might party with the Henry Fords, to alcoholic roisterings and poker games with fellow journalists.

He had no steady girlfriend. It was said that he had been in love with an English girl while at Oxford, but that she had broken it off after his return to the States and married another man. And so he squired, without commitment, various young beauties to social functions.

With his looks, money, and prestige, it was impossible to think of Johnny Knight as emotionally starved. If his private life harbored dark secrets, it was not evident to friends and associates. He spoke openly of using the services of female prostitutes. He drank heavily on occasion, but like his grandfather also went for periods of abstinence. He talked of spending $10,000 in a single year for psychiatric help. But in general, the scion of the Knight legacy seemed reasonably balanced.

Throughout his adult life, John S. Knight III had lived under intense career scrutiny. Despite his grandfather's insistence that he make it on his own, clearly the way was open for his ascension to power. Not that he was pressured to follow in Jack Knight's footsteps; on the contrary, the old man took pains to leave Johnny's options open and confessed that he himself had once harbored a youthful ambition to run a cattle ranch in Wyoming.

By the early 1970s Johnny III was on the staff of the *Free Press* in Detroit, doing general assignment work and covering the courts. He investigated overcrowding in the county jail and did some background work on the Knight Newspapers disclosure of Senator Thomas Eagleton's past mental treatments, which caused the vice presidential candidate to quit the Democratic ticket. He was sensitive to the opinions of colleagues. When plans emerged to shift John to editorial writing he told his grandfather, "Some people will have the attitude, 'There goes the boss's grandson off to the ivory tower.'" The change excited him, nonetheless.

Among executives at Detroit, some egos were bruised when Johnny went over middle-management heads to seek the direct counsel of Lee Hills. He expressed mixed feelings over such small abrasions. "I certainly did not want to appear pushy in what I did, but neither can I sit back and let others decide what is best for me without interjecting my own views," he wrote to his grandfather. "It is my life. I think I should have a primary role in determining how to live it."

If John expected sympathy, he was disappointed. Inscrutably, the elder Knight replied to this bit of self-evaluation with cold detachment, his numbered paragraphs lecturing rather than communicating. Newspapers, he noted caustically, did not assign jobs to employees to excite them but to use their skills. He advised his grandson to stop talking about his educational advantages (actually, Johnny rarely mentioned them) and to remember that many a Phi Beta Kappa wound up working on a copy desk. "As they say, it takes more than education." Knight carped on the idea that his grandson wanted to start at the top, without paying his dues. "Most successful newspapermen go through a lot of grubby work experience before they emerge at the top. I gather you don't care for that routine and prefer to avoid its self-discipline. . . ."

Johnny was stung, but replied with spirit. He did not intend to flaunt his Harvard and Oxford credentials. He was well aware that he would have to "grub it out" and in no way hoped to start at the top. "Where you surmise that I don't care for hard work," he protested, "is, quite frankly, an enigma to me."

By the following spring, 1972, Johnny was writing editorials full time. Editorial page editor Mark Ethridge, Jr., quietly passed along his written evaluation. Young Knight had energy and drive, broad knowledge, excellent vocabulary, and superb education, but was inclined to make harsh judgments of public officials. "He regards Mr. Nixon not as a misguided leader for resuming the bombing of Hanoi, but as a cretinous murderer. A wrong decision is not pardonable human error, it's unspeakable." He also displayed insight into human character, got along well with his peers, and researched editorial subjects extensively.

John's greatest weakness, professionally speaking, is that he is spoiled and has not determined, for good, what he wants to do. His attendance report shows 21 days ill, which is more than the rest of the staff combined. Frankly, I can't blame him. Tying down a rich young man who's been places and seen things is no small chore. There is no question but that John can do anything he wants to do. The question is whether he wants to.

By late summer, Lee Hills was outlining to Byron Harless, Knight Newspapers corporate psychologist and vice president for personnel, a two-year training program for young Knight in Detroit, to include circulation, advertising, and *Free Press* public relations. "After that I would see him moving to one of our other papers."

The following year, John S. Knight III went to the tabloid *Philadelphia Daily News* as assistant to managing editor David Lawrence, Jr.

He had lived well in Detroit, with an apartment on the river and a twenty-four-foot racing boat, which he swapped to an art dealer for a Picasso lithograph. In Philadelphia, he took a large apartment on the twenty-third floor of the fashionable Dorchester in Rittenhouse Square, at a rental of $1,050 per month. He hired an interior decorator to furnish the place and properly display his $140,000 art collection. He kept a well-supplied liquor cabinet and white fur rugs, a mirrored weight-lifting area, a closet filled with tailor-made suits, and a collection of guns and hunting knives.

His new bosses at the *Daily News,* managing editor David Lawrence and editor Rolfe Neill, were skeptical. "There was no question about his education, or his quickness and his intelligence," Lawrence would recall. "There were questions about how much drive he would put into his work and how the staff would react to him." But the reports from Detroit had been favorable. Knight seemed intent on doing his best. A penchant for tardiness was quickly corrected; Lawrence simply made it clear that one got to work on time, and Knight complied.

He was put to work on the news desk, editing and laying out pages. His first efforts were less than inspiring. Lawrence made brisk note of deficiencies:

You tend to miss detail. For instance, "4 years later" should be "four"; it's "Jan. 24 and Oct. 29," not "January 24"; it's "loneliness," not "lonliness"; the wall is "60 feet," not "sixty feet"; it's "Philadelphia," not "Phila."; "Social Security" should be capped. But overall, a good effort.

Knight studied the style book and began to improve. Noted Lawrence, "It was exciting to see him learn how to write a headline, edit a story and lay out a page. He did all of them well."

Lawrence and his wife, Bobbie, introduced John to their favorite Philadelphia restaurant, La Truffe. Among its special features, the restaurant would cook game brought by a customer from a hunting trip. Knight vowed to bring in his own pheasant.

He progressed well at the *Daily News* and by midsummer 1975 was ready for advancement. Rolfe Neill made him day news editor, in charge of editing the front page. Neill, who had worked up from the editorship of a Knight suburban paper in Miami, wrote a note to Johnny charged with enthusiasm: "When you give a man the front page, you give him everything. . . . You have the background to make your own monument, John."

Time was ticking away.

Early on the morning of December 8, Eddie Thomas received a long-distance telephone call in Akron from Gene Roberts, one of the Philadelphia editors. He listened to Roberts's report with sickened disbelief.

"But Jack's not even here in Akron," Thomas protested. "I think he's somewhere in Connecticut, visiting Betty Augustus's family. Besides, I'm not sure I'm the right person to tell him this. Shouldn't his brother do it?"

"We've talked about it, Eddie, and you're the logical man," Roberts insisted. "Nobody's closer to Jack. Nobody can do it better."

Thomas sighed heavily. "All right." He hung up the phone, feeling the weight of his seventy-seven years.

Knight had been keeping company with Elizabeth Augustus, the Cleveland widow. Friends knew that he was hopelessly in love. Betty Augustus was bright, attractive, and—from the estate of her late husband, industrialist Ellsworth H. Augustus—even richer than Knight. She kept a stable of Thoroughbred horses and owned rambling estates at Waite Hill, near Cleveland, and the twelve-hundred-acre Old Keswick Farm, near Charlottesville, Virginia.

It was said that they would soon marry.

With a heavy heart, Thomas called the number in Connecticut, identified himself, and asked for Jack Knight. The familiar voice came on the line.

Thomas came directly to the point.

"Jack, I have a report from Philadelphia that Johnny was murdered last night. I don't have too many of the details yet. I'm . . . I'm sorry to have to call you and tell you."

That was it. He waited for the response. There was no word from Knight. The seconds passed, and it was as if time itself had been choked off. A minute went by. Finally—"Life is rough, isn't it?" John S. Knight said.

Philadelphia was electrified. Fifty detectives were assigned to the case, swarming over Rittenhouse Square. The body of John Shively Knight III had been found bound, gagged, beaten, and stabbed repeatedly with one of his own scuba diving knives. He lay in a pool of blood in his bedroom. Blood spattered the bathroom and the hallway. The place had been ransacked, drawers dumped, plants broken, clothing ripped, lamps shattered. A shocked couple who had been his houseguests for the weekend, former college classmate Dr. John McKinnon and his English-born wife, Rosemary, gave sketchy accounts of what had happened.

Mrs. McKinnon told of being awakened by an intruder in the guest bedroom, and of her physician-husband's trying desperately to revive Knight without success. In the harrowing process, Rosemary had been slashed on the hand by an assailant who had remained after two companions left.

Detectives leaked rumors to the press that young Knight had been involved with homosexuals and visited gay bars. Headlines splashed the papers as the shocked Jack Knight and company executives arrived in Philadelphia. At Dorothy's wish, Johnny's body was shipped to Columbus, Georgia, for burial, while the Knight Newspapers pursued the story with a vigor equal to that of competitors.

The funeral was conducted at the Stiffler-Hamby Macon Road Chapel in Columbus. While police made copies of five hundred signatures in the chapel guest book, a minister eulogized Johnny as "a young man blessed by birth, circumstance and family. A young man with God-given gifts." His passing was unreal, the minister went on, like a bad dream. "But it is reality. And our first thought is, 'Why?' I can't answer. I can only comfort." In chill sunlight, the motorcade drove slowly to nearby Parkhill Cemetery. TV cameras filmed the scene from a hilltop. Dorothy stood in shocked silence as the coffin was lowered into the ground. Jack Knight remained in one of the automobiles, pale and withdrawn.

After the funeral, James Knight, his wife, Mary Ann, John McMullan, and J. Montgomery Curtis went to the home of Dorothy Knight. They gently told her of the events in Philadelphia. Jim Knight told Dorothy that rumors of Johnny's homosexuality were unfounded; such stories were sometimes circulated in order to set up innocent people for blackmail. She should report any strange contacts that were made to her. Dorothy listened in white-faced silence. "She was tremendously shocked," James later told his brother.

In Philadelphia four days later, one of Knight's slayers, Felix Melendez, was mourned at a wailing wake by his Puerto Rican family. He had been shot dead by one of his confederates in the Knight robbery-murder. Detectives continued to piece together a bizarre web of fact and speculation.

It was sensational news, interwoven with allegation and circumstance. Because the victim was John S. Knight III, the press felt a special obligation to dig for details. Mayor Frank Rizzo detested the Knight-Ridder *Inquirer* and *Daily News.* The usually closemouthed Philadelphia Police Department suddenly sprang leaks. Headlines traced the hunt for Knight's killers through Philadelphia's gay community. Gossip had it that young Knight was bisexual, using procurers to obtain both female and male prostitutes. There was talk of detectives' finding hard-core pornographic pictures in a locked footlocker in the victim's apartment, along with juicy entries in his personal diary. None of this was substantiated. The generally accepted version of the Knight slaying, however, went like this:

On Saturday night, December 6, Knight and several friends dined at La Truffe on four pheasants he had shot on a hunting trip. In the meantime, several miles away in a house on Beulah Street, twenty-year-old Isais (Felix) Melendez was shooting up on drugs with friends. The Beulah Street party wore on until long after midnight. When the drugs ran out, Melendez told two companions, Salvatore Soli, thirty-seven, a street hustler, and Stevie Maleno, twenty-five, a sheet-metal worker, that he knew a "rich fag" who could supply more and also had cash. He took them to the apartment of John Knight III. The bachelor's houseguests had gone to bed. Melendez rang the doorbell and pleaded to be admitted. Knight made the mistake of unlocking the door. Soli would later describe what happened next: "Felix runs in and cracks the guy. The guy's glasses fall off. The guy looked bewildered, confused. . . ." Melendez and Soli shoved Knight roughly into the bedroom, slugged him, pushed him to the floor, trussed him with neckties and belts. Soli and Maleno rummaged through the apartment for money and jewels, but found little. While they were busy, the drug-enraged Melendez grabbed up the diving knife and stabbed Knight five times.

Soli and Maleno found the McKinnons in bed. They forced Mrs. McKinnon to help them search the apartment for valuables, while her husband slept on. She saw Knight lying on the floor. An elderly night porter rang the doorbell with complaints about the noise. The smiling Melendez reassured him. The man left. Soli and Maleno, frightened, left too. Melendez remained, armed with a harpoon and the knife. Rosemary McKinnon awakened her husband, who attempted unsuccessfully to revive Knight. The phone wire had been cut, so Mrs. McKinnon started downstairs for help. She scuffled with Melendez in the elevator, and he cut her with the knife. He then fled into the dawn. Four days later, Melendez's dead body was found in New Jersey, shot.

The Knight murder case went on for months. Maleno pleaded guilty to the slaying of both Knight, as an accomplice, and Melendez and drew two concurrent life terms. Soli was found guilty of the Knight murder, escaping the electric chair by three votes of the jury.

After the funeral, with his own wounds fresh and deep, John S. Knight had flown to Boston and checked himself into Massachusetts General Hospital. He sought refuge and isolation. "I'm here to think," he announced. "I don't want to be disturbed." There, alone, he went through the process.

Nothing in his lifetime, not the deaths of Katie or Johnny, Jr., or Frank or even Beryl, had prepared him for this. He was eighty-one years old, tired and sick in body and mind, taking four nitro-glycerin pills a day against chest pain. Was he to blame for Johnny's tragedy? The thing made no sense to him at all. The very life-styles involved were alien. The boy had been given every advantage, every chance for education and preparation, and certainly all the money he needed. Life had been his for the taking. Where did things go wrong?

Five months later, in an interview with this writer, Jack Knight would analyze his own train of thought:

> I can't think of a time that I let him down. I got him out of a small town, exposed him to the finest education. We played golf. We could talk together for hours. If we were to live our lives over, I can't think of a thing that I would change. I said to myself, "I've been through this before. I see no reason to reprove myself. I am not going to let this destroy me."
>
> A minister came up to see me from Akron. But I realized that I didn't need a minister. I had to wage this discussion with myself, alone. I thanked the minister for coming. He went away.
>
> They had represented Johnny as heir to the Knight newspapers. He was never heir to anything like that. We are a publicly owned company. There is no heir. He would have to sell himself. As for myself, I had done everything I could to see that he reached a position to achieve what he could, no more and no less. So I said, "I am not guilty of Johnny's death. I am not going to adjudge myself guilty."
>
> "I will not be crushed."

After four days, he checked himself out of the hospital and asked Elizabeth Augustus to proceed with their wedding plans.

The mystery of John S. Knight III would never be resolved. But on the first anniversary of his death, there appeared in the rival *Philadelphia Bulletin* a story by reporter Ronald Goldwyn suggesting that in the rush of exposé and scandal, the murder victim might have had unfair treatment from the news media of which he was a part.

"Many details of Knight's private life, sad, sordid and gossipy, were leaked to the media and eclipsed the victim's public record as a rising young newspaper executive," Goldwyn reported. "A year later . . . there are indications that Knight's double-life reputation as a kinky perverter of young men is mostly a bad rap."

Without conclusive evidence, he went on,

> Philadelphia police sources leaked to the media reports of a sensational private collection of tapes and photos and a diary of sexual exploits found in Knight's apartment. But Assistant District Attorney Clifford Haines, who was chief of the district attorney's homicide unit when it organized prosecutions of Soli and Maleno, now says the tapes and photos never existed. "I don't know where that story came from," Haines said, adding that most of Knight's photos consisted of family snapshots, including some pictures of young men in bathing suits, and nude photos that are available commercially. "Nothing private that was, quote, pornographic, unquote. It was a gross exaggeration of not a great deal."

Elizabeth Augustus was one of those women who wear their age well. At seventy-six, she gave the impression of youthful vitality. "I never mention age," she said. "I'm lucky to feel as young as I do." Independent and strong-minded, she was a graceful hostess, traveled widely in her own prop-jet aircraft, and made money as an international breeder and seller of racehorses. Her father, Daniel Good, had founded a chain of five-and-dime stores that subsequently became part of the F.W. Woolworth Company. She was married to Ellsworth Augustus in 1920, and he died forty-four years later, a multimillionaire Cleveland industrialist and president of the National Council of the Boy Scouts.

The Knights and the Augustuses had been social acquaintances for thirty-five years. "We've known each other for so long," Betty said, "that I can't remember exactly when we met."

Jack's personal interest in her began in spring 1975, when each was invited to the Kentucky Derby as a guest of Leslie Combs II. Combs loaded up his luxury bus, the Blue Goose, with friends for the ride from Lexington to the track in Louisville, deliberately seating Knight and Betty Augustus side by side.

After that, they were constantly together at dinners and parties, holding hands, dancing cheek-to-cheek. "Jack fell madly in love with Betty Augustus," Eddie Thomas would remember. The relationship blossomed in Akron, Lexington, and Miami. They went to the horse sales at Saratoga, dined at the private La Gorce and Surf clubs in Miami Beach, weekended with friends or family at Cleveland, Charlottesville, or New York.

The wedding had been set for early January. With Johnny's murder, friends assumed it would be postponed. Betty gave Knight unblinking emotional support, spoke frankly of "this awful tragedy," and left the rest to him. It was Knight himself who decided to carry on as planned.

The ceremony was supposed to be small. "We'll just go around the corner and get married," Betty joked. Only the families would be there. But plans somehow kept expanding.

Akron Beacon Journal columnist Betty Jaycox visited Mrs. Augustus at her home, Cobble Court, south of Willoughby, Ohio. There was snow on the ground. Betty introduced a couple of resident dogs, a German shepherd and a curly-haired mixed breed. She nodded to the mixed-breed. "That's Peabody. We gave her a fancy name for status. She's a stray." The house was big and warm, with a garden room, picture windows, skylights, trellises, ivy cascading from holders, white chandeliers, and scenic antique wallpaper. Betty talked about her fiancé, with whom she shared a love of horses but not of dogs, and laughed. "It's the only thing in our relationship that isn't perfect."

More than one hundred guests attended the wedding in the chapel of the Church-by-the-Sea at Bal Harbour, Florida, near Miami Beach. The minister was an old friend of Jack Knight, the Reverend John L. Yenches. Candles guttered in brass candlesticks, and there were bouquets of iris and roses. The bride wore a long-sleeved gown of blue silk, the groom a dark business suit. Peggy Augustus was her mother's matron of honor. Landon Knight served as his father's best man.

Betty and Jack walked down the aisle together, arm-in-arm. Reverend Yenches kept his formalities brief. Knight tried to slip the wedding band on his bride's finger. There was chatting and giggling at the altar. She had forgotten to remove her engagement ring first. Reverend Yenches suggested that she transfer that ring to her right hand, making room for the wedding ring. "I can't put it on the other hand," she said. "It won't go on." The audience stirred. Betty looked apologetically at Jack. "I've blown it."

Finally, somehow, the ring exchange was made, the ceremony finished. As a photographer flashed pictures, they left the altar and started down the aisle. Knight stopped in midstride and went back to thank the minister, leaving the bride by herself. "Well, I'll just have to go it alone," she said. Laughter rippled through the crowd. Knight caught up with her, and they went out together.

Afterward, they all partied at Miami Beach's Indian Creek Country Club, drinking toasts and dancing while a trio played the music of their bygone youth.

"Where are you going on your honeymoon, Jack?"

"Hell, La Gorce Island. What's any better than that?"

Long after midnight, Knight's house at La Gorce in Miami Beach glowed with lights. A full moon lay a swath of silver across Biscayne Bay. There was a scent of jasmine. Two elderly lovers strolled out, arm-in-arm.

For the magic, breathless moment, time seemed to stop.

It was a fresh beginning. At eighty-one, he was five years older than his bride. Each of them had heart problems and doubtful prognoses. And yet life filled with unexpected new zest. They were in demand for dinners and parties. He enjoyed Betty's family, a son and three daughters and assorted grandchildren. He found in his wife both friendly warmth and mental toughness. His dark moods evoked in Elizabeth Augustus Knight neither sympathy nor terror; rather, she insisted that he be civil. He doted on her innate conservatism and told his daughter-in-law Cynthia, wife of Landon: "I always marry Thoroughbreds."

Doggedly he went about the business of acknowledging the messages of sympathy over Johnny's death. He kept things brief and pointed. (To John J. Gilligan, Washington, D.C.: "JSK III was an attractive and able young man. In reviewing our lives together, I can think of nothing that I would change. Therefore, I intend to move ahead.") In April, he surrendered his last official title as editorial chairman of Knight-Ridder Newspapers. Nominally, this left him as a director, but he was also the principal stockholder and living embodiment of the Knight side of the corporation.

Knight himself was done with it all, even weaned from the "Notebook." As the nation prepared for its bicentennial celebration in the summer of 1976, editors urged him to write something suitable. He declined. Miami cooked in a heat wave as he stood in his office and talked with an interviewer about his life, his hopes, his disillusionments.

"If I resumed writing, I'd see things all around that infuriate me," he said. "Don't misunderstand. I have no bitterness. I don't grind my teeth and pull out what little hair I have left. I've never been personally happier. I get up in the morning and feel great."

He was taking daily long walks and riding his bicycle around La Gorce Island. His Fourth Estate Stables had a dozen racehorses in training in Miami, New York, and Kentucky and was stocked with four excellent broodmares. He and Betty planned to take several Thoroughbreds to France for racing. "Marriage to her is absolutely great. She is attractive, high-spirited, loves life, loves the outdoors, loves animals. She's enthusiastic, good at everything. She doesn't try to change me."

He stared out the window at a passing sailboat on the bay. On distant islands, towering new buildings thrust skyward. Miami was in the midst of a new boom, and going heavily Latin. He had groused ineffectively about new trends—a Spanish-language section of the Miami paper, called *El Herald;* an expensive new experiment in home computerized electronic journalism, called Viewtron—and worried that the zeal for corporate profits would override good journalism. But in a broader sense, he worried that America was losing its individuality. Confiscatory taxation galled him. Free enterprise was a joke. Profit had become a dirty word. "When you tax beyond a certain point, you defeat incentive. Take away the vitality of business and everything suffers. If I was a young man today, knowing what I know, I wouldn't go into business."

Writing a column all those years had been good to him, as a craft; being a writer had given him an excitement granted to few men in their lives.

"People say, 'Why'd you quit?' And, 'Oh, you ought to write. You owe it to people to write something for the bicentennial, something for the Fourth of July.' I don't think so.

"What would I say that anybody would want to read?

"It's best to quit while you're ahead."

fortune seemed a little more evenhanded in its treatment of John S. Knight. He grew closer to his brother and son. The few honors that he had not already won as a journalist and a human rights advocate were heaped on his shoulders.

Then, on Aug. 8, 1974, his wife of 42 years died after a long illness. And there was more to come.

The news of the death of John S. Knight Jr. in Germany was kept from Johnny's wife, the former Dorothy Wells of Columbus, Ga., until after the birth on April 13 — about two weeks later — of a boy who was named John S. Knight III.

Knight. Through the medium of the Editor's Notebook they discussed the campus violence of the '60s and the course of the Vietnam War. They exchanged letters frequently, played golf together and ta...

Paul Janensch, managing editor of the Daily News, ... of young John, "He... was... sharing guy. He knew who he... he was an heir to a fortune and to a key job in the organization if he earned it. But he didn't take himself too seriously."

It was obvious that John S. Knight hoped through his grandson to see that...

John S. Knight III and lives, I can't think of change. I can't think ... down. So I am not myself guilty.

"I am not going to ...er me," he told Thom... start a new life."

He returned to Fl... her... his grandson's ... nounced he would ma... beth) Augustus. They 1976, in the chapel of Sea at Bal Harbour Lifestyle editor of the...

TWILIGHT'S GLEAMING

...pare for Harvard. He graduated from the latter cum laude in 1968 with a degree in history, then went on to study philosophy, politics and economics at Oxford University in England, where he earned a master of arts degree, with honors, in June 1970.

During high school and college he worked summer vacations at several Knight papers, including the Beacon Journal.

His first full-time newspaper job came at the Detroit Free Press in 1970. He gained experience in the circulation

center of Philadelphia, John S. Knight III was stabbed to death during a robbery by three men. There were homosexual overtones.

At the time, his grandfather was visiting at the home of Mr. and Mrs. Edwin C. Whiteheads of Greenwich, Conn. Mrs. Whiteheads is a daughter of the then Betty Augustus, widow of Cleveland millionaire Ellsworth H. Augustus. Knight and Mrs. Augustus had known each other for 35 years though a mutual interest in thoroughbreds and horse racing.

Mrs. Knight died th... while watching the Ro... the LaGorce Island ho...

WHEN HE STEPP... torial chairman of Kni... 1976, his title became Knight-Ridder and the His decision to qui... by Thomas and others Knight's position," Tho... ly that they stay on to hat the business can't

Friends would remember long afterward the brief, remarkable transformation of John S. Knight. "Betty brought sunlight back into his life," said *Akron Beacon Journal* columnist Polly Paffilas. "I said to her, 'Thank you for all you've done for him.' She replied, 'Well, he's done a lot for me.' " Lee Hills's wife Tina would recall: "He seemed to soften. He laughed more." Betty also took on a glow. She had a passion for the color blue, to match her eyes, and so she wore blue dresses, blue shoes, surrounded herself with things of blue. He bought her a blue Cadillac.

Strange, the gifts of circumstance. One could hardly place value on the ability to accept life's infirmities. And yet she gave him that, too. The health problems persisted, but his wife also had them, with a heart condition as bad as his own. "Betty did not talk about it, you see," Tina Hills remembered. "And after a while, he didn't either."

By mid-1977, Knight was back to something resembling his old stride. He spoke at ceremonies opening Akron's new city convention center at Cascade Plaza downtown, seeded with $200,000 from the Knight Foundation. He hoped that this kind of effort, along with such projects as the E. J. Thomas Performing Arts Center at the University of Akron, would revive the city's dying heart. "A renaissance of downtown," he liked to say. But he knew it would not happen in his lifetime.

In Miami, there was a management change for the rival *Miami Daily News*. Cox Newspapers announced that the new publisher would be David Kraslow, who for fifteen years had worked for Knight Newspapers in Miami and Washington, D.C., before moving on to executive jobs with the *Los Angeles Times* and Cox Enterprises. Kraslow was a strong, aggressive newsman. Knight wrote him a letter of congratulations and invited him to Akron for a day of shoptalk. Kraslow eagerly accepted. They talked in the old publisher's apartment and later over lunch at the Portage Country Club. "You've got a hell of a challenge down there, maybe an impossible one," Knight said. "There are too many one-newspaper towns in this country, an unfortunate trend. I'd like to see the *News* become a strong paper, a strong editorial voice. You've got a good background in the community, you've worked Miami, you understand it." He advised Kraslow to become active in town, be visible and identifiable as the *News* publisher. "Produce an editorial product that commands respect of the opinion makers." As for his relations with the *Herald* management, under the Joint Operating Agreement between the two papers: "Don't take any crap from them, Dave. Hang tough. You've got an interest to protect." It was a long, full day of talk, one-on-one. Kraslow, who took charge of the *News* on August 1, 1977, would never forget it. "It was such a tremendous, thoughtful thing for him to do," he would recall more than a decade later. "Jack hammered at me how essential it was for the *News* to be an independent editorial voice. He believed in, he insisted on, journalistic freedom."

In October, Knight made a speech at the Akron Press Club's annual awards dinner. An audience of three hundred saw flashes of the old Knight, blasting confiscatory tax laws that destroyed family newspaper enterprise. "A publisher can't leave enough negotiable securities to meet the death tax. His family must sell to big chains in order to pay off the government. It's disgraceful that other members of an owner's family can't have what was built up by their parents and grandparents."

He tore into mediocre television news programming, "so anxious to get to the commercial that nobody knows what's being said." He took a poke at lazy print journalism. "Too many editors and publishers are boring readers to death."

The crowd loved it. Applause was loud and long. Then, in a brief question-and-answer session, someone asked, "What's your golf handicap now?"

The illusion dissolved. He sadly shook his head. "Infirmity," he said.

His own family no longer interested him. What was done was done, and he had grown too old and battered to concern himself. Besides, there wasn't much family left. His surviving son, Landon, had married well, but seemed more concerned with breeding and betting on racehorses than making a mark as head of Portage Newspaper Supply Company, a Knight-Ridder satellite business based in Akron. Nor did he display interest in advancing up the Knight-Ridder hierarchy. Dorothy, mother of Johnny III, wrote infrequently from Georgia. Knight sent her checks, which went undeposited and uncashed. His other immediate family member was Beryl's daughter, Rita, whom he had adopted as a child. She, too, lived a troubled life.

Rita initially had matured into a headstrong young woman with dark eyes and a good figure. Her first marriage in 1945 to physician Robert L. Craig had produced two children, Robert and Tracy. She became a Chicago socialite and model for charity fashion shows. The marriage ended in divorce after eleven years. Rita then married Chicago insurance executive Edward N. Cheek, but that union also failed. Her third husband was Kenneth W. Hewitt, an attorney from Grand Rapids, Michigan.

By the mid-1970s she and Hewitt were living in Fort Lauderdale. Her health was failing, a condition that doctors blamed on alcohol and improper diet. By late summer 1976, the Hewitts were in Costa Rica, Central America, where at age forty-nine Rita deteriorated to skin and bones, her handwriting a childish scrawl. Knight sent George Beebe, associate publisher of the *Miami Herald,* to investigate. A Costa Rican physician, Dr. Oscar Ortiz, told Beebe: "I first saw her seven weeks ago. She looked like someone out of a Nazi concentration camp." Rita had been hospitalized in San José after a female neighbor found her isolated in her bed, soiled and starving. Both Hewitt and Rita insisted to Beebe that her illness was not alcohol-related. "Jack Knight has two CIA agents down here spying on me," Hewitt confided. "I know. I talked with one of them today."

In a lengthy report to Knight, Beebe summarized: "It all adds up to a sad and confused story. I am sorry that I couldn't come back with the problems solved. . . ."

Rita's husband kept Knight informed of the spiraling cost of her medical and nursing care. For 1977 alone, Knight paid nearly $65,000 and wrote exasperatedly to his adoptive son-in-law. "I have been very happy to help out, but the continuing appeals for more and more money are not to my liking. . . ." He established a large trust fund to meet her medical expenses. Beebe would make another trip to San José in spring 1980 and report back, sadly, "The picture is unchanged, and if there is a solution, I can't find one."

Professionally, the older generation was fading fast. Stuffy Walters was dead, Ben Maidenburg slowly dying. Lee Hills would retire in 1979 as Knight-Ridder board chairman, leaving Bernard Ridder, Jr., and Alvah Chapman in the top jobs. Bright young talent was everywhere, but Knight tended to focus from the perspective of old age. He tried to absorb the exploding amount of information from more and more newspapers, all progressively harder to read. Either his sight was dimming or the print was too small. Some papers seemed sloppily printed, with ugly black lines and distracting boxes. He expressed his chagrin in staff meetings to no avail and then began writing memos.

To J. Montgomery Curtis, Knight-Ridder vice president: I don't want to be a nuisance on this subject, but I think newspapers are fighting a losing battle. You can't attract subscribers by making publications harder to read.

☐   ☐

To John McMullan, executive editor, the Miami Herald: *Hopefully, one of these days you will come around to my point of view on type sizes.*

To Kurt Luedtke, executive editor, the Detroit Free Press: *People like to find newspaper reading a pleasure, not a chore.*

For an aging man, life was rife with physical indignities.

He had come to despise elevators, especially small, balky ones. An elevator in his house at Miami Beach stopped between floors, trapping him for ninety minutes until he was freed by a city rescue squad. In Akron, the *Beacon Journal*'s lobby unit sometimes simply refused to function. Knight was now eighty-three years old, suffering from a bad back and angina pains and had recently undergone surgical removal of eighteen inches of cancerous large intestine. He vented his displeasure to the *Beacon Journal* business department. "Four times this summer I have had to negotiate the three flights of stairs. The uncertain elevator is a disgrace to our company." A budget item was added for elevator repairs.

Nonphysical annoyances galled him. He could not understand the New Journalism. It was an unholy thing, in his view, when reporters could inject personal bias into a story, especially if it struck at one of his cherished institutions. One day as he scanned the *Lexington Herald,* Knight snorted, made an angry red pencil mark around an offending item, and fired off a note to publisher Creed C. Black. "I bring your attention to the coverage of the Lexington Ball. I found it an obvious attempt by a young reporter to evidence his distaste for 'the establishment.' This kind of juvenile writing almost makes me throw up."

It was an old rancor that had grated on him since long before the reporter was born. Franklin D. Roosevelt also had roused the publisher's ire in his lofty disdain for "economic royalists." But now, under the influence of age and medication, the angry Knight sent copies of his missive to both Hills and James K. Batten, Knight-Ridder vice president, fuming, "This negates some arguments for 'complete editorial independence.' " In earlier times, he would never have gone to such extreme over a trifle.

A newspaper was a living thing, both corporate and mortal, but the stuff that gave it purpose, news, was as temporary as a puff of smoke. Against constant deadlines, talented people poured their energies into the making of a daily newspaper. Great prose was written at a moment's notice and promptly forgotten. In the city room nothing was more vital than the next edition, nothing deader than the last. As midwives to the printed word, newspaper people daily brought to life a miracle, only to see it die as it rolled off the presses.

Knight had always drawn vitality from the process. For good or ill, theirs was the chronicle of life in all its glory and meanness. "The best newspaper crusade is not sensation-mongering," he liked to say, "but simply printing the truth."

One ignored the disciplines at peril. All his life he had respected discipline and goaded those who fell short. His ire often fell on the *Akron Beacon Journal,* for that paper—in the cynical view of his journalists—was the "mother church." The only truly successful editor there, besides Knight himself, had been Ben Maidenburg, who shrewdly ran it the boss's way: heavy on community service, boosterism, and society interest and mindful of Akron's pecking order in civic and social affairs. Still, Knight jotted his notes and nitpicked. "Memorandum, Aug. 2, 1977: Front page makeup inconsistent in appearance. Editorials flabby, little variety. Life / Style section performance uneven, little local copy, too much syndicated matter. Business pages fail to show much enterprise. . . ." And "Memo, June 6, 1979: The *Beacon Journal* seems to be falling into the classic liberal posture, out of line with editorial policies which have made it a distinctive Ohio newspaper."

Akron was tough. It could make or break a man.

Mark Ethridge, Jr., Princeton-educated, bright, liberal, product of a famous family—his father, Mark, Sr., was famed for his leadership at the *Louisville Courier-Journal;* his mother, Willie Snow Ethridge, was an author—arrived from the *Detroit Free Press* as Akron's new editor in 1973. It was a significant step, out of shirtsleeve editing at which he excelled into the murkier environs of management. Personable, with an attractive wife, Peg, and children, Ethridge brimmed with confidence. But Akron was conservative and set in its ways. Within eighteen months, Ethridge was having trouble. "He was an idealist, a liberal," Peg would recall years later. "He wanted to make changes overnight. Akron wasn't ready for that."

Derick Daniels arrived from Detroit to troubleshoot. He found Ethridge applying sophisticated standards of noninvolvement to a town accustomed to hands-on editors. The editor had a serious problem with community relationships. "I think Mark knows where he stands, although not in terms that he finds palatable," Daniels concluded. "Whether he can handle all that, time will tell."

Ethridge tried gamely. It vexed him, he said, to see stories killed because they displeased the Akron establishment. He tried to raise standards of objectivity. "Ben [Maidenburg], with the best of intentions, has run the paper as a shill for the community." Ethridge sought an end to civic "puffery." But others sensed his withdrawal, raising barriers between himself and the staff. His private life suffered. His marriage failed, ending in divorce. Knight asked departing managing editor Robert Giles to produce a private summary. Giles and Ethridge had been at odds. Giles wrote bluntly what he believed was the staff's consensus:

> *They consider Mark to be cold, withdrawn, rigid in his attitudes, impulsive in judging others, awkward in dealing with people, lacking a commitment to Akron. . . . Others said that in remodeling his office, the act of removing windows from the walls and door became a symbol of Mark's attitude toward the staff; he wanted to be sealed off from it.*

In July 1976, Mark Ethridge, Jr., resigned from the *Beacon Journal,* his enormous talent thwarted and his ambitions frustrated. He would die of cancer in North Carolina nine years later.

The new editor at the *Beacon Journal* was Paul Poorman, forty-five, a former managing editor of the *Detroit News.* Poorman would have his troubles too. Life under the thumb of John

S. Knight never ran smooth, what with complaints targeting everything from spelling and headlines to "small, unreadable type." (Memo to James K. Batten: "This is the kind of headline writing we get from our staff at Akron. Doesn't anyone edit newspapers any more?")

Knight-Ridder editors differed in their personalities and strengths, but John McMullan was a quantity all his own. Blunt-spoken, talented, and controversial, he returned to the *Miami Herald* as executive editor in 1976. The new job gave him authority over both news and editorials. Knight was lavish in his approval. Within a few months, however, the two were haggling over the freedom given to local columnists. Knight criticized sports columnist Edwin Pope's treatment of racing news. McMullan fired back with, "I am one of those who worries about the *Herald*'s speaking with only its one big institutional voice on every public issue." Knight replied testily, "Perhaps we ought to stop writing to one another, as it only seems to add to the confusion." But he was soon back, pressing for larger type size again. McMullan finally agreed to a "somewhat larger" font, to which Knight responded, "I hope 'somewhat larger' will not mean miniscule."

During the 1980 presidential campaign, the *Herald* threw its editorial support to independent John Anderson, in preference to Reagan or Carter. Knight seethed. "Anderson is not equipped to hold the presidency," he told McMullan. "You only confuse your readers." The editor refused to yield. And yet for all the bickering, Knight respected his stubborn man in Miami. And so at the end of some sulfurous note, he might add a disarming closure: "Otherwise, I'll see you in December." Or "I miss you."

It was not always the quality of a newspaper, just as it was not always the quality of a man, that assured survival. No paper in its day had been greater than the *Chicago Daily News*. Venerable, erudite, world-renowned, the *Daily News* had been called, among other things, the writer's newspaper. Purists still debated whether it reached its peak during the ownership of John S. Knight or simply succumbed to Stuffy Walters's marketing gimmickry. Certainly Knight had given it commercial success, with a record daily circulation of 614,098 in 1957. However, the 15 years of the Knight era, from 1944 to 1959, was but a brief part of the paper's 102-year existence.

Knight had seen the demise coming, prompting him to sell to Marshall Field IV. The latter would operate the *Daily News* until his unexpected death in 1965. Ownership then passed to Marshall Field V. Beset by management and union troubles, the newspaper was in a downhill slide from which it could not recover. Still, the end of the paper in March 1978, its daily sales down to 315,000, came as a shock. Among writers and editors there remained a resolute, spit-in-the-eye spirit even at final deadline. "The *Chicago Daily News* ends as it began, a momentous book of life," mourned M. W. Newman in the lead obituary story. "It took 102 years to finish and these are the final pages. We die knowing we did our job to the utmost. . . ." Columnist Mike Royko pondered the irony of a great newspaper that couldn't make it. "This is the toughest part of being on a tradition-laden newspaper that goes under. If it had been a cheap rag, its death would have been easier to take."

And yet, with that steady, unstaunched loss of readers and advertising, the *Daily News* had been doomed, "—no matter," concluded former reporter Dennis P. Leavy, "what happened in the newsroom." Knight himself offered a parting comment that the terminal elements had been self-contracted: "Editorial ineptitude and managerial malnutrition."

Lee Hills turned over chairmanship of the flourishing Knight-Ridder organization to Bernard Ridder. In thirty-seven years with Knight, Hills had lost none of his exuberance for the job. "There was not one day," he reflected, "when I didn't look forward to going to work." The ten years of public ownership had been rugged and, for the nation, sometimes traumatic. "But they've demonstrated again," he told the stockholders, "the free society's ability to adjust." In the process, financial growth had been phenomenal, their revenues up from $275 million in 1969 to $880 million a decade later. And the most recent foreign news bureau was now being opened by veteran *Miami Herald* correspondent William Montalbano in Peking.

Ultimately, Hills noted, it was not the balance sheets and

technology that counted most; ultimately the function of newspapers was to earn and hold the public trust. "The greatest imaginable tragedy for this democracy would be the loss of our tradition of open and unfettered discussion and debate. The free press is indispensable to that process."

Despite the financial successes, Knight was not wholly pleased with the direction of things. He had long insisted that the newspaper had a dual role: business and production on the one hand, editorial on the other. Management responsibilities for each must be kept apart. This "separation of powers" was basic to a Knight operation. But change was coming about, in the form of a single publisher for both types of function.

Knight had done his own share of compromising "separation of powers." In Detroit, he had given Hills clear authority over the *Free Press,* no matter what title he carried. In Akron, Ben Maidenburg had been publisher of the *Beacon Journal.* The trend to name publishers had quickened after Hills's rise to corporate leadership. By the time Alvah Chapman became chief executive officer of Knight-Ridder in April 1976, former Knight papers in Akron, Charlotte, Boca Raton, Bradenton, and Lexington were headed by publishers. Later that year all the former Ridder papers had publishers, and by 1979 fully seventeen of Knight-Ridder's twenty-two newspaper companies were similarly structured. Knight questioned the trend. Was separation of powers being jeopardized? Rare was the person gifted in both types of management. "Very different talents are required." Chapman defended his policies, insisting that most publishers came from the editorial ranks. Pressures on management had changed dramatically, he said. "Often there is no clear line of demarcation as to where editorial ends and business begins."

Rarely were top executives recruited from outside Knight-Ridder. When it did happen, the process could be painstaking. Knight, though no longer a titular participant, continued to be a potent force in decision making.

Dick Capen, forty-four, was a senior vice president of Copley Newspapers in San Diego. The chain published nine dailies and twenty-two weeklies in California and Illinois. He had been with them for eighteen years, except for a stint as an assistant to the secretary of defense in Washington, D.C. An energetic extrovert and graduate of Columbia University, Capen had a newspaper background that was based on the business side. As chairman of the United Press Advisory Board, he had become personally acquainted with Alvah Chapman. The two men had much in common as Protestant church lay leaders and strong community activists. Capen received a call from Byron Harless, Knight-Ridder vice president for personnel. Chapman would like to talk with him about an executive job with Knight-Ridder. Could Capen come to Miami?

This launched a series of Chapman-Capen meetings that would go on for two months, in New York and Miami, and cover some twenty-five hours of talk, one-to-one. The chief executive officer of Knight-Ridder politely grilled Capen about his management philosophy, personal objectives, background, achievements, family life, ethics, values, sense of teamwork. Between meetings they exchanged more questions and answers by mail, setting a kind of agenda for even further conversations. Capen also met with Lee Hills; Jim Knight; Knight-Ridder treasurer Robert Singleton; Byron Harless; Jim Batten, future president of the corporation; and Bernard Ridder, Jr., whom Chapman would soon succeed as board chairman. Finally, after three months, only one hurdle remained. Said Chapman, "I think we ought to fly to Akron and have lunch with Jack Knight."

Capen, Ridder, and Chapman made a morning flight from Miami. They arrived at midday at the double penthouse apartment of Jack and Betty Knight in Akron's Blair House. Knight and Eddie Thomas were waiting. Capen had seen the publisher at conventions but had never met him in person. Knight's greeting was brusque. In apparent ill humor, he began chastising board chairman Ridder. A cousin of Ridder had asked for tickets to the Kentucky Derby, which Knight had obligingly arranged. The tickets had gone unused. "Damned impolite, if you ask me," Knight grumbled. He next turned his ire on Chapman over some trifling issue. The group, including the now-uneasy Capen, then went to lunch at the Portage Country Club across the street, taking a reserved table in the large, nearly empty dining room. Capen kept a tight smile while they discussed subjects generally foreign to him, such as the upcoming Knightcap Golf Tournament, which Knight had sponsored for years for his friends. Attention finally turned to the new man, and it was Chapman's time to speak. The chief executive officer expressed confidence in Capen, reviewed his background, and described what some of his duties would be as a senior vice president, with initial responsibility for nineteen newspapers.

Knight's eyes narrowed. He observed that Capen's previous experience had been on the business side of Copley, not the news. Capen nodded. Knight wondered whether a man could jump from an operation the size of Copley into Knight-Ridder as a senior vice president without overextending himself. Capen sensed strong unspoken support from the others. It was not common for both the chairman and the president of a major company personally to accompany a prospective executive this far just to give him moral support. Years later, Capen would remember the experience as one of the most grueling of his life. "Jack Knight was a dominant personality. He challenged every man, from the board chairman on down. I suddenly realized that I would have a lot of proving to do."

Three years later, Capen would be named board chairman and publisher of the *Miami Herald,* flagship newspaper of the Knight-Ridder group. The job would catapult him into a new era of competition in explosive south Florida, where three-quarters of a million readers were leaving Dade County, displaced by Cuban refugees, most of whom preferred their news in Spanish. The *Herald* would be vying for readers in Miami as well as neighboring Broward and Palm Beach counties, against entrenched hometown newspapers. Capen's job would be to make it work.

In February 1980, Knight was honored with a testimonial dinner in Miami by Cornell University alumni, spouses, and guests. With Betty at his side, he was exuberant, reminding the crowd of 250 that his collegiate life had been inauspicious. "It proves that in this country, anything can happen." But he had gained something from college that proved priceless in later years, a sense of writing discipline, in gratitude for which he had given financial support to Cornell's writing program for undergraduates.

Today, however, he found glaring deficiencies in public education. "Curriculum has been diluted. Instead of history, language and composition, children are taught about venereal disease and how to drive an automobile. Foreign language has been virtually eliminated. Emphasis is on manual rather than intellectual skills. . . ."

They gave him a rousing ovation. Many were moved to tears. There was a sense of fading light. "I have been honored," he said, "far beyond what I deserved."

Health was failing, the idyll growing short. Betty and Jack spent time at their homes at Miami Beach; Old Keswick, Virginia; Cleveland, and Akron. They took long walks, rode bicycles, talked. Late in 1977 she had undergone a skin graft on her leg at Cleveland Clinic. Three years later, after the Cornell dinner, she was troubled with fatigue and shortness of breath. In September she suffered a blackout at her home near Cleveland and was rushed to a nearby hospital. Surgeons attached a pacemaker to her heart. Betty was then on her feet again, but slowed.

Knight sent her to Massachusetts General Hospital for more checkups. Dr. W. Gerald Austen discerned an obstruction of the aortic valve, light leakage of the mitral valve, and possible narrowing of the coronary artery. She was released for Christmas with plans for further tests in January. Austen recommended that she have modest exercise and that she be alert for palpitations and chest pressure. "We would hope that in time she will have some improvement."

They went to Miami Beach for the holidays. Betty was in good spirits, in the company of friends and family. They sent out one hundred invitations for a party to celebrate their fifth wedding anniversary.

It never took place.

On the evening of New Year's Day 1981, as the two of them watched the Rose Bowl football game on television in the house on La Gorce Island, Betty slumped in her chair, unconscious. Knight telephoned the rescue squad. She was taken by ambulance to Mt. Sinai Hospital in Miami Beach. Efforts to revive her failed.

Elizabeth Augustus Knight was dead at eighty-one.

The light of his life had gone out. On the day before their anniversary, she was buried in the Knight family plot at Rose Hill Cemetery in Akron. A minister told the mourners, "She and Jack built a marriage of rare beauty and extraordinary grace." The principal mourner went through the motions of the ritual, outwardly stoic as usual.

He flew back to Florida and was admitted to the hospital with worsening angina pains and abdominal distress. From Mt. Sinai, he began writing acknowledgments to inpouring messages of condolence. He left the hospital in late January, again facing major surgery for gallbladder trouble.

Depression dogged him. He lost weight. He brooded on the relentless toll of time on friends and loved ones. Monty Curtis, the genial talker and Knight-Ridder vice president, lost a leg to cancer and suffered a heart attack. Knight's longtime chauffeur, Gene Cecci, retired in failing health. On and on it went.

Eddie Thomas, ever the optimist, insisted that Knight's stubborn resiliency would pull him through; intellect alone, he believed, was a formidable force against adversity. Others, however, saw the dire finality at work. In Miami, reporter Gene Miller organized a luncheon for Knight with *Herald* newsroom veterans. "The Old Man is suffering," Miller said. "He's losing the will to live."

In February, at Massachusetts General, Dr. Austen saw to removal of the malfunctioning gallbladder. Knight's recovery was surprisingly swift. He was back in Miami three days earlier than expected, again taking slow walks around La Gorce Island as mechanical rainbirds flicked over rich green lawns and neighbors' yachts rocked gently at their moorings.

He managed to go out socially, attended the company's annual board meeting, and resumed a level of letter writing. Betty's death served to restore contact with his daughter-in-law Dorothy. After an exchange of letters, they talked on the telephone. Knight told her that she was included in his will. "You are terribly sweet to remember me," she wrote afterward, "but I'd rather forget the money and have you." For the first time in years, she signed her letters, "All my love. . . ."

In late April 1981, he left Miami for the last time. Despite his frail condition, he was in Detroit on May 4 for the Economic Club's luncheon celebrating the 150th anniversary of the *Free Press.* It was forty-one years since he had handed the check to

E. D. Stair. In a brief speech, he now concluded, "I shudder to think what would have happened if it had bounced."

He returned to Akron fatigued and out of sorts. May blended into June. The rolling hills of Summit County had never been greener. His links to the past seemed to strengthen. From the lofty windows of Blair House he looked out over the immaculate fairways of Portage Country Club, where he had golfed since boyhood and won the championship six times.

During the rides downtown, as he sat on the front seat beside chauffeur Bud Boggs, the car passed the gray stucco house he had shared with Katie and where all the boys had been born so long ago. It was the house he had locked and left after Katie's death, never to set foot in it again. To this day, he never looked that way, keeping his gaze straight ahead or deep in his newspaper as if the house did not exist.

Dr. Henry Kraus checked him over and offered the usual advice to take things easy. The cardiologist had often been a guest in Knight's home and had treated Beryl in her final illness. The doctor now saw his patient every day and was not happy with his state of mind. Knight was having accelerated angina attacks, not always responsive to medication. The doctor saw nothing to be gained by curtailing Knight's modest self-imposed work schedule and daily visits to the *Beacon Journal.*

They had been grateful in Detroit for his visit. Joe H. Stroud, now editor and senior vice president of the *Detroit Free Press,* expressed this in a letter that seemed almost a farewell. "Jack, those of us who edit these papers are always going to be struggling to live up to your standards. I hope we can be worthy heirs to a great tradition."

And so he still went to the office every day, to read and critique the paper and make life difficult for editor Paul Poorman. He still lunched with cronies at the Mayflower Club. He had given up hard liquor and drank only a little champagne or Dubonnet wine, one glass, no more. He dined from time to time with the widow Stella Hall, a bright companion, knowledgeable in art and one of the few mortals who could give him a necktie that he liked. Stella had even furnished her home at Portage Woods with some of his mother's furniture. Everyone in Akron knew that she loved him.

Early in the evening of Tuesday, June 16, he arrived at her door for a dinner date. She welcomed him and offered a half-glass of Dubonnet. "How do you like my new suit . . . ?" he asked.

Dr. Kraus was working late in his office at suburban Cuyahoga Falls when the telephone message came. He drove quickly down the rain-slick expressway to Stella Hall's home. Jack Knight's car and chauffeur were still parked in front. Kraus walked in and found Knight slumped, motionless. Stella was in shock. The physician checked the victim for life signs. There were none. After giving Mrs. Hall a sedative, he telephoned the Summit County coroner, Dr. A. H. Kyriakides. "You'd better come over right away. John S. Knight is dead."

Flowers bloomed in parks and schoolyards. The sky was flecked with cloud masses, threatening rain. For three days the Akron-Canton Airport was the scene of an ingathering as they arrived from across the nation to mark the passing of a patriarch. The very technology involved might have caught his fancy as worth a "Notebook" column. He had been born in an era of horse-drawn buggies and trains, when man's technology was measured in steam-driven engines and flickering electric lights. He had died eighty-six years later in the age of the jet aircraft, which whistled over the Summit County hilltops bearing his mourners from far-flung places. Black-suited and grave, they rode into the city in high-powered automobiles and later watched news pictures of themselves on color TV sets. The very moon, rising over the city that he had always called home, bore the footprints of man.

Tributes arrived by mail and telegram and were printed in the U.S. press. The *Philadelphia Inquirer* editorialized on the man's uniqueness: "He was, before and above all else, a reporter and editor. . . . He was tough, canny and skeptical, but could use words like 'ideals' and 'convictions' with comfort."

From Muscatine, Iowa, came a letter from a former Knight caddy at Portage Country Club, now William Catalona, M.D., who remembered how the publisher had helped pay his tuition to medical school as one of the first recipients of a Knight scholarship. "He made it possible for me to become a physician."

Old ideological adversaries came forth. Burr McCloskey,

once a socialist organizer in the rough-and-tumble of Akron's rubber wars, had often crossed swords with the boss of the *Beacon Journal.* But in time, as often happens between strong rivals, they had developed an accommodation and even grudging respect. Now, from his home in Dallas, McCloskey wrote: "John S. Knight wasn't born to power, he earned it. He was a fighter not easily put off, or down."

June 20, Saturday: Under lowering skies, the cars and limousines streamed to St. Paul's Episcopal Church. In the vaulted splendor of the thirty-year-old Greek Revival sanctuary, its hanging chandeliers lighted against the gloom, the family and closest associates occupied front pews and some six hundred others filled seats behind them. Ben Maidenburg, retired and in failing health, made his way on crutches, gaunt and ravaged. When first told of the death he had burst into tears, saying hoarsely, "I thought I'd go first."

The body of John S. Knight had been laid to rest an hour earlier in a small graveside service at Rose Hill Cemetery, with only a reading from the Episcopal Book of Common Prayer: "Everyone the Father gives to me will come to me; I will never turn away anyone who believes in me." They had handed Knight's son Landon a folded American flag, provided for the deceased as a military veteran. Now, at St. Paul's, there was only the memorializing to be done, in a mood of splendid austerity.

To Lee Hills fell the task of delivering the eulogy. He had spent nearly forty-five years in the service of Jack Knight. There were those who said that if Knight were the patriarch of the empire, Hills was its formative genius.

He ascended to the pulpit and looked out over the crowd. It consisted of a fine mix of people: princes of industry and finance, socialites, politicians, friends, neighbors, physicians, colleagues, everyday folk. Familiar faces lined the front pews—Bernard Ridder, Jr., Alvah Chapman, James and Landon Knight, Eddie Thomas, James Batten. Katharine Graham, owner of *The Washington Post,* was there, wearing a plain V-necked dress devoid of jewelry. "Jack was a great human being," she had commented earlier. "He was direct and honest." She had arrived with Allen Neuharth, board chairman of Gannett Newspapers.

A funeral was both sad and oddly stimulating, a gathering and a terrible leavetaking, not unlike a family reunion.

"We have come to bid our last farewell to a remarkable man," Hills said.

John Shively Knight was not a person you could easily forget. . . . He was a Renaissance man, entrepreneur, reporter, sportsman, business executive, writer, publisher, philanthropist, columnist. But first and last, he was an editor. He believed fiercely that newspapers must be independent editorially and economically. He practiced journalism with passion, energy and courage. He left a legacy of excellence.

That was the essence of it: excellence.

"We will cherish his memory."

In forty-eight turbulent years the wealth of John Knight had multiplied incredibly. At the beginning, in 1933, he had wrestled with hard realities of the Great Depression. At his death, Knight-Ridder Newspapers, Inc., was a $1 billion-a-year enterprise and flourishing, its operations including newspapers, publishing, television broadcasting, electronic distribution of commodity and financial news, newsprint production, and computerized information services.

The empire now counted thirty-two daily newspapers and part ownership in several other papers and supply firms.

Three days after Knight's death, the stock of Knight-Ridder sold at $38 a share on the New York Stock Exchange. Of 31.9 million shares of common stock outstanding, he had personally owned 6.35 million. At that day's price his holdings exceeded $200 million. The beneficiary would be the Knight Foundation and, through it, the public.

The foundation, too, was a far cry from its beginnings. The original Charles Landon Knight Memorial Education Fund had been created in 1940 to aid worthy students who could not afford a college education. In the first dozen years, $325,000 went out in interest-free student loans. Even after the project was expanded into the foundation in 1950, its benefits remained small.

By 1966 they totaled only about $600,000 for the entire twenty-six years. Not until Knight changed his will did the foundation begin to show vigor. From 1967 onward, his personal involvement quickened the pace of its development. With C. C. Gibson as president and administrator, foundation requests surged by one thousand per year. Chairman Knight had reviewed each application, with James Knight as vice chairman and Charles E. Clark, Knight-Ridder vice president, as treasurer.

"Our main concern," Knight declared, "is people and ideas, not bricks and mortar."

In the last year of his life, the foundation distributed ninety-one grants totaling $1,401,665. Recipients in Akron alone included the University of Akron, the Ohio Ballet, the Akron Art Museum, the symphony orchestra, Blossom Music Center, Civic Theater, Stan Hywet Hall, mobile meals for the elderly, a Catholic high school, a radio reading service for shut-ins. National grants went for press scholarships, inter-American press freedom, the American Red Cross, and the United Negro College Fund, as well as local projects in cities such as Charlotte, Detroit, Philadelphia, and Lexington; Miami, Boca Raton, Tallahassee, and Bradenton, Florida; and Columbus and Macon, Georgia. In 1982, after Knight's death, the foundation would award nearly $2.5 million in 114 grants to 110 organizations; in 1983, the outlay was more than $5.3 million in 118 grants—for art museums, literacy studies, orchestras, opera companies, hospitals, group counseling, colleges, crime fighting, literary festivals, historic preservation, and street missions. In 1985 there were 129 new grants worth $5,083,572, bringing the fifteen-year total to $28,530,007. A few years later, the level of *annual* grants would exceed $20 million. One $4 million gift put new vigor into Stanford University's prestigious but financially threatened midcareer journalism program, providing journalists a year to study the humanities or other subjects of choice. The program was renamed the John S. Knight Fellowships. Said Dr. Lyle Nelson, director, "Jack Knight set the example for highest standards."

On a warm, cloudy day one year after Knight's death, carpenters set up a small outdoor speaker's platform at the High Street entrance to the *Beacon Journal.* A new bronze plaque was affixed to the gray granite building. At midmorning, four hundred people gathered for a brief ceremony. Charles R. Novitz, national president of the professional journalism society Sigma Delta Chi, joined James Knight in dedicating the newspaper building as a National Historic Site. The plaque carried a message:

> Throughout his 67-year career as reporter, editor, columnist and publisher, Jack Knight called Akron and the Beacon Journal his home. Accorded virtually every journalism honor in existence, he was tireless in his dedication to serving the public. . . .

At a banquet that night, the speaker was a career journalist who had first met Jack Knight while caddying at Portage Country Club and then gone on to make his own mark in the field. Now James B. Reston, columnist for *The New York Times,* read his notes through half-moon spectacles, and over the years his hair had turned to silver. He ruminated on the pressures and constraints of newspaper work and deplored "police-blotter journalism" that bombarded readers with shallow news at the expense of depth and understanding. "People are beginning to question whether we are meeting our responsibilities as well as we might. But if Jack Knight were here, he might not agree with me. He was a tough and combative guy."

Afterward, editor Paul Poorman went off to Jack Knight's old office at the *Beacon Journal* to write a column for the coming Sunday. He was a big, handsome man out of Detroit, still trying to get the hang of Akron and finding that the task was not easy. People came and went in this business. He himself would hold the job until 1986, when he would be replaced and become professor of journalism at Kent State University. For now, however, Poorman occupied the old desk, at the old window, with the ghost of the former occupant still hovering about. He wrote with that presence strongly in mind:

> It is difficult for those of us at the *Beacon Journal* to be dispassionate about Jack Knight and his newspaper organization. We are part of it and part of him, shaped whether we like it or not by the standards and directions

he set for us. Our colleagues on 32 other Knight-Ridder newspapers across the nation are caught in the same compulsion, whether we know it or not. A 22-year-old beginning reporter in Wichita or San Jose or Philadelphia who never met Jack Knight and never personally felt the impact of his enormous presence, will still conduct himself differently and try harder because the legacy of the man lives on in his newspapers. . . .

The press of America is better today because he owned, edited and published newspapers and insisted that they strive to be great.

Jack Knight is gone, but he lives on in his newspapers and in the millions of people who, though they never knew him, live lives even slightly better because of a free and responsible press in a democracy. . . .

NOTES

CHAPTER 1: VOICES OF THUNDER

PAGE

5–6 "My father . . . university": John S. Knight (hereafter JSK) speech, "Fifty Years in Journalism," Akron, Ohio, November 16, 1964.

6 "I'm glad . . .": "The Life of C. L. Knight," *Akron Beacon Journal*, September 27, 1933.

6 ". . . C. L. Knight walked . . .": Ibid.

7 "All I inherited . . .": JSK, Chicago Tribune Archives interview, September 11, 1975.

7 Jefferson Davis: Landon Knight, *The Real Jefferson Davis* (Battle Creek, Mich.: Pilgrim Magazine Co., 1904).

7–8 Life in Bluefield, West Virginia: C. L. Knight obituary, *Akron Beacon Journal*, September 27, 1933.

8 From Bluefield to *Akron Beacon Journal* purchase: Ibid.; and James L. Knight interviews with author.

8–9 History of Akron: Karl H. Grismer, *Akron and Summit County* (Akron, Ohio: Summit County Historical Society, 1952).

9   thwarted lynch mob: Cloyd R. Quine, "The Akron Riot of 1900" (unpublished MS, Akron, 1951), University of Akron Archives.

9   "We are ourselves . . .": JSK, eighty-fifth birthday remarks, October 26, 1979.

10   C. L. Knight quotations: Obituary, *Akron Beacon Journal,* September 27, 1933.

10–   "Mother would have hired . . .": JSK, eighty-fifth birthday remarks.
11

11   Fight with bully: Ibid.

11   Schoolboy copybook quotations: Knight Collection, University of Akron Archives.

11   childhood . . . warmly remembered: JSK, "The Editor's Notebook," December 24, 1944, *Akron Beacon Journal.*

12   "According to my tastes . . .": Schoolboy copybook, Knight Collection.

12   "It is a grand sensation . . .": Ibid.

12   IWW strike of 1913: Grismer, *Akron and Summit County.*

13   age of innocence: Walter Lord, *The Good Years* (New York: Harper & Brothers, 1960); Mark Sullivan, *Our Times* (New York: Charles Scribner's Sons, 1936).

13   Akron Central High football: JSK, eighty-fifth birthday remarks.

13   "Taft has left his party . . .": C. L. Knight, "The Election Shambles," *Akron Beacon Journal,* November 15, 1912.

14   Start of World War I: Sullivan, *Our Times.*

14   The Cornell years: JSK speech to Cornell Alumni Dinner, Miami, Florida, February 15, 1980.

14   "a blundering . . . crime . . .": C. L. Knight, "The Mania for War," *Akron Beacon Journal,* January 1917.

15   Sedition Act and anti-German sentiment in Akron: C. L. Knight obituary edition, *Akron Beacon Journal,* September 27, 1933.

15   C. L. Knight quotations: Ibid.

15   American war fervor: The National Geographic Society, *We Americans* (Washington, D.C.: 1957).

16   "changing into rumpled . . . uniforms . . .": "The Editor's Notebook," *Miami Herald,* December 24, 1944.

16   Palming dice: Chicago Tribune Archives interview, 1975.

16   Knight war experiences: Knight Collection; Charles Whited, "Profile of John S. Knight," *Miami Herald,* April 26, 1963; JSK, Chicago Tribune Archives interview, 1975.

16–   Combat experiences of the 29th Division: U.S. Battlefield Memorial Com-
17   mission, *Official Records,* 1928.

17   "Don't mind if I do . . .": JSK, Chicago Tribune Archives interview, 1975.

CHAPTER 2: JOYS AND SORROWS

18– Katherine McLain, the early years: James S. Jackson, retired associate
19 editor, *Akron Beacon Journal,* interview with author, January 12, 1985;
    Ken Nichols, retired columnist, *Akron Beacon Journal;* interview, James
    L. Knight; letters of Katherine McLain, Knight Collection, University of
    Akron Archives.

19 "—the roar and growl and mutter . . .": Howard and Ralph Wolf, *Rubber*
    (New York: Civic-Friede, 1936).

19 C. L. Knight and Anti-Saloon League: Obituary, *Akron Beacon Journal,*
    September 1933; James L. Knight interview with author.

19 women of easy virtue: C. L. Knight's alleged dalliances were widely
    rumored in Akron; in a 1985 interview with author, retired *Akron Beacon
    Journal* publisher Ben Maidenburg said the elder Knight sometimes en-
    tertained women in his office behind locked doors.

20 "a lotus-eating life . . .": JSK, Chicago Tribune Archives interview, 1975.

20 "Father . . . fancied himself . . .": James L. Knight interview with author,
    January 1985.

20 "You're not selling . . .": Ibid.

20 "If I don't like the work . . .": Transcript, Larry King interview of JSK,
    WIOD radio, Miami, Florida, 1966.

20 "I discovered how little . . .": JSK speech, "Fifty Years in Journalism,"
    Akron, Ohio, November 16, 1964.

21 C. L. Knight talk with Harding: "Life of C. L. Knight," *Akron Beacon
    Journal,* September 27, 1933.

21 "If I can borrow . . .": JSK speech, Akron Press Club, October 6, 1977.

21 "Old C. L.'s a damn good newspaperman . . .": JSK speech, Cornell
    Alumni Association, Miami, Florida, March 13, 1980.

21 "My opponent has drawn . . .": From "Thousands Mourn Death of C. L.
    Knight," *Akron Beacon Journal,* September 27, 1933.

22 ". . . the county printing business.": Chicago Tribune Archives interview,
    1975.

22 "Oh, I love you . . .": Letters of Katherine Knight, Knight Collection.

22– Remembrances of Katie: JSK interview with author, 1963; James L.
23 Knight interview, January 1985; "Long Illness Fatal to Wife of Editor,"
    Akron Beacon Journal, January 16, 1929.

23 The Ku Klux Klan thrived . . .: JSK, Chicago Tribune Archives interview,
    1975.

24 C. L. Knight speeches in Congress: "Thousands Mourn Death of C. L.
    Knight," *Akron Beacon Journal,* September 27, 1933.

24 "More royalist . . . than the king.": JSK, speech, "Fifty Years in Journal-
    ism."

24 A jaded public: "Thousands Mourn Death of C. L. Knight," *Akron Beacon
    Journal,* September 27, 1933.

24 "I look forward . . .": C. L. Knight, press conference, Washington, D.C., November 23, 1922.

25 Death of Warren G. Harding: Frances Russell, *The Shadow of Blooming Grove* (New York and Toronto: McGraw-Hill, 1968).

25 The job of newspapers: JSK speech to Economic Club of Detroit, Detroit, Michigan, March 23, 1946.

25 "the gay Twenties . . .": "The Editor's Notebook," *Miami Herald*, October 27, 1947.

25 "Where we once . . . inquiring mind.": "C. L. Knight, Champion of Causes," *Akron Beacon Journal*, September 27, 1933.

26 "swaddling clothes": JSK, Chicago Tribune Archives interview, Akron, Ohio, 1975.

26 Katie's weakness, noted in diary of Clara Knight, March 1928. Knight Collection.

27 "Hell, for all I care . . .": JSK, Chicago Tribune Archives interview, 1975.

28 Sale of *Springfield Sun* and dice roll at Massillon: Ibid.

29 Katie's letters from the Greenbrier: Knight Collection.

29 Blanche Seiberling's visit to Katie: Letter, Blanche Seiberling to JSK, January 1929, Knight Collection.

29 The end came . . . : Final diagnosis from post-mortem pathology report to JSK by Dr. Alfred Taylor, Roosevelt Hospital, January 25, 1929, Knight Collection.

29 Death of Katie: "Long Illness Fatal to Wife of Editor," *Akron Beacon Journal*, January 16, 1929.

30 "A great sorrow . . .": Blanche Seiberling letter, Knight Collection.

30 Knight's golf game: "Application Brings JSK Golf Honors," *Akron Beacon Journal*, January 24, 1930.

30 "Life is a leveler . . .": "The Editor's Notebook," *Akron Beacon Journal*, December 26, 1965.

CHAPTER 3: TIMES OF TEMPEST

31 "We shall soon . . . this nation.": Speech, Herbert Hoover, March 1929.

32 Stock market crash: Roger Butterfield, *The American Past* (New York: Simon & Schuster, 1966).

32 This interval of life for Knight's sons from Charles Landon Knight II, interview with author, Akron, Ohio, January 1984.

33 Description of Beryl Knight: Columnist Ken Nichols, *Akron Beacon Journal*, August 9, 1974.

33 Beryl's background: Jack Alexander, "Up from Akron," *Saturday Evening Post* (August 18, 1945); Kenneth Stewart, "The Man Who Bought the *Chicago Daily News*," *PM* magazine (November 1944).

33 "... a light for both ...": Nichols, *Akron Beacon Journal,* August 9, 1974.

33 Letter from Beryl to Jack, March 14, 1944, courtesy James L. Knight.

34 The Depression in Akron: Karl H. Grismer, *Akron and Summit County* (Akron, Ohio: Summit County Historical Society, 1952).

34 Hundreds besieged his factory ...: James Jackson, interview with author.

35 C. L. Knight quotations: "The Life of C. L. Knight," *Akron Beacon Journal,* September 27, 1933.

35 "Let me first ... fear itself.": Roosevelt's first inaugural address, March 4, 1933.

35 "I tell you, C. L. ....": Letter, JSK to Cyrus Blumfeld, February 16, 1952, Knight Collection, University of Akron Archives.

35 Akron sweated ... around the clock: Grismer, *Akron and Summit County.*

36 Landon Knight described his polio affliction in an interview with author.

36 "A trained mind ... a decision.": Ben Maidenburg, "JSK, Man of the Hour," *Success* (March 1963).

37 "It is our duty ... cash-register editor.": C. L. Knight obituary edition, *Akron Beacon Journal,* September 27, 1933.

37– *Akron Beacon Journal* financial difficulties: Ben Maidenburg, interview
38 with author; JSK, Chicago Tribune Archives interview; James L. Knight interview, January 18, 1985.

38 Knight-Borah alliance: Letters, February 5 and 12, 1936, Knight Collection.

38 "which denies the people ...": JSK letter to Senator William Borah, March 2, 1936.

38 "John Knight dislikes ... over the nation.": George Fort Hamilton, "Ohio's Primary Fight," *Chattanooga News,* March 10, 1936.

39 FDR's ridicule of the Kansas sunflower: William Manchester, *The Glory and the Dream* (Boston: Little, Brown, 1974).

39 The Barberton strike: "Trouble in Barberton," *Akron Beacon Journal,* November 26, 1936.

39 trouble spread to Goodyear: George Knepper, *Akron, City at the Summit* (Tulsa, Okla.: Continental Heritage Press, 1981); James Jackson, interview with author, January 17, 1985; E. J. Thomas, interview, January 12, 1985.

40 "No Room for Vigilantes": JSK letter to Joseph Pulitzer, August 12, 1938, Knight Collection.

40 Knight's confrontation with Goodyear executives was described by E. J. Thomas, retired board chairman of Goodyear, in interview with author.

41 Knight nominated the *Akron Beacon Journal* for the Pulitzer Prize in a letter to Joseph Pulitzer in August 1938, Knight Collection.

41 "Far too many ... inspire the people. ...": JSK speech, University of Akron, October 12, 1936.

CHAPTER 4: "THE EDITOR'S NOTEBOOK"

42 "I'm a bleeder . . .": JSK interview with author, May 1976.

43 "Newspapers . . . like banks.": W. Sprague Holden, "Twenty-Five Years of Straight Talk," *Akron Beacon Journal,* November 26, 1961.

43 ". . . editor with fire . . .": Mark Ethridge, Sr., publisher and board chairman, *Louisville Courier-Journal.*

43 "I'm starting something new . . .": Holden, "Twenty-Five Years of Straight Talk."

43 "One wonders why . . .": "The Editor's Notebook," *Akron Beacon Journal,* December 2, 1936.

44 "Our speaker assured . . . 'everybody reads.' ": Ibid., December 4, 1936.

44 "It is all very . . . same platform.": Ibid., December 11, 1936.

45 "Sloppy reporting . . .": Ibid., December 21, 1936.

45 "Akron reminds me . . .": Ibid., December 23, 1936.

45 "I first knew . . . I wonder . . .": Ibid., February 8, 1937.

46 "Munsey contributed . . . per cent security.": Ibid., May 14, 1937.

46 Mail increased: Ibid., February 12, 1937.

46 "My telephone . . .": Ibid., February 16, 1937.

47 "geriatric paradise.": Ibid., April 7, 1937.

47 "Insignificant-looking Mert . . .": Ibid., April 21, 1937.

47 "Years of pioneering . . . failure.": Ibid., May 11, 1937.

48 "The President's . . . American journalism.": Ibid., June 8, 1937.

48 "Breakfast in Akron . . .": Ibid., July 8, 1937.

48 "It is a far cry . . .": Ibid., July 30, 1937.

48 "Highly unfortunate . . .": Ibid., August 20, 1937.

49 "These clubs . . . attendance.": Ibid., July 24, 1937.

49 "People who make me tired . . .": Ibid., September 28, 1937.

CHAPTER 5: GAMBLE IN MIAMI

51 Davis's views on radio purchase: Letter, Davis to JSK, August 8, 1936, Knight Collection, University of Akron Archives.

51 Main source on *Miami Herald* negotiations: Nixon Smiley, *Knights of the Fourth Estate* (Miami, Fla.: E. A. Seemann, 1974).

51– Background of Shutts and *Herald:* Ibid.
52

52 This Miami historical sketch is from Helen Muir's excellent book, *Miami, U.S.A.* (New York: Henry Holt & Co., 1953).

53 Annenberg's background: John Cooney, *The Annenbergs* (New York: Simon & Schuster, 1982).

53 *Tribune*'s advertising weakness: Letter, JSK to John H. Barry, November 5, 1937.

53 Conditions in *Herald* newsroom: From Smiley, *Fourth Estate;* author interview with Jack Anderson, *Herald* reporter.

53 "What's half a million . . .": Smiley, *Fourth Estate.*

54 John S. Knight in later years was fond of making disparaging comments about Shutts's abilities as a publisher and the condition of the *Miami Herald* generally. Shutts's daughter, Elinor Shutts Baker, refuted this image in a letter to the author April 12, 1988. She wrote, in part: "Frank Shutts loved the *Herald,* not only for the excitement and power but also because it was his tool with which to help build Miami into everything glorious he wanted it to be. He involved himself in the city's growth with gusto. He did *not* live beyond his means. He paid his bills scrupulously by the 10th of the month and scolded Mother if she didn't do likewise. In the summers we rented various houses in the Berkshires. Dad was a meticulous taskmaster. If you found any inaccuracies in the old *Herald,* he must have been out of town. He read every word of the bulldog edition, then got on the phone to correct any mistakes that came within his field of knowledge, which was prodigious. . . . The building was an old building, but once had been a source of pride. One elevator was enough. Sure there was sweat, everybody perspired; air conditioning wasn't in use until after World War II. As for mosquitoes being in the City Room, I believe that's nonsense. He loathed the pesky things. Dead-enders on the staff? Probably so, because Dad was kind. . . . In his sixties, his vigor waning, he looked for newer, younger management that would lift his beloved paper to its full potential and would be good for Miami. The Knights were the answer to his prayer, and the *Herald* was sold to them for a lot less money than Annenberg would have paid because Dad wanted them to have it, because he cared. . . . Maybe the front page looked 'dull' and 'gray' to Jack Knight, but enough people liked it so that the *Herald* outstripped all competitors, locally and statewide, in circulation."

54 It was another turbulent summer.: Karl H. Grismer, *Akron and Summit County* (Akron, Ohio: Summit County Historical Society, 1952).

54 Roosevelt programs, the first hundred days: Robert E. Sherwood, *Roosevelt and Hopkins, An Intimate History* (New York: Harper & Brothers, 1948).

54 Disagreement with Judge Wanamaker: "LaFatch Gang Sentenced," *Akron Beacon Journal,* June 12, 1937; "The Editor's Notebook," ibid.

54 Knight touted for governor: "Party Leaders Believe Knight Is GOP Hope," *Akron Times-Press,* July 8, 1937.

54 "He bought another comic strip . . .": JSK, Chicago Tribune Archives interview, 1975.

55 Shutts's debts, past attempts to sell: Smiley, *Fourth Estate.*

55 Shutts, fearing violence . . . : Elinor Shutts Baker, interview with author, April 14, 1988.

55– Stern-Annenberg feud: Cooney, *Annenbergs.*
56

56 Trip to New York for Stern visit: This section is drawn entirely from Jack Alexander, "Up from Akron," *Saturday Evening Post* (August 18, 1945). Knight never refuted the report, including his attack of cold feet and the chest pains.

56 Knight account of Louis-Farr fight: "The Editor's Notebook," *Akron Beacon Journal,* August 31, 1937.

57 *Herald* sale details: Smiley, *Fourth Estate.*

57 he had even stopped C. L. Knight . . . : Ben Maidenburg, interview with author.

58 James Knight in Miami: Smiley, *Fourth Estate.*

58 ". . . just, friendly and fair.": *Miami Herald,* October 16, 1937.

58 Miami evening life: Muir, *Miami, U.S.A.*

59 Annenberg competitiveness: Jeanne Bellamy, interview with author.

59 Jeans's death and aftermath: Cooney, *Annenbergs.*

59– Knight buys *Tribune:* JSK, Chicago Tribune Archives interview, 1975;
60 Smiley, *Fourth Estate.*

CHAPTER 6: CASTLES IN THE SAND

61– *Herald* newsroom and people: From interviews with former reporters
62 Jack Anderson and Jeanne Bellamy; Maidenburg; Nixon Smiley, *Knights of the Fourth Estate* (Miami, Fla.: E. A. Seemann, 1974).

62 Barry's housecleaning: Memo, Barry to JSK, November 3, 1937, Knight Collection, University of Akron Archives.

62 Knight introduction to Miami: "Factual Reporting Pledged by Knight," *Miami Herald,* October 20, 1937.

63 Random Thoughts: Smiley, *Fourth Estate.*

63 "I need at least a year . . .": JSK to McDowell, December 1937.

63– Ellis Hollums memos: Knight Collection.
65

65 *Akron Times-Press* failure: *"Times-Press* purchased," *Akron Beacon Journal,* August 29, 1938; Ken Nichols, "Knight Battled Grim Years," *Akron Beacon Journal,* July 3, 1975.

65 Knight-Howard coin flip: JSK letter to Jack Howard, April 29, 1964, Knight Collection.

65 "It was bad enough . . .": Roy Howard, letters, March 26, 1966, Knight Collection.

65 ". . . solely responsible . . .": Maidenburg interview.

66 ". . . A tremendous power . . .": "Power in JSK's Hands," *Akron Beacon Journal,* September 3, 1938.

66 ". . . This was Akron . . .": Knight speech, Chicago Federated Advertising Clubs, September 24, 1947.

66 Skeptics: Knight speech, Akron Audit Bureau, September 12, 1944.

66– Johnny, Jr., and the gunshot incident: *Akron Times-Press,* February 21,
67 1938.

67 ". . . the whole slant of my life . . .": Letter, Johnny to his parents, February 22, 1938, Knight Collection.

67 Barry arranges new school: Letter, Barry to JSK, February 19, 1938, Knight Collection. "It's all for the best, John. He will succeed, with that personality, in spite of all."

67 "a strange frontier.": John Pennekamp letter to JSK, 1963.

67 Miami Beach atmosphere: Jane Fisher, *The Fabulous Hoosier* (New York: Robert McGrath Publishing Co., 1947).

67 S & G syndicate: Jack Kofoed, *Moon Over Miami* (New York: Random House, 1955).

68 DuBose visit: JSK memo to Hollums, June 1938, Knight Collection.

68 *Herald* operations and critiques: Knight to Hollums, June–July 1938.

69 Maidenburg hiring for Miami: Maidenburg, interview with author, January 12, 1985.

69– Hollums memos: 1937–38, Knight Collection.
70

70 "Colonel Shutts . . .": Smiley, *Fourth Estate.*

70 Souvenir firm and dinner check incident: Knight memos, 1938–39, Knight Collection.

70 Bob Fredericks's steaks: Smiley, *Fourth Estate.*

71 "Free meals . . .": "The Editor's Notebook," March 31, 1940.

71 "I WON'T PAY: . . .": Ibid., March 5, 1939.

71 Raw milk: Smiley, *Fourth Estate.*

72 Maidenburg antics: Ibid.; and Jack Anderson, interview with author, February 9, 1985.

72– Maidenburg-Hollums dislike and Hollums life-style: Maidenburg inter-
73 view, January 1984.

73– Gambling story and Hollums departure: Ibid.
75

75 "Some of us . . . good broom": "The Editor's Notebook," March 2, 1940.

CHAPTER 7: THE *FREE PRESS*

76 Knight profile: Ward Morehouse, "Jack Knight Big Factor in Revitalization of Akron," *Editor & Publisher* (June 17, 1939).

☐ ☐

77 White-haired, secretive, and aloof: Frank Angelo, *On Guard: A History of the Detroit Free Press* (Detroit: Detroit Free Press, 1981).

77 His personal foibles: JSK speech, Akron, Ohio, July 16, 1968; also from Maidenburg interview with author.

77 Stair clearing of the lobby, from Maidenburg interview.

78 Disinclination to sell to chain: Letter, Smith Davis to JSK, December 22, 1939.

78 "We were taught . . .": "The Editor's Notebook," July 30, 1938.

78 "What are we doing . . .": Ibid., January 8, 1939.

78 "I wonder . . .": Ibid., July 16, 1939.

78 ". . . We're not quitters.": Ibid., October 9, 1939.

79 Knight remembered the visit to Stair in a speech to the Economic Club of Detroit, April 27, 1981.

79 Barry's bargaining: JSK letter to Barry, January 8, 1940.

80– History of the *Detroit Free Press:* Angelo, *On Guard.*
81

81– Knight's thoughts on a Detroit deal are detailed in a letter to Barry,
82 January 8, 1940, Knight Collection, University of Akron Archives.

82 ". . . police the world?": "The Editor's Notebook," *Akron Beacon Journal,* February 12, 1939.

82 "Life goes by . . .": Diary of Clara Knight, 1939, Knight Collection.

83 ". . . old Roman, always demanding his way.": Knight memo to Blake McDowell, January 27, 1940.

83 "Let the FBI . . .": "The Editor's Notebook," *Miami Herald,* January 28, 1940.

83 "Is he getting touchy on us?": Ibid., February 25, 1940.

83 "This will have to be negotiated. . . .": JSK to McDowell, March 12, 1940.

83– Guild troubles: Ibid.
84

84 Abrupt agreement with Stair's loan offer: JSK, Chicago Tribune Archives interview, 1975.

84 "I'll run it.": Angelo, *On Guard.*

85 ". . . routine people.": JSK to Barry, memo, May 1, 1940.

85 "Detroit . . . is going . . . long time": Bingay column, *Detroit Free Press,* May 3, 1940.

85 Knight's takeover style and activities: Angelo, *On Guard.*

85– "In our news columns . . .": JSK speech to Economic Club, Detroit, May
86 12, 1940.

CHAPTER 8: THE GATHERING FURIES

88 Maidenburg watched news films: Maidenburg interview with author.

88 "What luck . . .": Leonard Mosley, *Lindbergh: A Biography* (New York: Doubleday & Co., 1976).

88 "England and France . . .": "The Editor's Notebook," February 2, 1939.

88 "German panzers overran . . .": William Manchester, *The Glory and the Dream* (Boston: Little, Brown, 1974); "The Editor's Notebook," April 16, 1939.

88 "There can be no guarantee . . .": "The Editor's Notebook," September 17, 1939.

88– "The youths of many nations . . .": Ibid., December 24, 1939.
89

89 European visitor: Ibid., March 10, 1940.

89 By summer 1940: Manchester, *The Glory.*

90 ". . . tolerance and understanding . . .": "The Editor's Notebook," *Miami Herald,* August 11, 1940.

90 "It is natural . . .": Ibid., August 8, 1940.

90 Willkie in Akron: JSK, "Wendell Willkie as I Knew Him," *Akron Beacon Journal,* October 15, 1944.

91 "president was no stranger": "The Chief owns memberships in a list of well-stocked clubs as long as your arm." "The Editor's Notebook," July 18, 1937.

91 The Wagner Act: JSK, remarks to the American Society of Newspaper Editors, Washington, D.C., April 16, 1940.

91 Knight hailed Willkie: "The Editor's Notebook," May 12, 1940.

91 "The same old faces . . .": JSK, "GOP Convention Stuck in Groove," *Akron Beacon Journal,* June 24, 1940.

91 "I'm going to be nominated!": JSK, "Willkie as I Knew Him."

91 "Willkie represents youth and success": JSK, "Phenomenon in Philly," *Detroit Free Press,* June 29, 1940.

92 "Poor prophet . . .": "The Editor's Notebook," June 30, 1940.

92 "The President has courted . . .": Roger Butterfield, *The American Past* (New York: Simon & Schuster, 1947).

92 "Mr. Willkie is a victim . . .": JSK, "England's Plight Haunts Willkie," *Miami Herald,* September 22, 1940.

92 "As Americans . . .": "The Editor's Notebook," November 10, 1940.

92 ". . . insane tragedy . . .": JSK, "Smug in Our Beliefs . . . ," *Akron Beacon Journal,* June 10, 1945.

93 "We are already . . .": "The Editor's Notebook," January 12, 1941.

93 "This is not OUR war . . .": Ibid., February 9, 1941.

93 "It is difficult . . .": Historians differ on the questions of a people's being manipulated and propagandized into wars against their will. In her work *The Proud Tower: A Portrait of the World Before the War, 1890–1914,* Barbara Tuchman remarked, "It is misleading to rest on the easy illusion that it is 'they,' the naughty statesmen, who are always responsible for war while 'we,' the innocent people, are merely led. . . . To probe the underlying forces one must operate within the framework of a whole society and try to discover what moved the people in it."

93 "Mr. Willkie has sold . . . the river.": "The Editor's Notebook," January 19, 1941.

93 "How did it happen . . .": Ibid., December 14, 1941.

CHAPTER 9: THE WORLD TURNED UPSIDE DOWN

94 War in south Florida: Helen Muir, *Miami, U.S.A.* (New York: Henry Holt & Co., 1953).

94– "The vastness, scope and horror . . .": "The Editor's Notebook," June 7,
95 1942.

95 "We have no quarrel . . .": Letter to Byron Price, March 10, 1942, Knight Collection, University of Akron Archives.

95 "Whereas the British . . .": Memo, N. V. Carlson to Price, June 12, 1942, Knight Collection.

96 "Mark my words . . .": "The Editor's Notebook," September 13, 1942.

96 "Knight, things . . . get better.": Knight letters, October 1942.

96 Censorship activities: Price, letters to Knight, October–November 1942, Knight Collection.

97 Knight's reasoning for accepting Price's offer: Maidenburg, interview with author; JSK speech, Economic Club of Detroit, May 5, 1944.

97 ". . . I dread to think . . .": Diary of Clara Knight, June 7, 1942, Knight Collection.

98 "There is nothing to be gained . . .": "The Editor's Notebook," June 10, 1942.

98 "The winning . . . too high to pay": Ibid.

98 ". . . sooner or later . . .": George Seldes, *Lords of the Press* (New York: Blue Ribbon Books, 1938).

99 newsprint rationing: Nixon Smiley, *Knights of the Fourth Estate* (Miami, Fla.: E. A. Seemann, 1974).

99– Lee Hills hiring: Ibid.
100

100– Hills in Miami and Coconut Grove fire: Ibid.; Hills recollections, interview
102 with author, July 12, 1986.

102 John H. Barry personal description: James S. Jackson interview with author, Akron, Ohio, January 11, 1985.

102– Barry-Knight confrontation: Frank Angelo, *On Guard: A History of the*
103 *Detroit Free Press* (Detroit: Detroit Free Press, 1981).

103 "Discrimination against Negroes . . . ": Ibid.

103 James Knight's displeasure over Barry's payoff of the *Free Press* debt was expressed in an interview with the author: "Barry's decision cost us a lot of money in the long run."

104 "I wonder how . . . all gone.": Angelo, *On Guard.*

104 Decision to scrap *Herald* ads: Hills and James Knight, interviews with author; letters, John Barry to JSK, June 1944, Knight Collection.

105 "It's probably a good thing . . .": Letter, JSK to Barry, June 5, 1943.

105 Clara Knight diary entry, September 21, 1943.

105 London experiences: JSK speech, "Some Impressions Gathered in London," Economic Club of Detroit, May 5, 1944.

106 ". . . the English people . . .": Broadcast from London, July 24, 1943.

106 Knight's London contacts: "The Editor's Notebook," July 1, 1945.

106 "The code of the journalist . . .": JSK, "Memories of Lord Beaverbrook," *Miami Herald,* June 12, 1964.

106 "You deny free speech . . .": JSK, "Stage Ready for British Election Drama," ibid., July 1, 1945.

107 "A shocking condition . . .": "The Editor's Notebook," June 4, 1943.

107 "We all do our bit.": JSK speech, Akron War Loan luncheon, June 13, 1944.

107 Irving Berlin plays "Happy Birthday.": Letter, JSK to Barry, October 30, 1943, courtesy Blake McDowell, Jr., Akron.

108 "I have never thought more . . .": Letter, JSK to Barry, London, January 18, 1944, courtesy Blake McDowell, Jr., Akron.

108 Air raids, food shortages, and RAF outgoing raids: "The Editor's Notebook," May 21, 1944.

109 "When the invasion begins . . .": Letter, JSK to Allied High Command, London, February 1944.

109 "Be it in England . . . protected": "Knight Demands Free Postwar News," *Akron Beacon Journal,* November 18, 1943.

109 "The very idea of censorship . . .": "U. S. Alone Has Voluntary Censorship, Says Knight," Associated Press, Washington, D.C., April 22, 1944.

CHAPTER 10: THE *DAILY NEWS*

110 "It's the opportunity . . . gold rush": Letter, Smith Davis to JSK, May 12, 1944.

111 Conversation, JSK and Smith Davis: Chicago Tribune Archives interview, 1975.

112 "Queen and guttersnipe of cities . . .": Emmett Dedmon, *Fabulous Chicago* (New York: Atheneum, 1981).

112 Forty-seven-star flag: *Time* (June 2, 1961).

112 Knight visit to McCormick: JSK, Chicago Tribune Archives interview, September 11, 1975.

113 Bidders for the *Chicago Daily News:* Ibid.

113 Knight group's discussions of sale: Kenneth Stewart, "The Man Who Bought the *Chicago Daily News,*" *PM* magazine (November 1944).

113 Chicago fire: Bessie Louise Pierce, *A History of Chicago* (New York: Alfred A. Knopf, 1957).

113 ". . . nothing should be printed . . .": Raymond Moscowitz, *Stuffy* (Ames, Iowa: Iowa State University Press, 1982).

113 Victor Lawson era: Ibid.

114 foreign correspondents became the stars: John Hohenberg, *Foreign Correspondence: The Great Reporters and Their Times* (New York & London: Columbia University Press, 1964).

114 "What this paper needs . . .": Moscowitz, *Stuffy.*

114 *Daily News* financial complexities: Blake McDowell, letter to JSK, September 11, 1944, Knight Collection, University of Akron Archives.

114– Adlai Stevenson and bidding for the *Daily News:* Ibid.; also Arthur E.
15   Hall, "Adlai Backed Out of Buying the Paper," *Chicago Daily News,* January 17, 1976.

115 Interview by trustees: JSK, Chicago Tribune Archives interview, 1975.

116 Knight's withdrawal: JSK, Chicago Tribune Archives interview, September 11, 1975.

116 Lloyd Lewis's joke on the staff: *Time* (October 30, 1944).

117 "I am confident . . .": Ibid.

117 "John Knight has committed . . .": John M. Johnston of the *Chicago Daily News,* "Editor's Roll Call," *ASNE* [American Society of Newspaper Editors] *Bulletin* (1965).

117 "Loving a newspaper . . .": Ed Lahey, letter to JSK, June 12, 1952, Knight Collection.

118 "When we pay off the mortgage . . .": *Time* (October 30, 1944).

118 "You had your good times, Jack.": Harold Graves, interview with author, Akron, Ohio, June 12, 1985.

119 "John has . . . difficulty . . .": Colonel George L. Miller letter to JSK, March 21, 1939, Knight Collection.

119 Knight's travels and brown briefcase: Stewart, "The Man Who Bought the *Chicago Daily News.*"

119 Stuffy Walters: Moscowitz, *Stuffy.*

120 Walters reading studies and early successes: Ibid.

120 "Dr. George Gallup . . . keeps growing.": "The Editor's Notebook," April 30, 1939.

121 "I have just . . . dairy farmer.": Letter, Walters to JSK, November 11, 1943.

121 Walters's work on *Detroit Free Press:* Frank Angelo, *On Guard: A History of the Detroit Free Press* (Detroit: Detroit Free Press, 1981).

122 ". . . bobby sox on the Madonna.": Stewart, "The Man Who Bought the *Chicago Daily News.*"

122 "A paper has got to be read . . .": From Johnston, "Editor's Roll Call."

122– Competition in Chicago: Herbert Asbury, "Battle in Printer's Ink," *Col-*
23 *lier's* (June 30, 1945).

123 "Your first duty . . .": JSK memo to A. T. Burch, associate editor, *Chicago Daily News,* November 10, 1946.

CHAPTER 11: A CALL TO ARMS

125 "Some of us have children . . .": "The Editor's Notebook," *Miami Herald,* March 2, 1940.

126 "The work you are doing . . .": Letter to Johnny, Jr., January 21, 1943.

126 "Reward Landon well . . .": Johnny, Jr., letter to JSK, Tullahoma, Tennessee, June 22, 1944.

127 Knight interview: Kenneth Stewart, "The Man Who Bought the *Chicago Daily News,*" *PM* magazine (November 1944).

128 "Let us give full credit . . .": JSK, "Dewey Represents Faith in America's Future," *Akron Beacon Journal,* November 2, 1944.

128 "The administration suffers . . .": JSK, "Some Friendly Advice for Candidate Dewey," *Miami Herald,* November 5, 1944.

128 "Let's not be squeamish . . .": William Manchester, *The Glory and the Dream* (Boston: Little, Brown, 1974).

129 "My God!": Harry S Truman, *Year of Decisions* (Garden City, N.Y.: Doubleday & Co., 1955).

129 "The very qualities . . .": Stewart, "The Man Who Bought the *Chicago Daily News.*"

129 Knight blasts party-giver Elsa Maxwell: JSK, "This Is the Wrong Time for Gay Parties," *Detroit Free Press,* October 22, 1944.

130 Johnny Knight's combat experience from reporting by B. J. McQuaid, combat correspondent, *Chicago Daily News.*

130 "We might be fooling ourselves . . .": "The Editor's Notebook," March 2, 1945.

132 "That boy died . . .": "The Editor's Notebook," *Miami Herald,* April 1, 1945.

133 "We never had a chance . . .": B. J. McQuaid, "Lt. Knight Killed in Germany," *Miami Herald,* April 21, 1945.

134 ". . . The golf ball would suffice": JSK interview with author, Miami, Florida, March 19, 1976. Added details of the incident from James Knight interview, June 16, 1985.

134 "In a land as great . . .": JSK, "The U.S. Never Was a One-Man Country," *Akron Beacon Journal,* April 16, 1945.

136 "We have a covenant with the dead.": "The Editor's Notebook," April 22, 1945.

CHAPTER 12: DESTINY'S CHILDREN

138 "no shade of suspicion . . .": JSK, "Truman Works Hard at Being President," *Miami Herald,* June 17, 1945.

138 *Free Press* exposé of legislative payoffs: Frank Angelo, *On Guard: A History of the Detroit Free Press* (Detroit: Detroit Free Press, 1981).

138 "True journalism . . .": Letter to Malcolm Bingay, July 12, 1945, Knight Collection, University of Akron Archives.

139 Knight-Beaverbrook exchange: "British to Use All in Pacific," Associated Press, July 7, 1945.

139 "The hills and valleys . . .": JSK, "Leftover Japanese on Okinawa," *Akron Beacon Journal,* August 14, 1945.

140 "Little children on the sidewalks . . .": "Knight Lauds MacArthur," *Miami Herald,* August 20, 1945.

140 "An air of depression . . .": "The Editor's Notebook," *Akron Beacon Journal,* September 2, 1945.

140– Surrender ceremonies: JSK and William McGaffin, "Allied Stars Shine
41 Aboard *Missouri,*" *Chicago Daily News,* September 3, 1945.

142 "we must make our choice . . .": Speech, University of Akron, June 10, 1945.

142 Veterans' affairs column: Angelo, *On Guard.*

142 Walters intensifies crusade: Raymond Moscowitz, *Stuffy* (Ames, Iowa: Iowa State University Press, 1982).

142– Walters's rule of brevity: William Ferris, "Knight of the Short Sentence,"
43 *Chicago* (November 1955).

143 Howard Vincent's reading test: Moscowitz, *Stuffy.*

143 Not all the influx was welcome: "Kefauver Committee Probes Crime," *Miami Herald,* July 15, 1950.

144 Judges block gambling crackdown: Nixon Smiley, *Knights of the Fourth Estate* (Miami, Fla.: E. A. Seemann, 1974).

145 "an open effort . . .": Ibid.

145 "Without a free press . . .": *Wiseheart and Barnes* v. *Miami Herald,* U.S. Supreme Court, June 3, 1946.

145 "Force is the only thing they understand.": Harry S Truman, *Years of Trial and Hope* (Garden City, N.Y.: Doubleday & Co., 1956).

146 "The country fumes . . .": JSK, "How Do You Like It, America?" *Chicago Daily News,* June 23, 1946.

147 "A dull effort . . .": "The Editor's Notebook," *Akron Beacon Journal,* January 22, 1948.

147– Memorandum to A. T. Burch on editorial principles: November 10,
48 1946.

148 "Truman's mediocrity . . .": "The Editor's Notebook," *Akron Beacon Journal,* June 22, 1948.

148 "The reactionary . . .": William Manchester, *The Glory and the Dream* (Boston: Little, Brown, 1974).

149 "A vote for Dewey . . .": "The Editor's Notebook," *Akron Beacon Journal,* October 24, 1948.

149 Editors endorsed Knight's favorites: James S. Jackson, former associate editor of the *Akron Beacon Journal,* told the author, "We took the 'Notebook' as policy and followed its lead."

149 DEWEY BEATS TRUMAN: Manchester, *The Glory.*

149 Bingay's editorial predicting Truman's defeat: Angelo, *On Guard.*

150 "What's this about . . .": Ibid.

150 ". . . Truman painted the Republicans . . .": "The Editor's Notebook," *Akron Beacon Journal,* November 7, 1948.

150 "Dear Mr. Liebling . . .": JSK letter, November 13, 1948, Knight Collection.

151 "It is a rank, rotten story . . .": JSK, "Boss and Gang Followers Balk Chicago," *Chicago Daily News,* June 30, 1946.

151 "No city is ever any better . . .": Speech, Ohio Real Estate Convention, Akron, Ohio, September 20, 1946.

151 Union chieftains were outraged.: Smiley, *Fourth Estate.*

152 "You handle the strike, Knight . . .": Chicago Tribune Archives interview, September 11, 1975.

152 "We made our greatest circulation . . .": Ibid.

152– Material on start of the Miami strikes is based on "The Editor's Note-
53 book," *Akron Beacon Journal,* August 22, 1948; "Substitute Printing Discussed at Hearing," *Miami Herald,* June 20, 1948; interviews by author with James Knight and Lee Hills; Smiley, *Fourth Estate.*

153 James Knight scuffle with pressman: Though it is a part of *Miami Herald* legend, and described here by reporter Anderson in an interview with author, James Knight refused to confirm or deny that the episode ever occurred.

153 *Miami Herald* fire: From author interview with Lloyd McAvoy; article, *Fire Engineering* magazine (November 1949); Smiley, *Fourth Estate.*

CHAPTER 13: A WORLD DIVIDED

155– East German youth parade: JSK, "Report from East Berlin," *Akron Bea-
56 con Journal,* May 29, 1950; "Battle for Berlin Must Not Be Lost," June 4, 1950.

156– Description of visit to England: JSK, "Freer World Trade Needed," May
57 7, 1950; "British Press Talks Less of War," May 14, 1950.

157 French visit from "Notebook," *Akron Beacon Journal*, May 28, June 18,
June 25, 1950.

158 "Barely five years . . .": "Race in Chicago," *Time* (February 13, 1950).

158 ". . . best foreign service . . .": Letter, McGaffin in *Chicago Daily News*
London bureau to Stuffy Walters, January 6, 1950, Knight Collection,
University of Akron Archives.

158 John T. Watters letter, June 17, 1950, ibid.

159 "The newspaper is something apart . . .": Speech, Chicago convention of
Sigma Delta Chi, November 22, 1946.

160 "Jack always won . . .": Ken Nichols, interview with author, Akron, Ohio,
June 7, 1985.

160 "When you had cocktails . . .": Stella Hall, interview with author, Akron,
Ohio, January 14, 1985.

161 "The impatient among us . . .": Speech to World Brotherhood Conference, Paris, June 2, 1950.

161 Executive Order 9835, FBI probes of citizens, and actions against the
innocent are detailed in David Caute's excellent history of the era, *The
Great Fear* (New York: Simon & Schuster, 1978).

162 ". . . last bulwark of freedom.": JSK, speech at University of Missouri
School of Journalism, Columbia, Missouri, May 6, 1949.

162 "Wherever Jack Knight sat . . .": Lee Hills, interview with author, July 17,
1986.

163 "God was good to me . . .": Letter, Bingay to Knight, December 22, 1942.

163 Stuffy Walters's report on Landon: Letter to JSK, March 3, 1950, Knight
Collection.

163 Frank's childhood physical problems: Charles Landon Knight II, interview with author, January 14, 1985.

163– "Mr. Knight should live . . .": Report from Dr. F. J. Smith, Henry Ford
64 Hospital, Detroit, Michigan, July 27, 1950.

164 Illinois journalists' payoff scandals: Raymond Moscowitz, *Stuffy* (Ames,
Iowa: Iowa State University Press, 1982).

164 "It is vital . . .": "The Editor's Notebook," *Miami Herald*, July 2, 1950.

165 "Knight shoots a thousand dollars . . .": *Miami Morning Mail*, February
12, 1950.

165 Sheriff Sullivan's heated testimony: "Sullivan, Sultan of Sweat," *Miami
Herald*, July 16, 1950.

165– Hills's file material finally makes print: Lawrence Thompson, "Wide
66 Open Town Blasted," *Miami Herald*, July 1, 1948.

166 "He was alarmed for my safety . . .": JSK, note to Hills, August 1950,
Knight Collection.

167 ". . . Knight is a cynical hypocrite . . .": "Knight Admits Double Cross," *Miami Life* editorial, August 4, 1951.

167 Judge criticized *Free Press* race results: "Knight Defends Publishing Racing News," *Akron Beacon Journal,* April 8, 1951.

167 "I am in need of help . . .": Letter, JSK to Hills, November 7, 1951.

168 Keyes Beech reporting from Korea: "Marines Retreat in Frozen Hell," *Chicago Daily News,* November 29, 1950; also quoted in John Hohenberg, *Foreign Correspondence: The Great Reporters and Their Times* (New York & London: Columbia University Press, 1964).

168 "If the press is muzzled . . .": "The Editor's Notebook," *Akron Beacon Journal,* March 11, 1951.

168 ". . . every chiseling stinker . . .": JSK, "Politicians Attack Free Press," *Miami Herald,* September 30, 1951.

168 "Living or dead . . .": "The Editor's Notebook," *Akron Beacon Journal,* April 22, 1951.

168 ". . . the people's choice": "The Editor's Notebook," *Chicago Daily News,* July 22, 1951.

169 ". . . the next Republican nominee . . .": "The Editor's Notebook," July 12, 1952.

170 "This is the Knight decade in journalism": Memo, Walters to JSK, December 20, 1948, Knight Collection.

170 "I see a fallacy . . .": Memo, JSK to Walters, March 15, 1951.

170 "Regarding your misgivings . . .": Memo, JSK to Walters, January 29, 1951.

170– "Merchants today . . .": Memo, JSK to Walters, February 4, 1952.
71

171 The cooking experiment: JSK letter, August 18, 1955.

171 "I thought of you . . .": Undated letter, Bingay to JSK, Knight Collection.

171 ". . . difficulty in following these economists . . .": JSK memo, August 14, 1950.

171 ". . . old-fashioned idea.": Letter, June 31, 1949.

171 "Memorandum writing . . .": Letter, December 27, 1949.

171 "I was so badly burned . . .": Letter, February 3, 1950.

172 Charles Kettering comments: James L. Knight interview with author, January 16, 1985.

172– Knight circulation growth: *Newsweek* (August 31, 1953).
73

CHAPTER 14: THE POWER AND THE PRIZE

174 ". . . ornery as a goat.": James Knight, interview with author, June 18, 1985.

175 John S. Knight arrived at the age of sixty: "Knight of the Press: New Breed in a Tough Game," *Newsweek* (April 25, 1955).

175 Combined circulation: Audit Bureau of Circulation, 1955.

175 "We don't have any.": William Ferris, "Knight of the Short Sentence," *Chicago* (November 1955).

176 "The man was arrogant.": Kays Gary, interview with author, September 12, 1985.

177 "I am against . . .": Letters, James and John Knight, summer 1954, Knight Collection, University of Akron Archives.

177 "If you are not inclined . . .": James Knight letter, August 7, 1954.

177 Secrecy of Charlotte negotiations: Lee Hills, interview with author, March 13, 1986.

177 ". . . an impartial portrayer of the news . . .": "Knight Group Adds Fifth Newspaper," *Akron Beacon Journal*, December 30, 1954.

178 "You can't build morale . . .": Letter to JSK, March 5, 1949.

178– Limits on *Free Press* circulation: Hills, interviews with author, March 13,
79 1986.

179 long-range plan: from Hills reports to Knight; Hills interviews with author, June, July 1986; Frank Angelo, *On Guard: A History of the Detroit Free Press* (Detroit: Detroit Free Press, 1981).

180 "A Look Behind the UAW-Auto Curtain" column: Angelo, *On Guard.*

181 "Buenos Aires . . .": JSK, "Argentina Is a Police State," *Miami Herald*, October 2, 1954.

182 *Miami Herald* Clipper Edition: Nixon Smiley, *Knights of the Fourth Estate* (Miami, Fla.: E. A. Seemann, 1974).

182 "The voices of freedom . . .": Speech, Inter-American Press Association banquet, Rio de Janeiro, October 13, 1954.

182– ". . . Torino . . .": Edward R. Murrow dinner, Chicago, December 20,
83 1954.

183 "The threats to freedom . . .": Speech to Friends of the Chicago Public Library, May 21, 1955.

183 government search for Communists: William Manchester, *The Glory and the Dream* (Boston: Little, Brown, 1974).

184 Harry P. Cain resignation: Harry Cain interview with author, Miami, Florida, September 12, 1976.

184 Knight's ambivalence on McCarthy: "The Editor's Notebook," *Chicago Daily News*, June 7, August 9, 1953.

185 Death of John H. Barry: Maidenburg interview with author, January 12, 1985; "J. H. Barry, Builder of Newspapers," *Akron Beacon Journal*, November 4, 1955.

186 accosted by a distraught man: Knight interview with author, February 22, 1963.

187 The times were strange: Peter Lewis, *The Fifties* (New York: J. B. Lippincott, 1978).

187– The toll in Korea: JSK, "Korea's Frightful Price," *Detroit Free Press*, Au-
88 gust 7, 1954.

188 "a good and decent man": "The Editor's Notebook," *Miami Herald*, January 25, 1953.

188 For all Nixon's quirks: "The Editor's Notebook," *Chicago Daily News*, February 6, 1955.

189 "The language is clear . . .": Ibid., December 15, 1956.

189 "My father was born . . .": Ibid.

190 ". . . might cost us a few subscribers": Letter, C. A. McKnight to James L. Knight, March 1, 1956.

190 "The modern editor . . .": JSK, "Exposures by Newspapers Protect the Public," *Miami Herald*, July 22, 1956.

CHAPTER 15: FEAR NO EVIL

193 "Nobody ever worked harder . . .": Ken Nichols, *Akron Beacon Journal*, March 10, 1958.

193 "Will I ever stop . . .": Editorial, "Frank Knight," *Akron Beacon Journal*, March 10, 1958.

193 "A touch of the flu.": Ben Maidenburg, interview with author, January 12, 1985.

193 "Gran has a constant cough . . .": Letter to parents, March 3, 1958.

194 Frank Knight stricken: Maidenburg interview, January 1985.

194 "The autopsy showed": Loyal Davis, M.D., to JSK, March 13, 1958.

196 "I was surprised . . .": "The Editor's Notebook," *Akron Beacon Journal*, March 31, 1957.

196 "I don't say something . . .": *Time* (May 17, 1957).

196 "The myth . . . has collapsed.": JSK, *"Sputnik* Jars U.S.," *Miami Herald*, October 13, 1957.

196 "Unlike [*Time*] editor Henry Luce . . .": JSK, *"Time's* Press Criticism Not Supported by Facts," *Chicago Daily News*, March 31, 1958.

197 "Some men write . . .": Letter to E. J. Thomas, February 20, 1956, Knight Collection, University of Akron Archives.

197 "Today's woman . . .": Commencement address, Ethel Walker School, Simsbury, Connecticut, June 3, 1957.

197 "The business or professional man . . .": Ibid.

197 "The competition . . .": Commencement address, Culver Military Academy, Culver, Indiana, June 11, 1957.

198 Papers shutting down, mergers and trend to chains: "Why Newspapers Are Having Trouble," *U.S. News and World Report* (January 16, 1959).

198 Heiskell's reaction: Letter, Heiskell to JSK, January 7, 1959.

198 "For the first time . . .": This account of the sale of the *Chicago Daily News* is drawn from several sources, including Knight's interview for the Chicago Tribune Archives in 1975; a Knight radio interview with Larry King

in Miami, August 27, 1966; "Cancelled Check," *Time* (June 2, 1961); "The Editor's Notebook," *Chicago Daily News,* October 28, 1956; Raymond Moscowitz, *Stuffy* (Ames, Iowa: Iowa State University Press, 1982); JSK column, "A Farewell to Chicago," *Chicago Daily News,* December 15, 1959.

200 "The spirit and principles . . .": "The Editor's Notebook," *Chicago Daily News,* October 28, 1956.

200– Field as manic depressive and the closing of the deal: JSK, Chicago Tri-
202 bune Archives interview, September 11, 1975.

202– Background of purchase of the *Charlotte News* is drawn from "Charlotte
203 Is Knight's," *Newsweek* (April 20, 1959); contemporary notes by reporter Bill Emerson; letters of James and John Knight; C. L. McKnight, letters, Knight Collection; Jack Claiborne, *The Charlotte Observer, Its Time and Place, 1869–1986* (Chapel Hill, N.C.: University of North Carolina Press, 1986).

203 Racehorse venture: "Knight, Field Form New Stable," *Akron Beacon Journal,* November 25, 1959.

204 New Miami Herald building: Nixon Smiley, *Knights of the Fourth Estate* (Miami, Fla.: E. A. Seemann, 1974); Whited, articles on new plant, *Miami Herald,* April 26, 1963; Dick Capen, "Two Decades at Herald Plaza," *Miami Herald,* March 20, 1983.

205 Arrest and trial of reporter James Buchanan: *Miami Herald,* December 23, 1959; George Beebe, interview with author, March 12, 1985.

205 "The Cubans have some damaging evidence . . .": McMullan, letter to Beebe from Havana, December 14, 1959.

206 "We hold no bitterness . . .": "The Editor's Notebook," *Miami Herald,* December 27, 1959.

CHAPTER 16: THE DAYS OF LIGHTNING

209– Bombing of Shoemaker home: From confession of Donald Branch, Gene
10 Miller, "I'm Glad I Was Caught," *Miami Herald,* November 7, 1964; Shoemaker, interviews with author, June 12, 1985.

210 "No one questions . . .": "The Editor's Notebook," *Miami Herald,* February 25, 1962.

211– Boyhood of Johnny Knight III: From JSK letters, Knight Collection, Uni-
12 versity of Akron Archives.

212 "We need to face . . .": Hills, memo to *Miami Herald* editors, July 1960.

213 "Too many editorial . . .": Speech to Inland Daily Press Association, Chicago, March 10, 1960.

214 ". . . Harry Truman has made the round trip . . .": "The Editor's Notebook," *Miami Herald,* March 6, 1950.

214– Brautigam libel suit: Nixon Smiley, *Knights of the Fourth Estate* (Miami,
16 Fla.: E. A. Seemann, 1974).

216 "The greatest actor . . .": "The Editor's Notebook," *Miami Herald,* December 15, 1963.

216 "of mirrors and blue smoke.": Thomas O'Neill and William Novak, *Man of the House: The Life and Political Memoirs of Speaker Tip O'Neill* (New York: Random House, 1987).

216– "Jack Kennedy has . . .": "The Editor's Notebook," July 10, 1960.
17

217 Kennedy camp's denial: Pierre Salinger, *With Kennedy* (New York: Doubleday & Co., 1966).

217 " 'Twas a victory . . .": "The Editor's Notebook," November 13, 1960.

218 Detroit newspaper battles: Frank Angelo, *On Guard: A History of the Detroit Free Press* (Detroit: Detroit Free Press, 1981).

219 Launching of Family Edition: Angelo, *On Guard;* Hills, interviews with author, April and May 1986.

219– *Free Press* sale rumor: AP and UPI wires; transcript WXYZ news, January
20 8–9, 1962.

221 Hills incensed: *Detroit Free Press,* January 10, 1962.

221 "I must insist . . .": JSK, letter to AP, January 15, 1962.

221 ". . . proof that any union can black out the press . . .": Arthur Krock, "Jefferson Did Not Foresee the Picket Line," *The New York Times,* May 8, 1962.

221 "This column originated . . .": "The Editor's Notebook," *Akron Beacon Journal,* November 26, 1961.

221 "Some years ago . . .": Ibid.

222 "Journalism is both . . .": Ed Lahey, "Profile of John S. Knight," *New York Herald Tribune,* November 13, 1960.

222 "Phil is always unhappy . . .": "The Editor's Notebook," January 3, 1961.

222 "Grover Hall . . .": Ibid.

222 "The pure rot . . .": "The Editor's Notebook," *Miami Herald,* January 22, 1960.

222 Woman reader miffed by Lippmann interview: "The Editor's Notebook," September 10, 1961.

223 "Those who prate . . .": Ibid., December 24, 1961.

223 "I was born to the craft. . . .": Letter to Roy Poffenberger, February 3, 1962, Knight Collection.

223 Bay of Pigs background: Peter Wyden, *Bay of Pigs: The Untold Story* (New York: Simon & Schuster, 1979).

223 ". . . a hard lesson for Kennedy . . .": "The Editor's Notebook," January 27, 1963.

224 "The world applauds . . .": "The Editor's Notebook," November 4, 1962.

225 "It's simple . . .": James L. Knight, interview, *Miami Herald*, March 12, 1972.

225 "The nation was dotted . . .": JSK speech, University of Missouri, Columbia, Missouri, 1979.

225 "Mark Ethridge . . .": JSK to Neuharth, undated memo.

226 Knight and Shoemaker at the Hialeah races: Shoemaker interview with author, June 12, 1985.

226 Ludwig's port proposal: Shoemaker interview; Smiley, *Fourth Estate.*

226 "We need more . . .": JSK to Roy Hawkins, Miami, July 27, 1962.

227 "We just never spoke . . .": Shoemaker interview, April 12, 1985.

227 "A successful newspaper . . .": Speech to American Society of Newspaper Editors, April 1965.

227 "We thrive to wash . . .": Letter, Kraslow to JSK, 1963, Knight Collection.

228 Opening of new Herald building: *Miami Herald,* April 15, 1963.

229 "As old Ned Heiskell . . .": "The Editor's Notebook," April 13, 1963.

229 "My first newspaper . . .": Ibid., June 21, 1964.

229 Kennedy arrival: "Tight Security Marks JFK Visit," *Miami Herald,* November 19, 1963.

230 federal research spending: "The Editor's Notebook," September 29, 1963.

230 "This incredible snafu . . .": Ibid., October 6, 1963.

230 "a meretricious mountebank . . .": Letter, February 3, 1963.

230 ". . . super-patriot lunatic fringe.": Letter, March 12, 1963.

231 Kennedy remarks: *Miami Herald,* November 19, 1963.

CHAPTER 17: "THE BEARING OF A GENTLEMAN"

233 Knight-Thomas friendship: E. J. Thomas interview with author, Akron, Ohio, January 12, 1985.

233– Anecdotes: E. J. Thomas.
34

234 "He is independent . . .": Don Shoemaker column, *Miami Herald,* November 16, 1964.

235 "Johnny shows self-reliance . . .": Brodie S. Griffith to JSK, July 1963. (All letters quoted this section from the Knight Collection, University of Akron Archives.)

235– Comments on John S. Knight III: John J. Fatum to JSK, October 12, 1964.
36

236 "The *Free Press* . . .": Hills, open letter to employees, July 15, 1964.

236 "The problem of every newspaper . . .": "An Editor Remembered," compiled by Sigma Delta Chi, May 25, 1982.

237 Contract to produce *Miami Daily News:* Nixon Smiley, *Knights of the Fourth Estate* (Miami, Fla.: E. A. Seemann, 1974).

237 "I thought it was a bad deal . . .": JSK, Chicago Tribune Archives interview, September 11, 1975.

237 "Such venom-venting reportage . . .": "The Editor's Notebook," July 26, 1964.

238 ". . . palm of his hand.": Merle Miller, *Lyndon: An Oral Biography* (New York: Ballantine Books, 1980).

238– Johnson visit to Akron: *Akron Beacon Journal,* October 22, 1964; Maiden-
39   burg, interview with author.

239 "I shall vote for Barry Goldwater. . . .": Paid advertisement, Tom Horner, *Akron Beacon Journal,* October 28, 1964.

240 "South Vietnam continues . . .": "The Editor's Notebook," *Akron Beacon Journal,* January 3, 1965.

240 "There is precious little . . .": Ibid., May 2, 1965.

240 "the criminal scum . . .": Ibid., January 17, 1965; also Justice McBride.

241 "Lyndon Johnson thrives . . .": "The Editor's Notebook," March 28, 1965.

241 "An excellent university . . .": JSK to John S. Knight III, April 28, 1964.

242 "Oh, he was accepted.": E. J. Thomas interview with author.

242 ". . . when he arrives on campus with a Corvette.": JSK to Major Fatum, October 22, 1964.

242 "Anyone who can afford . . .": JSK to John S. Knight III, August 9, 1965.

242 "Ever since I began . . .": John S. Knight III to JSK, July 15, 1965.

243 ". . . preferential treatment.": Letter, February 16, 1965.

243 "I was much impressed . . .": Letter, March 4, 1965.

243 "I do not seek . . .": Letter, March 15, 1965.

244 JSK advice on getting to work on time and remarks about a local trial: Polly Paffilas, "About Town," *Akron Beacon Journal,* May 30, 1982.

245 ". . . use of the word 'rape' . . .": Memo to editors, January 1968, Knight Collection.

245 "They may impeach my ass . . .": Gene Miller, " 'Kirk Pressured Me,' Says Judge," *Miami Herald,* April 25, 1969.

245– Knight memories of Churchill: "The Editor's Notebook," January 31,
46   1965.

247 "Lady Astor and Churchill . . .": John S. Knight III to JSK, February 3, 1965.

247 Death of Clara Knight: *Akron Beacon Journal,* November 13, 1965.

247 "Youth is not a time of life . . .": Clara Knight diary, Knight Collection.

247– Critique of journalism: "What's Wrong with the Press?" *Newsweek* (No-
48   vember 23, 1965).

248 "Self-righteous screed! . . .": "The Editor's Notebook," November 28, 1965.

248 "I want above all . . .": Letter, September 26, 1965.

249 "There are many excellent buys . . .": Letter, March 4, 1966.

249– "The question of a profession . . .": Knight letters, March 24, 27,
50 1967.

CHAPTER 18: "AN AGE OF EXCESSES"

252 "The chief barriers . . .": Speech, Akron, Ohio, August 17, 1966.

252– Interview of Knight: *Editor & Publisher,* transcript of WIOD program
53 broadcast on August 2, 1966.

254 "All human beings . . .": Undated letter, Eleanor Roosevelt to Franklin
Delano Roosevelt, Knight Collection, University of Akron Archives.

254 "You are not telling . . .": Eleanor Roosevelt to JSK, August 12, 1937,
Knight Collection.

254 "Conflict too often . . .": Speech, December 26, 1966.

255 Thomas becomes director, criticizes Knight Newspapers: E. J. Thomas
interview with author, January 12, 1985.

256 restructuring company-level management: Interviews with Thomas,
Byron Harless, and Lee Hills.

257 John Peter Zenger Award speech: University of Arizona, Tucson, Arizona, 1967.

257 Rioting in Detroit: Frank Angelo, *On Guard: A History of the Detroit Free
Press* (Detroit: Detroit Free Press, 1981).

258 " 'Hoodlums, whatever . . .' ": John S. Knight III to Lee Hills, July 21, 1967.

258 "Progress [in civil rights] is painfully slow . . .": "The Editor's Notebook,"
Detroit Free Press, June 18, 1967.

258 "The frustrated . . .": Angelo, *On Guard.*

258 "We are living . . .": JSK to John S. Knight III, September 3, 1967.

259 ". . . sure of its virtues": Quotation from article by Karl E. Meyer, *Esquire,*
in JSK files.

259 "Either our government . . . politicians in power": The following are more
detailed excerpts from the Pulitzer Prize "Editor's Notebook" columns:

March 12, 1967—The U. S. command in Saigon has announced the highest casualties of any week in the Vietnam war. This dirty little war is
assuming proportions of a major conflict. American forces in Vietnam
total 417,000 and continue to increase. The blood, tears and sacrifice
leave us sick at heart. Who can have faith in leaders who have proclaimed
since 1954 that our assistance in Vietnam would be merely advisory and
no American boys would be sent to do, as President Johnson said, "what
Asian boys should be doing for themselves." One must conclude that
either our government has no well-defined policy or stands guilty of lying
to the people . . . or both.

April 9, 1967—I recall no protest among my classmates at Cornell University, no boil of discontent, in 1917. Many comrades fell in France. The lucky ones never forgot. If the young people of today are different from those of us who accepted World War I without question, it is because they dare to examine the causes of war and its morality. Theirs is a new generation which rightly challenges what their elders have done and vigorously doubts statesmen who piously talk of peace while sending them to an Asian war to "save democracy" in a most undemocratic land.

August 6, 1967—President Johnson is accelerating the troop buildup in Vietnam. The politicians, from the President on down, must accept responsibility. This war could drag on for years. We are not winning. If we do go all-out to win, bombing Hanoi to rubble, there is risk of bringing in Red China or Russia or both. The American people have been deluded by the commonly accepted theme that we are fighting to repel Communist aggression. If this be so, then our allies should join the effort. World opinion, however, is almost universally opposed to what we are doing. We alone cannot conquer the North Vietnamese or the Viet Cong. In the long run, the Asians will shape their own destiny and the white man's military presence will no longer be tolerated.

August 27, 1967—When the South Vietnamese go to the polls Sept. 3 to choose a president, vice president and members of congress, the principal purpose will be to legitimatize the government of South Vietnam. Should the election be a fiasco, the Americans will emerge as the real losers; or, as Keyes Beech of the *Chicago Daily News* has put it, "looking like bigger fools than they were for starting the whole thing in the first place." The American people, who read of bribery, corruption and graft in the Saigon regime, can't understand why the lives of our young men are being sacrificed to keep unscrupulous South Vietnamese politicians in power.

Sept. 17, 1967—Topping all other questions is this one: "You have been a persistent critic of our involvement in Vietnam. Have you changed your mind since going there?" The answer is no. As I warned on April 25, 1954, intervention in Indochina would find us fighting with virtually no support from our allies, and military victories alone will not resolve the situation in Southeast Asia. Now, 13 years later, 465,000 U.S. servicemen are in Vietnam, 13,129 have been killed in combat and 81,669 wounded. We are paying a tragic price for what may prove to be an unattainable objective.

Oct. 15, 1967—A corrosive side effect of the Vietnam war is the rise of anti-intellectualism in the United States. Although right of dissent is clearly set forth in our Bill of Rights, there are those who would deny this right to others who view U.S. involvement in Vietnam as a grim and unending tragedy. What escapes the simplicists is that the question of patriotism is not involved in discussions of the Vietnam war. In September of 1963, even President Kennedy said, "In the final analysis, it's their war. We can help them, we can send our men out there as advisers, but they have to win it." It is the history of our step-by-step involvement that self-anointed patriots choose to ignore.

260 "This may be indicative . . .": JSK, "Even With Clean Vote, Vietnam's Future Scary," *Miami Herald,* September 10, 1967.

260 "—a land of contrasts . . .": "The Editor's Notebook," *Miami Herald,* September 24, 1967.

260 Vietnam experiences: Ibid.

260 "I don't know why . . .": Letter, Stone to Hohenberg, January 30, 1968.

261 "Your stuff on Vietnam . . .": Harris to JSK, April 10, 1967.

261 "It is our obligation . . .": *Time* (May 17, 1968).

262 Three prizes: "John S. Knight Wins Pulitzer," *Akron Beacon Journal,* May 6, 1968; Ben Maidenburg, interview with author, January 12, 1985.

262 ". . .'Crusty' appears . . .": Interoffice memo, *Akron Beacon Journal,* May 18, 1968.

CHAPTER 19: FACING THE WRATH

264 "It's a subculture . . .": Note to Stuffy Walters, April 12, 1968.

264 "I felt sorry . . .": Letter, June 19, 1968.

264 ". . . I believe I am doing the right thing. . . ." John S. Knight III to JSK, November 28, 1969.

264 Annenberg party: John S. Knight III to JSK, July 22, 1969.

265 ". . . the generation gap is showing.": JSK to John S. Knight III, March 3, 1969.

265 "But it is a different world . . .": Ibid.

266 "There has never been . . .": John S. Knight III to JSK, May 22, 1970.

266 "Revolting . . .": JSK to John S. Knight III, November 17, 1967.

267 "Your attitude . . .": John S. Knight III to JSK, March 27, 1971.

267 "For you to allege . . .": JSK to John S. Knight III, April 4, 1971.

268 "He is heartsick. . . .": "The Editor's Notebook," April 7, 1968.

269 "His powerful, resonant oratory . . .": Ibid., April 14, 1968.

269 "Bobby Kennedy . . .": Ibid., June 9, 1968.

269 "Our landing . . .": JSK, "Fasten Your Seat Belts for Chicago," *Detroit Free Press,* August 27, 1968.

269 James Batten of the Washington Bureau: By the early 1980s, Batten would be president of Knight-Ridder Inc.

269 "A firm but fair . . .": "The Editor's Notebook," September 1, 1968.

271 His tone dismissed the Macon deal as unimportant.: John McMullan, interview with author, March 1985.

271 "I understand my brother . . .": Ibid.

271 "... We bought the two papers ...": JSK to John S. Knight III, September 30, 1964.

272 "Under our peculiar tax laws ...": Letter, JSK to Walters, September 21, 1965.

272 "Going public ...": Wolfson to JSK, March 1, 1966.

273 "I think we have objectives ...": JSK to James Knight, October 6, 1967.

273 "What criteria are ...": Memo to Executive Committee, July 12, 1968, Knight Collection, University of Akron Archives.

273 "Dear Tom ...": Knight Collection.

274 "Without the *Inquirer* ...": Gaetano Fonzi, "Annenberg," *Philadelphia* (April 1969).

274 "... to poison the political life ...": John Cooney, *The Annenbergs* (New York: Simon & Schuster, 1982).

275 "The son Walter ...": Letter from Richard E. Hanson, August 5, 1942.

275 $14 million in cash: Cooney, *Annenbergs.*

275 "At this stage ...": Letter, Hills to JSK, October 1969.

276 "To John Shively Knight ...": "John S. Knight, Man in the News," *The New York Times,* January 1970.

276 "As a fervent advocate ...": Speech, Athens, Ohio, May 10, 1970.

277 "The FBI ...": J. Edgar Hoover to JSK, July 31, 1970.

277 "We never thought ...": *Akron Beacon Journal,* May 4, 1971.

278 "The truly distinguished newspapers...": Speech to International Mailers Union, Akron, Ohio, June 20, 1971.

278 "I am doing my best ...": JSK to Stuffy Walters, February 12, 1971.

279 Company markets and plant expansions: Alvah Chapman, Jr., to Knight-Ridder board, April 1971.

279 "Will people really believe ...": To Virgil Pinkley, August 8, 1966.

280 Memo about Eugene Pulliam: To Knight Executive Committee, August 2, 1971.

281 "I prefer a top executive ...": Memo, August 1, 1972.

281 "No newspaperman ...": JSK to Hills, September 26, 1972.

282 "I do not share your apprehension ...": JSK to John S. Knight III, September 22, 1972.

CHAPTER 20: "THE MAN WHO CAME TO BREAKFAST"

284 Nixon visit to Akron apartment: "China Chat, GOP Jam," *Miami Herald,* August 8, 1971.

285 Nixon personal luxuries: William Manchester, *The Glory and the Dream* (Boston: Little, Brown, 1974).

285 "If you will pardon ...": "The Editor's Notebook," September 26, 1971.

286 "My own feelings . . .": Ibid., November 30, 1971.

286 "Knight being outvoted . . .": John Cooney, *The Annenbergs* (New York: Simon & Schuster, 1982).

286 "They go around bragging . . .": Ibid.

287 Knight-McMullan confrontation: John McMullan, interview with author, March 1985.

288 "I tried to be compassionate . . .": Ibid.

288 "McMullan's great shortcoming . . .": Bill Hutchinson and Adrienne Stokols, "John McMullan and the Press of Power," *Miami* (June 1977).

288– Rizzo responded . . . : John McMullan, interview with author, March
89   1985.

289 "Dear John . . .": Memo, February 23, 1972.

289 "Dear Lee . . .": Memo, February 28, 1972.

289– Dispute over Moses Annenberg story: John McMullan, interview with
90   author, March 1985.

290– Knight interview: "Conversation: John S. Knight, Publisher," *Cleveland*
92   (November 1973).

293– Memos on Lexington bargaining: Knight Collection, University of Akron
94   Archives.

295 "These horse and mule bankers . . .": James L. Knight letter, August 1, 1973.

295 "Confucius say . . .": JSK letter, August 3, 1973.

295 "Times change . . .": "The Editor's Notebook," October 1, 1972.

295– Break with Nixon complete: Ibid., October 29, 1972.
96

296– "The conservatives . . .": "Republic Will Survive," *Miami Herald,* August
97   4, 1974.

CHAPTER 21: "THE ONE CERTAINTY"

298– Knight's worsening health: Lee Hills, interview with author, April 15,
99   1985.

299 ". . .'what America needs is more shortages. . . .' ": "The Editor's Notebook," *Charlotte Observer,* November 24, 1973.

300 After the heart attack: Hills, personal notes and reflections, interviews with author.

300 ". . . I hope that the Notebook can be resumed": Note to readers, December 30, 1973.

301 "Ed Hoffman . . .": Stein memo to Sidney Weinberg, April 28, 1966. Weinberg queried Knight the following day by note.

301– History of the Ridder newspapers: From Bernard H. Ridder, Jr., retired
305 board chairman, Knight-Ridder Newspapers, interview with author, March 11, 1985.

305 "The free press in San Jose . . .": J. Montgomery Curtis report on Ridder personnel, June 25, 1974.

305 "Hills understood . . .": Bernard Ridder, Jr., interview with author, March 11, 1985.

305 ". . . the problem of thought control . . .": McMullan, memo to JSK, May 16, 1974.

306 "We believe . . . acquired": JSK, "In Defense of Group Ownership," *Editor & Publisher* (June 1973).

306 "If I were a younger man . . .": McMullan, interview with author, March 1985.

306 ". . . not only larger . . .": Chapman, interview with author, February 7, 1985.

307 "We were merging . . .": Ibid.

307 Details of merger: *Editor & Publisher* (November 16, 1974).

307 Note to employees: December 2, 1974, Lee Hills files.

308 Beryl's illness: Dr. Henry Kraus, Akron, Ohio, interview with author, June 3, 1985.

308 Closeness of Jack and Beryl Knight as she was dying: Cynthia and Landon Knight, interviews with author, February 3, 1985.

308 Death of Beryl Knight: James L. Knight and Lee Hills interviews with author; obituary, *Akron Beacon Journal,* August 8, 1974.

311 "If a large public . . .": Hills note, October 5, 1974, Knight Collection, University of Akron Archives.

312 ". . . bureaucrated to the point of absurdity . . .": "The Editor's Notebook," June 16, 1974.

312 "There's nothing free . . .": JSK, talks with author, March 9, 1974.

313 Knight's medications: Dr. Henry Kraus, interview with author, June 3, 1985.

314 "Do you take all this stuff? . . .": Thomas, interview with author, January 12, 1985.

314 "Death is as much a reality . . .": JSK to Henry Kraus, June 4, 1975, Knight Collection.

315 "I've always been an optimist . . .": JSK, Chicago Tribune Archives interview, September 11, 1975.

CHAPTER 22: "A YOUNG MAN BLESSED"

316 English romance ended: Landon and Cynthia Knight, interviews with author, February 10, 1985.

317 "Some people will have the attitude . . .": John S. Knight III to JSK, February 17, 1972.

318 "Most successful newspapermen . . .": JSK to John S. Knight III, March 2, 1972.

318 "Where you surmise . . .": John S. Knight III to JSK, April 2, 1972.

318 "John's greatest weakness . . .": Memo, Mark Ethridge, Jr., to JSK, June 15, 1972.

319 "There was no question . . .": David Lawrence, Jr., "You Would Have Liked John," *Akron Beacon Journal,* December 2, 1975.

319 "You tend to miss detail . . .": Memo, March 21, 1975.

320 "It was exciting . . .": Lawrence, "You Would Have Liked John."

320 Telephone call to Eddie Thomas: E. J. Thomas, interview with author, January 12, 1985.

321 "Life is rough . . .": Ibid.

321– Sources on the John S. Knight III murder include "Murder of John S.
22 Knight III," *Philadelphia* (February 1976); articles, Knight-Ridder News Service, *Philadelphia Inquirer;* Arthur Bell, *Kings Don't Mean a Thing* (New York: William Morrow, 1978).

322 James Knight and others visit Dorothy Knight: Letter, James Knight to JSK, December 11, 1975.

324 "I can't think of a time . . .": JSK interview with author, May 12, 1976.

325 "Many details of Knight's private life . . .": *Philadelphia Bulletin,* December 7, 1976.

326 "Jack fell madly in love . . .": E. J. Thomas interview, January 1985.

326 "It's the only thing . . . that isn't perfect.": Betty Jaycox, "Betty Augustus Looks Ahead," *Akron Beacon Journal,* January 6, 1976.

329 "It's best to quit while you're ahead.": JSK interview with author, June 5, 1976.

CHAPTER 23: TWILIGHT'S GLEAMING

330 "Betty brought sunlight . . .": Polly Paffilas, interview with author, January 14, 1985.

330 "He seemed to soften. . . .": Tina Hills, interview with author, March 12, 1985.

331 Management change for the *Miami Daily News:* David Kraslow, interview with author, May 15, 1988.

331– "A publisher can't leave . . .": Speech, Akron Press Club, October 26,
32 1977.

332– Rita Knight Hewitt's problems in Costa Rica: George Beebe report to JSK,
33 September 30, 1976.

333 "I have been very happy . . .": Letter, JSK to Kenneth Hewitt, February 22, 1978.

333 "I don't want to be a nuisance . . .": Memo, November 9, 1976.

334 ". . . type sizes": Memo, October 18, 1979.

334 ". . . not a chore": Memo, March 15, 1977.

334 ". . . The uncertain elevator . . .": Memo, July 22, 1978.

334 "I bring your attention . . .": JSK to Creed Black, May 2, 1979.

335 "The best newspaper crusade . . .": "The Editor's Notebook," March 2, 1952.

336 "He was an idealist . . .": Peg Ethridge, interview with author, January 1985.

336 "I think Mark knows . . .": Daniels memo to JSK, October 27, 1973.

336 "Ben [Maidenburg], with the best of intentions . . .": Ethridge to JSK, December 30, 1974.

336 "They consider Mark to be cold . . .": Giles memo to JSK, December 2, 1975.

337 "I am one of those . . .": McMullan memo to JSK, July 19, 1977.

337 "Perhaps we ought . . .": JSK to McMullan, July 27, 1977.

337 ". . . will not mean miniscule.": JSK to McMullan, September 3, 1980.

337 "Anderson is not equipped . . .": JSK to McMullan, October 21, 1980.

338 "It took 102 years . . .": "So Long Chicago!" *Chicago Daily News,* March 4, 1978.

338 "This is the toughest . . .": Mike Royko, ibid.

338 "—no matter what happened in the newsroom.": Dennis P. Leavy, "The *Chicago Daily News* Killed Itself," *Columbia Journalism Review* (July–August 1978).

338 "Editorial ineptitude . . .": Knight, "The Death of the *Chicago Daily News,"* *Akron Beacon Journal,* March 8, 1978.

338– Hills comments to stockholders: "Report to the Annual Meeting," April
39 1, 1979.

339 Trend of installing publishers; seventeen of twenty-two papers . . . similarly structured: Alvah Chapman, Jr., response to JSK critique of publishing philosophy, April 18, 1979.

339 "Very different talents . . .": JSK to annual meeting, April 17, 1979.

339 "Often there is no . . .": Chapman response, April 18, 1979.

339– Hiring of Dick Capen: Capen interview with author, April 10, 1985.
41

341– "Curriculum has been diluted. . . .": Speech, Cornell Alumni Dinner,
42 Miami, Florida, February 15, 1980.

342 Betty rushed to hospital: JSK letter to Hendrik J. Berns, April 29, 1980.

342 Betty's checkup results at Massachusetts General: Letters, Dr. W. Gerald Austen to JSK, December 1980.

343 "You are terribly sweet . . .": Dorothy to JSK, April 11, 1981, Knight Collection, University of Akron Archives.

344 During the rides downtown: Forrest Boggs, interview with author, June 9, 1985.

344 accelerated angina attacks: Henry Kraus, interview with author, June 1985.

344 ". . . worthy heirs to a great tradition.": Stroud to JSK, May 5, 1981.

344 Stella Hall furnished home with some furniture from Knight's mother: Stella Hall, interview with author, January 15, 1985.

345 "You'd better come over . . .": Kraus, interview with author, June 1985.

345– Tributes and funeral: "Death of John S. Knight," *Akron Beacon Journal,*
47 June 20–21, 1981.

347– The empire counted thirty-two daily newspapers and other firms. They
48 included the *Aberdeen* [South Dakota] *American News; Akron* [Ohio] *Beacon Journal; Boca Raton* [Florida] *News; Boulder* [Colorado] *Daily Camera; Bradenton* [Florida] *Herald; Charlotte* [North Carolina] *Observer* and *Charlotte News; Columbus* [Georgia] *Ledger* and *Columbus Enquirer; Detroit* [Michigan] *Free Press; Duluth* [Minnesota] *News-Tribune* and *Duluth Herald; Fort Wayne* [Indiana] *News-Sentinel; Gary* [Indiana] *Post-Tribune; Grand Forks* [North Dakota] *Herald; Lexington* [Kentucky] *Herald* and *Lexington Leader; Long Beach* [California] *Press-Telegram; Macon* [Georgia] *Telegraph* and *Macon News; Miami* [Florida] *Herald; New York Journal of Commerce; Pasadena* [California] *Star-News; Philadelphia* [Pennsylvania] *Inquirer* and *Philadelphia Daily News; St. Paul* [Minnesota] *Pioneer Press* and *St. Paul Dispatch; San Jose* [California] *Mercury* and *San Jose News; State College* [Pennsylvania] *Centre Daily Times; Tallahassee* [Florida] *Democrat;* and *Wichita* [Kansas] *Eagle-Beacon.* Circulation of these papers alone exceeded 3.6 million per day and 4.2 million on Sundays. In addition, the corporation owned a dozen suburban newspapers in California, Florida, and Georgia. Knight-Ridder controlled three television stations: WJRT-TV, Flint, Michigan; WPRI-TV, Providence, Rhode Island; and WTEN, Albany, New York. Its subsidiary companies included Adams, Inc.; American Quotation Systems, Inc.; Commercial Terminals of Detroit, Inc.; Commodity News Services, Inc.; Fisher Publishing, Inc.; Knight News Services, Inc.; Observer Transportation Co.; Portage Newspaper Supply Co.; Twin Cities Newspaper Services, Inc.; and Viewdata Corporation of America, Inc.

348 "Jack Knight set . . .": Lyle Nelson interview with author, May 12, 1985.

349– "It is difficult for those of us . . .": Paul Poorman column, *Akron Beacon*
50 *Journal,* May 30, 1982.

SELECTED BIBLIOGRAPHY

ANGELO, FRANK. *On Guard: A History of the Detroit Free Press.* Detroit: Detroit Free Press, 1981.

BELL, ARTHUR. *Kings Don't Mean a Thing: The John Knight III Murder Case.* New York: William Morrow, 1978.

BUTTERFIELD, ROGER. *The American Past: A History of the United States from Concord to the Great Society.* New York: Simon & Schuster, 1947.

CAUTE, DAVID. *The Great Fear: The Anti-Communist Purge Under Truman and Eisenhower.* New York: Simon & Schuster, 1978.

CLAIBORNE, JACK. *The Charlotte Observer, Its Time and Place, 1869–1986.* Chapel Hill: University of North Carolina Press, 1986.

COONEY, JOHN. *The Annenbergs: The Salvaging of a Tainted Dynasty.* New York: Simon & Schuster, 1982.

DEDMON, EMMETT. *Fabulous Chicago: A Great City's History and People.* New York: Atheneum, 1981.

FISHER, JANE. *Fabulous Hoosier.* New York: Robert McGrath Publishing Co., 1947.

GRAHAM, HUGH DAVIS, and GURR, TED ROBERT. *Violence in America: Historical and Comparative Perspectives.* New York: Bantam Books, 1969.

GRISMER, KARL H. *Akron and Summit County.* Akron, Ohio: Summit County Historical Society, 1952.

HART, CAPT. B. H. LIDDELL. *The Real War, 1914–1918.* Boston: Little, Brown, 1930.

HOHENBERG, JOHN. *Foreign Correspondence: The Great Reporters and Their Times.* New York and London: Columbia University Press, 1964.

————. *The Pulitzer Prizes.* New York: Columbia University Press, 1974.

JOHNSON, WALTER, AND EVANS, CAROL, eds. *The Papers of Adlai Stevenson.* Boston: Little, Brown, 1973.

KNEPPER, GEORGE W. *Akron: City at the Summit.* Tulsa, Okla.: Continental Heritage Press, 1981.

KNIGHT, LANDON. *The Real Jefferson Davis.* Battle Creek, Mich.: Pilgrim Magazine Co., 1904.

KOFOED, JACK. *Moon Over Miami.* New York: Random House, 1955.

LEWIS, PETER. *The Fifties.* New York: J. B. Lippincott Company, 1978.

LORD, WALTER. *The Good Years.* New York: Harper & Brothers, 1960.

MANCHESTER, WILLIAM. *The Glory and the Dream.* Boston: Little, Brown, 1974.

MARSHALL, BRIG. GEN. S. L. A. *History of World War I.* New York: American Heritage Publishing Co., 1964.

MILLER, MERLE. *Lyndon: An Oral Biography.* New York: Ballantine Books, 1980.

MOSCOWITZ, RAYMOND. *Stuffy.* Ames, Iowa: Iowa State University Press, 1982.

MOSLEY, LEONARD. *Lindbergh: A Biography.* Garden City, N.Y.: Doubleday & Co., 1976.

MOWRY, GEORGE E. *The Twenties: Ford, Flappers and Fanatics.* Englewood Cliffs, N.J.: Prentice-Hall, Inc., 1963.

MUIR, HELEN. *Miami, U.S.A.* New York: Henry Holt & Co., 1953.

NATIONAL GEOGRAPHIC SOCIETY. *We Americans.* Washington, D.C.: 1975.

O'NEILL, THOMAS, AND NOVAK, WILLIAM. *Man of the House: The Life and Political Memoirs of Speaker Tip O'Neill.* New York: Random House, 1987.

PIERCE, BESSIE LOUISE. *A History of Chicago.* University of Chicago Press, 1976.

PIERS, BRENDON. *The Life and Death of the Press Barons.* New York: Atheneum, 1983.

RUSSELL, FRANCES. *The Shadow of Blooming Grove: Warren G. Harding and His Times.* New York and Toronto: McGraw-Hill Book Co., 1968.

SALINGER, PIERRE. *With Kennedy.* New York: Doubleday & Co., 1966.

SELDES, GEORGE. *Lords of the Press.* New York: Blue Ribbon Books, 1938.

SHERWOOD, ROBERT E. *Roosevelt and Hopkins, An Intimate History.* New York: Harper & Brothers, 1948.

SMILEY, NIXON. *Knights of the Fourth Estate.* Miami, Fla.: E. A. Seemann, 1974.

SULLIVAN, MARK. *Our Times.* New York: Charles Scribner's Sons, 1937.

TRUMAN, HARRY S. *Memoirs (Year of Decisions* and *Years of Trial and Hope).* 2 vols. Garden City, N.Y.: Doubleday & Co., 1955–56.

TUCHMAN, BARBARA. *The Proud Tower: A Portrait of the World Before the War, 1890–1914.* New York: The Macmillan Company, 1966.

U. S. BATTLEFIELD MEMORIAL COMMISSION. "Official Records." Washington, D.C.: U.S. Government Printing Office, 1928.

WOLF, HOWARD, AND WOLF, RALPH. *Rubber.* New York: Civici-Friede, 1936.

WOODWARD, BOB, AND BERNSTEIN, CARL. *All the President's Men.* New York: Simon & Schuster, 1974.

WYDEN, PETER. *Bay of Pigs: The Untold Story.* New York: Simon & Schuster, 1979.

ACKNOWLEDGMENTS

The biographer is hard pressed to do justice to an individual whose life was as complex and far-reaching as John Shively Knight's. Understandably, there are some who will view this effort as inadequate. To those who took the time to share their memories with me, I apologize if the work falls short of expectations. As for those whom I failed to interview, please be assured it was not for lack of appreciation. Sometimes one's desire to cover everything is constrained by energy and time.

Numerous people contributed selflessly, and sometimes dramatically, to this work. I am especially indebted to Lee Hills, retired board chairman and chief executive officer of Knight-Ridder, Inc., who inspired the project and gave unstinting support. Because of the ages and health of other Knight contemporaries, I sometimes found myself in a bizarre race to capture their memories. There was Ben Maidenburg, retired publisher of the *Akron Beacon Journal*, gaunt and ravaged by illness, huddled in a shawl and chain-smoking cigarettes while he talked with me in his Akron living room. He died a few months later. And there was James Jackson, retired associate editor of the *Beacon Journal,* who with his wife, Margot, spent a weekend driving me around Jack Knight's hometown on a guided tour. Two days later he was dead of a heart attack.

I am indebted to Don Shoemaker, retired editor of the *Miami Herald,* and to Louis Heldman, *Herald* deputy managing editor, for reading the manuscript and offering numerous helpful suggestions for its improvement. Special thanks are due John V. Miller, director of archival services at the University of Akron, and his assistants, Suzanne Mann and Pauline May, who unlocked a treasure of half a million items of personal correspondence and memorabilia contained in the Knight Collection; Cathy Tierney, head librarian of the *Akron Beacon Journal,* for enduring my prolonged invasion of the premises and endless questions; C. C. ("Gibby") Gibson, president of the Knight Foundation, whose administrative skills were invaluable; former *Beacon Journal* editor Paul Poorman and his assistant editor at the time, David Boerner, for smoothing the way; C. Landon Knight II and his wife, Cynthia, John S. Knight's son and daughter-in-law, for candid interviews and unfailing cooperation; as well as James L. Knight, the publisher's brother, and George Beebe, retired associate publisher of the *Miami Herald,* for constant help and encouragement.

Numerous people provided essential glimpses into the life, work, and personality of John S. Knight for this book. They included his close friend and confidant E. J. Thomas of Akron, retired board chairman of Goodyear Tire and Rubber Company; Alvah H. Chapman, Jr., board chairman and chief executive officer; and James Batten, president, Knight-Ridder Inc., in Miami; Bernard H. Ridder, Jr., retired board chairman, Knight-Ridder; Larry Jinks, senior vice president for news, Knight-Ridder; Byron B. Harless, director and former senior vice president, Knight-Ridder; Dick Capen, publisher, the *Miami Herald;* John McMullan, retired executive editor, the *Herald;* David Kraslow, publisher, *Miami News;* Polly Paffilas, Ken Nichols, and Fran Murphy, columnists, the *Beacon Journal;* Henry Kraus, M.D., Akron; Elinor Shutts Baker, of Perrysburg, Ohio, daughter of the late Colonel Frank Shutts. I also wish to thank Tina Hills, Jeanne Bellamy, Jack Anderson, Lloyd McAlvoy, C. Blake McDowell, Jr., Forrest ("Bud") Boggs, Phil Meyer, Mrs. Karl Arnstein, Jack Claiborne, Kays Gary, Harold E. Graves, Stella Hall, Homer Wolfe, Peg Ethridge, Roger Mezger, Helen Coy, Dr. Lyle Nelson of Stanford University, and members of the Mayflower Club. Special thanks to my wife, Dorothy, for invaluable assistance in research and manuscript typing and to my daughter, Harriet Whited Kerge, for reading for errors of grammar and spelling.

Charles Whited

Coral Gables, Florida
March 1988

INDEX